An Acco.t of the Gene.ll Courts Comm.tee Proceedings In Granting And Letting out the Lands in the South Town ship Westward of And Contiguous To y.e Town of Groton in the County of Middx. Called Turky Hills By virtue of y.e Grant or Order of y.e Gen.l Court.

At a Great & General Court or Assembly for His Majesties Prov. of y.e Massachusetts Bay Held Nov.r 4. 1719

In y.e House of Representatives The Vote for Granting T. New Towns was brought Down from the Board With Amendm.ts Which Wear Read & Agreed to. And y.e Vote is as follows: viz, Voted that Two Towns Each Containing a Quantity of Land, not exceeding Six Miles Square to be Laid out in as Regular Forms as y.e Land Will Allow, to be Settled in a Defensive Manner On y.e Westerly Side of Groton West Line, And that William Samuel Thaxter, Francis Fulham & John Shipley & Mr. Benjamin Whittemore be a Comm.tee Fully Impowered to Allot & Grant out y.e Land Contained in Each of s.d Towns (a Lot not to Exceed Two Hundred & Fifty Acres) to Such P.sons & Upon Such as Will Effectualy Settle y.e Same Within y.e Space of three Years after Entering y.e Laying out & Granting Such Lotts by s.d Comm.tee Who are Instructed & Directed to Admitt Eighty Families or persons at Least Who Shall pay to y.e s.d Comm.tee For y.e Use of y.e Province the Sum of Five pounds for Each Allotm.t Which Shall be Granted & Allotted as Aforesaid And that Each P.son to Whom Such Lot or Lots, Shall be granted & Laid out Shall be Obliged to build a Good Dwelling House thereon & Inhabit it, & also to break up & Fence in three Acres of Land at y.e Least Within y.e Term of three Years, And y.t There be Laid out & Reserved for y.e first Settled Minister a Convenient Lot also A Lot for y.e School, And A Ministerial Lot for Harvard Colledge of Two Hundred & Fifty Acres Each & y.e Settlers be obliged To build A Convenient House for y.e Worship of God in Each of s.d Towns In The Term of four years, & to pay y.e Charge of Necesary Surveys & Comm.tee for their Service in & about y.e premises, And that y.e Comm.tee Give Publick Notice of y.e Time & place When they Will Meet to Grant All Allotm.ts
Consented to, Sam.l Shute

THE EARLY RECORDS

OF THE

TOWN OF LUNENBURG

MASSACHUSETTS

INCLUDING THAT PART WHICH IS NOW FITCHBURG

1719—1764

A COMPLETE TRANSCRIPT OF THE TOWN MEETINGS AND SELECT-
MEN'S RECORDS CONTAINED IN THE FIRST TWO BOOKS
OF THE GENERAL RECORDS OF THE TOWN

ALSO A COPY OF ALL THE VITAL STATISTICS OF THE
TOWN PREVIOUS TO THE YEAR 1764

COMPILED BY

WALTER A. DAVIS, CITY CLERK

FITCHBURG
PUBLISHED BY AUTHORITY OF THE CITY COUNCIL
1896

Notice

In many older books, foxing (or discoloration) occurs and, in some instances, print lightens with wear and age. Reprinted books, such as this, often duplicate these flaws, notwithstanding efforts to reduce or eliminate them. The pages of this reprint have been digitally enhanced and, where possible, the flaws eliminated in order to provide clarity of content and a pleasant reading experience.

Originally published
Fitchburg, Massachusetts:
1896

Reprinted by:

Janaway Publishing, Inc.
732 Kelsey Ct.
Santa Maria, California 93454
(805) 925-1038
www.janawaygenealogy.com

2008, 2011

ISBN 13: 978-1-59641-109-8

Made in the United States of America

FITCHBURG, MASS., Jan. 29, 1895.

TO THE HONORABLE CITY COUNCIL OF THE CITY OF FITCHBURG.

Gentlemen: The undersigned petition your Honorable Body, and respectfully represent that the preservation of the records of the town of Fitchburg, prior to its incorporation as a city, and also such records as may be obtainable of the town of Lunenburg and its early proprietors, prior to the formation of the town of Fitchburg, is a matter of great importance; and therefore they respectfully pray that the city council of the city of Fitchburg may take such measures as shall be deemed expedient to secure and preserve an additional copy or copies of said records, to be deposited in such fire-proof situation, other than the city hall, as may be authorized by your council.

    A. NORCROSS,   *Committee of*
    ARTHUR H. LOWE, *Fitchburg Historical*
    J. F. D. GARFIELD, *Society.*

IN BOARD OF ALDERMEN, Feb. 5, 1895.

 Referred to committee on education. Sent down for concurrence.

        WALTER A. DAVIS, *Clerk.*

IN COMMON COUNCIL, Feb. 5, 1895.
 Concurred.

        JOHN R. OLDFIELD, *Clerk.*

CITY OF FITCHBURG.

IN CITY COUNCIL, Feb. 19, 1895.

The joint standing committee on education, to whom was referred the petition of the Fitchburg Historical Society, relative to the preservation of early records of Fitchburg, and so much of Lunenburg as relates to Fitchburg, have attended to the business committed to them, and present the following report, and would recommend the adoption of the following order:

ORDERED, That the sum of $500 (five hundred dollars) be, and the same hereby is, appropriated for the purpose of copying and printing the early records of the town of Fitchburg prior to its incorporation as a city, and so much of the records of the town of Lunenburg as pertains to Fitchburg prior to its separation from Lunenburg, the work to be done under the supervision of the city clerk, who shall have authority to employ such assistance as he may need in doing the work, the amount to be charged to account of incidentals.

C. A. CROSS,
SAMUEL ANDERSON,
JAMES A. AUSTIN,
GEORGE F. COMLEY,
WILLIAM V. LOWE,
Committee on Education.

IN BOARD OF ALDERMEN, Feb. 19, 1895.

Report read, accepted, and order adopted. Sent down for concurrence.

WALTER A. DAVIS, *Clerk.*

IN COMMON COUNCIL, Feb. 19, 1895.

Adopted in concurrence.

JOHN R. OLDFIELD, *Clerk.*

MAYOR'S OFFICE, FITCHBURG, MASS., Feb. 21, 1895.

Approved.

EDGAR S. MOULTON, *Mayor.*

A copy of record. Attest:

WALTER A. DAVIS, *City Clerk.*

CITY CLERK'S OFFICE,

FITCHBURG, MASS., Nov. 1, 1895.

In compliance with the preceding vote, I immediately corresponded with the Selectmen and Town Clerk of Lunenburg, with a view to obtain the books containing the earlier records of the town, viz.: What was embraced between the years 1728 and 1764, or previous to the incorporation of Fitchburg as a town.

The value of these records cannot be estimated in dollars and cents, and the wisdom of the city council in taking measures to preserve them will become apparent as time advances.

It is intended that the following pages shall be an exact transcript of the original record, and every portion of the original is copied as far as possible.

The pagination of the original volumes is inserted in our text in brackets.

After considerable search and diligent inquiry, I succeeded in securing the book containing the proprietors' records. As there is so much matter, I have concluded to have them printed in a separate book, and consequently it will appear later.

These old records contain much information as to the names and possessions of the first settlers, together with an accurate idea of the power exercised by the old town governments, and furnishes much food for the student of social science.

This work was undertaken not in the interest of the historian, so much as for the use of the city; for its more familiar acquaintance with, and its surer preservation of, its own annals, and the bringing together in one place of so much of the Lunenburg records as are connected with, and are a part of, this city.

The idea of copying and printing the old records originated with the Fitchburg Historical Society and was

Introduction.

urged by their secretary, James F. D. Garfield, to whom I am indebted for many suggestions and references. Many cities and towns are having the same work done, and while it may take some time to do it and do it well, the value of the copy will be enhanced by having it accurately done.

The vital statistics in this book have been copied from a volume owned by the town of Lunenburg, which was carefully transcribed by John R. Rollins in or about 1849. Minutes have been noted down of such suggestions as he has made. These vital statistics have not been copied beyond 1764, except to complete the record of families, and to add such vital statistics as belonged in Fitchburg and were not recorded here. In the Lunenburg records these are included in the same volume with the town records. In the Fitchburg records, to be published later, they may be separated.

It is to be hoped that the work of copying the remaining records will continue, and that soon the time will come when all the vital statistics will be printed each year.

I desire to express my appreciation to Selectmen Hildreth and Jones and Town Clerk Stillman Stone of Lunenburg, for the many courtesies extended to me.

Walter A. Davis.

City Clerk.

SURVEY AND ALLOTMENT

OF THE

NEW SOUTH TOWN WEST OF GROTON CALLED TURKEY HILLS.

---

[1] An Acco^t of the Gen^{ell} Courts Comm^{tees} Proceedings In Granting And Lotting out the Lands in the South Town Ship Westward of And Contiguous To ye Town of Groton in the County of Midd^{sx} Called Turky Hills By Virtue of ye Grant or Order of ye Gen^{ell} Court.

At a Great & General Court or Affembly for His Majefties Province of ye Mafsachusets Bay Held Novr 4. 1719

In ye Houfe of Reprefentatives The Vote for Granting Two New Towns Was brought Down from the Board with Amendments Which Wear Read & Agreed to, And ye Vote is as follows: Viz Voted that Two Towns Each Containing a Quantity of Land not exceeding Six Miles Square to be Laid out in as Regular Forms as ye Lines Will Allow, to be Settled in A Defenfible Manner On ye Wefterly Side of Groton Weft Line, And that William Tailer, Samuel Thaxter, Francis Fullam Capt John Shiply & Mr Benjamin Whittemore be a Comm^{tee} fully Impowered to Allott and Grant out ye Land Contained in Each of ye said Towns (a Lot not to Exceed Two Hundred & Fifty Acres) to Such P^{r}Sons & Only Such as Will Effectualy Settle ye Same Within ye Space of three Years Next Enfuing ye Laying out & Granting Such Lotts by S^d

Comm^tee Who Are Inftructed & Directed to Admitt Eighty Families or perfons at Least Who Shall pay to ye S^d Comm^tee for ye Ufe of ye Province the Sum of Five pounds for Each Allottm^t Which Shall be Granted & Allotted as afforef^d And that Each P^rSon to Whom Such Lot or Lotts Shall be granted & Laid out Shal be Obliged to build a Good Dwelling Houfe theron & Inhabit it, & alfo to break up & Fence in three Acres of Land at ye Leaft Within ye Term of three Years, and y^t there be Laid out & Referved for ye firft Settled Minifter a good Convenient Lot alfo A Lot for ye School, And A Minifterial Lot & A Lot for Harvard Colledge of Two Hundred & fifty Acres Each & ye Settlers be Obliged To build A Convenient Houfe for ye Worfhip of God in Each of S^d Towns within The Term of four years, & to pay ye Charge of Necefary Surveye & ye Comm^tee for their Service in & About ye premifes. And that ye Comm^tee Give Publick Notice of ye Time & place When they Will Meet to Grant Allottm^ts.

         Confented to, Sam^ll Shute
 Copy Examined

[2] Whereas We John Farnworth Jonathan Boyden Jonas Prefcott Junr John Ames And Benjamin Prefcott Ware Chofen & Impowered by the Town of Grotton to Confer with the Honourable the Great Genarall Courts Committee Concerning the West Line of the Townfhip of Grotton, & Settle the Same With them, As by A Vote Or Act of the Inhabitants of f^d Town At there Meeting on the 4th Day of February 1719/20 Doth or May More at Large Appear.

Now Let All Men Know, by these Prefents That We (The Committee Before Named) having Confidered of the Premifes, & Taken Upon us the Charge of the S^d Buisnefs, Do Hereby Conclude Concurr & Agree [   ] Honourable Committee of the Genarall Court affore f^d, that th[Corner of the Town Shipp of Grotton be A Small Tree With a heap of Stones About it, Standing & Being on the Easterly side of Niftaqualothe* hill, (So Called) by

---

*Probably the same as Nissitissit. [W. A. D.

Whereas We John Farnworth, Jonathan Boyden, Jonas Prescott Junr, John Ames, And Benjamin Prescott Ware Chosen & Impowered by the Town of Groton, to Confer with the Honourable the Generall Courts Committee Concerning the West Line of the Township of Groton, & Sett the Same With them, as by a Vote or Act of the Inhab[itants] of sd Town at there Meeting on the 4th Day of February 1719/20 Doth or May More At Large Appear. —

Now Let All Men Know by these Presents, That We (the Committee Before Named) haveing Considered of the Premises & Taken Upon us the Charge of the sd Trust, Do Hereby Conclude Concurr & Agree w[ith the] Honourable Committee of the Generall Court afore sd, That the Corner of the Township of Groton be A Small Tree with a heap of Stones about it, Standing & Being on the Easterly side of Nissaquassitt hill, (So Called) by Dunstable Line: and that the Southwest Corner of sd Township, be A Stake and heap of Stones being Forty Poles south of A heap of Stones, about half a mile Southward of Cataconamoog Pond (So Called) and westward of a Brook Called Prescott Brook, Made in the Presence of Francis Fulham Esqr, Mr Benjamin Whitemore, & Mr [illegible] And that a Strait Line be Made from one of the sd Corners [to the other] Which Line Being so Made Shall be the West Line of Groton

Witness our Hands the Second Day of Aprill Anno Dom 1720.

John Farnworth
John Ames
Jonathan Boyden
Benja Prescott

Survey and Allotment of Turkey Hills.

Dunftable Line, and that the Southwest Corner of s^d Townfhip, be a Stake and heap of Stones being Forty Poles South of a Smal Heap of Stones about half a mile Southwad of Cataconamog Pond (So Called) and westward of a Brook Called Benith* Brook Made In the Prefents of Francis Fullam Efq^r Mr Benjamin Whitamore & Mr Jo[†] and that A Strait Line be Made from one of the S^d Corne[   ] Which Line Being So Made Shall be the West Line of Groton

Witnefs our Hands the Second Day of Aprill Anno Dom 1720.

      JOHN FARNWORTH
      JOHN AMES
      JONATHAN BOYDON
      BENJA PRESCOTT

[3] An Acc^t of Time & Expences in ye Survey of ye New South Town West of Groton Called Turky Hills

	£.	S.	d
To m^r Benj^a Whittemore, And Francis Fullam Who began S^d Service On Monday ye 21st of Decr 1719. And Ended Said Whittemore Service ye 31st of ye Same Month Ten Days	5	00	00
And S^d Fullams Ended ye firft Day of Jan^{ry} Eleven Days	5	10	00
Capt Shiply from ye 22^d of S^d Month of Decr to ye Laft 9 Days	4	10	00
⁂ ‡ ye Surveyer Mr Sam^{ll} Jones Who began S^d Service ye 21st of Decr 1719 & Ended ye 31 of ye Same Month Ten Days	4	10	00
To 4 Chainmen &c. Viz Liu^t Jonth Boyden, Wm Whitney Finehas Parker, & Thom^s Tarbul, Who began their Service the 22^d of S^d Dec^r & Ended ye 30th Day of ye Same Eight Days Each	8	00	00

---

*Probably Bennet Brook, a name which it still bears. [W. A. D.

†Brackets signify that a portion of the original has been destroyed. [W. A. D.

‡This character is undoubtedly meant for the word "Item." So says Dr. Samuel A. Green, Librarian of the Massachusetts Historical Society of Boston. [W. A. D.

Survey and Allotment of Turkey Hills.

Whittemors Expenc	To y^e General Expenc as Reckned at Concord Mr Whittemore p^d £1-7-2	1	7	2
	More p^d by Mr Whittemore on y^e Road 3/10^d	00	3	10
	More p^d by Capt Shiply £00 - 15^s = 00 at pages. More £00 - 12^s - 6	01	7	6
To y^e wch Fullams	General Expenc Sd ffullam p^d £1-7-1 More Expenc Going & Returning home 3-6 [	1	7	1
Expenc	More to Bisket & Cheefe to Carry into ye Woods in S^d Service [			
&c	To A Journy to Bofton to Search y^e Records of P^{r}ticuler Grant [			

& Expenc in S^d Journy 5^s. And 1/6$^{s/d}$ p^d for a Copy [

[4] The Comm^{tee} for y^e New Towns Westward of Groton Met on the 5th of April 1720.

April 5th 1720.   P^{r}Sent Coll^o Tailer, Capt Shiply, Mr Benj^a Whittemore Francis Fullam Who was then Appointed Clerk to S^d Comm^{tee}

The Comm^{tee} Confidering y^e Propofal of A Comm^{tee} Appointed by The Town of Groton On ye 4th of Feb^r Laft paft to Confer, & Settle Groton West Line With ye Courts Comm^{tee} Prefented by En^s John Farnfworth One of S^d Comm^{tee} for Gioton, Who Declared That ye Small Tree with A heap of Stones About it on ye Eafterly Side of Niftiquafit Hill is No Other, but ye Same Heap of Stons Where ye General Courts Comm^{tee} Began their Survey, And it being So Accepted & Understood f^d propofals Are Accepable, & ye S^d Line to be Run & finaly Settled According

Then ye Comm^{tee} agreed to Meet at Concord the 11th of May Next And y^t ffullam in ye Name of ye Comm^{tee} Write to ye Selectmen or pet^{rs} of Lancafter to Meete ye Comm^{tee} at Concord On Sd Day to Settle [   ] the Line

The Expense then p^d at Angers by ye Comm^{tee} was   £00 - 17^s - [

And On ye Road by ffullam 8^d 00 - 00 - [

Survey and Allotment of Turkey Hills. 11

4t: Coll⁰ Tailers Attendenc One Day   00 - 10 - [
4t: Cap.ᵗ Shiply Attendanc & Travil 3 Days   [
4t: Mʳ Whittemores Attendanc One Day   00 - 10 - [
4t. Francis Fullams Attendanc One Day   00 - 10 - 00
Expenc p.ᵈ by Cap.ᵗ Shiply On y.ᵉ Road ⅜/   00 - 03 - 00
More Expenc by Mʳ Whittemor on yᵉ Road
$\overset{\pounds}{0} - \overset{s}{0} - 6$ 00 - 00 - [
                                          ─────[
                  Totall   04 = 01 = [

    The Comm.ᵗᵉᵉ also Agreed to Meete at Concord, To goe to Groton to p.ʳfect [ ] yᵉ Survey of yᵉ Lines, And Settle yᵉ Line With Groton, On Saterday yᵉ 16ᵗʰ [ ] Day of April 1720.

    Memorandom yᵗ yᵉ North Town is Made Dʳ [ ] one half part of yᵉ Charge & Expence of S.ᵈ Meeting being [ ] The South Town is Dʳ for yᵉ Like Sum being─ ─ ─ [

[5]   P.ʳSuant to the Vote of yᵉ Comm.ᵗᵉᵉ Entred on yᵉ Other Side April 20.ᵗʰ 1720 Mʳ Whittemor &

April
5th
1720
Ended
  Fullam Sett out to Groton On Saterday yᵉ 16ᵗʰ Day of April 1720. Ther Staid Sabath. On Monday yᵉ 18ᵗʰ proceed With Cap.ᵗ Shiply, Mʳ Jones, yᵉ Surveye, & Chainmen & prop.ʳ affistance With Groton Comm.ᵗᵉᵉ viz

En.ˢ Farnsworth, Liu.ᵗ Prefcot & M.ʳ Boyden, To yᵉ Heap of Stones at Groton Nor west Corn.ʳ Thene began our Work

To Mʳ Whittemores from yᵉ 16, to yᵉ 23.ᵈ of
  April 7 Days   3 10 00
To Cap.ᵗ Shiply from yᵉ 18ᵗʰ to the 23.ᵈ 6 Days   3 00 00
To Francis Fullam from yᵉ 16ᵗʰ to yᵉ 23.ᵈ
  7 Days   3 10 00
To Mʳ Jones Surveyer from yᵉ 18ᵗʰ to yᵉ 23.ᵈ
  6 Days   2 14 00
To Liu.ᵗ Jon.ᵗʰ Boyden 4 Days & ½   1 2 [
To Wᵐ Lauranc, And Nath.ˡˡ Wood 4 Days &
  half Each   2 5 [
To Tarbul & finehas Parker 5 Days Each   2 10 [

Survey and Allotment of Turkey Hills.

To Mr Green One Day			00	5	[
Expences p^d at Greens in S^d Survey by Capt Shiply £1–00–10			1	00	10
by Mr Whittemore £1=00-10- More Expenc on y^e Road $^3/_6$			1	4	4
	By Fra: Fullam	£1 = 00-10			
	More at Pages	0 - 00- 6			
Fullams	At Concord p^d	0 - 01- 3			
Expenc	for Bifket, Cheese &	)0 - 6- 7			
	Jenger to Carry. Totall	1 - 9- 2	1	9	2
			22	10	10

Memorand^m y^t of y^e Sum Total of £22 : 10 : 1̇0̇ as Above The North Town is Made D^r for One half being £11 5 5
And y^e South Town is D^r for ye Like Sum of £11 5 5

[6]   Concord, May the 11TH 1720.

The Comm^{tee} Appointed, & fully Impowered by ye Great & Gene^{ell} Court Or Affembly of His Majesties Province of ye MaffachuSett Bay in New England At Their feffion, On ye 7th of Decr 1719 To Allott & Grant out ye Lands Contained, in Each of ye Two TownShips Laft Granted by ye Court Each Containing The Quantity of Six Miles Sqare Lying Weftward of, & Contiguous to ye Town of Groton &c.

Mett at Concord in ye County of Middlesex On Wednesday the Eleventh Day of May 1720. At ye Houfe of Mr Jonth Hoberd, In Order to Grant out Said Townships, Agreeable to ye Order & Direction of ye General Court (The Whole of S^d Comm^{tee} Viz.

Wm Tailer & Sam^{ll} Thaxter Efq^r Capt John Shiply Mr Benjamin Whittemore & Fra: Fullam P^{r}Sent)

And Accordingly Proceeded to Grant out said Lands to ye P^{r}Sons Whofe Names Are Under Written On ye Other Sides, On ye following Conditions & provifions And Not Other wife.

Survey and Allotment of Turkey Hills.

1ˢᵗ That Each & Every PʳSon to Whom A Lot is or Shall be granted (No Allottmᵗ or Share to Exceed yᵉ Quantity of 250 Acres) Shal be Obliged at yᵉ Entring his Name With yᵉ Commᵗᵉᵉ to pay Down yᵉ Sum of fifty Shillings in part, And at yᵉ Drawing of his Lott, or When yᵉ Same is Laid out, The Sum of fifty Shillings More in full of yᵉ five pounds for yᵉ ufe of yᵉ Province. And if any Pʳсулт Who Enters his Name, & pays yᵉ first fifty Shillings Shall Neglect or Refufe to pay yᵉ Laft fifty to Compleat yᵉ five pounds As Ordered by the General Court, When his Lott is Laid out & Redy for Draft, Every Such Pʳсулт Shal forfit his first payment And yᵉ Lott be free to be Granted to An Other proper perfon as yᵉ Commᵗᵉᵉ Shal See Meet.

2ᵈ That Every Pʳсулт to Whom a Lott is, or Shall be Granted Shall be, & is herby Obliged To build A good Dwelling Houfe on his Sᵈ Allottmᵗ And also to break up, & Sufficiently fence in three Acres of Land at yᵉ Leaft Within yᵉ Space of three years After yᵉ Sᵈ Lotts are Laid out & Drawn, And Do also pay & Do Each of their full proportions Towards yᵉ Building & Finifhing of A Convenient Houfe for yᵉ Publick Worfhip of God, in Such Town Where his Lott Shall fall, Sᵈ Houfe to be Finifhed in four Years According to yᵉ Order of yᵉ General Court, And Do also pay yᵉ Necefary Charge of yᵉ Surveys And yᵉ Commᵗᵉᵉ for their Servic in And & bout yᵉ Premifes.

3ᵈ

[7] 3ᵈ That Every Grantee to Whom A Lott is or Shal be Granted Shall be & is hereby Enjoyned Effectualy To Settle & Inhabit yᵉ Same In his Own Proper Pʳульту, And Not have Liberty in Any Way What So Ever to Sell or Alienate or Any Ways to Difpofe of His Interest or Allottmᵗ in Either of Said Towns to Any Pʳульту What So Ever Untill the Whole Conditions Enjoyned by yᵉ General Court be fully Complied With, & Pʳformed, Without yᵉ Leave & Approbation of The Commᵗᵉᵉ Or the Majer part of them. Nor to Any Pʳульту, or pʳульту But Such As They Shall Approve And to be Accepted by yᵉ Commᵗᵉᵉ

Survey and Allotment of Turkey Hills.

		£	s	d
1	John Fletcher — of Concord — — —	2	10	00
2	Nath^{ll} Harris — of Needham — — —	2	10	00
3	Moſes Smith — of Needham — —	3	00	00
4	Roberd Harris — of Needham —	2	10	00
5	Abra^m Woodward — of Brookline — — —	2	10	00
6	Aron Smith — — of Needham — —	2	10	00
7	Timothy Harris — of Roxbury — — —	2	10	00
8	Ephraim Sautle — — of Groton — — —	2	10	00
9	Mr Whittemor for his Son Nath^{ll} Concord —	2	10	00
10	Jonth Hubard — — of Concord — — — —	2	10	00
11	Joſeph Hubbard — — of Concord — — — —	2	10	00
12	Dan^{ll} Davis — — — of Concord — — — —	2	10	00
13	Jonth Hartwell — — — of Concord — — —	2	10	00
14	Mr Wm Keene — — — of Concord — — —	5	00	00
15	Elias Barron — — — of Concord — — — —	2	10	00
16	En^s John Warrin for his son John of Marlborough — — —	2	10	00
17	Jonth child of W — — — — — — —	2	10	00
18	Jacob Fullam of Weston — — — — — —	2	10	00
19	John Whitny of Watertown — — — — —	2	10	00
20	William Wood of Concord — — — — —	2	10	00
21	Liu^t Jones for his Son Joſiah of Weston —	2	10	00
22	Eleazer Green of Groton — — — — — —	2	10	00
23	Ephraim Peirce for His Son Ephraim of Groton	2	10	00
24	Nath^{ll} Holden of Groton — — — — —	2	10	00
25	Zachariah Sautle for his Son David of Groton —	2	10	00
26	Wm Whitny for his Son W^m of Groton	2	10	00
27	Isaac Stone of Groton — — —	2	10	00
28	Nath^{ll} Woods of Groton — — — —	2	10	00
29	Nath^{ll} Woods Ju^r of Groton — — —	2	10	00
30	Nathan Haward of Concord	2	10	00
31	Edwd Emerson Eſq^r for his Son Edward-Newbery	2	10	00
		80	10	00

Survey and Allotment of Turkey Hills. 15

		£	s	d
[8]	Brought Over From ye Other Side	80	10	00
32:	John Calfe of Boston — — — —	2	10	00
33:	Thomas Hale for His Son Joshua of Newbery — — —	2	10	00
34:	Dan^{ll} Thirston for His Son Jonth of Newbery — — —	2	10	00
35:	Phillip Goodridge of Newbery — — — —	2	10	00
36:	Jonth Poore of Newbery — — — — —	2	10	00
37:	Wm Blount for his Son David Blount of Andover —	2	10	00
38:	Henry Chandler Ju^r of Andover — — —	2	10	00
39:	Thos Pearly for Phillip Amey of Boxford	2	10	00
40:	Jer. Perly for John Amey of Boxford — —	2	10	00
41:	Jonth Woodman for his Son Stephen Woodman Bradford	2	10	00
42:	Thos Tailer of Reading — — — — —	2	10	00
43:	Nath^{ll} Stow for His Son Nath^{ll} Stow of Reading	2	10	00
44:	Walter Bees of Lancaster — — — —	2	10	00
45:	Wm Wheeler of Concord — — — —	2	10	00
46:	Peter Harwood of Concord for His Son Nath^{ll}	2	10	00
47:	Thos Woolly — Concord —	2	10	00
48:	Sam^{ll} Hartwell for His Son Isaac Concord	2	10	00
49:	Joseph Ball for his Son Joseph Watertown	2	10	00
50:	John Hastings Watertown	3	00	00
51:	Ebenezer Chadwick Weston	2	10	00
52:	Joseph Allen for his Son Weston	2	10	00
53:	Jonth Boyden for his Son Josiah Groton	2	10	00
54:	Benja Prescot Groton	2	10	00
55:	Phinehas Parker Groton	2	10	00
56:	Thos Tarbul Groton	2	10	00
57:	Joseph Gilson for his Son Jonas Groton	2	10	00
58:	Wm Laurance Groton — — —	2	10	00
59:	Jam^s Goold Salem — — —	2	10	00
60:	Mr Sam^{ll} Page of Turky Hills &	2	10	00
61:	S^d Sam^{ll} Page for his Son Joseph	2	10	00
62:	Capt Jam^s RichardSon Wooburn &	2	10	00
63:	for his Son Wm Wooburn	2	10	00

Survey and Allotment of Turkey Hills.

64:	Jonth Whitny of Concord	2	10 00
65:	Isaac Whitny of Concord	2	10 00
66:	Shadrik Whitny Concord	2	10 00
67:	Thos Kembal Ju^r	2	10 00
68:	Mr Wm Clark Bofton	2	10 00
69:	Jonth Shiply Groton paid page 15	00	00 00
70:	John Burrill Efq^r " " "	00	00 00
71:	Jonth Dows Efq^r " " "	00	00 00
72:	Jer Allen Efq^r — — — —	5	00 00
73:	Nath^{ll} Whitny Ju^r of Weston	2	10 00
74:	Edwd Hartwel of Lancafter Paid page 15	00	00 00
75:	Amos Brown of Stow " " "	00	00 00

181 00 00

[9]	Brought Over from ye Other Side	181	00 00
76	M Eleaze^r Flagg Wooburn Paid page 15	00	00 00
77	Capt Richd Kembal for his Son Joseph of Bradford	2	10 00
78	Mr James Burbeen for his Son James paid page 15	00	00 00
79	Finehas Richardson paid page 15	00	00 00
80	Liu^t Thos Perly paid page 15	00	00 00

Totall 183 10 00

£ s d

May 11th 1720. The Comm^{tees} Attendenc, Travil & Expencs in Granting out ye South Town Lotts For wch S^d Town is D^r

To Coll^o Tailer Two Days & half	1 00 00
To Coll^o Thaxter Two Days Attendance & Travil One Day	1 4 00
To Capt Shiply Two Days Attendanc & Travil	00 16 00
To Liu^t Whittemor One Day & half at 8^s	00 12 00
To Francis ffullam One Day & half	00 12 00
Expenc p^d by Capt Shiply	00 04 00
Expenc then p^d at Mr Hubbards Two pounds Seven Shillings And Sixpenc	2 7 6
p^d by Mr Whittemore at Concord £00 - 00 - $\frac{d}{10}$	00 00 10

6 16 4

Survey and Allotment of Turkey Hills.

S:d South, & North Towns Contr:a Creditt

		£	s.	d
Concord May 11th 12th & 13th 1720	By Bills of Credit Then Rec:d of y:e Grantees of both Towns Three Hundred & Twenty pounds	320	00	00

Viz of y:e South town Grantees One Hundred &
Seventy One pounds & Ten Shillings — 171 10 00
And of y:e North Town One Hundred & forty
Eight pounds Ten — 148 10 00
— 320 00 00

of y:e Which Sum there Was then p:d by y:e Com:tee for past Expences A Necefary Charges of Surveys Sixty Six pounds One Shi:ll & a peny — 66 01 01

as is More p:rticularly Sett Down in y:e North Town Acco:ts pag 10:th

The Remainder Sent To y:e Province Treaf:y viz

By y:e Hon:ble Coll:o Tailer Eighty Two pounds — 82 00 00
By Coll:o Thaxter Seventy Two pounds Twlve Shillings — 72 12 00
By Fra: Fullam Ninty Nine pounds Seven Shillings — 99 07 00

---

[10] South Town D:r £ s. d

Sept 10th To M:r Whittemore Who began his Service y:e 10:th Day of Sep:tr 1720
1720 And Ended y:e 17:th of y:e Same Month 7 Days at 8:s p:r Day — 2 16 00
To Cap:t Shiply 6. Days — 2 8 00
To Fra: Fullam began Monday y:e 12:th Ended Saterday 17:th 6 Days — 2 8 00
M:r Sam:ll Jones Sureyer from y:e 10:th to y:e 17 Day 6 Days & half — 2 12 00

chain- W:m Lauranc four Days & half at 4:s — 00 18 00
men Finehas Parker & Nath:ll Woods 3 Days & half at 4:s — 1 08 00

Survey and Allotment of Turkey Hills.

Expenc p^d at Groton p^d by Capt Shiply Eight Shillings & $^d_{11}$	0	8	11
p^d by m^r Whittemore 16^s & $^d_1$	00	16	01
p^d By Fra: Fullam Eleven Shillings & one peny	00	11	01
Sep^t 22^d Mr Whittemore A Day to Dorchester & Expence 1720	00	9	6
	14	15	7

Septr 26 At A Meeting of y^e Comm^{tee} Appointed by y^e
1720 Great & General Court or Assembly of y^e
Province of y^e Massachusetts &c. for y^e Two New Towns Last Granted Westward of Groton &c. At Cambridge the 26 Day of Sep^{tr} 1720

P^{r}Sent Wm Tailer Esqr Capt Shiply Benjamin Whittemore and Fra: Fullam,

1. Agred That ye Comm^{tee} or Majer part of them Do forthwith proceed to Allott out both ye New Towns if Time Will permit But First the South Town, No Lott to be Less then forty & five Acres And that to be ye Standard of ye best Land, & if Need Require to Add five or More Acres to Make Each Lott Equal in ye Judgm^t of ye Comm^{tee} The Lotts to be Laid in Half mile Ranges Where ye Land Will Allow it So to be

And y^t ther be Laid out Convenient Ways Not Less then Six Rods Wide, And that ye School Lott be Laid out as Near ye Center of ye house lotts as May be. That ye Ministerial Lott be also Laid as Near ye Center of ye house Lots as May be &c. That ye Lot for ye first Settled Minister be Laid as Conveni^t To ye Meetinghouse place as May be. That ye Colledg Lott be Laid out as Convenient as May be Without Incomoding y^e House Lotts In One Intire peice Two Hundred & fifty Acres together

Survey and Allotment of Turkey Hills.

[11] South Town Dr̄   £   s   d

Sept. 26   To: Collo Tailer One Day   8   00
1720   ⁂ Capt Shiplys Attendanc & Travil 3 Days $\frac{s}{8}$ 1   4   00
⁂ Mr Whittemore One Day   00   8   00
⁂ Fra: Fullam One Day   00   8   00
To Collo Tailers Expenc then at Cambridge 6/$\frac{d}{3}$ 00   06   3
To Capt Shiplys Expenc in ye Journy $\overset{s}{10} \overset{d}{11}$ 00   10   11
Mr Whittemores Expence $\overset{s}{7}$ 5   00   07   5
Fra Fullams Expence $\frac{s/d}{6/3}$ 00   06   3

     03   18   10

     £   s   d

Octobr 3d Survey in Loting out ye South Town
1720   Westward of Groton From Monday ye 3d of Octo 1720. To Saterday ye 22d of the Same Month.

Mr Whittemore 17 Days at 8s   6   16   00
Capt Shiply 16 Days — — —   6   08   00
Fra: Fullam 14 Days   5   12   00
Mr Samull Jones. 18 Days   7   4   00
Liut Jonth Boyden 10 Days   2   00   00
Finehas Parker 13 Days   2   12   00
Thomas Tarbel 16 Days   3   4   00
Wm Lauranc 11 Days   2   4   00
Expences then pd by Capt Shiply $\frac{£}{2}$/4s: 7$\frac{d}{?}$ 2   4   7
Mr Whittemore pd $\overset{£}{2}$. $\overset{s}{1}$. 11 penc. More 0–$\overset{s}{7}$. $\overset{d}{1}$ 2   9   00
Fra Fullam then pd £2: 3: 3. More on ye Road $\overset{d}{9}$ &   2   4   00
More for horfe Keeping 13 Days $\frac{s/d}{3/9}$ 0   3   9
Expenc pd Wm Lauranc for 19 pound & half of Beefe at 2½ pr pound   1   4   [
pd at Pages   ——— [

     Total   48   08   [

Survey and Allotment of Turkey Hills.

[12]   BOSTON MARCH 24TH 1720/1

March 24 At A meeting of y^e Comm^{tee} for y^e New Towns
1720/21 West of Groton P^rSent Coll^o Thaxter, Mr Whittemor & Fra: Fullam.

In Anſwer to ye Petetion of Timothy Harriſs of Rowley, Sam^{ll} Hale of Bradford, Richd Kimbel for his Son Joseph of Bradforde & Sam^{ll} Tennys of Bradford. Dated March 22^d 1720. Requeſting to be Lett into The South Town West of Groton to Take Up Lotts there if it Might be but if Not y^t they Might be Admitted into ye North TownShip the P^rforming ye Conditions that Others Do.

Voted ⅌ ye Comm^{tee} that ye A Bove Named Tim^o Harriss, Sam^{ll} Hale, Richd Kembel for his Son Joſeph & Sam^{ll} Tennys Requeſt Be So farr Granted y^t they be Admitted in to ye North Town if They Cannot be Admitted in to ye South, Which is almoſt full, Upon the paym^t of their Money as Others.

And y^t Any Two of ye Comm^{tee} be impowred to Lay out ye Lotts in Caſe Anything Extr^a prevent ye Attendance of three.

The Lotts to be Drawn On Tueſday ye 23^d Day of May Next at Concord, The Comm^{tee} to Meet there on the 22^d in ye Evening.

Mr Wm Clark Admitted	
Sam^{ll} Kendal of Wooburn Admitted p^d	2 10 00
Nath^{ll} Whitny Ju^r of Weston Admitted p^d	2 10 00
The Above Named Rich Kembal Hath p^d for himſelf	2 10 00
And for Mr Sam^{ll} Tenny	2 10 00
M^r Joſeph Plympton of Medfield for his Son p^d	2 10 00

Ten pounds of y^e Mony in m^r. Whittemores hands
And in fullams Hand Rec^d of S^d Whitny   £02 - 10 - 0
More by S^d ffullam of Mr Wm Clark   02 - 10 - 0
More by S^d ffullam of Mr Jer. Allen   05 - 00 - 0
                                         ─────────
                                         10 = 00 - 0

Survey and Allotment of Turkey Hills.

		£	s	d.
[13] March 31 1721	March 31, 1721 Expenc p̄ᵈ by Francis Fullam at boſton When Mett With Collo Tailer, Collo Thaxter & yᵉ Commᵗᵉᵉ	00	01	6
More to yᵉ Secretary for A Copy of yᵉ Court Order ⁴/₆		00	4	6
pᵈ by Capᵗ Shiply for Writing One Shilling		00	1	00
		00	07	00

		£	s	d
from April 10ᵗʰ 1721	April 10ᵗʰ 1721. South Town Dᴿ In Lotting Sᵈ Town To Mʳ Whittemor Who began yᵉ 10ᵗ· & Ended yᵉ 21 Day of yᵉ Same Month 10 Dayes at 8ˢ	4	00	00
	To Capᵗ Shiply. 9 Days	3	12	00
To Fra: Fullam begining yᵉ 10ᵗʰ & Ending yᵉ 21ˢᵗ 10 Days		4	00	00
To mʳ Surveyer Jones 10 Days		4	00	00
chain- men	To Thomas Tarbel. 9. Days. at 4ˢ ⅌ Day	1	16	00
	#. Parker & Lauranc. 8. Days Each	3	4	00
Expences pᵈ by mʳ Whittemor £01-12-10		1	12	10
pᵈ by Capᵗ Shiply £01=12-00		1	12	00
pᵈ by Fra: Fullam £1-12-00		1	12	00
	totall	25	15	10

[14] An Account of yᵉ Mony Recᵈ at Concord &c by yᵉ General Courts Commᵗᵉᵉ of the Several Grantees of yᵉ South Town Called Turky Hills, When, & Since they Drew Their Lotts the 23ᵈ Day of May. 1721.

		£	s	d
John Fletcher in part — — —	Lot No: 81 — — —	2	10	0
Nathˡˡ Harris in full — — — —	No: 71 — — —	4	5	0
Moses Smith in full — — — —	No: 64 — — —	3	15	0

Survey and Allotment of Turkey Hills.

Roberd Harris in full — — —	No: 23 — — —	4	5	0
Abra^m Woodward in full — —	No: 82 — — —	4	5	0
Aron Smith in full	No: 46 — — —	4	5	0
Tim^o Harris in full	No: 31 — — —	4	5	0
Ephr^m Sautle in full	No: 33 — — —	4	5	0
Jon^th Huburd in full	No: 51 — — —	4	5	0
Joseph Hubard in full	No: 24 — — —	4	5	0
Dan^ll Davis in full	No: 61 — — —	4	5	0
Mr Wm Keen in full	No: 56 — — —	1	15	0
Jon^th Hartwel in full	No: 73 — — —	4	5	0
Elias Barron in full	No: 32 — — —	4	5	0
En^s John Warrin in full	No: 18 — — —	4	5	0
John Child in full	No: 10 — —	4	4	6
Jacob ffullam — in full	No: 80 — —	4	5	0
Nath^ll Whittemor in full	No: 57 — — —	4	5	0
John Whittny — in full	No: 76 — —	4	5	0
Wm Wood — in full	No: 79 — —	4	5	0
Liu^t Jones — in full	No: 34 — —	4	5	0
Eleaz^r Green — in full	No: 20 — — —	4	5	0
Ephr^m Peirce — in full	No: 65 — — —	4	5	0
Nath^ll Holden in full	No: 42 — — —	4	5	0
Zachariah Sautle in full	No: 28 — — —	4	5	0
Ephr^m Peirce in Room of Wm Whitny in full	No: 68 — — —	4	5	0
Isaac Stone in full	No: 29 — — —	4	5	0
Nath^ll Wood of Groton in full	No: 58 — — —	4	5	0
Nath^ll Wood Ju^r in full	No: 53 — — —	4	5	0
Nathan Haward in full	No: 38 — — —	4	5	0
Edwd Emerſon Eſq^r in full	No: 78 — — —	4	5	0
John Calf. in full	No: 21 — — —	4	5	0
Thos Hale in full	No: 22 — — —	4	5	0
Dan^ll Thirston in full	No: 50 — — —	4	5	0
Phillip Goodridg in full	No: 70 — — —	4	5	0
Jon^th Poor in full	No: 54 — — —	4	5	0
Wm Blount in full	No: 55 — — —	4	5	0
Henry Chandler in full	No: 13 — — —	4	5	0
Thos Perly in full	No: 84 — — —	4	5	0
Jer: Perly for John Amy in full	No: 67 — — —	4	5	0
		165	4	6

Survey and Allotment of Turkey Hills.

[15]

		£	s	d
of Jon.th Woodman — in full	No: 17	4	5	00
of Thomas Tailer — in full	No: 4	4	5	00
Thos. Kembal Jur in full	No: 16:	4	5	00
Nathll Stow in full	No: 19	4	5	00
Walter Bees in full	No: 49	4	5	00
Wm Wheeler in full	No: 47	4	5	00
of Peter Harwood for his Son Nathll in full	No: 59	4	5	00
Thos. Wooly in part 50s. Reſt to be pd in 3 weeks	No: 74	2	10	00
Samll Hartwell for his Son in full	No: 26	4	5	00
Joſeph Ball in full	No: 45	4	5	00
John Haſtings in full	No: 63	3	15	00
Ebenezr. Chadwick in full	No: 15	4	5	00
Joſeph Allen in full	No: 30	4	5	00
Jonth Boyden in full	No: 35	4	5	00
Benja Prescot in full	No: 72	4	5	00
Finehas Parker in full	No: 12	4	5	00
Thos. Tarbul in full	No: 11	4	5	00
Ens. Joſeph Gilson in full	No: 43	4	5	00
Wm Lauranc in full	No: 44	4	5	00
Jams. Goold in full	No: 5	4	5	00
Mr Samll Page for Two Lotts in full	No: 41 & 52	8	10	00
Capt. James Richardson in full	No: 66	4	5	00
& for his Son Wm Richardson in full	No: 36	4	5	00
Jonth Whitny in part	No: 25	2	11	00
Isaac Whitny in full	No: 62	4	5	00
Shadrik Whitny in full	No: 6	4	5	00
Mr Wm Clark in full	No: 48	4	5	00
Jonth Shiply in full	No: 60	6	15	00
John Burrel Eſq	No: 3	6	15	00
Jonth Dows Eſqr. in full	No: 27	6	15	00
Jer: Allen Eſqr paid page 8	No: 40			
Nathll Whitny Jur. in full	No: 77	4	5	00
Edwd Hartwell in full	No: 37	6	15	00
for Amos Brown of Stow pd by Jabez Fairbank of Lancaſter in part	No 2		5	

Maj.r Eleaz.r Flag in full	No: 8 — — —	6 15 00
Cap.t Rich.d Kembal for his son Joseph in full	No: 75 — — —	4 5 00
of M.r Jam.s Burbeen for his Son Jam.s in full	No: 9 — — —	6 15 00
Liu.t Tho.s Perly in full	No: 7 — — —	6 15 00
John Perham of Littleton in full	No: 14 — — —	6 15 00
Finehas Richardson in full	No: 69 — — —	6 15 00

Highest no. 84 — 81 drafts.

Gone Nos 1 — 39 and 83

[16]

May 23.d   May y.e 23, 1721 the Comm.tee At-
1721   tendanc Travil & Expenc When
The Lotts Were Drawn at Concord, for w.ch y.e South Town D.r

	£ s d
To Coll.o Tailer Two Days	00 16 00
To Coll.o Thaxter Two Days & half	01 00 00
To m.r Whittemore Two Day:	00 16 00
To Cap.t Shiply Two Days	00 16 00
To Fra: Fullam Two Days	00 16 00
Expenc p.d at Hubbards at Concord £1-14=00	1 14 00
More To Cap.t Shiply Two Days to Marlborough & Expenc	1 2 00
To Fra: Fullam Two Days y.e Same Service & Expenc	1 00 00
total	08 00 00

[17] Page 17 left blank.

[18] Page 18 left blank.

[19]

June 8.th   South Town Is D.r To Francis Ful-
1721   lam for One Day of my Self &
Horse, To Concord to Notifie M.r
Whittemore, & M.r Jones, and Sending to
Cap.t Jonas P.rescot, & Writing to Cap.t
Ward to Attend y.e General Courts Comm.tee
As Ordered at Cambridge by Said Comm.tee   00 10 09
To ffullams Expenc then p.d $\tfrac{d}{9}$.

Survey and Allotment of Turkey Hills.

To m.r Whittemore half A Day y.e Same Time at Concord	00	5	00
M.r Whittemores Expenc then p.d	00	2	00
More to m.r Whittemore Attendenc On y.e General Courts Comm.tee at Cambridge as by them Ordered Two Days	1	00	00
Necefary Expenc In S.d Journy p.d by Whittemor	00	06	00
total	2	03	9

Dec.r 5 & 6th The Comm.tee Appointed by y.e Great & General
1721. Court or Affembly of His Majefties Province of y.e Maffachusetts Bay in New England at their feffion Nov.r 4th 1719.

For y.e Granting & Allotting out y.e New Towns Westward of and Contiguous to y.e Town of Groton.

Mett at Concord in y.e County of Middlesex on y.e 5th & Sixth Days of Dec.r 1721.

P.rSent Coll.o Tailer, Coll.o Thaxter Cap.t Shiply M.r Whittemor, & Fra: Fullam.

Orded, y.t M.r Sam.ll Jones as Surveyer With Sutable affiftance and Chainmen Under Oath Do With What Speed they Can Take an Exact Account of y.e Juft Quantity of Acres of Medows (Not alredy Laid out into Lotts) in y.e South Town Westward of Groton in Order to A Division of the Medows in Juft proportion to y.e Several Grantees in Said Town Also y.t there be a Second Divifion of Upland Laid out to Each Grantee With What Speed May be Each Division to Contain fifty or Sixty Acres as y.e Comm.tee Shall Think best And y.e Land Will bare. The Rev.d m.r Sam.ll Stow Upon his Motion to y.e Comm.tee Had Leave to Purchase A Lott in y.e South Town he Settling y.e Lot himSelf or by Such P.rSon as y.e Committee Shall Approve Who Shall performe Conditions As Other of y.e Grantees in f.d Town Are Obliged to do.

Survey and Allotment of Turkey Hills.

[20] South Town D[r] to y[e] Comm[tee] for Time Travel & Expenc

	£	s	d
Dec[r] 5 & 6th 1721. To Coll[o] Tailer 3 Days at Holdins in Concord & Travil	01	10	00
To Coll[o] Thaxter 4 Days	2	00	00
4. Cap[t] Shiply 3 Days with his Travil	1	10	00
To m[r] Whittemore Two Days	1	00	00
To Fra Fullam Two Days Attendenc	1	00	00
Expences then p[d] at Concord By Coll[o] Thaxter at Holdins £1-2-6 More at Hobbards 8/6	2	11	00
More p[d] by Coll[o] Thaxter ⅌ Traveling Expenc	00	9	6
Then More p[d] by Fra Fullam 4[s]/	00	4	00
Total	10	4	6

	£	s	d
Feb 12th 1721/2 South Town D[r] To m[r] Benja Whittemore Who with Surver Jones Sett out (to Take An Acco[t] of y[e] South Town Medows as Ordred) The 12th Day of feb[r] 1721/2 & Ended March 1st			
S[d] Whittemore 10 Days	5	00	00
Cap[t] Shiply 8 Days	4	00	00
M[r] Sam[ll] Jones Ten Days	4	00	00
chain Liu[t] Boyden 8. Days at 4s	1	12	00
men Jofeph Page 5. Days	1	00	00
Expenc then p[d] by M[r] Whittemore	1	5	1
And by Cap[t] Shiply y[e] Like Sum of	1	5	1
More Two Days Travil out & home of S[d] Whittemore and M[r] Jones being Drove off by ftrefs of Wether	1	10	00
More Expenc p[d] by f[d] Whittemore	00	8	1
And by Cap[t] Shiply More p[d]	00	4	5
	20	4	8
]g[st] 25, 30th To Benja. Whittemor for Time & Expenc About y[e] affair of Lancafter ⅌ Order South Town D[r]	1	6	8
	21	11	4

This Whole Side 31-15-10

Survey and Allotment of Turkey Hills.

[21] South Town   D^r

To Coll^o Tailer With y^e Comm^{tee} at Cambridge
Ap^r 19th 1723 on y^e Afairs of S^d

	£	s	d
April 19th 1723 Town One Day 10^s	00	10	00
To m^r Whittemor $00=10-00$, & Expenc One Shilling & four penc	00	11	4
To Fra: Fullam One Day	00	10	00
To Expenc then p^d by Coll^o Tailer at Cambridge 00–12–6	00	12	6
	2	3	10
The One half of this Charg being £1–$^s_1$–$^d_{11}$ to be p^d by y^e North Town. y^e Other half by y^e South Town being y^e Totall	01	1	11
	01	1	11

June 25th   CONCORD, JUNE 25TH & 26   1723
1723   At A meeting of the Comm^{tee} Apoynted by y^e Great & General Court for y^e Granting y^e Two Town Ships Westward of & Contiguous to The Town of Groton

P^{r}Sent Coll^o Thaxter, Liu^t Whittemore And Fra Fullam.

Finehas Richardson Moved to ye Comm^{tee} that Sam^{ll} Bennett Might be Admitted, in his Roome he having Sold his Lott to him in Turky Hills if the Committee Approve therof.

Ephraim Sautle Desires Leave to Sell his Lott in ye South Town to Timothy Gibson for his Son Timothy.

Wm Richardson Requests ye Favour. to be Entred to Lott N° 66. And y^t his Brother James be Admitted & Entred to Lott N° 36 and That Sam^{ll} Farnsworth May be Admitted Instead of f^d Wm Richardson upon Lott N° 66.

Nath^{ll} Stow Desires His Brother Thos Stow May be Entred And Admitted in his Room to Act & Settle

Advised & Proposed by ye Grantees of ye South Town That the Medows in S^d Town, As Soon as May be With Conveniancy, May be Laid out & proportioned to ye Grantees in One Division

                         2dly

Survey and Allotment of Turkey Hills.

[22] 2^(dly) That the Second Division Now to be Laid out (Each Divifion to Containe Sixty Acres) be Laid out, as Soone as May be With Conveniancy, And that ye Comm^(tee) Endeaver as Near as They Can to Ballanc ye Lotts & Divisions.

Voted by The Comm^(tee) That S^d Divisions be Made Accordingly Any Two of ye Comm^(tee) being P^rSent.

At ye Request of Mr Wm Keen the Comm^(tee) Voted to Admitt David Perlin of Concord to Settle on ye Lott of Said Keen in ye South Town S^d Perlin having bought S^d Lott of S^d Keen With ye Comm^(tees) Allowanc

		£	s	d
Jun 25^(th) South Town D^r				
& 26^(th) To: ye Comm^(tee) for their Attend-				
1723 enc, Travil & Expences				
To: Coll^o Thaxter 3 Days		1	10	00
To: m^r Whittemore Two Days		1	00	00
At Concord To: Fra: Fullam Two Days		1	00	00
Expence then Paid by Coll^o Thaxter		00	6	00
Gen^(ell) Expenc p^d by m^r Whittemor at Concord		1	9	3
Expenc p^d by Fullam 00—4—10		00	4	10
And by Whittemore 00—3—7		00	3	7
Totall		5	13	8

		£	s	d
[23]				
Jan^(ry) 3^d South Town D^r To ye Comm^(tee) for				
1723/4 Time & Expenc in Laying out 2^d				
Divifion Lands in Said Town from				
Jan^(ry) 3. 1723/4 Ending ye 22^d of ye Same				
Month				
To Fra: Fullam 15 Days & half at 10^s		7	15	00
To m^r Whittemore 15 Days fifteen Days		7	10	00
To Capt Shiply 14 Days at 10^s		7	00	00
To m^r Sam^(ll) Jones Surveyer 13 Days		5	4	00
Expence then p^d at Pages at Turky Hills by ye Com^(tee)		2	10	5
More p^d by m^r Whittemor		3	5	2
More then p^d by fra fullam at Reads 1/6 at Holdens 2/		0	3	6
		33	8	01

Survey and Allotment of Turkey Hills.

	£	s	d
Feb^r 1st More to S^d Com^tee from Feb^r ye first 1723/4 1723/4 & Ending ye 29 For Laying out 2^d Divisions in S^d Town			
To: Capt Shiply 24 Days	12	00	00
To: m^r Whittemore 25 Days	12	10	00
To: Fra Fullam 23 Days	11	10	00
Surveyer Jones 24 Days	9	12	00
To Jacob Fullam 17 Days	3	8	00
chainmen To John Shiply Ju^r 15 Days	3	00	00
Mr Joseph Page 9 Days & half	1	18	
To Mark Bignal 4 Days	00	16	00
Mr Sam^ll Bennett 3 Days	00	12	00
Jonas Gilson 8 Days	01	12	00
John Wood 7 Days	1	8	00
Walter Bees 1 Day 4^s & 3^s/ for Oats	00	7	00
Totall Expense.	92	01	01

	£	s	d
[24] South Town D^r for Necesary Expenc in ye Survey of the 2^d Division Lands from ye first Day of Feb^r 1723/4 To ye 29th of ye Same Month.			
Feb^r 1st To ye 29th 1723/4			
Expence p^d at m^r Pages Turk Hills Five pounds Nine Shillings	5	09	00

	£	s	d
March 6 South Town D^r 1723/4 To Capt Shiply for One Day & half Attendanc at Concord & half A Day for Travil March 6 &c 1723/4 to Make Some Recknings And Acounts About ye Surveys of ye 2^d Divisions Lands	1	00	00
To m^r Whittemore One Day & half	00	15	00
To Fra Fullam One Day & half	00	15	00
Expence then Paid at Concord by m^r Whittemore	00	18	4
More from March 9 to ye 17th Capt Shiply & m^r Surveyer Jones 8 Days each	07	4	00
To Joseph Page 3 Days & half. Jonas Gilson 2 Days Mark Bignal One Day	01	06	00
Expences p^d at pages fourteen Shillings & four penc	00	14	4

Survey and Allotment of Turkey Hills.

		£	s	d
March 30th 1724	More from Monday March 30th 1724 to Thursday y[e] 2[d] of April following.			
	To: Cap[t] Shiply 3 Days	1	10	00
	To: m[r] Whittemore 3 Days	1	10	00
	To: Fra: Fullam 3 Days	1	10	00
	Expenc then p[d] by Cap[t] Shiply			
	Expenc then p[d] by m[r] Whittemore			
	Expenc then p[d] by Fra: Fullam Ten Shillings & Eight pence	00	10	8
		?3	2	4

		£	s	d
[25] *April y[e] 8. 1724*	South Town D[r] To m[r] Whittemore for More Service Begining y[e] 8th of April 1724, and Ending y[e] 13th Day of y[e] Same Month: 5 Days	2	10	00
	To: Cap[t] Shiply 4 Days	2	00	00
	To: Fra: Fullam 5 Days	2	10	00
	Expenc then p[d] by M[r] Whittemore £1-4=9 to Hubard £1-5-0	2	9	9

April 20th 21st 1724:	More At Concord Two Days April 20th & 21st 1724 To Ballanc Lotts			
	Cap[t] Shiply Two Days & half	1	5	00
	To m[r] Whittemore Two Days	1	00	00
	To: Fra Fullam Two Days	1	00	00
	Expence then p[d] by M[r] Whittemore Comm[tees] Charge £1-6-7	1	6	7

		£	s	d
Jan[ry] 26 1725/6	More to Fra Fullam for a Journy to Dorchefter & Bofton to Coll[o] Tailer About Calling A Meeting for y[e] South Town Man Horfe & Necefary Expence in S[d] Journy	00	16	00
	Total	14	17	4

Survey and Allotment of Turkey Hills.

CONCORD FEB^RY 23.D & 24.TH 1725/6

Feb^r 23 & At A Meeting of ye Comm^tee Appointed by y^e
24— Gen^ell Court for ye New Towns West of Groton
1725/6 P^rSent Coll^o. Tailer, Coll^o. Thaxter Capt Shiply
Liu^t Whittemore & Fra: Fullam.

To Confider ye Affairs of ye Settlem^t of ye South & North Towns Weftward of And Contiguous to ye Town of Groton

1: Voted by ye Comm^tee That ye Clark procure Books for ye Entrys of The proceedings of ye Comm^tee for Each of ye Towns South, & North

2: Voted by ye Comm^tee That Notyfication be forthwith Isued ⍰ Order of ye Comm^tee for A Meeting of ye P^rSons Admitted to Lotts or Intereft in ye South Town, To Meet at Groton at ye Houfe of Liu^t Jon^th Hobbard On Wednefday ye 16th Day of March 1725/6

firft

[26] 1: To Inform ye Comm^tee How Far they have proceeded in the Settlm^t of ye Allottments in S^d Town in Complyanc With ye Order of ye Comm^tee

2dly To Inform ye Comm^tee What they Would have them Do Concerning The Lotts in S^d Town that Are Under Some Difficulty & Dispute

---

CONCORD FEB^RY 23 & 24. 1725/6

feb^r 23 & South Town D^r to ye Comm^tee for Travil At-
24, 1725/6 tendanc at S^d Meeting & Expence

To: Coll^o. Tailer 3 Days	1	10	00
To: Coll^o. Thaxter 4 Days	2	00	00
To: Capt Shiply Two Days & half	1	5	00
To: Mr Whittemore 2: Days	1	00	00
To: Fra Fullam 2: Days	1	00	00
To Fra Fullam One Day to Bofton for Advertism^ts & Difpercing them for S^d March Meeting Agreed on—00-10^s-00	00	10	00
FEB^R 24TH 1725/6 Expence p^d by Liu^t Whittemore at Balls ⍰ Order of the Comm^tee Was £3 = 15 = 11	3	15	11
More Expenc p^d by Coll^o Thaxter With Coll^o. Tailer	3	18	6
Total	14	19	5

[27] At A Meeting of y̰ Gen̰ell Courts Commtee With yᵉ Proprietrs of yᵉ South Town West of Groton Called Turky Hills.

P̰rSent Collo Tailer, Collo Thaxter, Capt Shiply, Liut Whittemore and Fra: Fullam.

At yᵉ Houſe of Liut Jonth Hubbard at Groton in yᵉ County of Middleſex On Wednesday y̰ᵉ 16th Day of March 1725/6 at Ten in The Morning

Mett in Order to Informe yᵉ Commtee How far they Have proceeded in y̰ᵉ Settlemts of y̰ᵉ Allottments in Complyance With The Order of the Commṯe̱e̱

And Also to Inform yᵉ Commtee What they Would have them Do Concerning The Lotts in Sd Town y̰t are (at Preſent) Under Some Dificulty & Diſpute.

The Information y̰ᵉ Settlers then Gave y̰ᵉ Commṯe̱e̱ Was that there was then 26 Houſes Raiſed & Ten of them Settled & Inhabited

1 Voted by yᵉ Commtee That No pʳSon Whatso Ever Shall Have Liberty to Box Any Pine Trees Growing on yᵉ Comons in yᵉ South Town.

2 That Fra: Fullam Cap̰t Shiply & Liut Whittemore, Or Any Two of them With Sutable Affiſtance Do Lay out yᵉ Aquivalent Land as Soon as May be.

Groton March yᴱ 16: 1725/6

	£	s	d
March¹⁵ 16 South Town is Dr To yᵉ Commtee *17. & 18* for their Attendenc Travil & Expe			
1725/6 To: Collo Tailer 4 Days	2	00	00
To: Collo Thaxter 5 Days	2	10	00
To: Capt Shiply 2 Days & half	1	5	00
To: mṛ Whittemor 3 Days	1	10	00
To: Fra: Fullam 4 Days y̰ᵉ 15th: 16th, 17th & 18th of March	2	00	00
Expenc pd by Mṛ Whittemore	7	19	11
More Expenc pd by Collo Thaxter	1	3	00
More pd by Collo Tailer	00	16	00
Totall	19	03	11

Survey and Allotment of Turkey Hills.

[28] At A Meeting of y:e Comm:tee of y:e South Town
Bo∫ton West of Groton Called Turky Hills In order
Decem:r to Settle Some Accounts Relating To S:d Town
7:th &c.
1726 P:rSent Coll:o Tailer Coll:o Thaxter Capt Shiply
Liu:t Whittemore, & Fra: Fullam

	£	s	d
Dec:r 7:th South Town is D:r to y:e Com:tee for 1726 Attendanc Travil & Expenc To Attend S:d Meeting			
To: Coll:o Tailer Day	00	00	00
To: Coll:o Thaxter Day	00	00	00
To: Cap:t Shiply 3 Days	00	00	00
To: M:r Whittemore 2 Days £1=00=00 & Expenc	01	12	00
To: Fra: Fullam 2 Days & Expenc	1	4	00
Totall	2	16	00

[29] The Comm:tee for y:e South Town West of Groton
Sep:t 28:th Mett at Cambridge The 28:th Day of Sep:t
1724 1724.
P:rSent Coll:o Tailer, Coll:o Thaxter, Cap:t Shiply
Liu:t Whittemore And Fra Fullam

	£	s	d
To Make up Some Acco:ts for past Service & Surveys &c.			
Then p:d by Coll:o Thaxter to M:r Sam:ll Jones Surveyer In full to that Time for his Service in South Town Thirteen pounds & One Shilling	13	1	00
More to Fra: Fullam in full to y:t Day for S:d Town	11	13	6
More to Cap:t Shiply in part	12	00	00
More to m:r Whittemore in part	3	1	4
More then Due to m:r Whittemore. to Ballance	11	7	9
More then p:d M:rs Anger for Victuals Drink & hor∫meat	2	1	6
Total	53	5	1

April 25th 1726

April 25 1726 An Acco^t of ye Charges & Expenc of ye Viewing ye Equivalent Land for Turk hills or South Town Agreeable to ye Order of ye Gen^{ell} Court

	£	s	d
To: Capt Shiply Who began S^d Service April 26th 1726, & Ended May ye 2^d 7 Days	3	10	00
To m^r Benj^a Whittemore beging April 25th & Ended May ye 3^d 9 Days	4	10	00
To m^r Sam^{ll} Jones Surveyer 9 Days	4	10	00
To: m^r Edwd Hartwell 6 Days at 5^s	1	10	00
chainmen To: Jonth Shiply 7 Days	1	15	00
To: Capt Willard for his Man 6 Days	1	10	00
Expenc in S^d Service then p^d by m^r Whittemore	4	2	9
	21	7	9

[**30**] Cambridge Sep^t 28th 1724. South Town D^r To ye Com^{tee} for Attendanc, Travil, & Expenc, viz

	£	s	d
To: Coll^o Tailer One Day Ten Shillings	00	10	00
To: Thaxter Two Days One pound	01	00	00
To: Capt John Shiply Two Days & half	01	05	00
To: m^r Benjamin Whittemore One Day	00	10	00
To: Fra: Fullam One Day Ten Shillings	00	10	00
Expenc then p^d at Cambridge for Victuals Drink & horfmeat by Coll^o Thaxter Two pounds One Shilling & Six pence	02	01	06
	05	16	06

[**31**] Page 31 left blank.

[**32**] Turky Hills South Town April 12th 1727.

April 12th 1727. At A Meeting of ye Comm^{tee} Appointed & Impowred by the Great & General Court At their at Bofton, Decr 7th 1719 To Allott & Grant out the Lands Contained in the South Townfhip Granted Weftward of & Contiguous to ye Town of Groton in ye County of Middlefex.

Survey and Allotment of Turkey Hills. 35

P^rSent ye Hon^{bla} Coll^o Tailer & Sam^{ll} Thaxter Efq^{rs} Capt John Shiply, Liu^t Benja: Whittemore & Fra: Fullam Efq^r.

S^d Committee being Mett at ye Houfe of Capt Jofiah Willard In S^d Turky Hills After Due Warning Given, As Well at ye Requeft of ye Settlers As to be Informed What progrefs Was Made in Setling Each Lott, as Injoyned by ye General Court, & S^d Comm^{tee}.

And finding that Several of ye Lotts in S^d Town Are Not Settled as injoyned by ye General Court, And their Comm^{tee} And Several that to this Day have Never Done Any Labour at all on Them, but y^t ye p^rfons Who Drew them Have hitherto Kept the Lotts from Others Likly to Settle them, And have Only Traded them from One Man to Another for Exceffive Gaine & Prices, Which Practice is Directly Contrary to y^e Written Conditions & Provisos Upon Which Each P^rSon had his Lott of y^e Comm^{tee} Which practice Tends Greatly to Retard y^e Settling S^d Town, And Opreffion of thofe Who muft finaly Do it.

Voted $\mathcal{P}$ y^e Comm^{tee} that Lott N° 19. Lott N° 45. Lott N° 25 and Lott N° 44. In y^e S^d South Town Are Declared forfitted, And Shall forth with be Granted to Such Sutable P^rSons as Will forthwith Settle them Effectualy No Lott to be Sold for More then fifty pounds Nor for Lefs then forty pounds.

The Comm^{tees} Attendenc, Travil, & Expenc at S^d Meeting

	£	s	d
To: Coll^o Tailer 5 Days	2	10	00
To: Coll^o Thaxter 6 Days	3	00	00
To: Capt Shiply 4 Days	2	00	00
To: m^r Benja Whittemore 5 Days	2	10	00
To: Fra: Fullam 5 Days To Turky Hills & Concord	2	10	00
To Expenc then p^d by Coll^o Thaxter with Coll^o Tailer	3	14	00
More by m^r Whittemore $\mathcal{P}$ Order	8	8	00
More To m^r Whittemore A Day to bring y^e Turky hill petition In Order for y^e Above Meeting	0	10	00
	25	12	00

[**33**] SOUTH TOWN TURKY HILLS APRIL 28TH 1727.

To Francis Fullam Esqr Clerk of y^e Comm^{tee} for Said Town, ⁓

We y^e Subscribers Have proceeded to Sell y^e four forfitted Lotts in S.^d Town; And y^e Conditions And Delivery Wear in y^e Words Following. (viz)

By Order of y^e Reft of y^e Comm^{tee} of the Honrd General Court for South Town So Called. We grant you, A: B = Pofsefsion of Lott N^o: — With all y^e Rights thereto be Longing in this Said Town, On Conditions & Not Otherwife That you Do forth with fullfil y^e General Courts Act by building a good Dwelling Houfe Breaking up, & fencing in Three Acres of Land theron &c And by Doing And fullfilling all Other Duties According to ye Directions of ye S.^d Courts Comm^{tee} in & A bout ye Same, On penaly of forfitting ye Same into ye Hands of ye Comm^{tee} Again.

April. 26th on S^d Day We Sold & Gave Pofsefsion of Lot N° 25. To Capt Joliah Willard for ye Sum of Fifty pounds. Wittnefs—Sam^{ll} Jones & Ephr^m Sautle We Sold and Gave Pofsefsion of Lott N° 19 to Josiah Baylee for ye Sum of fifty pounds. Wittnes m^r Sam^{ll} Jones, Mr Ephraim Sautle

April 27th We Sold & gave Poffeffion of Lott N° 44: To Jofhua Hutchins for The Sum of forty pounds. Wittnefs Sam^{ll} Jones Dan^{ll} Auftin

April 28th We Sold And gave Poffefsion of Lott No 45 to Jonth Whitny Ju^r for ye Sum of forty pounds Wittnefs Sam^{ll} Jones & Ephraim Sautle

       BENJ^A WHITTEMORE
       JOHN SHEPLE

The Amounts of ye S^d Sums is One Hundred & Eighty pounds £180. For Which ye S^d Benjamin Whittemore Makes HimSelf Debter to the Comm^{tee}

Rec^d for Entry May 2^d 1727. BENJ^A WHITTEMORE.

℈ FRA: FULLAM *Clerk.*

Survey and Allotment of Turkey Hills. 37

	£	s	d
The Charge of yᵉ Sale of Sᵈ forfitted Lotts			
To: mʳ Benja: Whittemore 3 Days & half	1	15	00
To: Capᵗ Shiply 2 Days & half	1	5	00
To: mʳ Jones 3 Day & half	1	8	00
To: mʳ Sautle 2 Days & half.	00	10	00
Expenc then pᵈ by mʳ Whittemor £1=11=7 & A Day to Make Return 10s	2	1	7
	6	19	7

[34] Page 34 left blank.

[35]   Concord Novᴿ yᴱ 6ᵀᴴ & 7ᵀᴴ, 1727.

At A Meeting of yᵉ General Courts Commᵗᵉᵉ for yᵉ South Town Called — Turky Hills West of Groton

Pʳſent The Honᵇˡᵉ Colloͦ Tailer, Capᵗ John Shiple, Liutᵗ Benjᵃ Whittemore & Fra: Fullam.

Novʳ 6 & 7 1727. Voted by yᵉ Commᵗᵉᵉ That yᵉ Proprietʳˢ of yᵉ Lott Lands in Said Turky Hills be Directed; This Winter Without further Delay to proceed to The Erecting, building, & finiſhing of A Sutable & Convenient Meeting houſe For yᵉ Publick Worship of God in Sᵈ Town, Not Leſs than forty and Five feet in Length, And thirty And five feet in Width, Nott Leſs then Eighteen feet, Nor More then Twenty feet between Joynts, And to be Sett on yᵉ Same Spott of Ground as Ordered by yᵉ Commᵗᵉᵉ Lying between The Houſe of Benoni Boynton and Horſmeat Medow in Sᵈ Town.

And that Meſurſ Samˡˡ Page, Capᵗ Joſiah Willard Edward Heartwell Benoni Boynton & Isaac Farnſworth be Deſired to be And Act as A Sub commᵗᵉᵉ to Accompliſh Sᵈ Work as before Directed Subject NevertheLeſs to yᵉ Order & Directions of yᵉ General Courts Commᵗᵉᵉ

And that there Shall be A Meeting of yᵉ Genᵉˡˡ Courts Commᵗᵉᵉ With yᵉ proprietʳˢ of Turky Hills (at Turky Hills) Some Time this Winter as Soon as May be In Order to Raiſe A Sutable Sum of Mony to Carry on Sᵈ Work

Survey and Allotment of Turkey Hills.

		£	s	d
Concord	South Town D^r			
	To Attendenc Travil & Expenc at S^d Meeting			
Novr 6th & 7	To: Coll^o Tailer Two Days & Expenc	1	3	00
1727	To: Capt Shiple Two Days	1	00	00
	To: Liu^t Benj^a Whittemore One Day & half	00	15	00
	To: Fra: Fullam One Day & half	00	15	00
	To Expences then paid by m^r Whittemor ꝑ order	2	12	1
Octo^r 31 1727	To: Fra: Fullam for A Journy to Dorchefter to Agree on S^d Meeting Man, Horfe & Expenc	00	12	6
		6	17	7

[36] *Bolton* Novr 30th & Decr 1st & 2^d 1727.

At A Meeting of the Comm^{tee} for ye South Town West of Groton Called Turky Hills Pr^{s}ent Coll^o Tailer, Coll^o Thaxter, Capt Shiple & Fra: Fullam The following Requeft of ye Selectmen of Wooburn was Read as followeth

WOBURN NOV^R Y^E 24TH 1727

To ye Honble Wm Tailer Sam^{ll} Thaxter & Fra: Fullam Esq^{rs} Mr Benj^a Whittemore And Capt John Shiple Gen^t

Thefe Are to Requeft of you, Either by your Selves or Some That you Shall Appoint to Meet us at y^e Houfe of Mr Edward Hartwell of Turky Hills On Wednesday y^e Sixth Day of Decr Next at Eight of y^e Clock in y^e forenoon to perambulate y^e Lines between the Two Thoufand Acres belonging to y^e Town of Woburn And y^e Lands be=longing to Turky Hills

Signed ꝑ JOSEPH WRIGHT ⎫
SAM^{LL} WALKER ⎬ *Selectmen of*
SAM^{LL} RICHARDSON ⎬ *Wooburn*
ROBERT CONVERSE ⎭

Decr 1st & 2^d 1727 In Anfwer to y^e Above Requeft The following Power Went forth

BOSTON DEC.R 1ST 1727

To Capt John Shiply Capt Jofiah Willard, Liut Edward Hartwell And mr Benoni Boynton

Gentn The Selectmen of Wooburn Having Requefted The Genell Courts Commtee Either by them Selves, or Such PrSons as they should Appoint to Meet at ye houfe of mr Edward Hartwell of Turky Hills On Wednefday ye Sixth Day of Decemr 1727 at Eight of ye Clock in ye Morning to Prambulate ye Lines between ye Two Thoufand Acres belonging to ye Town of Woburn And ye Lands belonging to Turky Hills.

The Commtee Mett at Bofton ye Day A bove And agreed To Defire & Impower You the Above Named John Shiply Jofiah Willard, Edward Hartwell & Benoni Boynton to Meet ye Sd Selectmen & Run ye Prambulation Lines as Above

P Ordr of ye Commtee FRA FULLAM *Clerk*

[37] South Town Dr to ye Commtee for Attendanc Travil & Expenc

		£	s	d
Bofton To: Collo Tailer Day		00	00	00
Novr 30th To: Collo Thaxter Day		00	00	00
—&— To: Capt Shiply 3 Days & half.		1	15	00
Decr 1st & 2d To: Fra: Fullam 3 Days		1	10	00
1727 Expenc then pd by Fra: Fullam		1	1	2
More pd by Capt Shiply		1	3	00
To: mr Whittemore One Day		00	10	00
		5	19	2

At ye Town Ship Called Turky Hills December 7th 1727 We the Subscribers, John Shipley Benoni Boynton With Several of the Inhabitants or Propriatrs of Turky Hills, Sd Shiply And Boynton being Appointed by by ye Genell Courts Commtee to Prambulate with Woburn Gentlemen Such as Sd Woburn Should Send, Which Was Samll Walker And Samll Richardson Round Woburn farme Lying in ye TownShip Above Said And We Mett On ye

Survey and Allotment of Turkey Hills.

Sixth Currant & Did Prambulate On ye Eaſt Side & North Eand And ye Bounds On ye Eaſt Side Are as Followeth

We began at An Old Whit Oak Above Capt Willards Saw mill, & ye firſt Mark was S^d Oak, And we Run Northerly ye Next Was a Pitch Pine, Cheſnut Whit Oak, Piller of Stones, Cheſtnutt, Red Oak & Burch Together, Cheſnut Piller of Stones at ye North Eaſt Corner. Alſo many Other Trees Marked on S^d Line though Not Named. Then We Turned & Run ye North Line, firſt A Burch then A Cheſnut, A Maple Two Cheſnuts Marked facing, Pople, Blak Oak, Piller of Stons, Cheſnut Cheſnut, Blak Oak, Whit Oak, Baſswood Trees Standing in a Hallow Whit Oak Cheſnut, Blak Burch, Cheſnut, Blak Oak, Piller of Stones, Whit Oak, cheſnut Black Oak, Whit Oak, Walnut, Blak Oak, Walnutt, cheſnut Walnut a Walnut at ye Northweſt Corn^r of S^d Farme, And there be Several More Marks on S^d Line though Not Named. And We prambulated On ye Weſterly Side of ye Pond Called Unkechewalom. We began at A Marked Cheſnut by S^d Pond that is between S^d Farme & Turky Hill Land & Run North weſterly About Eighty pole to A Cheſnut Tree Then We Turned & Run South Weſt^rly to a Piller of Stons y^t is a Corn^r. between Woburn farm and Dorcheſter farm, & A Side bounds to Turky hills, And to Confirm our perambulation We have Enterchangably Signed ye Day Above Said

JOHN SHEPLE	SAM^{LL} WALKER	Comm^{tee}
BENONI BOYNTON	SAM^{LL} RICHARDSON	
The propriators Wear	J Joſeph Burnap Was preſent	
Iſaac Farnſworth	And Affiſted in S^d Perambulation	
Joſhua Hutchins		

[38] To ye Comm^{tees} Attendenc, Travil & Expenc
June 12th When Ordered to Attend ye General Court On
  & 13th   ye Petetion of Jonth Whitny June ye 12th &
   1727   13th 1727

To: Coll^o Tailer Day	00 00 00
To: Coll^o Thaxter Day	00 00 00
To: Capt John Shiply 3 Days	1 10 00
To: Liu^t Benj^a Whittemore 3 Days	1 10 00

Survey and Allotment of Turkey Hills. 41

To: Fra: Fullam One Day & half	00 15 00	
To: Expenc, & Writings then Given in by Fra Fullam	00 10 00	
Expenc then Paid by mr Whittemore ᵽ Order & For Writings &c	3 16 7	
	8 1 7	

Decr 19th More to ye Commtee for their Attendenc Travil
1727 & Expenc To Wait On ye General Court as by them Ordred Decr 19th 1727

To: Collo Tailer	00 00 00	
To: Collo Thaxter	00 00 00	
To: Capt Shiply 4 Days & Expenc	2 12 00	
To: Liut Whittemore 3 Dayes	01 10 00	
To: Fra: Fullam 3 Days & Expence	1 16 00	
To: Expenc then pd by mr Whittemor	00 18 00	

Janry ye 4th More to ye Commtee for their Attendanc Travil
1727/8 & Expenc To Wait on ye General Court as Ordered Janry 1727/8

To: Collo Tailer	00 00 00	
To: Collo Thaxter	00 00 00	
To Capt Shiply 11 Days	5 10 00	
To: mr Benja: Whittemore 9 Days	4 10 00	
To: Fra: Fullam 9 Days	4 10 00	
Expenc then pd by Capt Shiply	2 7 00	
Expenc then pd by mr Whittemor	1 18 00	
To: Expenc then pd by Fra: Fullam for his horfe keeping to mr Edmunds	1 01 00	
To pocket Expenc & Writings	2 17 00	
To: A Day to Bofton to fetch ye papers & Expenc	00 11 6	
Febr total	38 2 1	

Survey and Allotment of Turkey Hills.

[**39**] Weston April 2ᴅ, 1728 South Town Dʀ   £   s   d

		£	s	d
April 2ᵈ 1728	To yᵉ Commᵗᵉᵉ for their Attendanc Travil & Expenc to prepare Accounts to Lay before yᵉ General Court as Ordered			
	To Capt Shiply Two Days £1 = 00-0 & Expenc	1	00	00
	To mʳ Whittemore One Day	00	10	00
	To Fra: Fullam One Day & Expence	00	14	00
April 1728	More To mʳ Whittemore One Day to Weſton on ſᵈ Servic	00	10	00
	Dittᵒ To Fra Fullam One Day With mʳ Whittemor	00	10	00
	More to Expenc by Sᵈ fullam	00	03	00
May yᵉ 3ᵈ 1728	Ditto Sᵈ Whittemore One Day at Weſton on ſᵈ Service	00	10	00
	Ditto to ſaid Fullam One Day & Expenc	00	13	0

Concord May yᴱ 16:ᵀᴴ & 17ᵀᴴ 1728

South Town is Dʳ To yᵉ Comᵗᶜᵉ for Attendance Travil & Expenc to prepare Accounts to Lay before yᵉ Genᵉˡˡ Court

	£	s	d
To Collᵒ Tailer for South Town Accoᵗˢ One Day at 10ˢ	00	10	00
Ditto: To Collᵒ Thaxter One Day & half	00	15	00
To: mʳ Benjᵃ Whittemore One Day	00	10	00
To: Fra: Fullam One Day	00	10	00
Expenc then pᵈ by Collᵒ Tailer at Concord charged to yᵉ South Town	00	5	3
Ditto there pᵈ by Collᵒ Thaxter	00	5	3
Ditto: by Mʳ Whittemor	00	5	10
Ditto then pᵈ by Fra: Fullam	00	5	10
	7	17	2

Survey and Allotment of Turkey Hills.   43

June 5   More to m^r Whittemore One Day
1728   at Wefton to prepare Accounts
         to Lay before y^e Gen^{ell} Court as
Ordrd With ffullam One Day at $\frac{s}{10}$ five shill^s
to y^e South Town   00 05 00
And 5$^s_\cdot$ to y^e North Town
Ditto to Francis Fullam One Day at $\frac{s}{10}$ Ex-
pen$c$ 4$^s_\cdot$ for y^e wch y^e North Town D^r for
7$^s_\cdot$ & y^e South Town for   00   7 00
                                                 ─────────
                                                  8   9 02
                                                 ─────────
                   South Totall   08 09 02
                                                 ─────────

[40]   Left blank.

[41] ⎫
[42] ⎪
[43] ⎬ Pages 41, 42, 43, 44, cut out.
[44] ⎭

[45]   Left blank.

[46]   Left blank.

[47]   Left blank.

[48]

THE BOUNDS OF Y^E SOUTH TOWN MEDOW LOTTS

Two Lotts of Medow No: 9 & 10

Two Meadow Lotts Ajoyning to Lott No: 5: In the Second Divifion Near Bennetts Both Makes up: 10: Acres and are Bounded As Followeth. Northerly on the Above S^d: 5th Lott Westerly on Said Bennitts Lot No: 69: in the First Divifion & Southerly Bounded on Meadow Lot, No: 8: Near the uper End of Cataconamog meadow & Easterly Bounded by Marks & Upland thefe are the most Northerly Meadows in Cataconamog Meadows, & Belong to Lotts No: 5: and : 6: in Second Divitions — — —

─────────────────────────────────

*The lines here printed in italics are in the original written in the margins. [*W. A. D.*]

Meadow Nº: 8 :—5 Acres

Meadow Lot, Nº: 8: In Cataconamog Bounded Northerly on the 10 acre of Meadow above S^d Westerly on Bennitt or the 69th Lot, in First Divifion, Southerly on the three Acres above ye Bever Dam, Easterly by Marks and Upland — —

Meadow No 7 5 Acres

Meadow Lot, No: 7: In Cataconamog Bounded Westerly on Marked Trees, Partly Southerly on Meadow Lot Nº : 6: and Easterly by marks by the Upland Northerly by marked Trees at the Angles — —

Meadow Nº: 6:

Meadow Lot Nº : 6: Bounded Westerly by Marks on the Upland 19: Rods - Southerly by the Meadow Nº: 5: in s^d Cataconamog Meadows Easterly by Upland, Northerly by Meadow Lot Nº : 7: in Cataconamog meadows

Meadow Nº —5— 5 Acres

Meadow Lot Nº: 5: in Cataconamog Bounded Northerly on Meadow Lot Nº : 6: Easterly on the Marks by the Upland, 16: Rods Southerly by Meadow Lot Nº: 4: and Southwesterly by Marks About 20: Rods

Meadow No —4— 5 Acres

Meadow Lot Nº 4: in Cataconamog Meadows Bounded Norwesterly on Meadow Lot Nº: 5: Easterly on the Upland: 10: Rods and Partly Southeasterly on Meadow Lot Nº: 3: & Southerly on Marks about 33 Rods

Meadow Nº: 3: 5 Acres

Meadow Lot Nº. 3. in Cataconamog above Mr Bormans Farm Bounded Westerly on the above Mentioned Meadow Nº: 4: Bounded Northerly & Easterly on Upland, & Southerly on Marks 39 Rods this Contains about Six acres by Reafon of the widnefs of the Brook that Runs through the Same —

Medow Nº 2 5 Acres

Meadow Lot Nº 2: in Cataconamog Meadow, Bounded Norwesterly on Marks Near 19. Rods Easterly on medow Lots Nº 4. & 5. Southerly on Staks & Westerly on Lot Nº 1. on Mafsapog Brook

5 Acres

Medow Lot No 1: in Cataconamog on Both Sids Mafapog Brook Bounded Northerly 34 Rods by upland & marks & westerly it Bounds: 20: Rods by marks & Southerly about 34 Rods by marks in Meadow Lands and Easterly it Bounds on Meadow Lot No: 2:

[49] *Nº: 1: above Mafsapog Where the Brook Comes into the Meadow 5: Acres*

An account of the Meadows above Mafsapog Pond Begining at Nº 1: Where Unchawalam Brook Comes into the Meadow by A Small White Oak Marked & from thence it Bounds South & Southwesterly on Marks & on Upland Near Forty two Rods to a Ded Pine Tree thence it Bounds Partly East 23 Rods to a Stake from thence it Bounds North on Meadow Lot Nº 2. & Norwesterly 20 Rods on Upland to the Small White Oak Where we Began — —

Meadow Nº —2: 5 Acres

Meadow Lot Nº 2. Bounds South Westerly on meadow Lot No 1. — Norwesterly it Bounds on Upland 28 Rods and Noreasterly it Bounds on Meadow Lot Nº. 3. & Southeasterly it Bounds about 27 Rods Rods on Upland. — —

Meadow Nº: 3: 5 Acres & 20 Rods

Meadow Lot No. 3. is 4 acres & 20 Rods Bounded South easterly on the: 2ᵈ: or Nº 2. Norwesterly on Marks & upland, Noreasterly on Marks & Common Swamp. & South easterly on Marks & Common Swamp alfo one acre more Lying at a Small Diftance Easterly from it Being 20 Rods Long & Eight Rods Wide at the North end is Two Stakes one at Each Corner & at the South End a Ded Popler Stump & a Small Marked Tree at the Southeast Corner

Meadow N<u>o</u> : 4 : 5 Acres

Meadow Lot N<u>o</u> 4. on the Northerly Side Maſsapog Pond Bounded North & Norwesterly 25 Rods on Marks & Upland Northeasterly it Bounds on Mr Gutrog 34 Rods Southerly Near the S^d Pond 33 Rods Westerly on Marks 28 Rods.

Meadow N<u>o</u> : 1 : 5 Acres

Meadows Below Mr Bormans Farm on Cataconamog Brook N<u>o</u>. 1. on the East Side the Brook Begining at Mr Bormans Farm Down to the Pond the Brook Being the South & Southwesterly Bounds, and the Upland the North and Easterly Bounds — — —

Meadow N<u>o</u> 2 : 5 Acres.

Meadow Lot No 2. Below Mr Bormans Farm & is Bounded on the Brook Northerly, & Easterly, & Westerly on Marks 28 Rods & Southerly it Bounds on Meadow Lot N^o : 4 : 30 Rods.

Meadow No. 3. 5 Acres

Meadow Lot No. 3. Bounds Norwesterly 25 Rods on Common Upland to a Stake, & Westerly it Bounds on Marks Southerly on Upland, Easterly on Meadow Lot N° 4.

Meadow N° 4—5 Acres

Meadow Lot N<u>o</u> 4 Bounds Westerly on Meadow N<u>o</u> 3. Northerly on Meadow No 2. & Easterly & Southerly it Bounds on Upland

[50] *Meadow N<u>o</u> 5 5 Acres*

Meadow Lot N<u>o</u> 5. Lyes Below the Ridge hill on the Southerly Side & adjoyning to Cataconamog Pond

Survey and Allotment of Turkey Hills. 47

Bounds Northerly by the Pond North easterly by the Brook. Southeasterly by Meadow Lot No 6 and Southwesterly by the Ridge hill or upland.

Meadow No. 6 5 Acres.

Meadow Lot Nº 6 Near Cataconamog Pond Bounded Norwesterly by meadow Lot Nº 5. North or North easterly by the Brook & Southeasterly by meadow Lot Nº 7 and Southeasterly by Upland. 18. Rods

Meadow No 7—5 Acres.

Meadow Lot No 7. Bounds Westerly on Lot Nº 6— & Northerly on the Brook Southeasterly on the Marks by the Upland & Southwesterly by Marks A Pich Pine & A Maple Marked

Meadow Nº. 1. 5 Acres

Medow, Turkey hill Medow, Lotts which are. 4. No. 1. Bounded Easterly by the 47th Lot in the First Division and Upland South & Southwesterly by Marks & by the Bever Dam & Marked Trees and the Upland, & North westerly it Bounds on meadow Lot No. 2. — —

Medow Nº. 2. 5 Acres

Medow Lot Nº 2. Bounds Partly Southeasterly by Meadow Lot Nº 1. & Westerly it Bounds on Marks by the Upland Northerly by Lot of Medow Nº. 3. & Northeasterly it Bounds on Lot Nº 47 in the First Divifion

Medow No 3. 5 Acres

Medow Lot No 3. Bounds Southeasterly by Meadow Lot Nº 2. Westerly by Marks by the Upland Norwesterly by a Medow Lot Nº 4: Noreasterly by the First Division — — —

Medow No 4, 5 Acres.

Medow Lot No. 4. Southeasterly by Medow Lot Nº 3. & Westerly by Marks, & Norwesterly by marks, & Noreasterly by Lot No 46. in the First Divifion.

Survey and Allotment of Turkey Hills.

Medow No 1. 5 Acres.

Medow Lotts in Horsmeet Medow No 1. Bounded Nor easterly on Lt Perleys or N° 7. in the first Divifion & Easterly on S^d 7th Lott South on Medow No 2. West on old m^r Hills Medow in the 15th Lot

Medow No. 2 5 Acres.

Medow Lot No. 2. in horfmeet Bounded on the North by medow Lot No 1. on the East by the 7th Lot in First Division, on the South by Medow No 3. on the West by the 15th Lot in ye First Divifion

Medow N°. 3. 5 Acres.

Medow Lot, No. 3. in Horsmeet Medow Bounded North by Medow Lot No. 2. Easterly by Lot No 7. in the first Divifion Southerly by the Ministeriall Lot. & West by Old m^r Hills Lot No: 15th in first Divifion

Medow N° 1. 5 Acres.

Medow Lot the First above the Bever Dam in Bever Pond medows is Bounded Easterly on Groton Line South-westerly on the upland & Norwesterly on a Line Crofs the Medow & North & Noreasterly it Bounds on a Poin Ridge by the Side of S^d Medow — —

[51] *Three Acres and 60 Rods.*

And their is on the Same Stream Below the Line of the above f^d Medow or the 5 acres 3 acres & 60 Rods Before the Stream Crofses Groton Line

Medow No: 1: 5 Acres

Medow Lot N^o: 1: in Clay Pitt Medows Bounded as Followeth Southeasterly on Marks & Southwesterly on Severall Marks by the upland, and Northwesterly on Medow Lot No 2. & Easterly & NorEasterly on Marks by the Upland

Survey and Allotment of Turkey Hills.

Medow No. 2. 5 Acres.

Medow Lot No: 2, in Clay Pitts Medow, Bounded Partly South East on Medow Lot No: 1: and Southwesterly it bounds on Common Upland 18 Rods & Norwesterly it Bounds on Medow Lot No 3. & Easterly on Common Land

Medow No: 3: 5 Acres

Medow Lot No: 3: Bounded South easterly on Medow Lot No 2: and South westerly it Bounds on Marks by the Upland; and Norwesterly it Bounds on Lot N°. 4, and Easterly it Bounds on Common Land.

Medow N°: 4: 5 Acres

Medow Lot N°: 4: Bounded Southeasterly on Lot N°: 3: South westerly on Marks by Common Upland, & Norwesterly it Bounds on Medow Lot N°: 5: & Easterly it Bounds on Common Land.

Medow No: 5: 5 Acres

Medow Lot N°: 5: Bounded South easterly on Medow Lot No: 4: and Common Land, South westerly on Marks 4 Rods wide at this end and Norwesterly it Bounds on Medow No: 6: and Easterly it Bounds on Common Upland 29 Rods.

Medow No: 6: 5 Acres

Medow Lot No: 6: in Clay Pit Medow Bounded Southeasterly on Medow No: 5: & Southwesterly it Bounds on Marks about 10 Rods & Norwesterly it Bounds on Lot N°: 7: of medow, and Easterly it Bounds on Common Land about 10 Rods Wide

Medow No: 7: 5 Acres

Medow Lot N°: 7: in Clay Pit Medow Bounded South easterly on Medow No: 6: and South westerly it Bounds on Marks Better then Ten Rods and Norwesterly it Bounds on Medow Land in Lot No: 40: in the First Divifion & Easterly on Upland

Medow No: 1: 5 Acres

Medow Lot N°: 1: in yᵉ Most Southerly Parts of

Mulpus Medows, Bounding Norwesterly on Daniel Thursting, & Easterly on Upland, & Southerly on Beefes 2 Acres an quarter of medow to Make Up his Medow Part and Westerly on Upland

Medow No: 2: 5 Acres

Medow Lot No: 2: Bounded Southerly by Lot of Medow No: 1 and Westerly on Daniel Thurstings Medow Land & Northerly on Medow No: 3: and Easterly by Upland

Medow No: 3: 5 Acres

Medow lot No: 3: Bounded Southerly by Lot of Medow No 2: & Common Land and Westerly on Marks by the Upland & Northerly by Medow lot No: 4 —

[52] *Medow No: 4 5 Acres*

Medow Lot No 4: Bounded Southerly on Medow N° 3: and Southwesterly Marks and Northerly by Medow No. 5: & Southerly by Common Land — — —

Medow Lot No: 5 6 Acres

Medow Lot No: 5 Bounded 20 Rods on or Near the Brook; South Easterly 14 Rods by Common Land & Southerly on Medow No: 4: and Northerly on Medow No: 6: at the west end it is but about 4 Rods wide this Medow Takes in at the East End A Pine Island of Near an Acre

Medow No: 6: 5 Acres.

Medow Lot No 6: Bounded Southerly by Medow No: 5: South westerly by Marks & Northerly on Medow N°: 7: and Easterly it Bounds on the Brook

Medow No: 7: 5 Acres

Medow Lot No: 7: Bounded Southerly on Medow N°: 6: Southwesterly on Marks, & Northerly it Bounds on Medow No: 8: and Easterly on the Brook

Medow No: 8—5 Acres.

Medow Lot No: 8: Bounded Southerly by Medow No: 7: & Westerly by Marks & Upland & Northerly

Partly on Medow No: 9: and the Brook, and Noreasterly on the Brook.

Medow No: 9: 5 Acres
Medow Lot No: 9: Bounded Southerly on Medow No: 8: Westerly on Marks, & Northerly on Medow No: 10: & Easterly on the Brook —

Medow No: 10: 5 Acres
Medow Lot No: 10 -: on the West Side the Brook Below the Falls is Bounded South on Medow No: 9: West on Marks & Upland and North on Marks and East on the Brook —

Medow No: 11: 4: Acres
Medow Lot No: 11: on the West Side the Brook, up to the Falls, Bounded South by the Medow Line No: 10: & West by Upland, & North on the Falls. & East on the Brook, & this Contains 4 Acres.

Medow No: 1: 5 Acres
Medow Lot N^o: 1: on the East Side the Brook, Beginning by the Falls and So Counting Down the Brook, Bounding West on the Falls & the Brook, North on the Marks, and the Upland, & East on Marks & Upland, South on Medow No: 2:

Medow No 2: 5 Acres.
Medow Lot N° 2: Bound North on Medow No: 1: & Marks Westerly on the Brook & Southerly on S^d Brook, & Easterly on Medow No: 3: & a Pine Ridge & Marks

[53] *Medow No: 3: 5 Acres.*
Medow No=3= Bounded Southerly on the Brook, & West on Medow No=2= & Norwest on Upland & Swamp, & East on Medow No: 4=, and Marks

Medow No: 4 5 Acres
Medow Lot No: 4: Bounded Southwest on the Brook & South on the Medow No: 5: & Southeasterly on Upland, & Northerly on A line & West & Nor west on Marks.

Survey and Allotment of Turkey Hills.

Medow No: 5: 5 Acres

Medow Lot No: 5: Bounds on Upland Down the Brook on Both Sids Till it Comes Near the East line of Lot No: 52 in Second Divifion

Medow No: 1 5 Acres.

Medow Lot No: 1: above the Falls, in Mulpus Medows this was Guest at, and is Bounded Southerly at the Falls & Upland, and Westerly on Fisk, & Joseph Page. & Northerly on Marks & Easterly on the Upland.

Medow No = 2 = 5= Acres.

Medow No: 2: in uper Mulpus on the Easterly Side of the Brook Cheafly & Bounded South on Upland & North East on Upland, North on Marks, & West on Medow No: 3:

Medow No: 3: 5 = Acres

Medow Lot No: 3: Bounded South on the Brook, & Westerly on Medow No: 4: & Northerly on Upland, & Easterly on Medow No: 2:

Medow No = 4 = 5 = Acres

Medow Lot No: 4: Bounded Southward on the Brook, & west on medow No: 5: and North on upland, & East on Medow No: 3:

Medow No: 5: 5=Acres

Medow Lot No: 5 = Bounded South westerly Partly on the Brook and Westerly on Medow No: 8: & North easterly on Upland & : 10 : Rods East on Medow No: 4: this Lott of Medow Lies on Both Sids the Brook

Medow No: 6: 5 = Acres.

Medow Lot No 6: Lies on the East Side Mulpus Brook Bounded Easterly on the Upland, & Northerly on Marks, and Westerly on a Strait Line Near the Brook.

Medow No: 1: 5 Acres.

Medow Lot No: 1: In Perhams Medow or Rock Medow. Begining at the Lower end of the Bever Dam.

Survey and Allotment of Turkey Hills.

Bounding Southerly by Marks by said Dam. and Westerly by Marks on the Upland, and Nor[ ] it Bounds on Medow, No: 2: and Easterly it Bounds On Marks by the Upland.

[54] *Medow No: 2: 5 = Acres.*

Medow Lot No: 2: in s^d Medow Bounds South on Medow No: 6: and West on Marks & North on Medow No: 3: and Easterly on Marks and Upland — —

Medow No: 3: 5 = Acres.

Medow Lot No: 3: in Perham's or Rock Medow, Bounds Southerly on Medow Lot No: 2: and Nor westerly it Bounds by Marks by the Upland and Northerly it Bounds cheafly on Marks in the Medow Land & Southeasterly it Bounds it Bounds on the Upland and Marks.

Medow No: 7: 5: Acres.

Medow & Swamp Lot No: 7: on the East Side Mulpus Brook Against & Bound Northward or Lot No: 10: in Second Divifion Upland and Easterly on Upland, & Southerly on Upland about: 8: Rods, & Westward it Bounds on Lot of Medow & Swamp No: 8:

Medow No: 8: 5 Acres.

Medow & Swamp No: 8: Bounds Northerly on Lot No: 11: in Second Devifion Upland Easterly it Bounds on Medow: No: 7: and South on Medow No: 6: and west on Undivided medow Land

Medow No: 8: 5 acres.

Medow Lot No: 8: on the Westerly Side Mulpus Brook, in Uper Mulpus Medows, a Triangler Lot and is Bounded Northerly on Lot No: 9: of Medow, and Southeasterly on Medow Lot No: 5: and South westerly on + Mark Trees and upland,

Medow No: 9: 5 Acres.

Medow Lot No: 9: Bounded Southerly on Medow No: 8: and Westerly it Bounds marks, Northerly, on Medow No: 10: and Easterly on Upland.

Medow No: 10: 5 Acres.

Medow Lot No: 10: with allowance for a Pine Ridg in it and is Bounded Southerly by Meadow Lot No: 9: and Westerly by Marks, and Northerly by Meadow Lot No: 11: & Eastward it Bounds on upland.

Medow No: 11: 5: Acres.

Medow Lot No: 11: Bounded Southward on Medow Lot No: 10: and Westward on Marks, & Nor west on Medow Lot No: 12: & Eastward Partly, on Medow No: 6: and Partly on Upland.

Medow No: 12: 5 Acres.

Medow Lot No: 12: Bounded Southward on Medow No: 11: And Westward on Marks & Northward on Medow Lot No: 13: and Eastward on Medow No: 6:

Medow No. 13: 5 Acres.

Medow Lot No: 13: Bounded Southward on Medow Lot No: 12: and Westward on Marks, & Northward on Medow: 14: & Eastward on Medow No: 6:

[55] *Medow No: 14: 5 = Acres.*

Medow Lot No: 14: Bounded Southerly on Medow No: 13: and Westward is Bounded on Marks. Northward it is Bounded on Medow No: 15: and Eastward it is Bounded on Medow No: 6: —

Medow Lot No: 15: 5 Acres.

Medow Lot No: 15: Bounded Southward on Medow No: 14: and Westward on Marks, & is about 28 Rods Shorter then the 14: Medow Lot, & it is 22 Rods Wide, and Bounds Northerly by a Strait Line by Common Land to a Larg White Pine Tree Taking in Two Points of Upland, & Bounds Easterly on Medow No: 6:

Thirteen Medow Lotts & one Acre and half is cont] the Bounds of other Lotts.

[56] Page 56 left blank.

[57] Page 57 left blank.

[58] HOLDING THE SOUTH TOWN LOTS.

John Fletcher	81		84	15	West uper Mulpus
Nathll Harris	71		66	5	Lower end of Mulpus
Moses Smith	64		19	3	above Borman's farm
Roberd Harris	23		36	11	West of uper Mulpus
Abrm Woodward	82		51	3	in horſmeet
Aron Smith	46		52	11	in Lower Mulpus
Timo Harris	31		37	12	west of uper Mulpus
Ephrm Sautle	33		34		Medow in first Diviſin
Jonth Hubbart	51		62	2	in Turkey hill Medow
Joseph Hubbart	24		30	2	in Perl hill Medow.
Daniel Davis	61		13	5	in Uper Mulpus
Wm Keen	56		10	7	E: of Uper Mulpus
Jonth Hartwell	73		89		Medow in the Lott
Elias Barron	32		35	8	W: of uper Mulpus
John Warrin	18	Not yet	74 Done	2	in perrams medow
John Child	10		29	4	E: Side of uper mulpus
Jacob Fullam	80		2d Diviſion 87		South of Mulpus Medow Joyns thereto
Nathll Whittemore	57		6	6	in Cattaconamog
John Whitney	76		22	1	in Perrams Medow
Wm Wood	79		3d Diviſion		South of Capt Perleys Lott 45 Acres 1 in horſmeet
Lt Josiah Jones	34		75	3	in Perhams Medow
Eleazr Green	20		33	2	E: of uper mulpus
Ephm Peirce	65		86	1	above Maſapoge
Nathll Holdin	42		3		Medow in the Lot
Zacheriah Sautle	28		26	1	W: of Uper Mulpus
Ephrm Peirce W:W:	68		87	5	in Cattaconamog
Isaac Stone	29		76	9	west of Uper Mulpus
Nathll Woods	58		11	8	in uper mulpus
Nathll Woods Junr	53	2d diviſin	37	3	in Turkey hill Medow
Nathan Hayward	38		73	9	above Bormans Farm
Edward Emerſon Eſqr	78		21	4	E: lower Mulpus
John Calf	21		27	3	E: lower Mulpus
Tho — Hall	22		38	1	S. of lower Mulpus
Daniel Thurstin	50		46		medow in the Lott
Phillip Goodridg	70		85		Medow in the Lott
Jonathan Poore	54		79	7	in Cattaconamog
Willm Blunt	55		81	3	Behind Turkey hills
Henry Chandler	13		50	4	Behind Turkey hills
Capt Tho Perley	84		58	1	On Maſapoge Brook
Jeremiah Perley	67	Changed	80 91	4	in Cattaconamog
Jonathan Woodman	17		40	2	in Cattaconamog.
Thomas Tailler	4		28	7	west of Lower Mulpus
Thomas Kimball	16		24	3	Cata: above Bormans

[59]

		] Poor
		] Captⁿ Jofiah Willard
	]nry Chandler	Daniel Aufting
	] Capt Thomas Perley	Sam^{ll} Aufting
	] Jeremiah Perley	Benjamin Goodridg
	] Jonathan Woodman	Jonathan Woodman
	] Thomas Tailer	Sam^{ll} Johnfon
	] Thomas Kimball	Thomas Kimball
	] Nath^{ll} Stow	Jofiah Bailey
	] Walter Bees	Walter Bees
	] William Wheeler	William Wheeler
	] Petter Heywood	Petter Harwood
] 14	Thomas Woolley	Alnathan Jones
] 26	Sam^{ll} Hartwell for Isaac	Jofiah Willard Efq^r
] N° 45	Joseph Ball	Jon^a Whitney Junr
]t N° 63	John Hastings	John Hastings
] Lot N° 15	Ebenezer Chadwick	Thomas Hill
] Lot N° 30	Joseph Allien	John Brewer
] Lot N° 35	Lt Jonathan Boyden	Feffeis in Truft for Maddam Willard
] Lot N° 72	Benj^a Prefcot	Timothy Gibfon Junr
] Lot N° 12	Phineas Parker	Finehas Parker
]e Lot N° 11	Thomas Tarbell	Wm Larrance
]fe Lot N° 43	Joseph Gilfon	Jonathan Whitney
]fe Lot N° 44	William Larrance	Jofhua Hutchens
] Lot N° 5	James Gold	Sam^{ll} Jonfon
] N° 41	Jofeph Page	Jofeph Page
] N° 52	Sam^{ll} Page	Sam^{ll} Page.
] N° 66	James Richardson	Sam^{ll} Farnsworths hiers
]t N° 36	Willm Richardson	David Gold
] Lot N° 25	Jonathan Whitney	Jofiah Willard
] Lot N° 62	Isaac Whitney	William Wallis
]fe Lot N° 6	Shadrach Whitney	John Haywood
] Lot N° 48	Mr Willm Clark	Mr Willm Clark

[60]

Houfe Lot N° 60	[	
Houfe Lot N° 3	John Burrill Efq^r	]
Houfe Lot N° 27	Jonathan Dows Efq^r	Jon^a Do[
Houfe Lot N° 40	Jeremiah Allien Efq^r	Jeremiah Allien Efq^r
Houfe Lot N° 77	Nath^{ll} Whitney Junr	Richard Estey
Houfe Lot N° 37	Edward Hartwell	Benjamin Cory
Houfe Lot N° 2	Amos Brown	Hilkiah Boynton
Houfe Lot N° 8	Maj^r Elea Flagg	the heirs of s^d Maj Flag.
Houfe Lot N° 75	Capt Richard Kimball	John Wood
Houfe Lot N° 9	James Burbeen	James Burbeen
Houfe Lot N° 7	Lt Thomas Perley	James Colbern
]fe Lot N° 14	John Perram	Sam^{ll} Page
] Lot N° 69	Phineas Richardfon	Sam^{ll} Benith

Survey and Allotment of Turkey Hills.

]infter	1	Hous Lott	
]terial	39	Hous Lott	
] Lot No 85		Wm Tailer Efqr	Wm Tailer Efqr
] Lot No 86		Samll Thaxter Efqr	Samll Thaxter Esqr
] Lot No 87		Fra: Fullam	Edward Heartwell
] Lot No 88		Capt John Shiply	Ephraim Peirce
] Lot No 89		Benja Whittemor	Jonth Willard

[61]

[62]

South Town House Lots	No.	The Names of thofe That first Drew them	The Names of those That Now hold them
Houfe Lot No	81	John Fletcher	Ebenr Wheeler & Jonth Ball
Houfe Lot No	11	Nathll Harris	by ye Heirs of Samll Farnsworth
Houfe Lot No	64	Mofes Smith	John Grout
Houfe Lot No	23	Robert Harris	Mr Andrew Gardner
Houfe Lot No	82	Abraham Woodward	Isaac Farnsworth
Houfe Lot No	46	Aron Smith	Mofes Goold
Houfe Lot No	31	Timothy Harris	Nathll Harris
Houfe Lot No	33	Ephraim Sautle	Timothy Gibfon
Houfe Lot No	51	Jonathan Hubbart	Samll Page
Houfe Lot No	24	Jofeph Hubbert	Robert Paul
Houfe Lot No	61	Daniel Davis	Benoni Boynton
]fe Lot No	56	Willm Keen	Jacob Stiles
] Lot No	73	Jonathan Hartwell	Edward Hartwell
] Lot No	32	Elles Barron	Archa Mackfeddres & John Scot
] Lot No	18	John Warrin	Samll Warren
]ufe Lot No	10	John Child	John Child
Houfe Lot No	80	Jacob Fullam	Benoni Boynton
Houfe Lot No	57	Nathll Whitemore	Jofiah Willard
Houfe Lot No	76	John Whitney	John Whitney
Houfe Lot No	79	William Wood	Jonathan Willard
Houfe Lot No	34	Lt Jofiah Jones	Lt Jofiah Jones
Houfe Lot No	20	Eleazer Green	John Hill
Houfe Lot No	65	Ephraim Pierce	David Peirce
Houfe Lot No	42	Nathll Holdin	John Fisk
Houfe Lot No	28	Zachariah Sautle	Nathan Towns
Houfe Lot No	68	Ephraim Peirce W: W:	Ephraim Peirce Junr
Houfe Lot No	29	Isaac Stone	John Goodridg
Houfe Lot No	58	Nathll Woods	Nathll Woods
Houfe Lot No	53	Nathll Woods Junr	Jonas Gilfon
Houfe Lot No	38	Nathan Hayward	Nathan Hayward
Houfe Lot No	78	Edward Emerfon Efqr	Edward Emerfon Efqr
Houfe Lot No	21	John Calf	John Calf
Houfe Lot No	22	Thomas Hale	Thomas Hale
Houfe Lot No	50	Daniel Thurstin	Daniel Thurstin

LUNENBURG TOWN RECORDS

THE EARLY RECORDS

OF THE

TOWN OF LUNENBURG.

A TABLE.

The first Town meeting for Choice of Town officers—
 Page, 1, 2

Money granted for yᵉ miniſters Sallery and for Building of a meeting House p. 3

Thunder Bolts 1749.

Annual meeting— P.—4
Annual meeting— P—5
A Reccord of High wayes P.—6, 12, 21, 22, 30, 33, 34, 35, 38, 41, ☞42.

Page Norcross

money granted for mending High wayes. Isaac Farnsworth to to make a book of records. Eighty pounds to be paid Mʳ Gardner p 7

Comᵗᵗᵉ choſen to build Seets and pulpit. money granted therefor. money granted for building a Pound. To build Pews a Comᵗᵗᵉ choſen to State places. a Comᵗᵗᵉ choſe to Reckon with mʳ Gardner—— p. 9:8

Thunder Struck before Noon.

Annual meeting p. 9
except accounts. 20 pounds ordered for mʳ Gardner 9.

A TABLE.

Cap.t Hartwell chofe to Joyn with y.e heirs of Kiby in a petition to Court.
Choice of Jury men   p. 10

Regefter for y.e County Treafurer for y.e County Jury men Isaac Farnfworth chofe to wait on y.e Court to get y.e Land Taxt— — —   P. 11—

Voted m.r Gardner a Difmiffion and y.e Select men power to pay and do anything elfe to perform it   12

a road from Northfield Road to the meeting house thro' ministerial land—

Annual Meeting   13

Money granted to by weights and measures and to pay y.e Towns Debts   p 12 & 15

Granted to m.r Gardner a Pew y.e com.tte for pews to appoint a minifteral Pew——   p. 15

a Record of M.r Gardner's Receipts and Request for a Dismifsion, & Discharge—   p. 16

Com.tte chofe to provide Preaching money Granted to pay Heywood— — — —   p 17

agreed to hire m.r Stearns 2 months Longer & Granted 50 £ for to Suply y.e Pulpit   p 17

Com.tte to hire a School mafter: ministerial and School Land to be put on Record: y.e Com.tte for hyring a minifter be Difmif.d & a book to be provided for y.e Selectmen   18

Choice of minifter: money Granted for Settlement & Sallery &c: P. 19.

Granting money: Choice of Town Officers & Excepting of High ways—   20–21–2

M.r Stearns ordination: Galleries in y.e meeting Houfe to be finished forthwith— — —   23.

money Raised to pay Co.ll willard for Entertaining y.e ordination Councell— — — — —   23

A TABLE.

200 £ Mr Stearns Settlement ½ on Poles & ye other half on Estats— — — — —	24
Mr Gardner, School for 3 months— — —	24
Preambelating Lins with Lancefter	24
Annual meeting. Granting money— —	25-6
Co^{ll} willard ajant to get ye Land Taxt	26
Confcerning a School ajants for a new County	40 £
Granted for High ways— — —	27
Laying Rates Granting money. Power to ye ajants for a new County altered.	28
Annuel meeting Granting money Excepting High wayes Selling Town Rode To pay for others.— — —	29, 30
Granting money Isaac Farnfworth to get ye money Due to building ye meeting House Juftice Hartwell to Take a Leas of ye Ground where ye meeting Houfe Stands. Two Tything men Chofen.— — —	31
Northfield road road by the bury-g place part discontinued.	33

---

[1]   In Council August 2, 1728.
ordered that Capt Josiah Willard a Principle Inhabitant of the Town of Lunenburg be and hereby is Impowered and Directed to Afsemble the freeholders and other Inhabitants of Said Town to Convene as Soon as may be to Elect and Chuse Town Officers there to Stand untill the Anniversary Meeting in March next.
     Sent Down for Concurrence.
        J. WILLARD *Secry*.

  In the House of Reprefentatives August 2, 1728
    Read and Concured
      W^M DUDLEY. *Spek^r*.

    Confented to, W^M BURNET

A True Coppy Examined ℔ J. WILLARD *Secry*.

By virtue of the above written order I have warned the freeholders and other Inhabitants of Said Town To Assemble at ye House of Ensigne Jonathan Willards on ye 19 day of August 1728

JOSIAH WILLARD—

Recorded by me ISAAC FARNSWORTH, *Town Clerk.*

[2] At a Legal meeting of ye freeholders and other Inhabitants of ye Town of Lunenburg (by an order from ye General Court) Afsembled August 19 : 1728.—

voted and Chose Capt Josiah Willard moderator.

Lt James Colburn
Capt Josiah Willard
m^r Hilkeah Boynton } Chofen Select men
m^r Ephraim Pearce
m^r Sam^{ll} Page

Isaac Farnsworth } Chofen Constables
Noah Dodge

Jofhua Hutchens
Jonathan Willard } Chofen Survayers of high wayes.
Nathan Haywood

Eleazer Houghton } Chofen Tything men
Sam^{ll} Johnson

L^t – Edward Hartwell } Town Treasurer.

James Jewell
John Fisk } Chofen Hoggreaves
Jeremiah Norcross

Jacob Stiles } Chofen fence viewers.
Jonathan Whittney

Recorded ⅌ me ISAAC FARNSWORTH *Town Clerk.*

[3] At a Legal meeting of the Inhabitants and freeholders of ye Town of Lunenburg Afembled—September ye 24: 1728 Capt Josiah Willard was Chofen moderator.

1ly voted and Granted ye Sum of Eighty Pounds money to be Levied on ye whole of ye Lands within Said Townfhip for ye minifters Sallery for ye Term of Six years next Comming.

2ly voted and Granted ye Sum of Two Hundred Pounds money to be Levied on Each Right or full Grant Equally to be proportioned for ye building and finishing of a meeting house in Said Town so far as it will do or anfwer there for.— — —

3ly. voted that Capt Josiah Willard and m^r Hilkiah Boynton wait on ye General Court for a Confirmation of ye aforefaid articals and also to obtain a Reccord of Said Town—

Recorded by me.   ISAAC FARNSWORTH *Town Clerk*.

At a Legal meeting of ye freeholders and Inhabitants of ye Town of Lunenburg Afsembled Janewary ye 27: 1728/9— — — —

Voted and Chose Capt Josiah Willard Agant for ye Town of Lunenburg aforefaid to Joyn with Such other men as ye Several neighbouring Towns Shall appoint to Consider what may be best in order to devide ye County of middlsex into two Counties.

A True Record ISAAC FARNSWORTH, *Town Clerk*.

[4] At a meeting of ye freeholders and other Inhabitants of ye Town of Lunenburg Afsembled March ye 31: 1729. Capt Josiah Willard was Chofen moderator

Sam^ll Jonson	
Ephraim Pearce	Chosen
Capt Josiah Willard	
Noah Dodge,	Select
Edward Hartwell	men.

Hilkiah Boynton } Constable

Sam^ll Jonson } Town Treasurer

Josiah Willard	
James Colburn	Chofen
Joshua Hutchens	Colectors

John Grout
nathan Heywood } Tything men.

John Heywood }
Jonathan Willard } Survayers of high
Nath.ll Harwood } —wayes—

Sam.ll Jonson }
Noah Dodge } Fence viewers

John Grout }
Jeremiah Norcross } Hoggreaves
Benj.a Corey }

Recorded by me   ISAAC FARNSWORTH *Town Clerk*

[5] At a Legal meeting of the freeholders and other Inhabitants of y.e Town of Lunenburg Afsembled March y.e 11. 1729/30. Cap.t Josiah Willard was Chofen Moderator.

Cap.t Josiah Willard }
L.t Edward Hartwell } Chosen
Isaac Farnsworth } Select   Sworn as
Ephraim Wetherbe } men   afsefsors
Jonathan Willard }

Isaac Farnsworth } Chosen Town Clerk & Sworn.

Daniel Austen } Chofe Constable & Sworn.

Edward Hartwell }
Josiah Willard } Chofen
Sam.ll Jonson } Survayers of high wayes—

Jonas Gillson }
David Gould } Tything men

Jacob Gould }
Joseph Page } Fence viewers.   Sworn.

William Jones }
Joshua Goodridge } Hogg reives.
Nath.ll Harwood }

Ephraim Wetherbe } Colector Chofen & Sworn.

Sam.ll Johnson } Town Treasurer.

At.s   ISAAC FARNSWORTH *Town Clerk*

[6]   LUNENBURG, Feb.r y.e 13: 1729/30.

An account of y.e Town wayes Laid out by y.e Select men of y.e Town above Said Beginning at y.e meeting House in Said Town and Running through Burbeans house Lott 64 Rods 4 Rods wide as it is now marked out and through Pools house Lott 120 Rods 4 Rods wide adjoyning on Burbeens Land to y.e way which is Called Northfield Rode, and also y.e northfield rode as it is Laid by y.e General Courts Com.tte from or near Pearl hill Brook to where y.e way is turned into Jonathan Whittneys Lot, and then Going through Said Whittney Lott 24 Rods, 4 Rods wide where it is now marked out. and Runing through Thurstins Lott 50 rod 4 Rods wide where it is now marked out. and then Running through Eleazer Boyntons meddow 31 rods one rod one half wide as it is marked out and Through Becths Land 96 rod 4 rods wide. and through Moses Willards Land 26 rods 4 rods wide with high way marks to where it Coms into y.e rode or way Left by y.e General Courts Com.tte and then running a Crofs the Corner of y.e Land Laid to Archiball Mackfatrich to Groton Line.: y.e ways as above mentioned is accepted and confiermed by y.e Town at y.e Annuell meeting in March held y.e Eleventh day in y.e year 1729/30

An account of y.e wayes or Town Rode Laid out by y.e Select men of Lunenburg beginning at Lancester Line and making high way marks on y.e westerly Side thereof to Lunenburg meeting house the Said way to be 4 rods wide as it is now Laid out. an account of y.e said way going through mens Lotts where there is no alowance made by y.e General Courts Com.tte Going through Ebenezer Richardson Land 100 rods Through Benjamin Coorys Land. 80 rods throug John Heywoods Land 64 rods Through Nathan heywoods And John heywoods Land 132 rods. Through Edward Hartwells Land 165 rods Through Goodridges Land 212 rods through harreses Land 50 rods through Gipsons Land 12 through Ephraim Pearces Land 94 rods &c. which rode is accepted alowed and Confiermed by y.e Town at y.e meeting above Said.

Recorded by me   ISAAC FARNSWORTH *Town Clerk.*

[7] At a Legal meeting of ye freeholders and other Inhabitants of ye Town of Lunenburg afsembled May ye 18. 1730 Capt Josiah Willard was Chofen moderator.

then voted that there be granted ye Sum of Twenty Shillings to be paid by Each full Grant for ye mending of high wayes

2ly. Voted and ordered that Isaac Farnsworth Town Clerk for ye time being be Impowered to Record all Such votes and orders that are proper to be Recorded (which hath ben here to fore past) fairly in a Town Book.

3ly. Voted that Eighty Pounds be paid to m^r Gardner out of ye money Granted by ye General Court upon ye Lands for ye Support of ye Gospell for ye prefent year.

Recorded by me ISAAC FARNSWORTH *Town Clerk.*

At a Legal meeting of ye freeholders and other Inhabitants of ye Town of Lunenburg afsembled Feb^r ye 8: 1730/31 Then Capt Josiah Willard was Chofen moderator

1ly. voted and agreed to build a body of Seets and a pulpit in ye meeting house.

2ly. voted and Chofe Isaac Farnsworth Jonathan Willard and Benj^a Goodridge. to be a Com^tte to build ye Seets and Pulpit afore faid.

3ly. voted and Granted ye Sum of Thirty Pounds money upon ye house Lotts to be Equally Proportioned and paid for the building of a body of Seets and a pulpit in ye meeting houfe.

4ly. voted and Granted ye Sum of five Pounds Twelve Shillings and Six pence money to pay m^r Sam^ll Page for building a Pound and for ye Land ye pound Stands on and a way to pafs and Repafs to it.

5ly. voted to build Pews in ye meeting house. so many as there is Conveniant Room for——

—6ly—

[8] 6ly. voted that Capt Josiah Willard Lt Edward Hartwell m^r Sam^ll Page m^r Ephraim Wetherbe and Lt James Colburn be a Com^tte to State Places for building of Pews in ye meeting house and order who Shall or may have them according to ye Direction of ye Town and it is further voted y^t ye Rule ye Com^tte Shall go by Shall be according to ye Inhabitants Improvements

and Stations and having Some Referance to Pay. it is also voted and agreed that yᵉ perſons preferred to have Pews Shall build them on their own Coſt and Charge

7ly. Voted and Choſe Capᵗ Josiah Willard Lᵗ Edward Hartwell Isaac Farnsworth James Colburn and Ephraim Wetherbe to be a Comᵗᵗᵉ to Reckon with Mʳ Gardner to See what yᵉ Town are Indebted unto him Since his ordination and make Return thereof to yᵉ next Town meeting.

Recorded by me   ISAAC FARNSWORTH *Town Clerk*

[9] At a Legᵘal meeting of yᵉ freeholders and other Inhabitants of yᵉ Town of Lunenburg Aſsembled March yᵉ 1: 1730/31 Capᵗ Josiah Willard was Choſen moderator.

Capᵗ Josiah Willard Mʳ Samˡˡ Page Mʳ Ephraim Wetherbe Lᵗ Edward Hartwell Dᶜ Samˡˡ Johnson	Choſen Selectmen. and aſeſsors.
Isaac Farnsworth	Choſen Town, Clerk, and Sworn.
Nathan Heywood	Choſen Conſtable. and Sworn.
Isaac Farnsworth	Choſen Colector, and Sworn
Ephraim Wetherbe Daniel Austen	Choſen Tythingmen. and Sworn.
Edward Hartwell Ephraim Pearce Josiah Willard Samˡˡ Johnson	Choſen Survayers of highwayes.
John Grout Jonathan Page	choſen fence viewers. and Sworn
Benjᵃ Cory Jonas Gillſon Jonathan Page	Choſen Hoggreives and Sworn.
Samˡˡ Johnson	Choſen Town Treasurer & Sworn

Voted yᵗ yᵉ Town accept of yᵉ accounts brought in by yᵉ Comᵗᵗᵉ appointed to Reckon with Mʳ Gardner

Voted and ordred that Twenty Pounds in bills of Credit yt is Raiſed upon ye unimproved Lands in Said Town to be paid to ye Revnd Andrew Gardner for his ſettle ment here in Said Town Provided Mr. Gardner doth Give a full Discharge of ye whole of his Settlement in all Particulars as he shall Claim as a promise from ye Town aforeſd

Iſ. FARNSWORTH *Town Clerk*—

[10] At a Legual meeting of ye Inhabitants and freeholders of ye Town of Lunenburg Aſsembled July 5: 1731 Lt. Edward Hartwell was Choſen moderator—then voted and Choſe Llt. Edward Hartwell Agant for ye Town of Lunenburg to Joyn with ye Gardean or heirs of James Kibby (or who ſoever shall Claim by from or under him) in a Petition to ye General Court for an Equivilent in ye Province Land for yt which is thought by Some to Lye within our Town Provided they will Relinquish their Claim in Said Town.

Atſ.— ISAAC FARNSWORTH *Town Clerk*

At a Legual meeting of ye freeholders and other Inhabitants of ye Town of Lunenburg aſsembled July 26: 1731

Then voted and Choſe Mr. Edward Hartwell Grand Jury man to Sarve on ye Grand Jury for ye year Enſuing

Atſ. ISAAC FARNSWORTH *Town Clerk*

At a Legual meeting of ye freeholders and other Inhabitants of ye Town of Lunenburg aſsembled August ye 20th 1731:

Then voted and Choſe Mr. Jonathan Willard Grand Juryman To Sarve on ye Grand Jury at a Superiour Court of Judicature Court of Aſsize and General Goal Delivery, To be holden at Worcester for ye County of Worcester on the Fourth Wednſday of September next 1731 and no Longer.—

Voted and Choſe Mr. Ephraim Wetherbe Petty Juryman to Sarve on ye Petty Jury at Court, Time, and Place afore Said. and no Longer.

Atſ. ISAAC FARNSWORTH *Town Clerk*

[11] At a Legual meeting of yᵉ Inhabitants and freeholders of yᵉ Town of Lunenburg afsembled September yᵉ 2 : 1731.

Then voted and Chofe Isaac Farnsworth modderator Voted and Chofe John Chandler Junʳ Esqʳ to be Regefter of Deeds for yᵉ County of Worcefter.—

Then voted and Chofe Mʳ Jonathan Houghton To be Treasurer for the County of Worcester.

Atˢ   Iᶜ Farnsworth *Town Clerk*

At a Legual meeting of the Inhabitants and freeholders of yᵉ Town of Lunenburg Afsembled October yᵉ 25 : 1731 Voted and Chofe Mʳ Ephraim Wetherbe Petty Jureyman To Sarve on yᵉ Jury of Trials at an Inferiour Court of Common Pleas to be holden at Worcester for yᵉ County of Worcester on Tuesday yᵉ Seccond Day of November next Ensuing yᵉ Date hereof &c.

At A Legual meeting of the Inhabitants and free holders of yᵉ Town of Lunenburg Afsembled December yᵉ 6:ᵗʰ 1731

Mʳ Samˡˡ Page was Chofen Modderator.—

1ly. Voted and Chofe Isaac Farnsworth To wait on yᵉ General Court in behalf of yᵉ Town with a Petition that the Land In Said Town may be Taxed for yᵉ Support of yᵉ Gospel—Both Improved and unimproved farms Grants and Devifions, &c:

And for anything Else that Shall be Thought Proper

Atˢ   Iᶜ Farnsworth *Town Clerk*

[12] At a Legual meeting of the Inhabitants and freeholders of the Town of Lunenburg Afsembled Febʳ yᵉ 7ᵗʰ 1731/2 Voted and Chofe Josiah Willard Efqʳ modderator Then voted and Granted yᵉ Reverand Andrew Gardner a Dismifsion from his Paftoral or minifterial office in Said Town According to his Request

2ly. Voted. and ordred that yᵉ Select men or their Suckfefsers be vested with Power for and in behalf of the Town to Pay Mʳ Gardner all and what foever yᵉ Town are Indebted unto him and also do and Perform any thing or things Else Reffering to his Dismifsion from his Paftoral office and obligation in Said Town as Soon as can be Conveniantly Performed

    At^s I. FARNSWORTH *Town Clerk*

  An account of a High way or Town Rode Layed out by ye Select men of ye Town of Lunenburg March ye 4th 1731/2 Beginning at a Rhode Called northfield Rhode. marked on ye Eafterly Side of Said Rhode four Rods wide firft Running through Jofiah Bayley Land on ye fore Side of his new dwelling Houfe, then Running through Jeremiah Norcrofs,es Land, Running by ye fore Side of Said Norcrofs,es Houfe, Then Running Through ye Land of Sam^{ll} Davis at one Corner of his Lot.

  Then Running Through ye minifterial Land. Then Running Through Jonathan Pools Land to ye Corner of a Rhode Laid out to ye meeting Houfe Through Ephraim Wetherbes Land.

  The above Said Rhode Excepted and allowed by ye Town at their Annual meeting in march held ye 6 day : 1731/2

  Recorded here in ye Twelveth Page of ye Book being an empty fpace for want of room in ye Thirteenth Page.

       ISAAC FARNSWORTH *Town Clerk*

  [13] At a Legual meeting of ye Inhabitants and freeholders of ye Town of Lunenburg Afsembled March ye 6 : 1731/2

  Dec. Sam^{ll} Johnson was Chosen modderator

Benj^a Goodridge
James Colburn
John Heywood   } Chofen Select men and Sworn as Afsefsors
Hilkiah Boynton
Daniel Austen

Isaac Farnsworth } Chofen Town Clerk and Sworn

Mr Edward Hartwell } Chofen Town Treasurer. and Sworn

Mr Sam^{ll} Page } Chofen Collector. and Sworn

The Early Records of the Town of Lunenburg.

Jeremiah norcrofs } Chofen Conftable: and Sworn

Jonathan Houghton } Chofen County Treasurer.

William Jones
Eleazer Houghton } Chofen Survayers of high ways
Nath.ll Harwood and Sworn.

Jonathan Willard
Hilkiah Boynton } Chosen Tything men. and Sworn.

Sam.ll Davis } Chofen Fence viewers. and Sworn.
Benj.a Coorey.

David Pearce
Nath.ll Page } Hogg reives. and Sworn.
Benj.a Fofter
John Hill

Voted that ye Hoggs in Said Town Shall run at Large.

M.r Sam.ll Page } Chofen Pound Keeper.

At^s   ISAAC FARNSWORTH *Town Clerk*

[14] At a Legual meeting of ye Inhabitants and freeholders of ye Town of Lunenburg Afsembled March ye 13 1731/2

Voted and Chofe M.r Hilkiah Boynton Modderator

1ly. Voted and Granted ye Sum of Six Pounds money for the Buying of Weights and Measures for Standards for Said Town

2.ly Voted and Granted ye Sum of Eight Shillings for building of a pair of Stocks.

3ly. Voted and Granted ye Sum of four Pounds four Shillings to pay M.r Edward Hartwell for Sarvice done for Said Town

4ly. Voted and Granted ye Sum of Six Shillings to pay M.r Jonathan Willard for Sarvice done for Said Town

5ly. voted and Granted ye Sum of Ten Shillings to pay M.r Ephraim Pearce for Sarvice done for Said Town

6ly. voted. and Granted ye Sum of Twenty Shillings to pay M.r Ephraim Wetherbee for Sarvice done for Said Town

7ly. voted and Granted ye Sum of thirteen Shillings to pay Mr Sam^ll Page for Sarvice done for Said Town

8ly. voted. and Granted ye Sum of Three Shillings to pay Mr. Daniel Austin for Sarvice done for Said Town

9ly. voted. and Granted ye Sum of Six Shillings to pay Mr Hilkiah Boynton for Sarvice done for Said Town

10ly. voted. and Granted ye Sum of nine Shillings to pay M.^r nathan Heywood for Sarvice done for Said Town

11ly. voted. and Granted ye Sum of Six pounds Thirteen Shillings and one penney to pay Isaac Farnsworth for Sarvice done for Said Town

HILKIAH BOYNTON *moderator*

[15] At a Legual meeting of the Inhabitants and freeholders of the Town of Lunenburg Afsembled Sep^tr ye 18th: 1732

Voted and Chofe Mr Sam^ll Page Modderator

1ly. voted and Granted ye Sum of Thirty Two Shillings To pay Co^ll Jofiah Willard for Eight dayes Sarvice Done for Said Town at Laying of Rates and Laying out High wayes for time past ——

2ly. voted and Granted ye Sum of Sixteen Shillings to pay Mr Sam^ll Johnson for Sarvice done for Said Town Time 4 dayes

3ly. voted and Granted ye Sum of Twenty Two Shillings to pay Mr Jeremiah Norcrofs for Sarvice Done for Said Town

4ly. voted and Granted ye Sum of five Pounds to pay Isaac Farnsworth for his Collecting or Gathering of Rates for ye year 1731

5ly. voted and Granted ye Sum of Three Pounds to pay Mr Ephraim Wetherbe for his Collecting or Gathering Rates for year 1730.

6ly. voted and Granted ye Sum of Three Pounds Eighteen Shillings for ye ufe of Mr Nathaniel Page for fencing in the burying Place

At.^s   ISAAC FARNSWORTH *Town Clerk*

At a Legual meeting of ye Inhabitants and freeholders of ye Town of Lunenburg Afsembled October ye 30.th 1732

(A Record of) a Receipt Given By the Revnd Mr Andrew Gardner of Lunenburg in full Discharge to ye Town for his Settlement and Sallery there. ———

Then Received of the Select men for the Town of Lunenburg the Sum of three Hundred Ninety and four Pounds Twelve Shillings and three Pence which is in full for my Settlement and Sallery there I Say Received p me
         Andrew Gardner Pastor

Lunenburg October ye 27 1732

A True Record from ye originall Attest
       Isaac Farnsworth Town Clerk

(A Record of) a Request from ye Reverand Mr Andrew Gardner To this Church in Lunenburg for his Dismission

To the Brethren of ye Church of Christ in Lunenburg
Beloved Brethren I Cannot but Think from what I have heard and also from what I have observed of ye transactions and behaviour of this People Relating to me and my affairs that there is not that affection born toward me that there Should be from a People to their Gospell minister, or that there is where a People are likely duly to profit under their minister, ye consideration whereof has been very Grevious and discouriging to me and therefore think it best to Seperate. I Do therefore propose a Sepperation and if effectual Care be Taken yt my dues be honestly paid me, ye first ministers Lott with its appurtenances put upon Record and Attested and a Sufficiant Pew at ye Right hand of Going in at ye Great doors of ye meeting House I Shall be free to be Dismissed from my Pastoral Relation and office obligation to you as Soon as it Can Regularly be performed.

from your Loving Pastor who wisheth you ye Divine Direction and blessing and desires your Prayers for ye Same to him. —— Andrew Gardner Pastor

Lunenburg Septr 18. 1730 ——
according to church warning then ye Church met at ye meeting house and received his acquittance from his Pastoral Relation to us as Attest his hand. Andrew Gardner Pastor

Lunenburg November ye 3: 1732
A True Record from ye originall Isaac Farnsworth Town Clerk

voted. and Chofe Mr Hilkiah Boynton Modderator

voted To ye Revn.^{d} Mr Andrew Gardner a Place in ye meeting houfe at ye Right hand of ye Great Doors to build a Pew

voted that this meeting be ajourned to fryday next at one of ye Clock in ye afternoon:

Voted. That ye Com^{tte} appointed for Stating Places for Pews in ye meeting houfe be Directed and ordered to State, order and appoint, a place for a menifterial Pew adjoyning to ye foot of ye Pulpit Stairs at ye Right hand of ye Pulpit.

At.^{s} — Isaac Farnsworth *Town Clerk.*

[16] (A Record of) a Receipt Given By the Revn.^{d} Mr Andrew Gardner of Lunenburg in full Discharge to ye Town for his Settlement and Sallery there.

Then Received of the Select men for the Town of Lunenburg the Juft Sum of three Hundred Ninety and four Pounds Twelve Shillings and three Pence which is in full for my Settlement and Sallery there: I say Received p.^{r} me

        Andrew Gardner *Paftor*

Lunenburg October ye 27: 1732

 A True Record From ye originall Att.^{s}

    Isaa Farnsworth *Town Clerk*

(A Record of) a Request from ye Reverand Mr Andrew Gardner. To his Church in Lunenburg for his Dismifsion.

To the Brethren of ye Church of Christ in Lunenburg—

Beloved Brethren. I cannot but Think from what I have heard, and alfo from what I have obfarved of ye tranfactions and behaviour of this People Relating to me and my affairs that there is not that affection born towards me that there should be from a People to their Gospell minifter—or that there is where a People are Likely duly to profit under their minifter ye Confideration whereof has been very Grevious and discouriging to me and there fore think it beft to Sepperate I do therefore propofe a Sepperation and if affectual Care be Taken y^t my dues be honeftly Paid me: ye first minifters Lott with its appurtenances put upon Record and Attefted and a Sufficiant Pew at yᵉ Right hand of Going in at yᵉ Great dooers of yᵉ meeting House I shall be free to be Difmifsed from my Paftoral Relation and office obligation to you as Soon as it Can Regularly be performed.

from your Loving Paftor who wifheth you yᵉ Divine Direction and blefsing and defires your Prayers for yᵉ Same to him.

Lunenburg Sepᵗʳ 18. 1730   ANDREW GARDNER *Paftor*

according to Church warning then yᵉ Church met at yᵉ meeting houfe and received his acquittance from his Paftoral Relation to us as Atteft his hand.

ANDREW GARDNER, *Paftor*

Lunenburg november yᵉ 3: 1732
A True Record from yᵉ originall

ISAAC FARNSWORTH *Town Clerk*

[17] At a Legual meeting of the Inhabitants and freeholders of yᵉ Town of Lunenburg afsembled Nouʳ yᵉ 10ᵗʰ : 1732

Voted. and Chofe Capᵗ Edward Hartwell modderator

Voted. that Dec. Samˡˡ Johnson Dec. Ephraim Pearce and Mʳ Isaac Farnsworth be a Comᵗᵗᵉ to Provide a minifter from time to time to Supply yᵉ Town with Preaching till further order, and to aggree with him in yᵉ Towns behalf what he Shall have for his Sarvice.

Voted. and Granted yᵉ Sum of Sixteen Shillings to pay Mʳ John Heywood for Going to Court to anfwer to yᵉ Towns Prefentment

Atˢ   ISAAC FARNSWORTH *Town Clerk*

At a Legual meeting of Inhabitants and freeholders of yᵉ Town of Lunenburg Afsembled Decembʳ yᵉ 4:ᵗʰ 1732

Voted. and Chofe Coˡˡ Jofiah Willard modderator

Voted. and aggreed that yᵉ Comᵗᵗᵉ appointed. hire Mʳ Stearns Two months Longer after yᵉ Term is out which yᵉ Comᵗᵗᵉ appointed to Supply yᵉ Town with Preaching hath hired him.

Voted. and Granted yᵉ Sum of Fifty Pounds to Defray yᵉ Charge of Supplying yᵉ Pulpit in Said Town

Recorded Pʳ me   ISAAC FARNSWORTH *Town Clerk*

The Early Records of the Town of Lunenburg. 77

[18] At a Legual meeting of ye freeholders and other Inhabitants of ye Town of Lunenburg Afsembled December ye 11 : 1732

Voted and Chofe Capt Edward Hartwell modderator

voted. that Co^{ll} Jofiah Willard Capt Edward Hartwell and Mr Benjamin Goodridge be a Com^{tte} to Provide a School and School Mafter for to teach Children and youth to Read and write & if the Com^{tte} See Good to hire a Gramer School mafter, they Shall have ye Liberty. Provided they Pay ye over Plus Charge of what ye Keeping of a Gramer School would be more yⁿ ye charge of Keeping an Englifh School:—

Voted, that ye Com^{tte} appointed to Lay out the first Devifion Seccond Devifion or meddow Lott or any Part thereof to any y^t shall need, be alfo a Com^{tte} to take a Survay & Lay out ye minifterial and School Land with Mr Nathan Heywood Survayer and make and Return a Plan thereof to ye Propriators Clark in order to have ye Same put upon ye Propriators Book of Reccords, and make Return to the Town of ye Charge thereof. — — —

Voted y^t ye Bill of ye Com^{tte} appointed to hire a minifter from time to time be alowed which is £3–10–0–

Voted. y^t ye Com^{tte} for hyring a minifter be Difmifsed from their further Sarvice in y^t affair.

Voted. that there be a book Provided for ye Select men to Record ye Town Rates in and how they are ordred out in order to Prevent miftakes

    At^s Isaac Farnsworth *Town Clerk*

[19] At a Legual meeting of ye freeholders and other Inhabitants of ye Town of Lunenburg Afsembled February ye 12th 1732/3.

Then voted and Chofe Deacon Sam^{ll} Johnfon Modderator

Voted that ye Town meeting be Ajourned to fryday ye 23 day of february Currant at Two of ye Clock in ye afternoon. at which time ye Town being meet and formed Proceeded to Bufinefs.

1ly. Voted and Chofe Mr David Stearns to be our Gospel minifter to Carry on ye work of ye miniftrey in Said Town.

2ly. Voted and Granted yᵉ Sum of Three Hundred Pounds for yᵉ ufe of Mʳ David Stearns for his Settlement in yᵉ work of yᵉ miniftrey in Said Town.

3ly. Voted and ordred that Two Hundred of yᵉ above Said Three Hundred Pounds be paid to Mʳ David Stearns yᵉ first year of his Settlement and yᵉ other Hundred yᵉ Seccond year of his Settlement which in yᵉ whole makes up yᵉ above Said Sum of Three Hundred Pounds.

4ly Voted and Granted yᵉ Sum of one Hundred and Twenty Pounds in Bills of Credit to be Paid Mʳ David Stearns in yᵉ first year of his Settleing and yᵉ Sum of Five Pounds more of Like money to be added yearly till in yᵉ whole it amounts to yᵉ Sum of one Hundred and Fourty Pounds yᵉ money to be quallified according to yᵉ Prefent value and ·to be Paid yearly for his Sallery in Proportion as afore fᵈ

5ly. Voted and Chofe yᵉ Two Deacons namely Mʳ Ephraim Pearce & Mʳ Samˡˡ Johnfon, and Jofiah Willard Efqʳ to be a Comᵗᵗᵉ to wait on yᵉ Reverand Mʳ David Stearns with yᵉ Towns Propofals.

    Atˢ·   Isaac Farnsworth *Town Clerk*

[20] At a Legual meeting of yᵉ Inhabitants and freeholders of yᵉ Town of Lunenburg Afsembled march yᵉ 5ᵗʰ 1732/3

Voted and Chofe Mʳ Benjamin Goodridge Modderator

1ly. voted and Granted yᵉ Sum of Three Pounds Ten Shillings To pay Deacon Samˡˡ Johnfon and Isaac Farnfworth for Going to Hire a minifter for Said Town

2ly. voted and Granted yᵉ Sum ot Nine Shillings to Pay Mʳ Jeremiah Norcrofs for warning nine Town meetings

3ly. Voted and Granted yᵉ Sum of Three Pounds Seven Shillings and Eight Pence to Pay Mʳ Andrew Gardner for Keeping the Minifters and Deligates on yᵉ Bufinefs of yᵉ Town

4ly. voted and Granted yᵉ Sum of Five Pounds to pay Mʳ Samˡˡ Page for his Collection. of Rates for yᵉ year 1732.

5ly. voted and Granted ye Sum of Twelve Shillings to pay Mr Sam^ll Page for Keeping Six Horſes on ye Towns occaſion

6ly. voted and Granted ye Sum of Thirteen Shillings to pay Mr Nathan Heywood for Keeping of School in Said Town

7ly. Voted and Granted ye Sum of Eight Shillings to pay Mr Benjamin Goodridge for Keeping of School in S^d Town

8ly. voted and granted ye Sum of Three Pounds to pay Mr Hilkiah Boynton for Keeping of School in Said Town

9ly. voted and granted ye Sum of Three Pounds to pay M^r Joſiah Willard Junr for Keeping of School in Said Town

10ly voted and Granted ye Sum of fourty Shillings to pay Mr Benjamin Goodridge for Sarvices done for Said Town

11ly. voted and Granted ye Sum of Twenty Two Shillings to pay Mr James Colburn for Sarvice done for Said Town

12ly. voted and Granted ye Sum of Twenty Shillings to pay Mr Daniel Auſten for Sarvice done for Said Town

13ly. voted and Granted ye Sum of Fourteen Shillings to pay Mr John Heywood for Sarvice done for Said Town

14ly. voted and Granted ye Sum of Thirty Six Shillings to pay Mr Hilkiah Boynton for Sarvice done for Said Town

15ly. voted and Granted ye Sum of Six Shillings to pay Mr Daniel Auſten for his hors to Worcester on ye Town occaſion

ye other buſineſs of ye above Said meeting Entred on ye other Page

[21] March ye 5th 1732/3 Annual meeting

Mr Benjamin Goodridge.
Mr James Colburn.
Mr John Grout.
Mr Jonas Gillſon.
Mr Hilkiah Boynton

Choſen Select and Sworn Aſsesors men

Isaac, Farnſworth, Town Clerk. and Sworn
M.̠ James Colburn. Town Treaſurer and Sworn
M.̠ John Grout. Choſen Conſtable & Sworn
M.̠ William Jones. Choſen Collector & Sworn

M.̠ Sam.ˡˡ Page
M.̠ William Jones } Choſen Survayers of
M.̠ Joſhua Goodridge High wayes Sworn

M.̠ Sam.ˡˡ Johnſon
M.̠ Jonathan Page } Choſen Tythingmen

M.̠ Joſiah Bayle
M.̠ Eleazar Houghton } choſen Fence viewers

M.̠ Sam.ˡˡ Farnſworth
M.̠ Jonathan Whitney }   Farnsworth
M.̠ Jonathan Gould   Choſen Hoggreives: Gould Sworn

Voted that yᵉ Hogs Shall Go at Large in S.ᵈ Town
M.̠ Ephraim Pearce Choſen Sealer

    Atˢ: — Isaac Farnsworth *Town Clerk*

An account of High wayes Excepted at yᵉ above Said meeting one High way Laid out from Will.ᵐ Wallaces land to yᵉ Rode that Goeth from Lunenburg to Groton: which Road begins at the Corner of yᵉ Said Wallace's Land, Lying Two Rods Eastwardly and Two Rods Westwardly from a white oak Tree mark,t being yᵉ Said Wallaces Corner and So runing by yᵉ Line between yᵉ Said Wallaces Land, & Mitchel Land on a Strait Line taking of Two Rods from Each mans Land for Said High way, till it Comes to Nath.ˡˡ Pages Land and
               and

[22] And so Runing between the Said Mitchels Land and yᵉ Said Pages Land taking Two Rods wide from Each mans Land till it comes to a Stake there making an angle & then Coming into yᵉ Said Mitchels Land and then mark,t on the Northerly Side to a Pine Tree Mark,t in Jonathan Pages Land and So Runing Through yᵉ Said Pages Land till it Comes to M.̠ Clarks Land four Rods wide and mark,t on yᵉ Easterly Side till it Comes to a White oak Stump Standing in or near the Roade that Leads from Lunenburg to Groton. Also Laid out a High way from where yᵉ Rode began at Jonathan Whitneys

Land & So Runing as yᵉ General Courts Committe Laid it out between Thirſtons Land and Jacob Goulds Land and So between Thirſtons and George Wheelers Land. Alſo Laid out a bridle way across Eleazar Houghtons Land and William Wallaces Land ſaid way beginning at yᵉ Countrey Rode and Runing by yᵉ South Weſterly Side of Coˡˡ Willards fence and So to yᵉ End of yᵉ fence and then up the Ridge to a Tree mark,t on yᵉ Eaſterly Side of Said way and So mark,t and So mark,t yᵉ Same Side of Said way till it comes to David Pearces Land. Also we have Taken a view of yᵉ High way that Runs acroſs Jonathan Whitneys Land by his Deſire and we think it as Conveniant for yᵉ way to Go Round yᵉ Said Whitneys Land Saving four Rods at yᵉ Southerly Corner which he offers to Give yᵉ Town for a High way. Provided that they will Throw up the other way: which Land ſo Left out, begins at a Great White oak Stump, and ſo runs on a Strait Line to yᵉ Cauſeway: or whether yᵉ Town will Give ſaid Whitney Six Pounds for yᵉ way as it now Lyeth. (Voted yᵗ yᵉ alteration be alowed.) Alſo yᵉ High way being a Little altered between Leiuᵗ Colburns Land and Hilkiah Boyntons Land by Reaſon of yᵉ Said Boytons Setting his Houſe in yᵉ High way through a mistake and hath ſince purchaſed ſome Land of yᵉ ſaid Colburn for to be added to ſaid way in Stead of what Land yᵉ ſaid Boynton hath Taken up: we there fore yᵉ ſaid Colburn and Boynton deſire yᵉ Town to Confierm yᵉ Land which is Left out of yᵉ ſaid Colburns Land for part of yᵉ Highway aforeſaid.

(Excepted by yᵉ Town)

Atˢᵗ Isaac Farnsworth *Town Clerk.*

[23] At a Legal meeting of yᵉ Inhabitants and freeholders of yᵉ Town of Lunenburg Aſsembled March yᵉ 19ᵗʰ 1732/3

Voted and Choſe Isaac Farnſworth Modderator

1ly. Voted that yᵉ Third Wedenſday in April next which will be on yᵉ Eighteenth day of ſaid month ſhall be yᵉ Day for ordaining yᵉ Rev.ⁿᵈ Mʳ David Stearns in yᵉ work of yᵉ miniſtrey in ſaid Town

2ly. Voted that Col̄l̄ Joſiah Willard Shall make Sufficiant Proviſion for yᵉ ordination Councell: miniſters and Schollers and Mʳ Stearnſ-es Relations, and yᵉ Charge thereof ſhall be Paid on Demand.

3ly. Voted yᵗ yᵉ Galleries in yᵉ meeting Houſe ſhall be forth with finiſhed and yᵉ Stears. built up into yᵉ Galleries.

4ly. voted yᵗ Jonathan Willard Benjᵃ Goodridge and Isaac Farnſworth Shall be a Comᵗᵗᵉ To Carry on yᵉ work aforeSaid. at yᵉ Towns Charge

Isaac Farnsworth Town Clerk

At a Legall meeting of yᵉ freeholders and other Inhabitants of yᵉ Town of Lunenburg Aſsembled May yᵉ 22ᵗʰ 1733——

Voted and Choſe Lᵗ Jonathan Willard—Modderator

Voted yᵗ Col̄l̄ Willards account for Entertaining yᵉ ordination Counſell and others be alowed which is Twenty Three Pounds Eighteen Shillngs and Two Pence.

Voted and Granted yᵉ Sum of Twenty Three Pounds Eighteen Shillings and Two Pence as above ſᵈ to pay Col̄l̄ Joſiah Willard for Entertaining yᵉ ordination Councell and others as heretofore hath ben voted.

Voted that yᵉ money Granted as above ſaid be Raiſed yᵉ one Half on Pools and yᵉ other half on Eſtates

Atˢ. Isaac Farnsworth Town Clerk

[24] At a Legal Town meeting of freeholders and other Inhabitants of yᵉ Town of Lunenburg aſſembled Sepᵗʳ yᵉ 13ᵗʰ 1733 Mʳ Hilkiah Boynton Choſen Modderator.

1ly at yᵉ above Said meeting it was agreed and voted that yᵉ one half of yᵉ Two Hundred Pounds Granted to yᵉ Revⁿᵈ Mʳ David Sterns for part of his Settlement in Said Town for yᵉ firſt Payment) Shall be Laid on Poles and yᵉ other half on other Ratable Estate.

2ly. voted at Said meeting that Mʳ Jacob Gould Shall have Two Pounds Eight Shillings Paid by Said Town for putting Pillers under yᵉ Galleries and making Ladders and for putting up Rails in yᵉ meeting Houſe in yᵉ Galleries.- Hilkiah Boynton Modderator

Atˢ ⌐ Isaac Farnsworth Town Clerk

At a Legall meeting of ye Inhabitants and freeholders of ye Town of Lunenburg affembled December ye 31: 1733

Voted and Chofe Coll Jofiah Willard Modderator

1ly. Voted to hire a School mafter Three months from: ye Time ye School mafter begins his School. ——

2ly. Voted that ye School Shall be kept at ye Houfe of Mr Gardners ye Three months aggreed on to keep a School:

3ly. Voted and Chofe Mr Andrew Gardner to be ye School mafter to keep ye School ye Term of Three months as afore faid in faid Town or Such other as he Shall Provide therefor.

Ats   ISAAC FARNSWORTH *Town Clerk*

Lunenburg December ye 25th 1733. Then Edward Hartwell Efqr and Mr Benja Goodridge by order of ye Select men of Lunenburg. Met ye Com-tte appointed by Lancefter Select men at ye Houfe of Thomas Houghtons in Lancefter to preambulate ye Lines between ye Town of Lancefter and ye Town of Lunenburg as ye Law Directs. and alfo performed ye Bufinefs: as by Return made to me may appear.

ISAAC FARNSWORTH *Town Clerk.*

[25] At a Legall meeting of ye Inhabitants and Freeholders of ye Town of Lunenburg Afsembled March 4th 1733/4

voted and Chofe Capt Jonathan Hubbard Modderator

Coll Jofiah Willard
Mr Benja Goodridge
Dec. Samll Johnfon   } Chofen Select men
Capt Jonathan Hubbard
Mr John Grout

Isaac Farnfworth } Chofen Town Clerk & Sworn

Isaac Farnfworth } Chofen Sealor of Weights & Meafures & Sworn

Mr James Colburn } Chosen Town Treafurer & Sworn

William Jones } Chofen Collector

Nathaniel Harwood } Chosen Constable

Dec. Sam:ll Johnson
Dec. Ephraim Peirce } Chosen Survayers of Highways & Sworn
and Jonas Gillson

Hilkiah Boynton
Ephraim Wetherbe } Chosen Tything men & Sworn

Jacob Gould
John Farmer } Chosen Fence viewers

Sam:ll Davis
Sam:ll Commings } Hogg Reives
Joseph Dodge

Voted that Hoggs Shall Run at Large in S:d Town

M:r Sam:ll Page } Chosen Pound Keeper

The other Busines acted and Done on y:e above said Day is Recorded on y:e other Side of y:e Leaf

[26] March y:e 4 : 1733/4

Voted. and Granted y:e Several Sums to y:e Several Persons heafter named. for Sarvices Done for Said Town.

1ly. Granted. To Col:l Josiah Willard Three Pounds Ten Shillings

2ly. Granted. To Edward Hartwell Esq:r Two Shillings —

3ly. Granted. To M:r Sam:ll Page Ten Shillings —

4ly. Granted. To Isaac Farnsworth Four Shillings —

5ly. Voted. To Give Isaac Farnsworth Twenty Five Shillings for Taking Care of the meeting House for y:e year Past and y:e year to Come — — — —

6ly. voted & Granted y:e Sum of Twenty Four Shillings To Josiah Willard Jun:r for Sarvice Done for Said Town ——

7ly. Granted To Benj.a Goodridge Thirty Four Shillings

8ly. Granted. To Hilkiah Boynton Twenty Two Shillings.

9ly. Granted. To Jacob Gould Six Shillings and Three pence.

10ly. Granted. To John Grout Twenty Five Shillings —

At:s   ISAAC FARNSWORTH *Town Clerk* —

The Early Records of the Town of Lunenburg.

At a meeting of ye Inhabitants and freeholders of ye Town of Lunenburg Afsembled June 3^d 1734 Capt Jonathan Hubbard Chofen Modderator

2ly. Voted and Chofe Co^ll Jofiah Willard Ajant for ye Town of Lunenburg to wait on ye General Court in ye Towns Behalf: To pray y^t ye unimproved Lands Lying in ye Town aforef^d may be Taxed at one penny p^r acre p^r Anum for ye Space of Three years next Coming after ye Time is Expired of ye Laft Tax,

    At^s Isaac Farnsworth *Town Clerk*

[27] At a Legall meeting of ye Freeholders and other Inhabitants of ye Town of Lunenburg Afsembled September ye 2th 1734

Voted and Chofe Edward Hartwell Efq^r modderator

1ly. voted that Co^ll Jofiah Willard Edward Hartwell Esqr and Mr John Grout be a Comitte to provide a Lawfull School to be kept at ye Houfe of Lieu^t James, Colburn. Lieu^t Jonathan Willards and at Juftice Hartwell or as near to Each of ye Said places as may be and that by Some Sutable perfon at Such price as ye Said Com^tte Shall agree for — —

2ly. voted and Chofe Co^ll Jofiah Willard Edward Hartwell Esqr Capt Jonathan Hubbard Isaac Farnfworth and Mr Benj^a Goodridge to be a Com^tte for and in behalf of ye Town of Lunenburg who is hereby fully Impowered and Directed to Confer and act with ye other Comittes that Shall be Sent by any of ye Towns in ye County of Middle and Worcefter in order for ye Errecting and making a new County. Provided that the Town of Groton be ye County or Shire Town and alfo that ye Town of Lunenburg aforef^d be free from Coft and Charge in ye firft Settlement of ye Said County —

and upon thefe Conditions ye Com^tte are hereby Directed to act in all purticulars in order to bring forward ye Said County as they Shall Think moft proper, and they are hereby wholy forbiden to act any Thing to ye Conterary whatfoever ——

3ly. Granted ye Sum of Fourty Pounds for ye mending of High ways and voted that any Inhabitant in Said

Town have Liberty to work out his Rate or proportion of ye Sum of Fourty Pounds aforeſd at Three Shillings pr Diem for a man, and Two Shillings and Six pence pr Diem for a pair of oxen and Cart. — — — — —

Ats. Isaac Farnsworth *Town Clerk*.—

[28] At a Legall meeting of ye freeholders and other Inhabitants of ye Town of Lunenburg Aſsembled December ye 16:— 1734

Voted and Choſe Major Jonathan Hubburd Modderator

Voted That ye one Hundred Pounds for ye Last part of Mr David Stearns Settlement be Levied—d and aſseſſed ye one half on Poles and ye other half on Real and Perſonall Estate.

Voted and Granted ye Sum of Fifteen Pounds nine Shillings and Eight Pence to make up what is wanting in ye other Rates for ye Defraying of Town Charges.

Voted and Granted ye Sum of Fourty Pounds for ye Charge of a School for ye year paſt and Preſent.

Whereas at a Legall meeting of ye Inhabitants Town of Lunenburg held at ye Publick : meeting Houſe in Said Town on Septr. 2 yc 1734 Coll. Joſiah Willard Edward Hartwell Esqr Capt. Jonathan Hubburd Isaac Farnſworth & Mr Benja. Goodridge was Choſen a Comtte for and In Behalf of ye Town of Lunenburg aforeſd To Confer and act with other Committes that Should be Sent by any of ye Towns in ye Countys of Middleſex and Worceſter in order for ye Errecting and making a new County. Provided that ye Town of Groton be ye County or Shire Town and alſo ye Town of Lunenburg be free from Coſt and Charge in ye first Settlement of ye County. which Power and Restrictions Given to ye ſaid Comtte is found to be Inefectual and of Ill Consequence. Be it therefore voted That ye Said Restrictions and Power Granted ye Said Comtte be and hereby is fully Repealed and made null and void- and That ye Said Comtte namely Coll. Joſiah Willard Edward Hartwell Esqr. Capt. Jonathan Hubburd Isaac Farnſworth & Mr. Benja. Goodridge or any Three of them be veſted with Power for and in Behalf of ye Town of Lunenburg afores^d to Do and act any thing or things Respecting ye making of a New County out of ye northerly Parts of ye Countyes of Middlesex and Worcester as they in their wisdom Shall think most Proper and Conducing to ye welfare thereof. ——

    At^s. ISAAC FARNSWORTH *Town Clerk*—

[29] At a Legal meeting of the freeholders and other Inhabitants of ye Town of Lunenburg Assembled at ye Publick meeting House in Said Town on March 3.th 1734/5

 Voted and Chose Co^ll Josiah Willard Modderator

Co^ll Josiah Willard
Edward Hartwell Esqr   Chosen
Mr Nathan Heywood   Select   And Taken ye oath
Lieu^t James Colburn   men   of assesors
Isaac Farnsworth

Isaac Farnsworth Chosen Town Clerk Sworn
John Heywood   Chosen Constable, & Sworn
Isaac Farnsworth Chosen Survayer of Hemp & flax & Sworn

 Lieu^t Jonathan Willard ⎱ Chosen Survayers of High
 Mr Josiah Bayle   ⎰   ways Sworn

 Decon. Sam^ll Johnson ⎱
 Decon. Ephraim Peirce ⎰ Chosen Tything men

 Mr Ephraim Wetherbe ⎱
 Mr Amos Robinson ⎰ chosen Fence Viewers Sworn

 Major Jonathan Hubburd Chosen Town Treasurer Sworn

 Major Jonathan Hubburd Chosen Collector.

 Mr Jeremiah Norcross ⎱
 Mr Benjamin Bellows ⎰ Chosen Hoggreives. Sworn.

 Voted that Hoggs Run at Large. in S^d Town

 Then voted that ye Business and other Articles Contained in ye warrant for ye above s^d meeting be Adjourned to ye Third monday in march Currant at ye Publick meeting House in Lunenburg at Eight of ye Clock in ye forenoon.

     ISAAC FARNSWORTH *Town Clerk*

[30] Brought over — — — — — — — —
John Fisk Chosen Constable & Sworn.
Isaac Farnsworth Chosen Seeler of Waits & measures

Voted that ye Rode Called northfield Rode Runing through ye Town be Sold To pay for Sum other Rode or Rods that is or Shall be Laid out in Said Town not yet paid for Excepting Four Rods wide yet to Lye and Continue for a Town Rode or High way. (and that Co^{ll} Josiah Willard Edward Hartwell Esqr and Major Jonathan Hubburd be a Comitte fully Impowered to Sell and Give Title of ye Same to Such person or persons as Shall appear to buy ye Same &c : ——

Voted that ye Rode Laid out through Jeremiah Norcrofs Land Sam^{ll} Davifs Land ye menifterial Land and Amos Robinfons Land be accepted which is as followeth. begining at a heap of Stones at ye north eaft Corner of Jofiah Bayley Land and So runing as ye mark Directs firft to a Chefnut y^n to a Beach y^n to a Chefnut marked y^n to a Chefnut Logg. with an heap of Stones thereon y^n to a Black oak before Jeremiah Norcrofses Door & from thence to a Chefnut Tree upon Sam^{ll} Davifes Land marked 162 Rods &c: from y^t Chefnut Tree to a white oak marked y^n to another white oak 44 Rods on Sam^{ll} Davifes Land then runing acrofs ye minifterial Land untill it Comes to Amos Robinfons Land and Runs forty one Rods and there Comes in to ye other Rode or High way by ye Corner of Said Robinfons Fence ye Rode Lying on ye South westerly Side of ye marks through ye Said Lands. Also a Rode begining at ye Corner of William Joneses fence & So Runing upon John Scotts Lott to a heap of Stones upon a Rock near ye Brook So Extending acrofs y^e Brook to Two Trees marked and then Runing upon y^e East Side of John Scotts Lott into north field Rode marked on y^e westerly Side of Said Rode. Laid out February 24th 1734/5 by Jofiah Willard Benjamin Goodridge and Jonathan Hubbard Select men of Lunenburg. — — — — —

Granted y^e Sum of $^{£\ s}_{1\text{-}4}$-0 to pay Benj^a Goodridge for making Rates & Laying out High ways

Granted y^e Sum of 1-2-0 to pay John Grout for making Rates & Laying out Highwayes

Granted to Juftice Hartwell 4 Sh. for Renewing Bounds with Groton Selectmen

Granted to Ephraim Pierce 4 Sh. for Renewing Bounds as aforef^d

Granted to Nathan Heywood 6 Sh. for y^e aforef^d Sarvice — — — —

Granted to Amos Robinson 1=5=0 to take Care of y^e meeting Houfe Church Bafon & Cloth and keep all Clean and in good order — for y^e year—1735 — — —

ISAAC FARNSWORTH Town Clerk.

[31] At a Legall meeting of y^e freeholders and other Inhabitants of y^e Town of Lunenburg Afsembled March y^e 17th 1734/5

Voted & Chofe Co^{ll} Jofiah Willard Modderator

Granted ye Sum of Fourty Pounds for Building of Stairs up into ye Galleries in ye meeting Houfe & for Building or making of Seats in the Galleries

Granted ye Sum of Eight Pounds nine Shillings & Six pence to pay Mr Ephraim Wetherbe for what he hath Expended in building ye meeting Houfe in Said Town over & above his Proportion.

Voted that Isaac Farnfworth be fully Impowered for and in behalf of ye Town of Lunenburg to wait on ye General Court with a Petition Praying for Direction and order to make Such grantees or owners of Houfe Lotts in S^d Town who has not paid their part & proportion to build ye meeting Houfe in Said Town forth with to pay ye Same: or to use & take Such other method as he Shall think proper.

Voted that Edward Hartwell Esqr be Impowered for and in behalf of ye Town to Take a Leafe of Mr Ephraim Wetherbe of ye Ground where ye meeting Houfe Stands So Lond as a meeting Houfe for ye Publick worfhip of God Shall Stand there

Voted that ye Select men be a Comitte fully Impowered to make Due Provifion and provide for a School in Said Town according to ye beft manner for ye Towns Safety & Interft.— —

At^s ISAAC FARNSWORTH Town Clerk —

At a Legall meeting of ye freeholders and other Inhabitants of ye Town of Lunenburg Afsembled at ye Publick meeting Houfe in Said Town Sep.^tr ye 15.th 1735 —

Voted and Chofe Edward Hartwell Efq^r Modderator—

Voted & Chofe Jofiah Bayle & John Divel Tything men

Voted that ye Town wayes for ye Future be mended by a Town Rate

Voted & Granted ye Sum of Forty Pounds for ye mending of Town wayes for this prefent year.

Voted y^t any Inhabitant have Liberty to work out their proportion of ye Forty pounds before Grantend for ye mending of Town ways at Three Shillings Pr Diem a man: and alfo Three shillings p^r Diem for a pair of oxen & Cart.

Isaac Farnsworth *Town Clerk* —

[32] At a Legall meeting of ye Freeholders and other Inhabitants of ye Town of Lunenburg Afsembled Jan^r 26,^th 1735/6

Voted and Chofe Co^ll Jofiah Willard modderator

Nothing done at Said meeting

At a Legall meeting of ye Freeholders and other Inhabitants of ye Town of Lunenburg Afsembled March ye 1th 1735/6

Voted and Chofe Isaac Farnfworth Modderator —

Voted and Chofe

Co^ll Jofiah Willard
Isaac Farnsworth
D^c Sam^ll Johnfon } Select men Sworn as Afsefsors
Mr John Heywood
D^c Ephraim Pierce

Isaac Farnfworth } Chofen Town Clerk & Sworn

Mr Benjamin Goodridge } Chofen Conftable & Sworn

Mr Jonathan Whitney } Chofen Conftable & Sworn

Major Jonathan Hubburd } Chofen Town Treafurer & Sworn

The Early Records of the Town of Lunenburg.

Isaac Farnfworth—Chofen Survayer of Hemp & flax & Sworn

Benj^a Goodridge—Chofen Collector & Sworn

James Colburn ⎱ Chofen Tything men
David Pierce ⎰ Pierce Sworn

Jonathan Willard ⎱ Willard Sworn
Jofiah Bayle ⎰ Survayers of High wayes

John Gibfon ⎱
Jofhua Goodridge ⎰ Fence Viewers : Sworn

Eleazar Houghton ⎱ Houghton Sworn
Amos Robinson ⎰ Hogreaves

[33] Hilkiah Boynton ⎱ Field Drivers.
Benjamin Cory ⎰

Isaac Farnfworth ⎱ Sealer of Waits & meafures

Voted. that Joseph Turner be Difcharged of his Rates Two years past

Voted. that Ezekel Wyman take Care of ye meeting Houfe & keep it Clean, take Care of ye Church Bafon & Cloath for Baptifm and Bring water therefor when Defired for 25 Sh.

Granted ye Sum of £1–10^s 0^d to Isaac Farnfworth for Sarvice Done for Said Town

Granted ye Sum of 0–12–0 to James Colburn for Service Done for ye Town

Granted ye Sum of 0–6–3 to Isaac Farnfworth for Laws Bought for ye Town

Granted ye Sum of-0–15–0 to Isaac Farnfworth to pay for mending ye meeting Houfe glafs.

Benj^a Goodridge ⎫
John Heywood ⎪
Jonathan Whitney ⎬ Chofen a Com^{tte} to Seat ye meeting Houfe in S^d Town upon their own Coft and Charge. according to ye Inftructions that Shall be Given them from ye Town — —
Hilkiah Boynton ⎪
Nathaniel Harwood ⎭

Voted that ye Inftructions ye Com^{tte} appointed to Seat ye meeting Houfe in Said Town Shall be according to ye Inhabitants Pay or Rates accounting or Looking Back Four years —

2ly voted that ye afore S^d Com^{tte} for Seeting ye meeting Houfe in Said Town Do and perform ye Bufinefs thereof on or before ye first Day of April next.

Voted that all that part or Bredth of Northfield Rode So Called Runing through part of yᵉ Town Except Four Rods wide of Said Rode yet to Lye and Continue for a Rode &c be Discontinued from being a Rode or part of a Rode as afore ſᵈ

and also all that part or Bredth of yᵉ Rode from Jonathan Willards Runing to Andrew Flemings Except four Rods wide as aforeſaid. and Except that part of Sᵈ Rode that Lyes by yᵉ Buring place. yᵗ to Lye and Contain its full Bredth as before : yᵉ other part of yᵉ Said Rode Excepting as before Excepted be hereby Discontinued from being a Rode or part of a Rode as afore ſᵈ ——

[34] Brought over.

Voted and Choſe Major Jonathan Hubbard Mʳ Jeremiah Ballard and Mʳ Ephraim Pierce to be a Comitte fully Impowered for and in behalf of yᵉ Town to make Sale of all yᵗ part or Bredth of Northfield Rode So Called as within mentioned & Diſcribed & Discontinued and alſo yᵉ Rode from Jonathan Willards Runing to Flemings in Said Town that is Diſcontinued as within is Diſcribed, to Such perſon or Perſons as Shall appear to buy yᵉ Same, and Give and Paſs Good and abſolute Deeds in yᵉ Law to yᵉ Purchaſer thereof; and yᵉ aforeſᵈ Comᵗᵗᵉ is hereby ordered and Directed upon Sale of Such Land, forth with upon Sale thereof to Return yᵉ money yᵉ Land Shall be Sold for into yᵉ Town Treaſure — — — — — —

£ s d
12 0 0 Granted yᵉ Sum of Twelve Pounds to pay Jeremiah Norcroſs for a Town Rode Laid out acroſs his Land in Said Town

3 =   Granted yᵉ Sum of £-0-0 to pay Samˡˡ Daviſ for a Town Rode Laid out acroſs part of his Land in Said Town —

3 = 10 = 0 Granted yᵉ Sum of Three Pounds Ten Shillings to pay Amos Robinſon for Land taken for a Town Rode &c —

Voted that Major Jonathan Hubburd be Discharged from his Collection yᵉ year Paſt and that he be alowed Five Pounds out of his Collection which he hath in his hands for his Sarvice therein.

Voted and Chose Major Jonathan Hubburd Benja Goodridge and Isaac Farnsworth to be a Com{tte} to Examine and Settle accounts with William Jones Collector for time past and James Colburn a Former Treasurer fo. Said Town

0-10-0 Granted ye Sum of Ten Shillings to pay Benja Goodridge for Sarvice Done

A Town or By Law. Whereas of Late years there hath been brought into our Town many Cattle and Horses not properly belonging to ye Inhabitants thereof, and Turned out into ye woods in ye Town whereby ye feed has ben So Eaten up that ye Cattle & Horses belonging to ye Inhabitants of ye Town are in Dainger of Suffering, if ye matter as afore sd be not Speedaly Redrefsed.

For Redrefs whereof. — — — — — — — — — —

Voted that whatsoever Person or Persons from and after ye first day of April next one Thousand Seven Hundred and thirty Six Shall bring take or Receive into our Town Directly or Indirectly by any wayes or means what Soever any Cattle or Horses of Either Sort being not of their own property or Estate Shall for Every ox, Cow, Stear, or Heifer, [35] Hifer-Hors, mare, or Colt. brought in taken or Received as afore said. forfit and pay to ye ufes of ye Poor of the Town ye Sum of Ten Shillings to be Recovered in manner as by Law is Directed &c. Except oxen for Labour or Cows that Give milk—them. to be taken into the Town by any of ye Inhabitants thereof for their ufe and Benifit. &c — — —

Voted and accepted of a Town way or Rode Laid out by order of ye Select men of ye Town of Lunenburg May ye 29th 1735 begining at ye South west Corner of Old Mr Whites House Lot on which he now Dwells and So runing Between Said Whites Land and Elisha Smiths Land on Said Smiths Land Two Rods wide Down to ye Lower or Easterly End of ye Said Smiths Land then Runing on Said Smiths Land Two Rods wide as ye High way marks Directs Down to Mullipus Entervail marked on ye Southerly Side of ye Rode, and then Runing acrofs a narrow peice of Entervail of Aberaham Sanderson Two Rods wide marked on ye Easterly Side of ye Rode, to ye Corner of John Trulls Land and Said Sanderfons upland, and then Runing on Said Trulls Land and Sanderfons Land Two Rods wide a Rod on Each mans Land to Townfhend Line. &c

the Bufinefs on ye four Laft pages Done at ye Annual meeting in March 1735/6

Att.^s Isaac Farnsworth *Town Clerk*

At a Legal meeting of ye freeholders and other Inhabitants of Said Town Afsembled April y^e 5th 1736

Voted & Chofe Co^ll Jofiah Willard — Modderator

Granted y^e Sum of Twenty Pounds to make up Mr Stearns Sallery for y^s Prefent year with what is Laid in y^e penny acre Rate.

Granted to Justice Hartwell for his Sarvice y^e Last year & Laying out y^e minefterial Land £3 = 15 = 6

Granted to Jona^th willard for Laying out of minifterial Land, 6 Sh.

Granted y^e Sum of £3—4—0 to Nathan Heywood for Survaying y^e minifterial Land. & Sarvice y^e year past

voted that y^e Com^tte appointed to Reccon with Lt Colburn & Mr Jones make their Report to y^e Select men.

voted & Chofe ye Select men for this prefent year a Com^tte to provide for ye keeping of a School in Said Town for ye Prefent year. & to Hire School Dames as they Shall se meet.—and otherwife as ye Law Requires —

[36] Brought over —

The Report and Return of ye Comitee Chofen to Seat ye meeting Houfe in Said Town is accepted as by ye Said Comittes Paper of Seeting, in ye Town Clerks office—may appear —

voted and Granted all that Room behind ye Seets in ye Front Gallery in ye meeting Houfe in Lunenburg to Jonathan Wood. Sam^ll Reed. Phinehas, Osgood. Ezekel Wyman. David, Page. Stephen Boynton. John Fitch. Jonathan Abbit, for to Build a Long Pew or Seet for them felves and wives for Ever. (To Set in) &c. Provided ye Perfons aforenamed Build ye Said Seat within Four months from ye Date of this Grant.

Att.^s Isaac Farnsworth *Town Clerk*—

At a Legal meeting of yᵉ freeholders and other Inhabitants of yᵉ Town of Lunenburg Afsembled June yᵉ 21ᵗʰ 1736

Voted and Chofe Edward Hartwell Esqʳ Modderator

voted yᵗ yᵉ Committe Chofen to Sell a Part of northfield Rode So Called Runing Through part of yᵉ Town be Difmift from yʳ office and Truft in yᵉ Premifes & alfo from Selling any part of yᵉ Rode from Jonathan Willards Runing to Flemings &c.

Voted that

be a Committe fully Impowered for & in behalf of yᵉ Town of Lunenburg

This Meeting void

At a Legal meeting of yᵉ freeholders and other Inhabitants of yᵉ Town of Lunenburg Afsembled November yᵉ 22ᵈ 1736

Voted and Chofe Jofiah Willard Esqʳ modderator

Granted. yᵉ Sum of Twenty Pounds for yᵉ ufe of yᵉ School in Sᵈ Town — —

voted that Major Hubburds Houfe in Said Town be one of yᵉ Places afsigned and appointed for yᵉ Keeping of a School in Said Town.

voted that yᵉ Houfe of Mʳ Benjᵃ Bellows in Sᵈ Town be afsigned and appointed (for a Place) to Keep School in Said Town or on non procurement thereof: then Such other Place as near to yᵉ meeting Houfe as may be in Sᵈ Town as Shall be provided by yᵉ Comᵗᵗᵉ appointed for Providing for a School in fᵈ Town.

ISAAC FARNSWORTH *Town Clerk*

[37] At a Legal meeting of yᵉ freeholders and other Inhabitants of yᵉ Town of Lunenburg Regularly Afsembled March yᵉ 7ᵗʰ 1736/7

voted & Chofe Jofiah Willard Esqʳ Modderator

Jofiah Willard Esqʳ
Benjᵃ Goodridge
Ephraim Wetherbe } Chosen Select men
John Grout
Major Jonathan Hubburd

Benjᵃ Goodridge } Chofen Town Clerk

Edward Hartwell Esq.r \
Benj.a Goodridge } Chofen Afsefsors \
John Grout

James Colburn \
Jacob Stiles } Chofen Conftables

Major Jonathan Hubburd } Chofen Town Treafurer

Major Jonathan Hubbard } Chofen Collector

D.r Sam.ll Johnfon } Chofen Survayor of hemp & flax

D.r Sam.ll Johnfon } Chofen Sealor of weights & meaf- ures.

Benj.a Fofter \
John Divel } Chofen Survayors of High wayes \
Jeremiah Ballord

Noah Dodge \
Jonas Gillfon } Chofen Fence viewers

Jeremiah Ballord \
Daniel Auften } Chofen Tything men

Jacob Gould \
Moses Willard } Chofen Hogg reives

Voted that Hoggs Shall Run at Large in Said Town

Nathan Heywood \
John Scott } Chofen Field drivers \
Ezekiel Wyman

Ephraim Wetherbe Chofen to Sweep y.e meeting Houfe in S.d Town to Carry Water for Baptizen for y.e year Enfuing for £1-5-0 — — — — —

[38] Brought over.

Granted to Isaac Farnfworth £4 = $^{s}_{4}$-$^{d}_{10}$ for Sarvice done for S.d Town

Granted to John Heywood - 0-18-0 for Sarvice done for S.d Town

Granted to D.r Sam.ll Johnfon - 0-10-0 for Sarvice Done for S.d Town

Granted to D.r Ephraim Pierce - 0-08-0 for Sarvice Done for S.d Town.

Voted y.t That part of y.e Town Rode (Runing from north field Rode, So Called to William Jones,es) that Turns in to y.e Land of John Scots and Runs acrofs y.e north Eaſt Corner of his now Dwelling House Lot be Discontinued and Ceaſe to be a Rode or part thereof—

yᵉ other part of Said Rode Remain a Rode notwithstanding. Runing on yᵉ East Side of Said Scotts Land from north field Rode So Called over to Wᵐ Jones Houſe

Voted that ye other affairs and Buſiness of this meeting as Contained in yᵉ warrant for yᵉ Sam be adjourned to yᵉ Fourth Monday of May next.

                  ISAAC FARNSWORTH *Town Clerk*

At a meeting of the freeholders and other Inhabitants of the town of Lunenburg June the 27ᵗʰ 1737

Voted and Choſe Major Jonathan Hubburd Modderator

Voted that yᵉ School be Moved to four places in Said town

Voted that John Heywood John Grout and Nathniel Harwood be a Committe to hire a School Master and to provide places for yᵉ School to be kept in this preſent year

Voted that the Committe be paid for their time in spent in hireing a School Master

[39] At A meeting of the freeholders and other Inhabitants of the town of Lunenburg Aſsembled July the 11ᵗʰ 1737

Voted and Choſe Mʳ Nathan Heywood Modderator

Voted that the School be keept in four places for the Space of one year Next Enſuing

Voted that Mʳ John Grout Mʳ Jacob Gould and Mʳ David Parce be a Committe fully Impowered to hire a lawfull School Maſter for the town of Lunenburg and to provide four Conveniant places for the School to be Keept in where it May Beſt Conven the Inhabitants the time of keeping in Each place to be proportioned according to yᵉ Number of Schoolers for the Space of one year Next Ensuing

Voted that Mʳ Samvel Page Edward Hartwell Eſqʳ Mʳ James Colburn Benjᵃ Goodridge and Mʳ John Heywood be a committe to Examine the Town tearsurers accounts and others that has any of ye town money in their hands and Report thereof to the town and to Confer and agree with the Revend Mr David Stearns about ye Quallification of ye money in order for his Discharging the town of his Sallarys by Giveing Receipts in full

Voted and Granted the Sum of fifty pounds for ye ufe of ye School

Voted that this meeting be adjourned to the frift Monday of August Next at four of ye Clock in ye afternoon at ye meeting houfe

August ye first 1737 Mett by adjornment and upon hearing the report of the Committe Voted and Granted the Sum of fifteen pound to the Rev^nd Mr David Stearns an equeilent for the moneys not Beeing so Good as when he was fettled for ye year 1736

Voted and Granted ye Sum of ten pound to pay ye towns Debts

Voted and Granted the Sum of fourty pound to Mend Highways withall

At a meeting of the freeholders and other Inhabitants of the town of Lunenburg Afsembled November the fourteenth 1737

Voted & Chofe Edward Hartwell Esqr Modderator

Voted and Granted the Sum of twenty five pounds to make up Mr Stearns Sallary for the year A. D 1737

Voted that the High way Rate be worked out at five Shillings ⅌ Day from the first of May to the first of September and from the first of September to the first of may at three Shillings ⅌ day and two Shillings ⅌ day for a pair of oxen and one Shilling per Day for a Cart at any time of year

Recorded ⅌ BENJ^A GOODRIDGE *Clerk*

[40] At a meeting of the freeholders and other Inhabitants of ye Town of Lunenburg Regularly Afsembled March ye Sixth A D 1737/8

Voted & Chofe Edward Hartwell Esqr Modderator

Edward Hartwell Esqr
Benj^a Goodridge
Mr Jeremiah Ballard } Chosen Selectmen
Mr Samvel Johnson
Mr James Colburn

Benj^a Goodridge Chosen Town Clerk

Jeremiah Ballard
John Divol } Chosen Surveyors of highways
Benj^a Forstor

Maj Jonathan Hubburd Chosen town Treasurer

Eleazer Houghton
Josiah Bayley } Chosen Constables

Samvel Johnson Chosen Surveyor of Hemp & flax

William Snow
Joseph Fuller } Chosen Tydingmen

Amos Robinson
Benj^a Bellows ju } Chosen fence viewers

Jonathan Smith
John Fitch } Chosen Hogg reives

Samvel Johnson Chosen Sealer of weights and measures.
John Heywood Chosen Sealer of Leather

Jonathan wood
Samvel Cummings } Chosen feilder drivers

[41]

Voted and Granted to Edward Hartwell Esq	–0–12–0
Granted to Benj^a Goodridge	1– 6–0
Granted to Major Jonathan Hubburd	0–16–0
Granted to Mr Ephraim Wetherbe	0– 8–0
Granted to Mr Hezekiah Wetherbe	0 4–0
Granted to Mr John Grout	1– 4–0
Granted to Mr Benj^a Bellows ju^r for Sweeping the meeting house for ye year ensuing	1– 5–0

Voted that ye way from John Divols house Lott Between Joshua Goodridges and John Fitchs Land to ye way that Comes Lancaster and gos to ye meeting in Lunenburg be Excepted and Confrimed a privet way as it was laid out and marked by ye General Courts Committe five rod wide

Voted that this meeting be adjorned till ye Last tusday in April Next at one of ye Clock in ye afternoon at ye meeting house

Voted that this meeting be further adjorned untill ye third munday of May next at two of Clock in ye afternoon at ye meeting houfe this further adjornment was enterd In a rong place by a mistake.

At a meeting of the freeholders and other Inhabitants of the town of Lunenburg Afsembled the twenty-fifth Day of April A D 1738

Voted and Chofe Mr Samvel Johnfon Modderator

Voted that Hoggs run at Large in Said town for ye prefent year

☞ Voted that thofe perfons that Give ways through their land to the town Shall not pay any thing to the Buying of other ways in Said town untill Such time as the town has Bought So many as Shall amount to an Equal proportion of what Shall be Given Such ways to be Eftimated by the Select men that lay out the Same and Excepted by the town in the town meeting when the ways are excepted

Voted and Granted the Sum of fourty pound to mend town ways withall

Recorded P̃ Benj^a Goodridge *Clerk*

[42] At a meeting of ye freeholders and other Inhabitants of ye Town of Lunenburg held by adjornment on ye third Monday of May A D 1738 from an adjornment on ye Laft tuesday of April last past then Voted that a town way be Excepted from ye way Between the meeting houfe and Col^{ll} Jofiah Willards houfe Begining at ye End of the lane as it is now fenced and runs by the fence on ye Southerly Side of Said Lane untill it comes to Mr Seccartary Willards land two Rod wide. 108 Rod. then Runs acrofs Mr Secar Willards Land one hundred and twenty Rod on Said Willards land and is marked on trees on ye Southerly Side of Said way which is two Rod wide then truns into Jonathan Abbotts land and runs acrofs one Corner of Said Abbotts land fifty one Rod two Rod wide to a two Rod way Between the firft and Second Range of Lotts in woburn farm and is marked upon trees on ye Southerly Side and from Said way one hundred and Sev-

enty Six rod acrofs Mr Ephraim Wetherbes Land to a two Rod way Between ye Second and Third Rang of lots in Woborn farm and from Said way on Mr Jofeph Fullers land one hundred and twenty four Rod untill it Comes to Mr Jacob Stileses land then runs Between Said fullers and Stiles land a rod on Each mans land twenty Six Rod till it Comes to ye pond and is marked on trees on ye Southerly Side then runs fifty two rod by the Side of ye pond on Said Stiles land then makes an Angle at a Certain tree marked and on ye Southerly Side of Said Stilese Barn one hundred & twenty two Rod till it Comes to a heep of Stones which is the Corner of Samvel Commins and John Haftings jun land and is marked on trees on the Southerly Side and is two rod wide then runs between Said Commins and Haftings land a rod on Each mans land

Alfo voted that a town way Be accepted Begining at a two rod way at or neer the line Between Mr Seacretary Willards land and the land of Co^{ll} Jofiah Willards runing across a corner of Mr Secr. Willards land and runing acrofs the land of Mr Jeremiah Ballard by the Eafterly Side of Mr Secr Willards Land untill it comes neer the Brook then Crofsing the Brook neer the place where ye path now goes and leaving a corner of said Ballards land on the west Side of Said way untill it comes to a two rod way Between ye first and second rang of Lotts in woburn farm the Said way is two rod wide and markd on trees on the Eafterly Side

At a further adjornment of S^d meeting on Monday the twenty third day of october A. D. 1738

Voted that a town way Be accepted from the End of the way that runs acrofs Mr Ballards Land acrofs the land of Mr Thomas Cartter and then acrofs the Land Belonging to one Woodard untill it Comes to the Land of Benjamin Goodridge and then runs acrofs Said Goodridge-s Land untill it Comes to his Houfe S^d way is is two rod wide and marked on trees on ye Eafterly Side of Said way

[43] At a meeting of the freeholders and other Inhabitants of the the town of Lunenburg Afsembled May the 22nd 1738

Voted and Choofe Major Hubburd Moddrator

Voted that the Seats in the Gallary be moved forward so that there may be two Seats more Built Behind round the Gallary

Voted that the Seats be raised higher that are to be Built

Voted alfo that the alley Between ye Seats Below in the meeting House be made into Seats.

Voted that Mr Samvel Johnfon Mr Jeremiah Ballard Mr Samvel Page Be a Committe to lett out Sd work

Recorded ℔ BENJ GOODRIDGE *Clerk*

At a meeting of the freeholders and other Inhabitants of the town of Lunenburg Afsembled Sept ye 12th 1738

Voted that ye town will provide a School mafter for the firft six months and School Dames for ye other six months for the year enfuing

Voted that ye School be Keept in three places the firft six months

Voted that ye School be Keept in Six places the laft six months

Voted that Mr Jeremiah Ballard Mr John Heywood Mr John Grout Mr Samvel Page and Mr Jacob Gould be a Committe to Regulate ye Same

Voted that the Sum of Sixty pound be raifed and granted to Support the School with all for ye year enfuing

Voted that Seven pound be Granted to Build ye Seats Behind In ye Gallary

At a meeting of the freeholders and other Inhabitants of the town of Lunenburg afsembled october ye 23th 1738

Voted and Choofe Mr Samvel Johnson modderator

Voted yt the Sum of fifteen pound Be Granted to ye Revd Mr David Stearns an addition to his Sallary for ye year 1737

Voted that ye Sum of fifteen pound be granted to ye

Rev.ᵈ Mʳ David Stearns an addition to his Salary for the year 1738

Recorded ℞ Benjᵃ Goodridge Clerk

[44] At a meeting of the freeholders and other Inhabitants of the town of Lunenburg Aſsembled March the thirteenth A D 1738/9.

Voted and Chooſe Major Jonathan Hubburd Modderator

Edward Hartwell Esqʳ
Benjᵃ Goodridge
Mʳ Ephraim Wetherbe
Mʳ Samvel Johnſon
Mʳ John Heywood
Chooſen Select men and Sworn Aſseſsors

Benjᵃ Goodridge Choſen town Clerk and Sworn
Major Jonathan Hubburd Choſen town Treaſurer
Jonas Gillſon
Benjᵃ Bellows Junʳ
Choſen Constables and Benj. Bellows Sworn.

Edward Hartwell Esqʳ
Samvel Johnson
Benjᵃ Goodridge
James Litch
Jeremiah Norcroſs
Samvel Page
Choſen Surveyers of High ways

Sworn

Samvel Johnson Choſen Sealer of waights & Meaſures & Eleazer Houghton Choſen Sealer of Leather

Ezekeil Wyman
John Heywood
Choſen tying men

Jonathan Willard
Jeremiah Norcroſs
Choſen fence veiwers

Ezekeil Wyman
David Page
Chosen Hogg reives

Joſiah Bayley Choſen Surveyer of Shingles

Voted that Samvel Johnson Benjᵃ Goodridge and John Heywood be a Committe to fill up all the Vaccant Room in the meeting Houſe with Seats in yᵉ Best manner that can be with Convenince

Voted that yᵉ Sum of fourteen pound be Granted to Sattisfy the Coſt occationed thereby

Voted Samvel Johnſon be a perſon apointed to buy a burying Cloth

[45] Voted that the Sum Seven pound ten Shillings be Granted to Buy a burying Cloth withall

Voted and Granted to Edward Hartwell Esqr ye Sum of -1-4-0

Voted and Granted to Benjn Goodridge ye Sum of 1-0-0

Voted and Granted to James Colbourn ye Sum of 0-8-0

Voted and Granted to Samvel Johnſon ye Sum of 0-6-0

Voted and Granted to Jeremiah Ballard ye Sum of -0-8-0

Voted and Granted to Joſiah Baylay ye Sum of -0-3-6

Voted that ye Town way Be Discontinued where it went neer Thomas Harkneſs-s Land on flatt hill and that ye way Be allowed where it is now Laid out in Lieu thereof

Voted that a Town way be Excepted two Rods wide Begining at a heap of Stones and a Stake on the Eaſterly Side of the Road in Dea Ephraim Parces Land and runs acroſs a little Strip of Said parces Land two Rod wide to ye land of John Gibson and then runs two Rod wide through Said Gibſons land to ye Said Ephraim parces Second Diviſion and then runs through Said Parces 2^d Diviſion two Rods wide to Eleazer Houghton Second Diviſion and then runs through Said Houghton Second Diviſion to David Parces Land two Rod wide then through Said David Parces Land two Rod wide to ſaid Gibſons Second Diviſion and to David Carliles Land and all ye Said way is Deſcribed by marked trees which are on ye weſterly and Southerly Side of ye Said way.

And also there is another Short way of two Rod wide Laid out from this S^d way in ye Said Houghtons Second Deviſion to ye farm where Mr James Litch and Robert Ruſſell now Dwells upon for their Convenince to Bring them in to this Road as it is Deſcribed by marked trees

Voted that a bridle way of one rod wide be Excepted from Jethro Wheelers land on ye eaſt Side of Joſeph Dodges land that was to ye way by John Swans houſe

At a meeting of the freeholders and other Inhabitants of the town of Lunenburg afsembled May the Twenty first A D 1739

Voted and Choofe Mr John Heywood modderator

Voted that the Sum of fifty pound Be Granted to mend Highways withall to Be worked out in the way and manner of a former vote of this town

At a meeting of ye freeholders and Inhabitants of the town of Lunenburg afsembled auguft the fourtenth A. D 1739

Voted and Choofe Maj Jonathan Hubburd Modderator

Voted and Granted the Sum of five pound to bye Meafures withall and if fd Sum be to much the over plus to go into the treafury and if any be wanting to take it out of the treafury

these meetings Recorded ꝑ Benjᴬ Goodridge *Clerk*

[46] At a legal meeting of the freeholders and other Inhabitants of the town of Lunenburg afsembled November the nintenth one thousand Seven Hundred and thirty nine

Voted and Choofe Mr Samvel Johnfon Modderator

Voted and Chofe Mr Nathan Heywood and Mr Jonathan Smith to Enfpect the Killing of Deer at an unfeafonable time of the year as the Law Directs

Voted that the heads pay two third parts of the Afsfsments and the Eftates the other third part thereof

Voted and Chofe Mr William Jones to hire a lawfull School mafter for the town of Lunenburg for three months to Begin at Janvary next

Voted that the School be Keept at Mr Ephraim Parce's old Houfe six weeks

Voted that the School be Keept at the Houfe of Mr. John Jenifones or at Judge Dowses Houfe the other Six weeks

Voted and Granted the Sum of twenty pounds In Bills of the old tenor for the poor

Recored ꝑ Benjᴬ Goodridge *Clerk*

[47] At a legal meeting of the freeholders and other Inhabitants of the town of Lunenburg Afsembled March the third 1739/40

Voted and Chofe Edward Hartwell Esqr modderator

Edward Hartwell Esqr
Mr Benja Goodridge
Mr John Grout
Mr Ephraim Wetherbe
Capt Jonathan Bradftreet
} Chofen Select men and Sworn afsefsors

Benja Bellows Junr } Chofen Town Clark and Sworn

John Divol } Chofen Conftable Benja Bellows Jur Sworn in his Rome

Jacob Gould } Chofen Conftable & Sworn

Mr John Grout Chofen town Treafurer and Sworn

David Parce
Samll Comings
Ezekil Wyman
John Scot
Hilkiah Boynton
} Chofen Suveyers of high Ways Parce Wyman & Comings Sworn

Samvel Johnfon } Sealer of Waights and Meafurs

Benja Gould
Jonathan Abbot
Hezikah Wetherbe
John Gibfon
} hogg Reives & Sworn

Daniel Aften
Jeremiah Norcrofs
} Tything men

Elezer Houghton } Sealer of Leather

Jacob Stiles
Jofeph fuller
} Chofen fence viewers & Sworn

Benja Bellows Ju{r}
Jonathan Smith
} to profecute Such Perfons as Shall Kill Deer Contatry to Law and Sworn

Edward Hartwell Esqr
Benja Goodridge
Jacob Stiles
} be a committe to Examin the town Treafurers accompt and to Give him a discharge for ye payments he has advanced and make report thereof to ye town

[48] Voted that the Bridle way be discontinued that runs Acrofs Elezer Houghton Land

Voted that this meeting be Ajorned tell the third monday of May next at two of the Clock in ye afternoon at the meeting houfe in Lunenburg

Ats. BENJ^A BELLOWS JUR *town Clark*

at a metting march ye 3th 1740

Voted and Exepted of a way Laid out two Rod Wide through John Wyman and Ezekil Wymans Land a rod on Each mans one Hundred thirty four rod then runing Acrofs Ezekiel Wymans feild thirty Seven Rod then runing acrofs Stephen Boynton feild twenty rod to ye two Way betwen ye firft and Scond Rang of Lotts in Woborn fairm then Acrofs S^d two rod way thence between Holts Lotts one hundred and Sixty rod to ye miniftreal Land then acrofs ye miniftrail Land to ye Way by Amos Robingfon

Attest BENJ^A BELLOWS JU^R *town Clerk*

May ye 19th 1740 met by adjornment and upon Hearing the Report of the Commettee Chofen to Recken With Maj Jonathan Hubburd Town Treafurer and thay Report to the town that on the day above S^d that thay Reckned With him and find that he has Rec^{cd} of the towns money the Sum of £797-17^{sh}-1^d- out of Which he has Paid by Order the Sum of £795-15^{sh}-0^d and thare Remains in his Hands the Sum of 2-2^{sh}-1^d-

We find allfo in Conftable HarWoods hands the Sum of 2-6-3 and alfo in Conftable Whetneys hands y^e Sum of 1=11=6 and alfo in the hands of Maj^r Hubburd Collecter the Sum of 20=14=10 and in the hands of L^{tt} James Colburn Conftable the Sum of 8=9=2 and in the hand of Jacob Stiles Conftable y^e Sum of 1=17=8 and in the hands of Benj^a Goodridge Conftable the Sum of 16=5=9 and in the hands of Conftable Bayley the Sum of 21=9=3 and in the hands of Benj^a Bellows Conftable the Sum of 16=13=3

Voted and Granted to Maj Jonathan Hubburd for two years Collection 10$^£$-0^{sh}-0^d.

Voted to Mr Benj.^{a} Goodridge for one years Collection 5=0=0=

Voted to Edward Hartwell Esqr for Sarvices done for the town 1=18=0

Voted to Mr Benj.^{a} Goodridge for Sarvis done the Town 1=18=0

Voted to Mr John Heywood for Sarvis done the Town 0=8=0

Voted to Benj.^{a} Bellows Junr for Sarvis done the Town 3=0-0

Voted to Maj.^{r} Jonth Hubburd for Being Treafurer 5 years 2=0=0

Voted that L^{tt} Ephraim Wetherbe & Mr John Heywood & Mr Mofes Willard be a Commettee to Provide a Lawfull School & School Mafter for the this Prefent year.
Attest.
BENJ^A BELLOWS J^{UR} *Town Clerk*

[49] At a Meeting of the freeholders and other Inhabitance of the town of Lunenburg } June ye 2th 1740

Voted and Chofe Maj.^{r} Jonathan Hubburd modderator

Voted that thay Abate 1—7—11 of Benjamin Goodridge Rates Whoe was Conftable for the year 1736

Voted that thay Abate 1—17—8 of Jacob Stiles Rates Whoe was Conftable for ye year 1736

Voted that thay Abate 4-16-3 of Joliah Bayley Rates Whoe was Conftable for the year 1738

Voted that thay Rafe thirty Pounds for Defraing the School

Voted to the Rend Mr David Stearns the Sum of thirty Pounds to make up his Salery for the year 1739 & the year 1740

Granted fourty Pounds to mend Hieways with all
Attest   BENJ^A BELLOWS JUN^R *town Clerk*

At A Meeting of the Freeholders and Other Inhabitance of the Town of Lunenburg held on the 29th of September A D 1740.

Voted and Chofe Mr Benjᵃ Goodridge Modrator

1ly Voted that thay Build two School Houfen in Said town one to be by Decon Ephraim Pearce the other to be on the Eaft Side of Mr Jeremiah Norcrofses as Near as may be to the Road—

2ly Voted that the School Houfen be twenty three feet in Lenth and Eighteen feet in Wedth and Seven feet Stud

3ly Voted that Mr William Jones & Mr Jeremiah Norcrofs & Mr Jofiah Bayley be a Committee to Buld the North End School Houfe

4ly that Decon Ephraim Pearce & Mr John Divol & Mr John Gipfon be a Committee to Buld the South End School Houfe

5ly Voted that the School Houfen be Borded and Shingled and the Loar floor be Laid Down and the Chimney be Built and the Houfen under Pend & A partion maid & doors maid and Hung

6ly Voted that thay Rafe one Hundred and twenty Pounds to Buld the the School Houfen & to Defray the Charge of the School

    Attest Benjᴬ Bellows Junᴿ *Town Clerk*

[50] At a Legual Meeting of the freeholders and other Inhabitance of the Town of Lunenburg Held on the firft monday of November A D 1740

Voted and Chofe Majr Jonathan Hubbard Moddrator

firft Voted to Buld but one School Houfe in Said Town & that to Stand as near the Said meeting Houfe as the town Shall appoint and that all the Inhabitance of the Said town that Lives above two Miles diftance from the Place Whare the Said School Houfe Shall be Built the two miles all ways to be Estimated as the Roads go and that all the Inhabitance that Live above two miles as above Said Shall from time to time & at all times hereafter have the Whole of each of thare Refpective Share Sum or Sums that thay Shall hereafter pay towards any School Rate or tax Whatfoever repaid to them again out of the Town Treasurie to Provide Schooling And School houfen for them Selves thay dividing into

Companies and making it to Appear to the Select men that thay have Laid out So much money for the End aforefaid and alfo that all the Schools Within the Said Town at the Same Time Shall be free for any of the Inhabitance to Send Whare they Pleafe and alfo that the town meeting Wich Was on ye twenty ninth day of Laft September and Every Article and Claufe therein mentioned Shall be repealed and annulled to all Intents and Porpofes Whatfoever

2ly Voted that the School Houfe Be Set in the Corner of Mr Thomas Prentices Land Whare the Lain turns to ye to Capt Bradftreets Houfe out of the Road

3ly Voted that thay Rafe one Hundred Pounds of the old tenner for the Use of Town

4ly Voted that the Town meeting be Warned by the Conftables going about and notifying the People by Word of mouth for the futer

5ly Voted that the Afsefsors Lay two thirds of the tax on the Heads and one third on the Eftates

6 Voted that the Town Treafurer Call in the Town Debts Dirict

Attest BENJ^A BELLOWS JUN^R *Town Clerk*

[51] At a legall meeting of the freeholders and other Inhabitants of the town of Lunenburg Afsembled March the Second A D 1740/1

Voted and Chofe Maj^r Jonathan Hubbird Modderator

Edward Hartwell Esqr ⎫
Benj^e Goodridge ⎪
Mr Thomas Prentice ⎬ Chofen Selectmen
Mr Nathaniel Harwood ⎪
Mr Samvel Johnfon ⎭

Benj^a Goodridge town Clerk & Sworn

Mr Thomas Prentice.–town Treafurer & Sworn

Mr John Gibfon ⎫
Mr William Jones ⎬ Chosen Conftables & Sworn

Mr Jofeph Fuller ⎫
Mr Mofes Mitchael ⎪
Mr Ephriam Parce ⎬ Chofen Surveyers of Highways
Mr Amos Robbingfon ⎪
Mr Jacob Gould ⎭

Mr John Grout } Chofen tying men
Mr Jeremiah Norcrofs

Mr Benjᵃ Bellows junr Chofen Sealer of weights & Meafures & Sworn

Mr Jeremiah Norcrofs }
Mr John Jenifon } Chofen fence Viewers

Mr Eleazer Houghton Chofen Sealer of Leather

Mr William Snow }
Mr Abraham Sanderfon } Chofen Hogreves & Sworn
Mr Nathanael Page

Mr Ezekiel Wyman }
Mr Samvel Reed } Deer officers

2ndly Voted that the town way be Excepted as it is Laid through Jofhua Goodridges Land In Exchange for yᵉ town way where it was formerly laid through Sd land the new way to be four rod wide and is Defcribed by markt trees on the Eafterly Side thereof and and the former way is discontinued accordingly also

turn over

[52] Alfo Excepted a town way from Andrew Mitchaels Houfe two rod wide being one rod on william wallases Land and one rod on Mitchaels Land till it comes to the Highway Laid to Said Wallases Land.

Voted and Granted to Mr Samvel Johnfon yᵉ Sum of 0-14-0

Voted and Granted to Mr John Grout the Sum of 0-8-0

Voted and Granted to Mr Ephriam Whetherbe yᵉ Sum of 0-6-0

Voted and Granted to Edward Hartwell Esqr yᵉ Sum of 1-2-0

Voted and Granted Capt Jonathan Bradftreet yᵉ Sum of 0-4-0

Voted and Granted to Mr Benjᵃ Bellows junr yᵉ Sum of 2-0-0

Voted and Granted to Benjᵃ Goodridge yᵉ Sum of 1-0-0

Recorded ℔ Benjᵃ Goodridge *Clerk*

At a legall meeting of the freeholders and other Inhabitants of the town of Lunenburg Afsembled May the twenty fifth 1741

    voted and Chofe maj^r Jonathan Hubbaird Modderartor.

    1th Voted that the Select men provide a place to keep the School in

    2^{ndly} Voted and Granted the Sum of Six pound to Build a pound withall

    3^{rdly} Voted that major Hubburd and Mr Benj^a Bellows jr Be a committe to Lett out ye pound to be Built

    4^{thly} Voted that Hoggs run at Large this prefent year

                Recorded ℞ BENJ^E GOODRIDGE *cler*

[53] LUNENBURG March 9th 1740

Then Received of Mr Thomas Prentice Town Treaf^r The Sum of one Hundred Sixty one Pounds Two Shillings and Three Pence which Is In full for my Salary for the years 1739 and 1740

                  Received p^r me DAVID STEARNS

                LUNENBURG

March 9th 1740 1 The Subfcriber Hereby acknowledge That I Have Received of the Town of Lunenburg The full of my Salary from the time of my Settling with them for ye work of ye miniftry To the Prefent Day

                  Received p^r me DAVID STEARNS

Received alfo the full of what was granted to me for Settlement

                  Received p^r me DAVID STEARNS

Janvary the fourth 1741 then the Selectmen and treafurer Reckned with Mr James Colbuorn Constable for the year 1737 and find that he has paid the whole of his Rates for said year

At the time Reckned with Benj^a Goodridge Conftable and Colector for ye year 1736 and Conftable and Colector for ye year 1736 and conftable for ye year A. D 1738 and find that he has paid the full of his Collections for both ye years aforefaid

[54] At a Legall meeting of the freeholders and other Inhabitants of the town of Lunenburg Afsembled the Eleventh Day of January A D 1741/2

1th Voted and Chofe Mr Samvel Johnfon Moddrator for the Government of Sd meeting

2ndly Voted and Granted the Sum of Eighty pound In the old tennor for the ufe of the School

Recorded ℞ BENJ GOODRIDGE
town Clerk

At a Legual meeting of the freeholders and other Inhabitants of the town of Lunenburg afsembled March the 15th A D 1741/2

Voted and Chofe Mr John Grout moderator for the Government of the meeting

Benjamin Goodridge
Mr John Grout
Capt Jonathan Braudftreet
Mr John Heywood
Mr William Jones
} Chofen Selectmen and Sworn Afsefsors

Benja Goodridge Chofen town Clerk and Sworn

Mr Thomas Prentice Chofen town treafurer and Sworn

Mr Joshua Goodridge
Mr Jonathan Page
} Chofen Conftables and Sworn

Mr William Jones
Mr John Gibfon
Mr Benja Bellows Junr
Mr Thomas Brown
} Chofen Surveyers of Highways

Mr Benja Bellows junr Chofen Sealer of weights and meafures

Mr Eleazer Houghton Chofen Sealer of Leather

Mr Jacob Stiles
Mr Jofeph Fuller
} Chofen tying men

Mr Jeremiah Norcrofs
Mr Amos Robinfon
} Chofen fence Viewers

Mr Jofeph Fuller
Mr Nathanel Page
} Chofen Deer reves

[55] Mr David Goodridge
Mr Patrick White
} Chofen Hogg reves and Sworn

Voted and Excepted of a town way as Reported of by the Seelect men begining in the former way in Joseph

Fullers Land and turning into Said Fullers feild by a white pine tree in his fence and runing through said Fullers Land in al one hundred and Seven rods two rods wide then through Ephraim Wetherbes Land one hundred and five rod then on Thomas Carters Land fifteen rod then through S^d Wetherbe-s Land ninty rod then through Said Carters Land twenty one rod to the road that Leads from Benjamin Goodridge = s to the meeting houfe in S^d town the said road is Laid out two rod wide and is Defcribed by certain marks and the Several owners of the said Land say they will freely give the Land for the said way whare they are Laid out purfuant to the town vote Concerning thofe that shall Give there Land to town ways &c provided the said town shall Discontinue ye former Road where this new road is Laid out in Leiu of that.

Voted and Excepted alfo of one other town way as Reported of by the Selectmen viz beginning at Mr William Clarks Land and runing through his Land Sixty two rod two rod wide through William Moffetts Land sixty nine rod two rod wide through Nathanel Harwood Land Seventy seven rod two rod wide through Mr Allens Land ninty rod two rod wide through Thomas Littles Land one hundred and fifty two rods two rod wide then through Mofes Willards Land by Groton line a few rods two rod wide and the said way is Defcribed by markt trees on the Right hand as the way Leads to Groton the above named William Clark Esqr Jeremiah Allen and Mofes Willard we have not seen but the other Gentlemen that owns the Land where the ways are Laid out are free and willing to give the Land for the Same perfuant to the vote of the town Concerning Highways &c

Alfo voted and Excepted of another town way as Reported of by the Selectmen viz Begining at the Houfe of Mr Hezekiah Wetherbe and runs ten Rod on S^d Wetherbe,s land as the Lane runs South on Land of Daniel Auftin Eighty two Rod Southerly by markt trees and on Common Land forty eight rod by markt trees on land of Jofeph Page one hundred and Eighty Rod by markt trees Eafterly and Southerly all which way is two rod wide and is Given by the owner of the land according to the vote Concerning town ways &c

Voted that way Be Discontinued from the white pine tree where the new way turns into M^r Joſeph Fullers feild where it runs acorſs fullers Wetherbes Abbotts and Willards Land till it comes into ye road between Capt Broadſtreets cauſeway and ye corner of Jonathan Hubburd ju land &c

Turn over

[56] Voted and Granted to Mr Thomas Prentice 1-16-0

Voted and Granted to Mr Samvel Johnſon 1-6-0

Voted and Granted to Benj^a Goodridge 2-18-0

Voted and Granted Mr Nathanel Harwood 0-16-0

Voted and Granted to Edward Hartwell Esqr 2-16-10

Voted that the Selectmen provid a School Maſter and places to Keep School in for the year enſuing

Recorded ℞ BENJ^A GOODRIDGE *town Cler*

At a legual meeting of the freeholders and other Inhabitants of the town of Lunenburg Aſsembled May the ninteenth A. D. 1742

Voted and Choſe Mr John Heywood modderrator

Voted and Granted the Sum of twenty pounds to mend High ways withall

Voted that men be allowed two Shillings per Day from this Day to the Laſt Day of September for this preſent year and one shilling and sixpence from then to the first day of March next and that nine pence be allowed for a pair of oxen a day and three pence for a Cart

Voted that the Repairing of the meeting houſe be Committed to Mr Samvel Johnſon and that he Bring an account of the Coſt thereof to the next town meeting

Voted that Swine go at Large this preſent year

Recored ℞ BENJ GOODRIDGE *Cler*

At a legual meeting of the freeholders and other Inhabitants of the town of Lunenburg Aſsembled September the 13th A. D. 1742

116   *The Early Records of the Town of Lunenburg.*

Voted and Chofe Major Jonathan Hubburd Modderrator

Voted and Granted John Jenifon 1 = 15 = 0 old tennour

Voted and Granted forty two pound ten shillings for the Revd Mr Stearns es Sallary for y^e year 1742

Voted and Granted y^e Sum of three pound fifteen Shillings to the Revd Mr Stearns to make good his Sallary for the year 1741

Voted and Granted the Sum of two pound ten Shillings to Benj^a Goodridge and John Grout to pay Capt Stevens for Service done.

Recorded p̃ BENJ^A GOODRIDGE *Clerk*

[57] At Legual meeting of the freeholders and other Inhabitants of the town of Lunenburg Afsembled Janvary the thirty first 1742/3

Voted and Chofe Mr John Heywood Modderator

Voteded and granted to Mr Nathanael Page the Sum of five Shillings for Building the pound in S^d town

Voted and Granted to Mr Samvel Johnfon for repairing the meeting house the Sum of eight Shillings

Voted and Granted to Mr Benjamin Bellows ju^r for a lock and key for the pound one Shilling and eight pence

To Mr Thomas Prentice Town Treafurer for the town of Lunenburg or his Succefsor in faid office S^r this may Certify to you that we have afsefsed the Sum of Sixty pound seven Shillings and nine pence on the Inhabitants of the town of Lunenburg and have Delivered one Lift to Joshua Goodridge Constable of thirty three pounds and three pence and to Jonathan Page Conftable a Lift of twenty Eight pound Seven Shilling and Six pence which Sums you are to Demand and Receive and to pay out as follows (viz)

To the Revd Mr David Stearns the Sum of
$\frac{£}{42}$ = 10 - 0 for his Sallary for this prefent year
and three pound fifteen Shillings to make
the money Good for the year paft — —   3-15-0

To Thomas Prentice for Being an afsefsor for y^e
year seventeen hundred and forty one —   0- 9-0

To Nathaniel Harwood for Ditto	0- 4-0
To Samvel Johnson for Ditto	0- 6-0
To Benjª Goodridge for Ditto	0-14-6
To Edward Hartwell Esqʳ for Ditto	0-14-2½
To John Jeniſon for taking care of yᵉ meeting house	0- 8-9
To Nathanael Page for building yᵉ pound in Lunenburg	0- 5-0
To Samvel Johnſon for repairing the meeting houſe	0- 8-0
To Benjamin Bellows Jʳ for a lock and key for yᵉ pound	0- 1-8
To Samvel Davis for making two Jury Boxes	0- 0 4½
To Benjª Goodridge and John Grout to pay to Capᵗ Stevens	2-10-0

[58] At a legal Meeting of the freeholders and other Inhabitants of the town of Lunenburg Aſsembled March yᵉ Seventh A D 1742/3

Voted and Choſe Mʳ Thomas Prentice Moddr.

Edward Hartwell Esqʳ
Benjª Goodridge
Capᵗ Jonathan Willard
Mʳ John Grout
Capᵗ Jonathan Bradſtreet
} Were Choſen Select men

Benjª Goodridge Choſen Town Clerk & Sworn
Mʳ Thomas Prentice Choſen Town Treaſurer & Sworn
Mʳ Jonathan Page
Mʳ Jonathan Hubburd jr } Choſen Conſtables and Sworn

Mʳ Ezekeil Wyman
Mʳ David Parce
Mʳ John Martin
Edward Hartwell Esqʳ
Mʳ Eleazer Tarbal
Mʳ Jonathan Smith
Mʳ William Snow
Mʳ Thomas Brown
} Choſen Surveyers of High ways and Sworn

Mʳ Benjª Bellows junr Choſen Sealer of waits & meaſures Sworn
Mʳ Solomon Stewart
Mʳ Samvel Comings } Choſen Tyding men
Mʳ John Grout
Mʳ Samvel Davis } Choſen fence veiwers & Sworn

Mr Joshua Goodridge }
Mr Jacob Gould } Chofen Deer rives & Sworn
Mr Jofeph Fuller }
Mr Thomas Brown } Chofen Hogg reves and Sworn
Mr Nathan Heywood }
Mr William Jones } Chofen to take of fire & Sworn

[59] Voted that Mr Thomas Prentice Mr William Jones and Mr Jeremiah Norcrofs be a Committe to provide a school mafter and to appoint and provide places to Keep the School in for ye year Enfuing.

Voted and Granted the Sum of twenty five pound for the ufe of the school.

Voted and Granted the Sum of two pound ten shillings for Deacon Johnfon to repair the meeting houfe withall

Voted and Granted to Mr Benj^a Bellows for Service done for the town ten Shillings

Voted and Granted to Mr John Grout Six fhillings

Granted to Benj^a Goodridge Eleven fhillings

Granted Mr John Heywood Six Shillings

Granted to Capt. Jonathan Bradftreet three Shillings

Granted to Mr William Jones three fhillings

Granted to Mr Jonathan Page ten pence

Granted to Mr Thomas Prentice five pence half peny

Voted and Excepted of a town way Laid out by ye Selectmen Begining at Benjamin Goulds northwest corner on the South fide of north field Road and so runs about weft by John Fisks fence Being on ye South Side and then on Joseph Page^s fence till it comes to the corner of Bellows s meddow to a Black oak Stump then to a heap of Stones near ye meddow then to a great Stone about five rod South weft from the houfe where William Cannada lives then to a Black oak tree markt d then to another Black oak tree markt then to a white oak tree markt on or about ye head of houfe Lott No 6 in S^d town and then about weft till it comes over ye Stone Bridge into ye old way ye faid way to be four rod wide on ye north Side of S^d Marks

Voted and Excepted of a town way Laid out by acommitee appionted Begining about the Eaft Side of

Abraham Sanderſons Land at the Eaſt end of yᵉ Line Eaſt of Sᵈ Sanderſons houſe & So runing by Sᵈ Sanderſons houſe & then to a heap of Stones then by yᵉ north ſide of yᵉ Swamp to a white oak markt and then by other trees markt till it comes to Mulpus and then over Mulpus by markt trees till it comes to yᵉ other way at Abel Plattss Corner Sᵈ way to be two rod wide the markt trees and other marks are on the north and weſt sides

      Recorded ℔
      Benjᴬ Goodridge *town Cler*

[60] Att a Legual meeting of the freeholders and other Inhabitants of the town of Lunenburg aſsembled auguſt the 9ᵗʰ 1743

Voted and Choſe majʳ Jonathan Hubbard moderator for ſᵈ meeting

Voted that a committe be choſen to mark out away to the weſt Line of our town from the way already Excepted to the weſt end of the wyman Land

Voted that Edward Hartwell Eſqʳ Mʳ Ephraim Wetherbe and Mʳ Jonathan Page be a Committe for the purpoſe aforeſaid

Voted that Mʳ Ephraim Wetherbe with a Eleven Hands with him go on Monday next to Clear ſaid way and that Mʳ Wetherbe overſee ſaid work

Voted that the hands aboveſaid have two Shillings and Six pence ℔ Day each man

Voted and choſe Edward Hartwell Eſqʳ and Mʳ John Grout to make Reply to Collᵉ Berryˢ Complaint at Worceſter Court for our not having away to Dorchester Cannada or to the weſt Line of our town

    Recorded ℔ Benjᴬ Goodridge *Cler*

Att a legual meeting of the freeholders and other Inhabitants of the town of Lunenburg Aſsembled September yᵉ 12ᵗʰ A D 1743

Voted and Choſe Majʳ Jonathan Hubbard modderartor

Voted that they will Chuſe a Committe

Voted and Choofe Maj^r Jonathan Hubburd Mr Nathan Heywood and Capt Jonathan Bradftreet a committe to Lay out and mark away to the Weft Line of our town in order to anfwer the Requeft of the Honorable Thomas Berry Efq^r in Behalf of Ipswich Cannada and to accomodate Dorchefter Cannada and the new towns above us and make return to the town as foon as may Be where they have Laid it —— —— —— ——

[61] Voted and Granted the Sum of twenty pounds to be workt out at faid way at three Shillings ₱ Day & if any man Dos not work when warned he Shall pay his money and if any over plus be to be workt out as other ways

Voted & Granted to the Revd Mr David Stearns fo much as will make his Sallary fifty pounds in Bills of the Last Emifsion for this prefent year

Voted and Granted ye Sum of ten pound to make Good any Deficiences in the Treafurey

Voted and Granted to Mr John Grout the Sum of four fhillings for Service Done for ye town

Recorded ₱ Benj^a Goodridge *Clerk*

At a Legal Meeting of the freeholders and other Inhabitants of the town of Lunenburg Afsembled September ye twenty feventh A. D 1743

Voted and Choofe Mr Hilkiah Boynton Modderator

Voted that ye Report of ye Committee Be Excepted which is as follows

Lunenburg September ye 17th 1743 We the Subscribers being appointed by faid town to Lay out a Highway from Some part or particular place of Some Road already Laid out in Said town to the weft Line thereof &c In purfuance whereof we have made Search and viewed the Land where we thought it moft probable faid Highway could be made and our opinions are that to Begin at the Road Laid out Between Ezekiel and John Wymans Land and fo to Mr David Pages and then in or near the Road where people now pafs to Dorchefter Cannada about a mile and a half then turn out of Said old Road to y^e

Right hand by a Black oak tree marked and going by or near trees marked till it comes to ſaid old Road again near Uptons Land there corſsing ſaid old Road and going over ſaid Uptons Land and

turn over

[62] And then by trees marked about three Quarters of a mile and coming into ſaid old Road again and Continuing in ſaid old Road to the Line of Lunenburg will be much the beſt way much the Cheapeſt made and much the eaſieſt to maintain and will beſt accomodate the new towns which we are to have particular Regard to all thing Conſidered

Voted that the ſaid way be two Rod wide   Jonathan Hubbard ⎫
Nathan Heywood ⎬ Com^{tte}
Jonathan Bradſtreet ⎭

Recorded ℘ BENJ^A GOODRIDGE *Clerk*

At a meeting of the freeholders and other Inhabitants of the town of Lunenburg Aſsembled March ye fifth A D 1743/4

Voted and Choſe Maj^r Jonathan Hubbard Modderator
Voted and Choſe

Maj^r Jonathan Hubbard ⎫
Mr Jonathan Wood ⎪
Mr Joshua Goodridge ⎬ Selectmen
Mr Hilkiah Boynton ⎪
Mr John Grout ⎭

Benj^a Goodridge Choſen town Clerk and Sworn

Mr Thomas Prentice chosen Treaſurer and Sworn

Mr David Parce ⎱
Mr William Page ⎰ Choſen Conſtables   Voted that Mr Benjamin Bellows jun be Excepted Constable in the rome of ſaid Parce and Page

Mr John Buſs ⎫
Mr Benj^a Bellows jun ⎬ Surveyers of high ways
Mr Joseph Fuller ⎭

[63]   Mr Abraham Sanderſon ⎫
M^r Joſiah Dodge ⎪
Mr Jacob Gould ⎬ Choſen Surveyers of high ways and Sworn
Mr Jonathan Page ⎪
Mr Nathanael Page ⎭

Mr Benjamin Bellows jun Sealer of weights and meaſures

Mr Eleazer Houghton Sealer of Leather

Mr Benjamin Bellows }
Mr Jeremiah Norcroſs } fence viewers

Mr Solomon Stwart }
Mr Jonathan Abbott } Deer reves and Sworn

Mr William Snow }
Mr John Gibſon } tying men

Mr John Fisk }
Mr Jacob Gould } Hogg reves

Mr William Jones }
Mr John Fitch } Choſen to take care of fire

Voted that Edward Hartwell Eſq^r Capt Jonathan Bradſtreet and Mr Benjamin Bellows jun be a Com^{tte} to take care of the School and to provide a School Maſter for ye year enſuing

Voted that Mr Hilkiah Boynton Capt Jonathan Bradſtreet and Mr John Grout Be a Committee to agree with Major Jonathan Hubbard aboute Exchanging apeice of the miniſtreal Land with ſaid Hubbard for apeice of his Land and to Joyn with Mr Stearns in Giving a Deed of Exchange if they think proper and as they shall Judge Beſt

Voted that Mr John Jeniſon take care of ye meeting houſe ye year enſuing and granted to S^d Jeniſon for ſd service   0-10-0

Voted and Granted Maj^r Hubbard   0- 5-0

Voted & Granted to Mr Nathan Heywood   0- 5-0

Voted and Granted to Capt Bradſtreet   0 5-0

                                                              turn over

[64] Voted and Granted to Edward Hartwell Eſq^r 0- 2-6

Voted and Granted to Mr Ephraim Wetherbe   0- 2-6

Voted and Granted to Mr Jonathan Page   0- 2-6

Voted & Granted to Edward Hartwell Eſq^r 0- 9-0

Voted & Granted to Mr John Grout   0- 4-0

Voted & Granted to Capt Bradſtreet   0- 1-6

Voted & Granted to Capt Willard   0- 1-6

Voted & Granted to Benj^a Goodridge   0-16-6

Voted & Granted to Mr Benj Bellows   0-12-6

Voted & Granted to Mr Thomas Prentice   0- 0-9

Voted that a town way be Excepted of from M^r Joſeph Fullers Land to ye Great Streem of ye north Branch as Laid out by the Committee appointed Begining at ſaid Fullers Land and Runing through Mr Jacob Stiles Land one hundred and twenty Rod two Rod wide and marked on ye north Side and then Runing Between Mr Samvel Cumings es & Mr John Martins Land twenty Rod and then through Said Cumingses Land half a mild two Rod wide & marked on the north Side and then on Land of Juſtice Hartwell fourteen Rod and then on Land of Mr Prescut Eighty Seven Rod and then on Land of Mr Jacob Stiles forty Rod and then a few Rods on Common Land and then on Land of David Goodridge Eighty Rod all which way is two Rod wide and markt as aforeſaid and Laid out by

             Joſeph Fuller
             John Martin
             Jacob Stiles   } Com^{ttec}
             Samvel Cumings

Voted that ye way through Mr Jacob Stiles Land where it was formerly Laid out Be Discontinued from Being a way any Longer

Voted that a town way be Excepted Between Mr Ephraim Wetherbes and Mr Thomas Carters Land one rod on Each man's Land

Voted that ye town way as it was formerly Laid out on Mr Wetherbes Land Be Discontinued from Being away any Longer

[65] Voted that the way be Discontinued from Benjamin Bellows Land at ye Corner of ye meddow to John Fisks Corner all But two Rod wide next to fowlers Land to four rod upon ſaid Fisks Land and that ye way be Excepted as it Lyes by Joſeph Pages Barn provided Said Page make the way agood paſſable way by Caſaring so that it may be Good paſsing for teams to the Exceptence of ye Selectmen By the firſt of July next

           Recorded ℔

                 BENJ^A GOODRIDGE *Clerk*

At a meeting of the freeholders and other Inhabitants of the town of Lunenburg Aſsembled September the Seventeenth A D 1744

Voted and Granted to the Revd Mr David Stearns the Sum of fifty one pound five Shilling In Bills of the Last Emmiſtion for his Sallary this preſent year

Voted and Granted the Sum of twenty five pound for the uſe of the School

Voted that Maj^r Jonathan Hubbard Edward Hartwell Eſq^r and Mr Jonathan Page be a Committe to Reckon with the town treaſurer and to Give him a Diſcharge for So much as he has paid on the towns account

[66] At a meeting of the freeholders and other Inhabitants of the Town of Lunenburg Aſsembled March the fourth A D 1744/5

Voted and Choſe Mr Hilkiah Boynton Moddr of Said meeting

Edward Hartwell Eſq^r
Benj^a Goodridge
Mr John Grout } Choſen Selectmen and
Capt Jonathan Willard
Mr Eleazer Tarbal

Benj^a Goodridge Choſen town Clerk & Sworn

Thomas Prentice Eſq^r Choſen town treaſurer

Mr Samvel Cumings
Mr Jonathan Wood } Choſen Constables and Sworn

M^r Joſiah Dodge
Mr Joseph Fuller
Mr Samvel Davis
Mr Jacob Gould } Choſen Surveyers of Highways and Sworn
Mr John Wyman
Mr Ezekiel Wyman
Mr Nathanael Harwood

Mr Thomas Brown
Mr Nathanael Harwood
Mr John Grout } Choſen fence veiwers and Sworn
Mr Samvel Davis

Mr Thomas Brown
Mr Joseph Fuller } Choſen Deer reives and Sworn

Mr Ezekiel Wyman
Mr John Martin } Chosen tying men

[67] Mr John Grifin
Mr Stephen Boynton } choſen Hogg reives and Sworn

Mr John Jenifon Chofen Sealer of Leather and Sworn
Mr Benjamin Bellows jr } Chofen Sealer of waits and meafures and Sworn

Mr Solomon Stewart }
Mr Benjamin Gary } Chofen to take care of fire

Majr Jonathan Hubburd Chofen Surveyer of Shingles and Sworn

Mr Nathanael Harwood }
Mr Samvel Larrabee } Chosen to take care of fire

Voted that Major Jonathan Hubburd Mr Nathan Heywood & Mr William Jones be a Committe to provide the town with a School Mafter for the year enfuing

Voted and Granted unto Mr Jacob Gould the Sum of Eleven pound Seventeen Shillings and nine pence for his Extraordinary Coft at the Courts with Andrew Flemin provided he Settle accounts with the town

Voted and Granted unto Mr John Grout ye sum of 1 - 0 - 0
Voted & Granted unto Mr Hilkiah Boynton   0 - 3 - 6
Voted & Granted unto Mr Jofhua Goodridge   0 - 1 - 6
Voted and Granted to Mr Benja Bellows ju   0 - 7 - 0
Voted & Granted to Majr Hubburd ye Sum of   0 - 7 - 6
Voted & Granted Jonathan Hubburd junr   0 = 11 = 3
Voted & Granted to Mr Samvel Johnfon   0 - 1 - 6

[68] An acount of way Excepted at Sd meeting Namly A two Rod way Begining at Dupees Land and Runing upon walkers and Carltons Land 53 Rod and then upon Walkers and Hazeltines Land 22 Rod and then Begining at Mr Stewarts Land and Runs Between Walkers and Woods Land to the faid Road 93 Rods & then Runing all on Hazeltines Land 44 rod and then all on Woods Land 66 Rods and Between Mr Stones and Mr Fullers Land 193 Rod unto the two Rod way and about ten Rod a crofs Mr Wetherbes Land and then Between Mr Wetherbes and Mr William Stearns Land 164 Rods and then through Mr Benjamin Forfters Land 55 Rods all markt on the North Side and then acrofs Mr Jenifons Land to the Road 124 Rods markt on ye South fide

      Laid out by us   Hilkiah Boynton } Select
                           Jonathan Wood } men of
                           Jofhua Goodridge } Lunenburg

Alſo a two Rod way Laid out By us the Subſcribers Begining at the Road that comes from Hezekiah Wetherbes and Runs upon Mr Benj^a Bellows and Daniel Astins Land and Between the ſaid Auſtin and John Fiſks Land and acroſs ſome common Land and acroſs the miniſtreal Land and acroſs Mr Preſcotts Land and acroſs Dunsmores Land and acroſs Mr Noah Dodges Land to Groton Line meeting with thier Road all markt on the north Side —

 Laid out by   Joſua Goodridge
               Hilkiah Boynton

Voted that this way be Eccepted provided the Land be Givin

[69] And alſo a two Rod way Being origainally Left for away by Mr Israel Reed and others purchaſers of Woborn farm Begining at or near John Divols Swamp Between Mr Dodges and Benj^a Goodridges Land & So on a ſtrait Line Between the firſt and ſecond Ranges of Lotts in ſaid farm till it comes John Hills Land alſo another two Rod way Left By ſaid Reed and others as aforeſaid Begining at Jonathan Pages Land Between William Holts and John Wymans Land and So Between the Second and third Ranges of Lotts till it comes to Unchechewalunk pond Between the Land of Thomas Carter and Joſeph Fuller

 Laid out by us   Joseph Fuller } Com^tte
           Samvel Reed }

And alſo away Laid out from the north River Begining at Said River by markes on the weſt ſide ſ^d way being two Rod wide and So runing through David Goodridges Land and then through Eleazer Houghtons Land and then through Sergants Land then though Juſtices Harrises Land & So Coming to the old path at the foot of a great hill and So runing in the old Path to Leominſter Line and So Continuing in the old path up to James Pools

    Laid out by   Jonathan Hubburd } Com^tte
          Hilkiah Boynton }

All which ways are Excepted as above Deſcribed and Recorded   P̃ Benj^a Goodridge
                  town Clerk

[70] Att a meeting of the freeholders and other Inhabitants of the Town of Lunenburg Afsembled Sept the ninth A D 1745

Voted and Choofe Maj^r Jonathan Hubburd Moderator of faid meeting

Voted and Granted the Sum of fifty two pounds ten Shillings to the Rev Mr David Stearns for his Sallary for the present year ——

Voted and Granted the Sum of twenty five pound for the ufe of the School in Said town

Voted that the men that Live within the Bounds of Major Hartwells Company Build the Bridge over the North Branch in way as it goes to David Goodridges and the Bridge over ye said north Branch in the way that goes to David Pages

And that the men that Live within the Bounds of Capt Willards Company Build the Bridge over Mullepus in the way by or neer Hezekiah Wetherbes and the Bridge over Said Mullepus in the way that goes to Townfhend Below the widdow Whites mill

Recorded 㲻 BENJ GOODRIDGE *Cler*

At A meeting of the freeholders and other Inhabitants of the Town of Lunenburg Afsembled March the third A D 1745/6

Voted and Chofe Thomas Prentice Efq^r Modderator

Voted and Chofe

Edward Hartwell Efq^r
Capt Jonathan Willard
Benj Goodridge } Selectmen
Mr Jacob Gould
Mr John Grout

[71] Benj^a Goodridge Chofen town Clerk & Sworn
Thomas Prentice Chofen Town Treafurer

Mr Thomas Brown
Mr Eleazer Tarbal } Chofen Conftables & Sworn

Mr Samvel Johnson
Mr Arington Gibfon
Mr Joseph Fuller } Chofen Surveyers of Highway & Sworn
Mr Jofiah Dodge
Mr David Page

Mʳ Ezekiel Wyman ⎫
Mʳ Thomas Carter ⎭ tyding men

Mʳ Jofiah Bayley ⎫
Mʳ John Jenifon ⎭ Chofen fence viewers & Sworn

Mʳ Thomas Carter Chofen Sealer of Leather

Mʳ Benj Bellows jun Chofen Sealer of weights & meafures

Mʳ Jonathan Abbot ⎫
Mʳ Benj Gary ⎪
Mʳ Thomas Little ⎬ Chofen Hogg reves
Mʳ Obediah Walker ⎪
Mʳ Afael Hartwell ⎭

Mʳ Philip Goodridge ⎫
Mʳ Samvel Davis ⎭ Chofen Deer reves

Mʳ David Goodridge ⎫
Mʳ Jofeph Wood ⎭ Chofen to take care of fire

Mʳ Jacob Gould ⎫
Mʳ Thomas Brown ⎪
Mʳ Ezekiel Wyman ⎬ Chofen Feild Drivers
Mʳ Joseph Fuller ⎭

[72] Voted and Chofe
Benj Goodridge ⎫
Edward Hartwell Efqʳ ⎬ Afsefsors
Capᵗ Jonathan Willard ⎭

Voted and Granted the Sum of twenty five pound in Bills of the Laft Emifion for the ufe of the School

Voted & Granted to Capᵗ Willard — 0- 7-6
Voted & Granted to Capᵗ Willard   0- 4-6
Voted & Granted Mʳ Jofiah Dodge   0-10-0
Voted & Granted to Mʳ John Grout   1- 0-0
Voted & Granted to Benj Goodridge   0- 9-0
Voted & Granted to Mʳ John Heywood 0- 1-6
Voted & Granted to Mʳ Eleazer Tarbal 0- 4-6
Voted & Granted to Juftice Prentice 0- 1-6

Voted that a town way Be Excepted as Laid out by the Selectmen and Reported to the town Begining at the Bridge over Pearl hill Brook and runs acrofs Collonel Downe Land near Hutchins Celler (so called) to a white oak markt then to a pitch pine markt then to another pitch pine tree markt then to a white oak tree markt then by two yellow oak trees markt then to a white oak tree markt Near Deacon Bancrofts Land then through said Bancrofts Land by trees markt till it comes to the Line Between Benjamin Garys and Timothy Bancrofts Land Said way to Be two Rod wide on ye Southerly Side of Said marks then runs a rod on each Side of ye Line Between [73] Said Gary & Bancroft till it comes to the top of the Hill Between their Houses and then turns northward to a white oak tree markt then to a Stub with a heap of Stones then to a Gray oak markt then to a Chesnut tree markt then to a yellow oak tree markt on said Garys Land then to a maple tree markt on John Mansfeilds Land then to a Chesnut tree on the Line Between said Mansfeilds and John Peirces Land said way to be two Rod wide on the southwesterly side of said marks and said Mansfeild Gary and Bancrofts Gives their Lands for said way —— ——

Recorded ⅌ BENJ GOODRIDGE Clerk

At ameeting of the freeholders and other Inhabitants of the town of Lunenburg Assembled may ye twentieth A D 1746

Voted and Chose Maj^r Jonathan Hubburd Modderator

Voted and Chose Mr Nathan Heywood Mr Jonathan Wood Mr Jacob Stiles Major Jonathan Hubburd Mr Eleazer Tarbal a Committe to provide a school Master for the year Ensuing and to move the school as they think Best

Voted that Mr John Grout Mr John Heywood and Benj Goodridge Be a committe to Reckon with the Treasurer or Treasurers of ye twon and to Report thereon to ye next town meeting

Voted that Hoggs go at Larege the present year

Recorded ⅌ BENJ GOODRIDGE Clerk

[74] At a Legual Meeting of the freeholders and other Inhabitants of the town of Lunenburg Assembled November the tenth A. D 1746

Voted and Chose Mr John Heywood Modderator

Voted and Granted the Sum of three pound for the use of School in s^d town ———

Voted and Granted the Sum of fifty three pound Fifteen Shillings for the Rev Mr David Stearn-s- Sallary for the Prefent year

Voted that Town Meetings for the future be warned By the Conftables pofting up a Notification (under his hand) upon a poft to be fet up for that porpofe within two Rods of the meeting houfe faceing the Road Setting forth the articles of f^d meeting and to ftand Pofted as aforefaid fourteen Days at Leaft ———

Voted and Granted ye Sum of twelve Shillings and fix pence to Mr Benjamin Bellows ———

Voted and Granted ye Sum of two Shillings and Six pence to Mr Benjamin Bellows jun ——

     Recorded p̃ BENJ GOODRIDGE *Clerk*

At a Legaul Meeting of the Town of Lunenburg Afsembled March ye 2nd A D 1746/7

Voted & Choofe Major Jonathan Hubburd Modderator

Benj Goodridge
Maj^r Jonathan Hubbard
Capt Jonathan Willard } Selectmen
Thomas Prentice Esqr
Mr John Gibfon

Benj Goodridge town Clerk

Thomas Prentice Efq^r town Trerfurer

[75] Mr Solomon Stawart
  Mr Philip Goodridge } Constables

Mr Francies Buttrick
Mr James Leitch } Tyding men
Mr David Chaplin

Mr Jonathan Bradftreet jun
Mr Ezekiel Wyman
Mr Jonathan Wood } Surveyers of high ways
Mr Samvel Reed
Mr Joliah Dodge
Mr Samvel Larrabee

Mr Joseph Fuller
Mr Thomas Brown } fences veiwers

Mr David Goodridge
Mr Benj Gary } Hogg reives
Mr John Darlin
Mr Jonathan Hartwell

Mr Benj Bellows jun Sealer of Weights & meaſures
Mr Eleazer Houghton Sealer of Leather
Mr Amos Kimbal }
Mr Samvel Larrabe } to take Care of fire
Mr Samvel Davis }
Capt Jonathan Hubburd } Cullirs of Shingles
Mr Nathanel Harwood }
Mr Zechariah Whitney } to take care of Deer

Voted & Granted to Edward Hartwell Eſqr — 0-2-3
Voted & Granted to Benj Goodridge ——— 1-2-6
Voted & Granted to Capt Jonathan Willard — 0-2-3
Voted & Granted to Samvel Davis ——— 0-3-0

Voted that the town Discontinue the way from the way by Joseph Pages to Mulpus Brook and Except of the way Laid out from the way Between the Houſe william Kannady Lives in and Joſeph Pages Houſe to Mulpus two Rods wide as Laid out By Mr Jacob Gould and Mr Hezekiah Wetherbe

turn over

[76] and Reported to the Towon Provided Mr Joſeph Page Give Leave to the widow Mary Lane and her heirs to paſs and Repaſs with their Creatvers to ſaid way by the Bridge through Bars or Gates the which ſaid Joseph Page Conſented

Voted that that part of the way which gos to John Mansfeilds Between Timothy Bancrofts and Benja Garys Land Be Diſcontinued and the way through Benja Garys Land Be accepted in the Room therof Begining at a Black oak tree on the North ſide of ſd way and Runing through ſaid Garys Land two Rod wide till it comes to John Mansfeild Land as it is now fenced ———

Recored ⅌ BENJ GOODRIDGE *Cler*

At Meeting of the freeholders and other Inhabitants of the Town of Lunenburg Aſsembled May the Ninteenth A. D. 1747

Voted that Major Jonathan Hubburd be Modderator of ſaid Meeting

Voted the preſent Committe for the School be a committe to provide a ſchool Maſter for the town and to order where the School fhall be Kept the year Enfuing Saving that Nathanel Harwood be Joyned with faid Committee in the Room of Eleazer Tarball who is moved out of town

Voted that the Swine run at Large the prefent year

Recored ℗ Benj Goodridge.

At a Legual meeting of the freeholders and other Inhabitants of the town of Lunenburg afsembled March the 3rd 1745/6

Voted and Excepted of a two Rod town way through Mr William Jones Land on the Eaft fide of his houfe and Barn from Justice Harrises Land till it comes to Mr John Scots Land where the way now is—this way by a Mistake is Recored in a wrong Place

℗ Benj Goodridge.

[77] At a legual Meeting of the freeholders and other Inhabitants of the town of Lunenburg Afsembled September the 21th 1747

Voted and Choofe Majr Jonathan Hubburd Moddr for Sd meeting

Voted & Granted the Sum of two Hundred and Eighty pound old tenour for the Rev. Mr David Stearns Sallary for the prefent year ———

Voted and Granted the Sum of one Hundred and forty pound old tenour for the Suport of the School in Said town ———

Voted and Granted the Sum of ten Shilling to Mr Jofiah Dodge for making the Stocks

Recorded ℗ Benj Goodridge *Clerk*

At a Legual Meeting of the freeholders and other Inhabitants of the town of Lunenburg Afsembled March the Seventh A D 1747/8

Voted and Choofe Majr Jonathan Hubburd Modderator ———

Voted that ye Report of ye Committe to Reckon with ye town Treasurer be Excepted so far as they have proceeded.

The Early Records of the Town of Lunenburg. 133

Voted and chofse
Mr John Grout
Benj: Goodridge
Capt Jonathan Bradftreet } Selectmen
Mr Benj: Forfter
Mr Jonathan Wood

Benj Goodridge Choofen town Clerk & Sworn

Mr Jofiah Dodge Chofen town Traefurer and Sworn

Mr Samvel Davis
Mr Afhael Hartwell } Chofen Constables & Sworn

Mr John Heywood
Mr Abraham Sanderfon were Chofen
Mr Solomon Stewart
Mr William Page   Surveyers of
Mr Philip Goodridge   High ways
Mr Amos Kimbal   &
Mr Nathanael Page   Sworn
Mr John Martin

Turn over

[78] March meeting march ye 7th 1747/8

Mr Joseph Fuller
Mr Thomas Brown } Chosen fence viewers & sworn

Maj^r Jonathan Hubburd Chofen fealer of weights & meafures & Sworn

Mr Eleazer Houghton Chofen Sealer of Leather

Mr James Leitch
Mr Francis Buttrick } Chofen Tyingmen

Mr Isaac Gibfon
Mr Ephraim Whitney } Chofen to take care of Deer

Mr David Goodridge
Mr James Colman
Mr Joseph Page   } Chofen Hogg reives
Mr Edward Hartwell jun

Mr Jacob Gould   } Chofen Surveyors of Shingles
Mr Philip Goodridge   Claborad ftaves &c & Sworn

Mr David Page   } Chofon to take care of
Mr Timothy Bancroft   fire and Sworn

Voted and Choofe

Maj^r Jonathan Hubburd
Mr Mofes Mitchael   a committe to provide the
Mr John Gibfon   } town with a School Mafter
Mr John Martin   and to provide places to
Mr William Snow   Keep the School in &c

Voted that the town ways for the future be mended by a Rate.

Voted that the wages from the firſt of may to the Last of September be four Shillings ⅌ Day for a man and Two Shillings ⅌ Day for a yoke of oxen and Six pence ⅌ Day for a cart and two Shillings ⅌ Day for a Great Plow and all other Materials to be found by the owners without pay and that from yᵉ firſt Day of october to the Laſt Day of April one half of yᵉ wages above mentioned for men oxen cart and plow ——

Voted that the Sum of one Hundred pound be Raiſed to mend the ways withall

[79]   March meeting march yᵉ 7ᵗʰ 1747/8
Voted that the old Meeting Houſe Be Repaired and that
 Mr Samvell Johnson
 Mr John Grout
 Thomas Kimball Eſqʳ
 Mʳ John Gibſon and
 Majʳ Hubburd
Be acommittee to Repair the old meeting Houſe

Voted the Rome in the meeting House Between Mʳ Clarks Pew and the Stairs be Granted to Mʳ Samvel Reed ——

Voted and Granted the Sum of twenty pound old tennor To Repair the old meeting Houſe with ——

Voted and Excepted of a town way Laid out by order of the Selectmen Begining at the South end of Appletree Hill at the old way Runing through a peice of Common Land and over the Bridge and through Amos Kimballs Land and Ephraim Kimballs Land ſaid way was Laid out by

    David Page ⎫
    Amos Kimball ⎬ *Committee*
    Ephraim Kimball ⎭

and ſaid Kimballs gave the Land for ſaid way to the town ſaid way is two Rod wide ——

Voted and Excepted of a town way from James Pooles too the Line of Narraganſsett No 2 Begining at ſaid Pooles where the way is Laid too and Excepted by the twon at a former meeting and is Defcribed by markt Trees on the Northerly fide of faid way till it comes to faid Narraganfett Line faid way was Laid out by

Maj^r Jonathan Hubburd } *Selectmen*
Capt Jonathan Willard } *of*
and Thomas Prentice Efq^r } *Lunenburg*

Voted and Excepted of atown way Laid out through Mr Secratary Willards Land Begining at the End of Northfield Road (so called) and is two Rod wide then through Mr Samvel Reeds Land on the Southerly Side of Reeds Houfe and than through more of f^d Willards Land and through Mr Crockers Land and Mr Samvel Johnfons Land   turn over

[80] and through Mr Isaac Gibsons Land and through some part of Mr Reuben Gibsons to his Houfe and is Defcribed by markt trees and faid Road is partly throug The firft Land of faid Willard and Through faid Reeds near where the Road now is Traveled in Northerly on faid Willard Land northerly Through faid Crockers Land North-Easterly through faid Johnfons Land and northeasterly Throug Land of faid Isaac Gibsons and partly Eafterly through faid Reuben Gibfons Land under the Pearl Hills So called.

the above way was Laid out and Defcribed by

Mr John Gibson } *Select*
& Thomas Prentice Efq^r } *men*
Recorded ℔ BENJ: GOODRIDGE *Town Cler*

At A Legaul Meeting of the freeholders and other Inhabitants of the Town of Lunenburg Afsembled May the 23rd 1748

Voted and Chofe Maj^r Jonathan Hubbard Modderator

Voted that Swine go at Large the Prefent year

Voted that Town Meetings for the future be warned by a notification Being pofted up Fourteen Days Before the time appointed for the meeting

Voted and Granted ye Sum of Thirty pound for the ufe of the School.

Recorded ℔ BENJ: GOODRIDGE *Cler*

[81] At a Legall Meeting of the freeholders and other Inhabitants of the Town of Lunenburg Afsembled Sept ye Sixth A D 1748

Voted Chofe Mr John Heywood Modderator

Voted and Granted ye Sum of one Hundred pound for the Rev Mr David Stearns Sallary for this Prefent year

Voted and Granted ye Sum of Twenty pound for ye ufe of the School

Voted and Granted to Mr Bellows for Sweep-
   ing the Meeting Houfe two years ——— 1-10-0-
Granted to Mr John Heywood ——— 0- 2-6
Granted to Mr Afahel Hartwell ——— 0- 2-6
Granted to Mr Philip Goodridge —— 0- 4-0
Granted to Benj Goodridge ——— 0-12-0
Granted to Thomas Prentice Efq^r —— 0-10-0
Granted to Capt Jonathan Willard — 0- 2-0
Granted to Mr John Gibfon ——— 0- 2-0
Granted Maj^r Jonathan Hubburd — 0- 4-0

Voted and Granted ye Sum of one pound to pay the Committe for Reckening With the Treafurers. ———

                Recorded ⅌ BENJ: GOODRIDGE *Town Cler*

[82] At A Legall meeting of the freeholders and other Inhabitants of the Town of Lunenburg Afsembled March the Sixth A D 1748/9

Voted and Chofe Mr Samvel Johnson Modderator

Voted and Chofe ———

Benj Goodridge
Mr Samvel Johnson
Mr John Grout   Selectmen
Capt Jonathan Bradftreet
Mr Jonathan Wood

Benj Goodridge Chofen Town Clerk

Thomas Prentice Efq^r Chofen town Treafurer

Mr Ezekiel Wyman
Mr Samvel Reed   Chofen Conftables

Voted that Mr Jonathan Willard jun be Excepted to Serve as Constable in the Room of Mr Samvel Reed faid Reed having hired him ———

Mr Ephraim Whitney
Mr Stephen Boynton
Mr Mofes Mitchael — Chofen Surveyors
Mr Mofes Ritter — of
Mr Patrick White
Mr Thomas Brown — High ways
Mr Ephraim Parce
Mr William Jones
Mr Benj Fofter

Mr Jofiah Bayley
Mr Samvel Reed — Chofen fence veiwers

Mr Thomas Carter Chofen Sealer of Leather

Mr William Jones
Mr Nathanael Page — Chofen Tydingmen

Mr Jofeph Wood
Mr David Goodridge — Chofen Deer Revees

[83] Mr Jeremiah Norcrofs
Mr Gabriel Ponchee — Chofen Hogg reves

Mr Jacob Gould
Mr Philip Goodridge — Chofen Surveyors of ftaves and Shingles &c -

Mr Jofeph Fuller
Mr Thomas Brown
Mr William Jones
Mr Amos Kimball — Chofen to take care of fire and to burn ye woods &c.
Mr Isaac Gibfon
Mr Samvil Larrabee
Mr John Darlin

Edward Hartwell Efq^r
Thomas Prentice Efq^r
Mr John Martin — Chofen acommittee to provide The Town with a School Mafter and to order where the School fhall be Kept for the ye year Infuing
Mr John Bufs
Mr Eleazer Tarbal

Voted John Darlins Rates be forgiven him

Voted and Granted to Capt Jonathan Bradftreet -   0- 4-0
Granted to Mr Jonathan Wood   ———   0- 4-0
Granted to Mr Benj Fofter   ————   0- 6-0
Granted to Mr John Grout   ———   0- 8-0
Granted to Benj Goodridge   ———   1-15-0

Voted and Granted the Sum of fifteen fhillings for the taking care of the Meeting Houfe ye year Infuing Voted and Granted the Sum of one pound to mend the pound withall

Voted a Town way be Excepted off from yᵉ way Between Obediah Walkers and David Woods Land to Solomon Stewards Houſe Between ſaid Stewards and ſaid Walkers Land ſaid way is two Rod wide and ſaid Steward gives the Land for ſaid way

     Recorded ⅌ BENJ GOODRIDGE *town Clerk*

Voted and Granted at the above meeting one Hundred pound to mend the town ways withall

     Recorded ⅌ BENJ GOODRIDGE *Town Clerk*

[84] At A Legal Meeting of the freeholders and other Inhabitants of the Town of Lunenburg Aſsembled May the 22ⁿᵈ A D 1749.

Voted and Choſe Mʳ Samvel Johnſon Modderator for ſaid meeting

Voted that they will Build A New Meeting Houſe in ſaid Town

Voted that ſaid new Meeting Houſe be Built as Neer the old Meeting houſe as may be with convenience Not to bee above five Rod from the old Meeting Houſe

Voted that Benjamin Goodridge Edward Hartwell Eſqʳ and Mʳ Joſiah Dodge Be aCommitte To agree with Mʳ Benjamin Bellows junʳ for apeice of Land to Build a new Meeting houſe upon and to Stake out the ſame and to conſider how Bigg ſaid Meeting Houſe ſhall be Built and in what form and Report the Same to the Town for their Acceptence

Voted that the Swine go at Large this preſent year

Voted that this Meeting Be ajorned to the Laſt Tueſday of June Next at two o Clock in the afternoon.

Tuesday June yᵉ 27ᵗʰ 1749 the freeholders & other Inhabitants of the Town of Lunenburg Being Met by ajournment Voted that the meeting be further ajourned to the firſt Tuesday of September Next at ten of the Clock in the forenoon

Tuesday September yᵉ 5ᵗʰ 1749 The freeholders and other Inhabitants of yᵉ Town of Lunenburg Being Met by a Journment Voted y^t the meeting be further a Journ-d till two o Clock in the afternoon and then met and Voted that the Meeting Houſe be Built Sixty feet Long and forty five feet wide and twenty five feet poſt Between Joynts

Voted that the Sum of three hundred pound new tennour Be Granted to Build a new Meeting Houſe withall and to be imediately Aſseſed one half thereof to be paid in Six Months the other half to be paid in twelve Months

[85] Voted that Benjamin Goodridge Mr Samvel Johnſon and M^r Joſiah Dodge be a committe to manage the affair and then voted that the meeting be Still further ajournd till Monday Next at two o Clock in the afternoon

Monday Sept the Eleventh 1749 the freeholders and other Inhabitants of the town of Lunenburg Being Met again by a Journment

Voted that the Committe to manage the affair of Building a new Meeting Houſe Let out the work to ſome one man that will Do it Cheapeſt and Beſt

Recorded ℞ Benj Goodridge *Town Cler*

At a Legual meeting of the freeholders and other Inhabitants of the Town of Lunenburg Aſsembled & Met September the fifth A D 1749

Voted and Choſe Mr John Grout Modderator and then Voted that the Meeting be a Journ d till Monday Next at one of the Clock in the afternoon : Monday Sept the Eleventh 1749 the freeholders and other Inhabitants of the Town of Lunenburg Being met by a Journment —

Voted and Granted the Sum of Twenty five pound for the uſe of the School in ſaid Town —

Voted and Granted the Sum of one Hundred pound for the Rev Mr David Stearns Sallary This preſent year

	£	s	d
Voted and Granted to Thomas Prentice Eſq	0-	2-	0
Voted and Granted to Mr Eleazer Tarball ——	0-	14-	9

Voted and Granted the Sum of ten pound to make good Deficences in the Town Treaſury

Voted that fifty pound be Raised to Build two Bridges on the way To Narraganfet No 2. one over the River by David Goodridges and one over the River Between James Pooles and faid Narraganfet N⁰ 2 to be workt out at five Shillings ℔ Day

Recorded ℔ BENJ GOODRIDGE *Cler*

[86] At a Legal Meeting of the Freeholders and other Inhabitants of the Town of Lunenburg Afsembled December the 21th A D 1749

Voted and Chofe Mʳ John Grout Modderator

Voted that the town will Shew Caufe why the prayer of the Petition (praying that the mile on the Eaft fide of the Town may be Set off to Joyn with thofe on the weft fide of Groton River) Should not be Granted

Voted that Benjamin Goodridge Mʳ Jofiah Dodge Mʳ John Grout Mʳ John Gibfon and Mʳ Mofes Mitchael be a Committe to Draw up Reafons to Shew why the prayer of the faid petetion Should not be Granted

Voted that two men be fent to Bofton to Make anfwer to faid petetion

Voted and Chofe Benjamin Goodridge and Mʳ Jofiah Dodge to Go to Bofton to make anfwer unto faid petetion

Voted that the Sum of ten pound in yᵉ Laft Emifion Bills be Granted to Enable faid Goodridge and Dodge to go to Bofton and make anfwer to yᵉ faid petetion

Recorded ℔ BENJ GOODRIDGE
town Clerk

[87] At A Legal meeting of the Freeholders and other Inhabitants of the Town of Lunenburg Afsembled March the fifth A D 1749/50

Voted and Chofe Mʳ Samvel Johnson Modderrator for faid Meeting

Benj Goodridge
Mʳ Samvel Johnson
Capt Jonathan Bradstreet } were Chofen Selectmen
Mʳ Jofiah Dodge
Mʳ Solomon Steward

Benj Goodridge was Chofen Town Clerk and Sworn

The Early Records of the Town of Lunenburg. 141

Thomas Prentice Esqr was Chosen Town Treasurer
Mr Thomas Cartter ⎫
Mr William Snow ⎭ were Chosen Constables

Voted that Mr Ezekiel Wyman be Excepted to serve as Constable in the Room of Mr Thomas Carter

Mr Josiah Dodge
Mr Thomas Brown
Mr John Griffin
Mr Arington Gibson
Mr Philip Goodridge ⎬ Were Chosen Surveyers of Highways.
Mr Josiah Bayley
Mr Moses Mitchael
Mr George Kimbal
Mr David Wood

Mr Josiah Bayley ⎫
Mr Samvel Davis ⎭ were chosen fence veiwers

[88] Mr Nathanael Page ⎫
    Mr Samvel Hunt ⎭ were Chosen Tyding men

Mr Joseph Wood ⎫ were Chosen to take Care
Mr Isaac Gibson ⎭ of Deer

Mr Josiah Dodge junr ⎫
Mr Ephraim Kimbal ⎬ were Chosen Hogreves
Mr David Carlile ⎭

Mr Samvel Davis ⎫ were Chosen Surveyers
Mr Josiah Bayley ⎭ of Shingles

Mr Eleazer Houghton was Chosen Sealer of Leather

Mr John Martin ⎫
Mr Nicholas Dike ⎭ were Chosen Surveyers of Staves

Mr William Jones ⎫
Mr John Scott ⎬ were Chosen to
Mr David Goodridge ⎭ take Care of fire

Voted that the School be Kept in four places in the town three mounths at aplace in the year for the future

Voted yt Mr Benjamin Bellows junr Mr Nathan Heywood Mr Eleazer Tarbal Mr Solomon Steward and Mr William Snow be a committe to appoint the said four places and also to appoint places to Build four School Houses in and make Report of their Doings to the Town at Next May meeting

Voted that Mr Benjamin Bellows junr Mr Solomon Steward and Mr Eleazer Tarbal

be

[89] Be a committe to provide a School Marſter for the Town for the year Inſuing

Voted and Granted the Sum of Seventy five pound Laſt Emiſsion Bills for the Support of the School in ſaid Town

Voted that David Goodridge appoint a Day for thoſe that have not workt out their Rates at the High ways and that they work out their Rates under his Direction at the Bridge by his Houſe Between now and the Last of april next

Voted and Granted to Mr John Martin ——   2 = 5 = 0
Voted & Granted Thomas Prentice Eſq^r ——   1 = 4 = 0
Voted & Granted to Benj : Goodridge ————   1 - 5 - 0
Voted & Granted to Capt Jonathan Bradſtreet — 0 - 17 - 6
Voted & Granted to Mr Samvel Johnſon ——   1 - 5 - 0
Voted & Granted to Mr Jonathan Wood ——   0 - 12 - 6

Voted that Nathanael Harwoods Highway Rates be abated

Voted that it Be Left with the Selectmen to abate ſuch Rates as Shall appear to them to Be Reaſonable —— and then

Voted that the meeting be a Jorned to to morrow morning nine o Clock

Tueſday March ye Sixth nine o, clock A. M. A. D 1749/50 then the freeholders and other Inhabitants of the Town of Lunenburg Being met by ajornment

Voted that the new meeting Houſe that the Town of Lunenburg is about to Build be Built and Set up in the End of the Lane by the School Houſe the place already voted notwithstanding

voted

[90] Voted that the Committe to manage the affair of Building a new Meeting Houſe agree with Mr Benjamin Bellows jun and with Juſtice prentice for a ſuitable Diſtrick of Land for to Set the meeting Houſe upon and for Conveniences about the Same and Report the Same to the Town at Next may meeting for their acceptance

Voted that the Town Will Shew Cauſe why the prayer of the petetion Should not Be Granted and that the Committe appointed to anfwer the petetion of those praying to Joyn with thofe of Groton Shew Caufe why the prayer of the petetion of Edward Hartwell Efq^r and Eight others praying to be annexed to the Town of Leominster as part of that Townfhip fhould not Be Granted

Recorded ⱣBENJ GOODRIDGE town Cler

At a Legaul meeting of the freeholders and other Inhabitants of the town of Lunenburg Afsembled May the 21th 1750 Voted and chofe Mr John Heywood Modderator for f^d meeting.

Voted and Granted the Sum of fifty three pounds Six Shillings and eight pence to mend the town ways withall —— Voted that the wages for men be two Shillings & eight pence Ᵽ Day from May till the laft of auguft and a pair of oxen two fhillings and a cart eight pence Ᵽ Day from May till the Laft of auguft

Voted that the Selectmen Impower A a Surveyer to take a fuitable Number of hands and Cut the trees out of the way to Dorchefter Cannada

Recorded ⱣBENJ GOODRIDGE town Cler

[91] At a Legall Meeting of the freeholders and other Inhabitants of the Town of Lunenburg Afsembled November the Ninteenth A D 1750

Voted and Chofe Mr John Heywood Modderator

then Voted and Granted the Sum of Eleven pound Sixteen Shillings and Eight pence Lawfull Money to pay Mr Benjamin Bellows and Thomas Prentice Efq^r for the Land that the New Meeting Houfe Stands upon and for Conveniences about the Same

Voted and Granted the Sum of two pound fifteen Shillings to pay for the Rum ufed at the Raifing of the new meeting Houfe

Voted and Granted to Mr Jofiah Dodge the Sum of Eighteen Shillings and Eight pence for the ufe of his Rope to Raife the new Meeting Houfe withall and then voted that the Meeting be ajournd to too Morrow Morning at ten O Clock tuesday November the 20th 1750 ten o Clock the freeholders and other Inhabitants of the Town of Lunenburg Being met by a Journment

Voted and Granted to Thomas Prentice Efq^r the Sum of ten Shillings and five pence for Rum and other articles ufed at the Raifing of the New Meeting Houfe

Voted and Granted the Sum of fifty three pound Six Shillings and eight pence to ye Rev Mr David Stearns for his Sallary for the prefent year

Voted and Granted to Mr John Grout the Sum of two pound

Voted and Granted to Mr Robert Speer the Sum of Eight Shilling

Voted and Chofe Mr Benjamin Bellows Mr John Grout and Mr Philip Goodridge a committe to Reckon with the Treafurer and to Give him a Discharge for what he has payed by orders for the towns ufe

Voted that the Report of the committe for placing the School Houfes be Excepted

Recorded ℔ BENJ GOODRIDGE *town Cler*

[92] At a Legal Meeting of the freeholders and other Inhabitants of the town of Lunenbug Afsembled December the eighteenth A D 1750

Voted and Chofe Mr John Heywood Modderator for Said Meeting

Voted that thirty Eight pews be Built on the Lower floor of the new meeting Houfe

Voted that twenty one pews be Built on the Gallary floor of the new Meeting Houfe

Voted that Edward Hartwell Efq^r Mr Jofiah Dodge Benj Goodridge Mr Nathan Heywood and Mr Jonathan Wood be a committe to place the pews in the new meeting Houfe

Voted that the pew Ground in the New Meeting Houfe be fold

Voted that the pew Ground on the Lower floor be Sold to the Highesth Biders

Voted that the pew Ground in the Gallerys be fold to the Highest Bidders

The Early Records of the Town of Lunenburg. 145

Voted that Edward Hartwell Efq^r Benj : Goodridge and Mr Samvel Johnſon be acommitte to Sell the pews to the Highest Bidders

Voted that the town Reſerve one pew for the uſe of the Town or aminiſtreal pew

Voted that the Committe Sell but one pew to any one Man

Voted that the Committe take Money Down or notes on Demand of the perſons they Sell the the pews to

Voted that Major Edward Hartwell take Deeds of Mr Benjamin Bellows and of Thomas Prentice Efq^r of the Land that the New meeting Houſe Stands upon and for Conveniences about the Same In behalf of the town

Voted and Granted to M^r Joſiah Dodge ———	0 = 16 = 0
Voted and Granted to M^r Joſiah Dodge ———	1 - 4 - 0
Voted and Granted to M^r Joſiah Dodge ———	0 - 18 - 8
Voted and Granted to Benj Goodridge ———	2 - 8 - 9
Voted and Granted to Mr John Gibſon ———	0 - 7 - 10

Recorded ℔ BENJ GOODRIDGE *town Cler*

[93] At a Legaell Meeting of the freeholders and other Inhabitants of the town of Lunenburg aſsembled Janvary the Eighth 1750/51 Voted and Choſe Mr John Heywood Modderator for ſ^d meeting

Voted that they will come into anew Regulation concerning the Pews in the New Meeting Houſe notwithstanding any former vote.

Voted that two Hundred pound Lawfull money be Raiſed on the pews Ground on Lower floor and the perſons that have them to take them for their Seats any former vote to the Contrary Notwithstanding

Voted that thirteen pound Six Shillings and Eight pence Lawfull money be Raiſed on the pew Ground in the Gallarys and the perſons that have them to take them for their Seats any former Vote to the Contrary notwithstanding

Voted and Granted that one Hundred and Sixty pounds Lawfull money be Raiſed to finish the New Meeting Houſe Withall

Voted that the Highest payers on Real Eſtates Looking one year Back be perferred to have pews in the New Meeting Houſe

Voted that Edward Hartwell Eſq' Capt Jonathan Bradſtreet Capt Jonathan Willard M' John Heywood and M' Jonathan Wood be a committe to Diſpoſe of the pews and to take Securety for the money in Behalf of the Town

Voted that the Committe Give three months payment to thoſe that Do not pay money Down

Recorded P̃ BENJ GOODRIDGE *town Cler*

Whereas Wee the Subscribers on ye 8th Day of Jany A. D. 1750 by a vote of the Town of Lunenburg at a Legal Town Meeting ware appointed a Committe to Dispose of the pew: Ground, On the Lower floor in the New Meeting house in S^d Town and to take Security for the same &c and also at a Legal meeting in S^d Town on the twenty Seventh of August A D : 1751 then the S^d Town voted that the Committe affore ſ^d proſeed to Sell the Rest of the S^d pew Ground on the New meeting house on the floor of S^d house to the Next highest payers on Real Eſtate in purſuance of S^d votes wee have Sold the third pew Ground on the Left hand Going in at the front Dore adjoining to Daniel Austens : to Docter John Dunſmoor his Heirs & Aſsigns & have taken Security for the Sum of four pounds fourteen Shillings & nine pence.

Jonathan Bradſtreet ⎫
John Heywood ⎬ *Committe*
Dated Septm^r ye 30th 1751 Edward Hartwell ⎭

A True Record pr Jonathan Low
 Town Clerk
  Rec^d on Record November ye 21 : 1770

[94] LUNENBURG Janvary the 8th 1750

At a meeting of the freeholders and other Inhabitants of the Town of Lunenburg at the publick Meeting Houſe in ſaid town

Whereas it is propoſed in Consequence of the firſt Article of ſaid Meeting to Raiſe or Lay a a Certain Sum of

Money on the pews or on So much of the New Meeting houfe floors as they have voted to Build pews upon We hereby Decently Object against any Sum or Sums of Money Whatfoever Being in any ways or Manner Laid upon S^d pews or upon the S^d floors for Building S^d pews

  Benj^a Bellows
  John Gibfon
  John Grout

Alfo it is propofed in Confequence of the Second Article to vote who Shall be preffered to have the pews in the New Meeting Houfe we hereby Decently object against any other Rule or Method but only that the Highest payer towards Building the New Meeting houfe Draw the firft pew & the Next Highest payer to Draw the next pew & So on in that Method through out the whole Diftribution of pews in S^d meeting Houfe

  Mofes Mitchael
  John Grout
  Samvel Reed
  Nathaniel Page
  Eleazer Houghton

[95] At A Legal meeting of the freeholders and other Inhabitants of the Town of Lunenburg Afsembled March the 4th 1750/1

  Voted and Chofe Mr Nathan Heywood Modderator

Mr Nathan Heywood ⎫
Mr Jonathan Wood ⎪
Mr John Gibfon   ⎬ Chofen Selectmen and
Mr Amos Kimbal   ⎪   Since Sworn
Mr Jofiah Bayley   ⎭

Benj Goodridge Chofen Town Clerk
      and Since Sworn

Thomas Prentice Efq^r Chofen Town Treafurer

Mr Nathanael Page ⎱
Mr Zechariah Whitney ⎰ Chofen Conftables

Mr Jacob Gould ⎱
Mr Mofes Ritter ⎰ Chofen Tydingmen

Mr James Leitch
Mr Moſes Mitchael
Mr Jonathan Taylor
Mr Obediah Walker } were choſen Surveyors of the Highways
Mr John Buſs
Mr Joſeph Fuller
Mr Samvel Hunt
Mr Jacob Gould
Mr Joſiah Dodge
Mr Noah Dodge

Mr Samvel Comings
Mr Jeremiah Norcroſs } Choſen fence veiwers

Mr Ephraim Whitney
Mr Timothy Bancroft } Choſen to take Care of Deer

Mr Joseph Fuller
Mr Gabrial Pouchee
Mr Timothy Bancroft } Choſen Hogg reives
Mr Abraham Sanderſon

Mr Philip Goodridge
Mr Jacob Gould } Surveyors of Boards and Shingles &c

[96] Mr John Martin
Mr Nicholas Dike } Choſen Surveyors of Staves

Mr Eleazer Houghton Choſen Sealer of Leather

Mr Noah Dodge
Mr Nathanael Calton } Choſen to take care of fire
Mr David Goodridge

then Voted that the Meeting be ajorned to the Laſt Wenſday of this Inſtant March at nine of the Clock in the morning

At ameeting of the freeholders and other Inhabitants of the town of Lunenburg Held by ajorment on the Laſt wenſday of March 1751

Voted that they will come in Some other Regulation concerning the pews in the new meeting Houſe

Voted that the twelve pews in the Body of Seats be flung up to Build Seats upon the Room

Voted that the pews in the Gallary be flung up

Voted that all the pews on the walls Except the Miniſtreal pew be Dismiſt for the preſent

Voted that the article of making the Highway Rate on the old Valluation be Dismiſt

Voted that Sixty pound be Granted to mend town Ways withall

Voted that the wages for aman from the firſt of april to the Laſt of august for working at the Highways be two Shilling ⅌ Day and one Shilling for apair of oxen and Sixpence for a cart

Voted that the Sum of four pound be Granted Mr Thomas Brown and others for mending the Bridge by David Goodridges to Be Subducted out of the Highway Rate this preſent year

Voted that the Laſt article in the warrant be be Dismist

Voted that the meeting be further ajorn-d to to the third Tuesday of May next at three of ye clock in the afternoon

[97] May the twenty firſt A D 1751

the freeholders and other Inhabitants of the Town of Lunenburg Being met by ajornment the Question was put whither the Town will proceed upon the article of the way Between the Lands of Thomas Prentice Eſq^r Mr Benjamin Bellows and Mr Daniel Auſtin and it paſed in the affirmative and after a Debate Voted that the article be Dismiſt

Recorded ⅌ BENJ = GOODRIDGE
town Cler

Voted that the Town way be altered which Runs through Eleazer Houghtons from where it now gos Begining at the Land of the Heirs of David Parce and Runs upon ſaid Houghtons Land two Rod wide as it is Deſcribed by Markt trees on the weſterly ſide of ſ^d way the ſaid way being three Rods wide against Darius Houghtons Houſe and it Runs part of the way on the Land of Epharium Parce Junr as it is Deſcribed by markt trees on the weſterly ſide of ſaid way

It was alſo voted at the firſt ajornment of the above Meeting that a Bridle way be Excepted of by the town provided the perſons that own the Land Give the Land for the ſaid way which way is Deſcribed as follows Begining ſtanding in or neer the Line Between William Henerys and Capt Goulds Land and Run throug ſ^d Henerys

Land and and through afmal corner of David Parces Land in the old path and through Georges Ruffells Land in the old path to Mʳ James Leitches Land and through faid Leitches Land in or neer the old path and through the Land of the widdow Mary Ruffell then through the Land of Mʳ James Gordon and through acorner of the Land of Andrew Mitchael by the Bever Dam then on the fide of Francis Buttricks Land to the corner of Nathan Platts Land neer turkey Hill Brook then on fᵈ Buttrick by the fide faid Platts es Land then turning on fᵈ Buttricks Land on the foutherly fide of his Houfe then as the old path Gos to the Land of Nathan Platts and thro acorner of fᵈ platts Land to the Land of Mʳ Jofiah Dodge and through fᵈ Dodges Land to the Land of Capt Willard to the corner of the Buring Place and fo by the weft fide thereof into the Road

     Recorded p̃ BENJ GOODRIDGE *town Cler*

[98] At A Legal meeting of the freeholders and other Inhabitants of the Town of Lunenburg Afsembled March the 27ᵗʰ 1751

 Voted and Chofe Mʳ Nathan Heywood Modderator
 Voted and Chofe

Mʳ Jofhua Goodridge	a committe to Hire
Mʳ John Grout	a School Mafter
Mʳ William Snow	and to order where
Thomas Prentice Efqʳ	the School fhall be
Mʳ John Martin	Kept

 Voted and Granted the Sum of Twenty Six pound thirteen Shillings and four pence for the Support of the School

                £ sh d

Voted and Granted to Jofeph Goodridge 0-8-0
Voted and Granted to Philip Goodridge   0-2-0
Voted and Granted to Jonathan Bradftreet Jun 0-2-0

 Voted and Granted the Sum of two pound for the ufe of the poor

 Voted that the former Committe Continue to be acommitte to profecute the affair of finifhing the new Meeting Houfe and Lay out the Money that is Afsefsed and Raifed for that porpofe

At A Legal Meeting of the freeholders and other Inhabitants of the town of Lunenburg Afsembled May the 27th 1751

Voted and Chofe Mr John Heywood Modderator

Voted and Granted the Sum of four pounds to Build a pound withall in fd town

Voted that Edward Hartwell Efqr and Benj: Goodridge Be added to the Committe to Reckon with the Town Trefurer

Voted and Granted to Mr Nathan Heywood — 0-5-4

[99] At a Legal meeting of the freeholders and other Inhabitants of the Town of Lunenburg Afsembled Auguft the the twenty Seventh A D 1751

Voted and Chofe Mr Samvel Johnfon Modderator

Voted and Chofe Mr William Stearns Town Treafurer

Voted and Granted the Sum of fifty three pound Six Shillings and Eight pence for the Rev Mr David Stearns Sallary for the prefent year

	£ Sh d
Voted and Granted to Mr Nathan Heywood —	0-4 0
Voted & Granted to Mr Jonathan Wood ——	0-4-0
Voted & Granted to Mr Jofiah Bayley ——	0-4-0
Voted & Granted to Benj : Goodridge ——	1-7-0
Voted & Granted to Edward Hartwell Efqr —	0-2-0
Voted & Granted to Mr Philip Goodridge —	0-2-0

Voted that the Committe appointed to fell the pew Ground on the Lower floor in the New Meeting Houfe in faid Town be Directed forthwith to Call in the Money Due for the pew Ground and proceed to Sell the Reft to the Next Highest payers on Real Eftates in cafe thofe that have the first offer Refufe to Give the money afsefst on them by the Committe

Voted that the Committe aforefaid be Directed to pay Decon Johnfon for the Nails Bought of Mr Blair forthwith and that the Remainder of the money be paid to the Committe appointed to manage the affair of Building the new meeting Houfe or their order to be by them applyed to finish the faid new meeting Houfe withall exclufive of Building the pews

Voted and Excepted of alift of Jury men to be put into the Box for the Superiour Court

Voted and Excepted of alift of Jury men to be put into the Box for the Inferiour Court

Voted that the Selectmen abate the Rates of fuch perfons as fhall appear Reafonable to them –

[100] At A Legal Meeting of the freeholders and other Inhabitants of the Town of Lunenburg Afsembled March the 2nd A D 1752

Voted and Chofe Mr John Heywood Modderator

Mr John Gibfon
Mr Jofiah Bayley
Mr Amos Kimball } Chofen Selectmen
Mr William Downe
Mr William Snow

Benj Goodridge Chofen Town Clerk

Mr William Stearns Chofen Town Treafurer

Mr James Leitch }
Mr John Griffin } Chofen Conftables

Voted that Mr Philip Goodridge be Excepted Conftable in the Room of Mr John Griffin

Mr Jofiah Dodge
Mr Daniel Auftin
Mr Caleb Taylor
Mr Thomas Carter
Mr Thomas Dutton
Mr Ebenezer Going
Mr Mofes Mitchael
Mr Amos Hazeltine
Mr John Heywood
Mr William Gilchreft
Mr Samvel Reed
Mr Abraham Ireland
Mr Hezekiah Wetherbe
were Chofen

Surveyers of Highways

Mr Francis Buttrick }
Mr Samvel Davis } Chofen Tydingmen

Mr Nathanael Page }
Mr Jeremiah Norcrofs } Chofen fence veiwers

Mr Thomas Carter Chofen Sealer of Leather

Mr Samvel Davis Culer of Shingles & Clabords

Mr John Martin Culler of Staves

[101] Mr John Fitch
Mr Thomas Brown } Chofen Hogg reives
Mr Joseph Fuller
Mr Ephraim Whitney

Mr Isaac Gibson
Mr Samvel Hunt } Chofen to take care
Mr Thomas Dutton of Deer

Mr Jofeph Fuller
Mr Ephraim Kimball
Mr Abraham Sanderfon } to take care of fire
Mr Mofes Mitchall
Mr Reuben Gibson

	£-s-d
Voted and Granted to Mr Zechariah Whitney the sum of ——	0-4-0
Voted & Granted to Mr Nathaneal Page	0-1-0
Voted & Granted to Mr Nathan Heywood	0-8-0
Voted & Granted to Mr John Gibson ——	1-5-0
Voted & Granted to Mr Jofiah Bayley	0-4-0
Voted & Granted to Mr Amos Kimball	0-3-6
Voted & Granted to Mr Jonathan Wood	0-4-6
Voted & Granted to Mr Samvel Poole	0-2-8
Voted & Granted to Mr James Poole	0-2-8

Voted that the Third Article in the warrant be Dismift

Voted that any Person Being an Inhabitant that Shall Kill any Woffe within the Bounds of the Town Shall have twenty Shilling Reward out of the Town Treafury

[102] Voted and Excepted of A town way Laid out by order of the Selectmen Begining at Groton Road by Jacob Goulds Houfe on the Wefterly end of Thirfton Original Lot and Runing by Isaac Fofters Houfe till it comes to Land fd Fofter Bought of william Moffatt Alfo another Peice of way Begining at the Northweft Corner of the Widow Randals Land at Groton Road and Runing on Benjamin Bellows Land by the widow Randals Land on the Wefterly fide of the fd widow Randalls Land till it comes to Daniel Austins Land two Rod wide Being ten Rod and one Quarter on one fide and feven Rod and one Quarter on the other fide the above peice of way is excepted provided the Land be Given

the above ways were Laid out by
     Daniel Austin }
     Jacob Gould Committe

Alfo an other town way Begining at the South Weft corner of the Land of Nathanael Harris Efq^r and Running about forty Rods on f^d Harris es Land and then turning unto Jofiah Bayleys Land and Runing Strait to the South weft Corner of Nathanael Carltons Land faid way to be two Rod wide and is Excepted away provided the Land be Given and was Laid o By the Selectmen

Voted that the meeting be ajorned to the fecond Monday of May Next at two of the Clock in the afternoon

Monday May the Eleventh 1752 the Town of Lunenburg Mett By Ajornment

[103] Voted that they will mend the Bridges on the way to Narragansett N° two

Voted and Granted the Sum of fifteen pound to mend the Bridges and way to Narragansett N° two withall

Voted that the Money be workt out at two fhilling and Eight pence ₱ Day for aman

Voted that the wages for a pair of oxen be two fhillings and Eight pence ₱ Day and Eight pence for acart

Voted that Lt Jofiah Dodge over fee the work

Voted that Lt Dodge Notifie the feveral Surveyors to Bring their proportion of men

Voted that the meeting Be further Ajornd to Monday the twenty fifth Day of this Inftant May at four a clock in the afternoon

May the the 25th 1752 the freeholders and other Inhabitants of the Town of Lunenburg Met by a further Ajornment and the Meeting was Difmift

Recorded ₱ BENJ GOODRIDGE *town Cler*

At a Legal meeting of the freeholders and other Inhabitants of the Town of Lunenburg Afsembled May the 25th 1752

Voted and Chofe Mr Jofiah Bayley Modderator—

Voted that they will Choofe acommitte to Seat the New Meeting Houfe

Voted that they will Choofe five men for acommitte to Seat the New Meeting Houfe

Voted and Chofe
Mr Nathan Heywood
Mr William Snow
Mr Amos Kimbal
Mr Jofiah Bayley
Mr James Leitch
} a committe to Seat the New Meeting Houfe

[104] Voted that the New Meeting Houfe Be Seated upon the Real Eftates that paid toward the Building of fd Houfe

Voted that after the perfons are Seated that Have Real Eftates thofe perfons that have no Real Eftates shall be Seated upon their perfonal Eftates according to their pay and that all polls that have been paid for towards Building the new Meeting Houfe fhall have afeat

Voted that they will meet in the New Meeting Houfe Next Sabbath Day come fortnight to attend the publick worfhip there

Voted and Chofe
Mr William Snow
Mr Jacob Gould
Mr Afahel Hartwell
} A Committe to provide the town with a School Mafter

Voted and Granted the Sum of thirty five pound for the ufe of the School

Voted that the Selectmen Abate Such Rates as they think proper

Voted and Granted the fum of fifty pound to Mend the Highways withall and that the wages be

for a man be ———	0 = 2 - 8
for a yoke of oxen ———	0 - 1 - 4
and for a cart ———	0 - 0 - 8

and that the money be workt out by the Laft of September Next

Voted that Hoggs Run at Large the prefent year

Recorded ℔ BENJ GOODRIDGE Town Cler

[105] At a legal Meeting of the freeholders and other Inhabitants of the Town of Lunenburg Afsembled Auguft ye 10th 1752

Voted and Chofe Benjamin Goodridge Modderator

Voted and Granted the Sum of fifty five pound for the Rev Mʳ David Stearns Sallary for the prefent year

Voted and Granted the Sum of two pound to Buy Weights & Meafures withall

Voted and Granted the Sum of fifteen pound to Mend the way withall from Mʳ Hunts to the weft Line of the Town the wages yᵉ fame as on Narraganset Road

Voted & Granted to Mʳ William Snow ——   0-1-4
Voted & Granted to Mʳ Afahel Hartwell ——   0-1-4

Voted that they will Build Long pews Behind the Seats in the Gallarys in the New Meeting Houfe

Voted that they will Keep the old Meeting Houfe for town meetings &c and yᵗ Lt Jofiah Dodge take care of the old Meeting Houfe and Stop up the Windows &c

Recorded ℗ Benj Goodridge *town Cler*

[**106**] At a Legal meeting of the Freeholders and other Inhabitants of the Town of Lunenburg Afsembled March 5ᵗʰ: A: D: 1753

Voted and chose Mʳ John Heywood Moderator

Mefsʳˢ John Gibson
Willᵐ Downe
John Grout
Jonathan Wood
Samuel Reed

Chosen Selectmen and sworn ———— Afsefsors.

William Downe chosen Town Clerk and sworn
Deacon William Stearns chosen Town Treafurer

Mefsʳˢ Ephraim Peirce
John Bufs

chosen Constables

Voted that Mʳ Philip Goodridge be accepted Constable in the room of Mʳ John Bufs.

Voted that Mʳ Jonathan Page be accepted Constable in the Room of Mʳ Ephraim Pierce

Mefsʳˢ Josiah Dodge
Samuel Cummings
William Stearns
Moses Ritter
Willᵐ Jones
Moses Mitchell
Abraham Saunderfon
Ephraim Kimball
Isaac Gibson

Surveyors of Highways

The Early Records of the Town of Lunenburg.

Mess.rs John Martin
    Arrington Gibson
    Patrick White
    Jonathan Hartwell } Tything Men

Mess.rs David Goodridge
    Timothy Parker
    Joseph Wood
    Reuben Gibson } Hog reeves

Mess.rs Ezekiel Wyman
    Abijah Stearns } Fence Veiwers

[107] Mess.rs Reuben Gibson
    Samuel Hunt } Chosen Deer Reeves

M.r Thomas Carter chosen Sealer of Leather

Mess.rs Jacob Gould
    Philip Goodridge } chosen Surveyors of Boards Shingles Clabboards and Staves.

Mess.rs Amos Kimball
    Samuel Pool } chosen to take care of Fire

A Certificate signed by the Selectmen of the Town of Lunenburg informing s.d Town, that y.y had attended at Deacon W.m Stearns Town Treasur.r & examined his acco.ts find, that the Sum of $462\text{-}19\text{-}4\text{-}2^{qrs}$ had been ordered into his hands out of Sum he had rec.d from y.e Severall Con.stables $290\text{-}1\text{-}3\text{-}0$ and by orders from the Selectmen & Meeting house Com.te he had paid the Sum of $289\text{-}17\text{-}9\text{-}$ and that there still remains y.e following Sums in the hands of the Severall Con.stables Viz.t Due from Ezekiel Wyman $28\text{-}4\text{-}3\text{-}3^{qr}$ From W.m Snow £6-5- from Jon.a Willard jun.r $15\text{-}15\text{-}7\text{-}3\text{-}$ From Zech.h Whitney $15\text{-}10\text{-}5\text{-}2$ from Nath.a Page 5-17-11-3 and also from said Page 17^{sh} and $\frac{d}{4}$ from James Leitch £53-7-8-1 from Philip Goodridge 46-19-8-1 the amount in Const.as Hands 172-18-1-3

After reading The above certificate Voted y.e acceptance of it

A way two Rod wide from the House of M.r Reuben Dodge where M.r John Fitch formerly lived, down by the House of M.r W.m Jones in order to accomodate the said Dodge & others w.th a convenient Road to come into the Town and w.ch was laid out at the Desire of the Selectmen — — Not accepted

The above Road is laid out from S^d Houfe of Mr Dodge and is markt on the South Side of the Way and runs in and near the Old Troden path as Attested by

The above Road not accepted by Reafon y^t Mr Benoni Wallis objected ag^nst its going as proposed through his Land

Willm Jones
Reuben Dodge
John Fitch

The Committee to lay out S^d Road

[108] A Road laid out two Rod wide and 107 Pole in length beginning at Narragansett Road by James Pooles Land and running thro S^d Pools Land to Thos. Stearns Land, then turning and running between f^d Stearns & Pooles Land two Rod wide about Thirty Rod to ye Town Line —

Voted not to be accepted.

—— By order — one other Road laid out beginning at the Foot of the hill below Saml Pooles Land and running near a Brook (called Monusnut Brook) about fourscore Rod, then crofsing the Brook and running about Thirty Rod to the Town Line through land of Esqr Harris —

Voted that the S^d Road be accepted provided the land be given and that the old Road running thrô S^d Harris Land be difcontinued

— The above Roads being laid out by

Amos Kimball
Saml Pool
James Pool

Com^tte

Voted that there be a Bridle Road as laid out through part of Mr Samuel Hunts Land to Wm Hendersons land, Beginning at a Stake by the Road about ten Rod North east of Mr Hunts Houfe & then runs North west about Twenty Rod to a Stake and Stones by the fence, then runs as the Fence now ftands to ye said Hendersons Land and so along in a lane fenced out through said Hendersons Land between his houfe & Barn

Laid out by order of ye Selectmen p^r

Willm Snow
Amos Kimball

Com^tee

Voted that the above road be accepted — and the abovenamed Sam!. Hunt & W͟m Henderſon have consented thereunto & given the land abovementioned — as given under their hands —

Voted and accepted of a Road lay'd out by order of the Selectmen : Beginning at the End of the Road that runs up to the Land of the Heirs of David Peirce & running on a ſtrait Line with the Old Road at the North : East End of the Houſe till it strikes the Stone Wall and then bounds on the Wall on the South Easterly side of the Road and so runs to a Chestnut Tree into the Old Road, the Road being two Rod wide   accepted if y͟e land be given

     Eleazer Houghton ⎫
     Josiah Dodge ⎬ being y͟e
     John Gibson ⎭ Comm͟tte

Voted that the Article in the Warrant respecting the Road laid out by the Selectmen between Leiu͟t Bellows Land & Land of Thomas Prentice Esq͟r at y͟e Request of Jacob Gould & others —— be dismiſed

[109] Voted and accepted of a Road laid out by the Selectmen mark'd as follows. Beginning at a Stake at Groton line running on M͟r Goings Land to a white Oak Stump mark'd near his houſe then to a Rock in the Fence, then to white oak Tree these marks on the North side of said Way, then to a White Oak Tree mark't on the South side of s͟d Way on Robert Moffatts Land, then to a White Oak Tree mark'd, then to a Rock, then to a Stake and Stones between Going & Moses Gould, S͟d Way to be four Rod wide —— ——

Then the said meeting was adjourned to the Third monday of May next at one of the Clock afternoon

    Recorded p͟r WILLIAM DOWNE *Town Clerk*

May 21͟th Anno Domini. 1753 The Freeholders and other Inhabitants of the Town of Lunenburg being mett by Adjournment

Voted and Granted to Tho͟s Prentice Esq͟r   0- 2-11-$\frac{15}{12}$
Voted and Granted to M͟r James Leitch — 0- 3- 0 —

Voted and Granted to Mr Ezekiel Wyman —   0- 1- 0
Voted and Granted to Mr Ezekiel Wyman —   0-16- 0- 0
Voted and Granted to Deacon Wm Stearns }
    for his Service Two Years as Treaſurer   2- 0- 0- 0

Voted that there be a Com^{tte} chose to treat wth & examine the acco^{ts} of Capt Benj^a Goodridge, Deacon Saml Johnſon & Leiu^t Josiah Dodge the Meeting Houſe Committee

Voted that Major Hartwell Leiu^t Nathan Heywood — Willm Downe, John Grout, Jonathan Wood, be a Com^{ttee} for the purpose afore s^d

Voted that Jeremiah Norcroſs be one of the s^d Committee in the Room of Leiu^t Heywood who refuses ——

Voted that the Comm^{tte} be impowered to inquire of Capt Benj^a Goodridge, Deacon Saml Johnson Leiu^t Josiah Dodge the Meeting Houſe Com^{te} what Sums of Money they have received out of the Severall Sums granted and ordered for building and finishing the New Meeting Houſe and how they have disposed of the Same

                                         —— verte.

[**110**] Voted that the s^d Committee make return to the Town Clerk of their Proceedings by the middle of June next.

Voted that the Sum of Sixty pounds be raised and that the Inhabitants of the Town of Lunenburg be aſſeſſed the s^d Sum to be workt out at the Highways, the Method as to raising the Money and the price of Labour to be the same as the last year — — — —

The Ninth Article in the Warrant being read, respecting the releiving & providing for Mr Sam^{ll} Stow —— and Mr Stow being present and representing his Case & Circumſtances before the Town —— Voted — That the Selectmen deal with Mr Stow in the steps of the Law —

Voted & granted the Sum of Four pounds for the uſe of the Poor in s^d Town

                Recorded p^r WILLIAM DOWNE *Town Clerk*

At a Legall meeting of the Freeholders and other Inhabitants of the Town of Lunenburg Aſſembled July the 9th A. D. 1753

Voted and chose Mr John Gibson Moderator

The Report of a Comm^tee chosen to treat with and examine the acco^ts of Capt Benj.^a Goodridge, Deacon Sam^ll. Johnſon & Leiu.^t Josiah Dodge the Meeting Houſe Com^tte was Read ——

It being put to vote whether the Town will choose a Comm^tee to settle ye acco^ts of ye Pew Committee ——— paſsed in the Negative

The Third Article in the Warrant being put to Vote to See whether the Town will chooſe Agents & instruct and impower them to bring an action in Common Law ag^nst Capt Goodridge & others ye Meeting Houſe Committee

————————paſsed in the Negative

Voted and granted the Sum of Sixty Pounds lawfull money to the Revd Mr David Stearns for his Salary this preſent year ——

[111] Voted and chose Meſs^rs. Joshua Goodridge, Moses Mitchell Ephraim Whitney & Deacon W^m. Stearns to be a Com^tee to provide a School master ——

Voted and granted the Sum of Fifty Three pounds six shill^s. and eight pence Lawfull Money for the use of Schooling in said Town

Voted that the School be kept in the Quarters of the Town as it has already been till further orders ——

Voted that Notifications for Town Meetings for the future be posted up within Three foot of the South East Corner of Major Hartwells Horſe Stable

Recorded ℗ : Wm Downe *Town Clerk*

Att a Legall Meeting of the Freeholders and other Inhabitants of the Town of Lunenburg Aſsembled October 22.^d 1753.

Voted and chose Mr Jonathan Wood Moderator

Voted that the Grammar School in S.^d Town be kept in the four Quarters of the Town as formerly and that the Remainder of Money already voted for the uſe of Schooling be improved by the School Com^tee in said uſe in such parts of the Town as S.^d Committee ſhall judge most beneficial ——

The 2ᵈ Article in Warrant respecting granting Money to mend yᵉ Road beyond Mʳ Samˡˡ Hunts to the West Line of Sᵈ Town, being put to Vote — — — not Voted —

Voted that Mʳ Amos Kimball be joyned to the Comᵗᵉᵉ for hiring a School master

The 4ᵗʰ Article in yᵉ Warrant being put to Vote. to see Whether yᵉ School Houfes Shall be built in the places already appointed for that purpofe ——— No Vote.

and then the sᵈ meeting was dismifsed ——

Recorded pʳ Wᴹ Downe *Town Clerk*

[112] At a Legall meeting of the Freeholders and other Inhabitants of the Town of Lunenburg afsembled March 4ᵗʰ 1754

Voted and chose Deacon William Stearns Moderator

Capᵗ Benjamin Goodridge
Deacon John Heywood
Mefsʳˢ Solomon Steward } Select men Sworn Afsefsors
Moses Ritter
John Bufs

William Downe   Town Clerk Sworn

Deacon Thoˢ Reddington   Town Treafurer

Mefsʳˢ David Chaplin
John Hill } Constables

Upon a Motion made and seconded Voted that Mʳ John Hill be excused serving as Constable and Mʳ Arrington Gibson was chose in his Room & Sworn

Capᵗ John Gibson
Mefsʳˢ William Jones
Moses Ritter
Charles White
Samuel Pool
Joseph Spafford } chosen Surveyors of Highways
Thoˢ Carter
Moses Mitchell
David Wood
Abijah Hovey
Samuel Larrabee

Mefsʳˢ Benjamin Garey junʳ
Eleazer Houghton
Josiah Dodge junʳ } chosen Tything Men
Patrick White
Samuel Hammond

Mess.rs Zebulon Dodge } chosen Hogreves
Timothy Bancroft

Mess.rs Samuel Hunt } chosen Deer. Reeves
Isaac Gibson

Mess.rs Timothy Parker } chosen Fence Veiwers
Samuel Hunt

[113] M.r Thomas Carter chosen Sealer of Leather

Leiu.t Jacob Gould } chosen Surveyors of
M.r Josiah Dodge jun.r Boards shingles and Clabboards

Mess.rs Jon.a Wood jun.r } chosen Cullers of Staves
Paul Crocker

Mess.rs Ephraim Kimball } chosen to take of Fire
Reuben Gibson

Voted and Granted M.r Philip Goodridge one Shilling for his warning Mathew Davis out of Town —

Voted and Granted M.r Joshua Goodridge four shill.s for his going to procure a School Master

Voted and granted M.r Moses Mitchell Two shill.s for the use of his Horse in the s.d Service —

Voted and accepted of M.r Patrick White to be a Constable in the Room of M.r David Chaplin and he was Sworn to y.e faith full Discharge of his office.

Voted to choose a Committee to reckon with the Town Treasurer

William Downe }
Mess.rs Amos Kimball } Committee chosen for
John Grout } the Said Purpose —

The 4.th 6.th 8.th 9.th 10.th 11.th Articles in the Warrant being Read, and the Town Voted not to act upon any of the said Articles.

Voted that Swine run at large this Year —and then said meeting was dismissed —

Recorded p.r WILLIAM DOWNE *Town Clerk*

[114] At a Legall Meeting of the Freeholders and other Inhabitants of the Town of Lunenburg Assembled April 16.th A: D. 1754 —

Voted and chose M.r John Heywood Moderator

Mess.rs Josiah Bayley } a committee to
William Stearns } examine the acco.ts
Chose   Asahel Hartwell } of the Committee
appointed to manage the affairs

of building the New Meeting Houfe
and make Report to the Town at their
next Town meeting.

Voted that the Sum of Thirty pounds be granted and work't out between Mr Hunts and the West line of the Town ——

Voted that Ten pounds be raised and workt out from the South Side of the River to Narragansett Line — —

Voted and Granted the Sum of Sixty pounds to mend the Town Ways withal —— —— ——

Voted that the Wages from Mr Hunts to the West Line of the Town be 2-8 p^r Day and the same from the River to Narragansett Line and 0-1-6 p^r Day for a yoke of oxen and 0-0-8 for a Cart —— and 0-2-0 p^r Day for a man & 0-1-4 for a yoke of oxen & 0-0-8 for a Cart in Town —— and 0-1-4 p^r Day for a Plow, the whole of the Money to be workt out by the last of September next :. —

The above Attested by John Heywood Moderator and Recorded p^r WILLIAM DOWNE *Town Clerk*

At a Legall meeting of the Freeholders & other Inhabitants of the Town of Lunenburg Afsembled May 20th A: D. 1754 —

Voted and chose Deacon Benj^a Foster Moderator

Voted and chose Mr Abijah Stearns Town Treafurer in the Room of Mr Thos Reddington who was chosen in March last and has refused to act in that Capacity ——

Report of the Committee appointed to reckon with Deacon William Stearns late Town Treafurer being read, Voted that the same be accepted.

as sett forth in S^d Report

Dated May 3^d 1754 — reference to ye same being had may appear

Report of the Committee chosen to reckon with the Com^{tee} formerly appointed to manage the Affairs of building the New Meeting Houfe, being Read & put to Vote whether the Said Report be accepted, and y^t ye s^d Com^{tee} be discharged ye Sum of 521-19-5-1 & that ye said Committee be allowed the Sum of 1-19-5-1 as by s^d Report appears to be Due to said Committee to Ballance

———— NO Vote ⁓

[115] The 4th Article in the Warrant being Read —
Voted that Capt Willard, Mr Auftin & Mr Natha Page be appointed to rectify the Fence round the burying Yard and clear up the Brush in sd burying place and bring in their accounts at the next Town Meeting —

Voted that Mr Bufs, Mr George Kimball & Mr Ireland be appointed to look out a place for a burying Yard and agree about the Price & report at ye next Town Meeting and then the said meeting was dismifsed —

Recorded pr WILLIAM DOWNE *Town Clerk*—

At a Legall meeting of the Freeholders & other Inhabitants of the Town of Lunenburg Afsembled Sepr 10th 1754

Voted and chose Willm Downe Esqr Moderator

Voted and granted the Sum of Sixty pounds Lawfull Money for the Revd Mr David Stearns's Salary for this present year —

Voted and granted the Sum of Thirty pounds for the School.

Voted and chose Mefsrs Ezekiel Wyman & David Wood, Capt John Gibson, Leiut Jacob Gould & Mr Benja Garey junr a Comt to provide a School Mafter or Mafters or Miftrefses

Voted and granted the Sum of Eight pounds to repair the Bridge by Mr Paul Wetherbee's —

Voted and granted the Sum of Six pounds to repair the Bridge between ye Great Bridge and Mr Amos Kimballs and also voted that the said Sums for repairing the said Bridges be work't out as usuall and the Work to be done by the middle of October next — — — —

Voted and granted the Sum of Four pounds for ye ufe of ye Poor.

Voted and granted to Leiut Josiah Dodge the Sum of one pound nineteen fhills and five pence one farthing being Due to him, for what he has done to ye New Meeting Houfe —

The 8th Article in the Warrant being put, pafsed in the Negative — — —

Verte

[116] Voted That Mr John Heywood the Representative of the Town petition the Great & Generall Court in the behalf of the Town, that the unimproved Lands belonging to Perſons out of Town and who are now refidents may be taxed to mend the High ways from Mr Saml Hunts to Dorchester Canady and from David Goodridges to Narragansett N{o} 2 at one half penny per Acre or such other Sum as yr shall think proper for the Term of Five Years — — —

Voted and granted the Sum of one pound Six shill{s} & 8 pence to Deacon Willm Stearns for his Services as Treaſurer of the Town for the year 1753 — — — —

Voted and granted the Sum of one pound Six shill{s} & 8d to Mr Ezekiel Wyman for his taking care of the New Meeting Houſe one year & one Quarter ——

Voted and granted the Sum of one pound Six ſhill{s} & 8d to ye Aſseſsors for ye Year 1752 for yr Service in sd Year

Voted and granted the Sum of one pound six ſhill{s} & 8d to the Aſseſsors for ye Year 1753 for their Service in sd Year

The 11th Article in ye Warrant respecting the providing a Suitable place in the Westerly part of the Town for a burying place, with the report of a Committee thereon being read —— referred for further Consideration at the next Town Meeting — — — —

The 12th Article, vizt to hear an Extract of the excife Bill prepared by the Generall Court & now lying for the Governours Consent and to hear the Govern{rs} Speech thereon & to shew their minds whether they would have said Bill paſs into a Law —— being read & putt to Vote —— paſsed in the Negative —— and then said Meeting was Diſmiſsed ——

Recorded pr Wm Downe *Town Clerk*

[117] Worcest{r} ſc: Anno Regni Regis Georgij secundi magno Brittanice Francice & Hibernice viceſsimo Octavo

Att a Court of Genll Seſsions of Pease begun and held at Worcester within and for the County of Worcester the first Tuesday of November being the fifth Day of said Month A. D. 1754 — — —

Mefs.rs Jonathan White and Thomas Wilder both of Leominster in said County a Committee appointed in august last on the Petition of John Scott of Lunenburg in the County of Worcester Husbandman to lay out a Way or private Road agreable to the Report of the Committee of Lunenburg for laying out the Same as p.r s.d Committees Report to the Town of Lunenburg at their annual meeting in March last appears which way described as follows, beginning at the land of the S.d John Scott, and running North Eaft on John Bridges land described by mark'd Trees, then on land of M.r Mead then on land of Joseph Eaton, then on land of Joseph Spafford to the Road that comes from Isaac Gibsons said Road described by mark'd Trees, and the Road to be on the South Side of s.d mark'd Trees & to be two Rods wide

Reported that having veiwed the s.d Road have laid out the same to y.e great Satisfaction of M.r John Scott, and the owners of the land the Road goes through, who freely gave their Land for the Road and the Road to be on the South side of the mark'd Trees ——

Which Report was read and accepted by the Court & order that the Said Road for y.e future be deemed a private Road, Provided the said John Scott pay all the Charge relating to the affair, and upon his so doing order the same to be recorded ——

    Copy examined p.r TIMO.y PAINE *Clerk*

A True Copy of a Copy
    Attest   W.M DOWNE *Town Clerk*

[118] At A Legal Meeting of the freeholders & other Inhabitants of the Town of Lunenburg Afsembled March y.e 3.d A D 1755

 Voted and Chofe M.r John Heywood Moderator

Benj: Goodridge
Cap.t Joshua Hutchins   Selectmen and
M.r Jonathan Wood   Sworn Afsefsors
M.r Afahel Hartwell
M.r Samvel Davis

Benj: Goodridge Town Clerk and Sworn
M.r Abijah Stearns Town Treafurer & Sworn

Mr Mofes Mitchel \
Mr Abraham Sanderfon ∫ were chofen Conftables
                  & Sworn

Mr Joseph Fuller \
Mr Ezekiel Wyman
Mr Obediah Walker
Mr Daniel Auftin
Mr Amos Kimbal   were Chofen Surveyors
Mr David Taylor   of the Highways
Mr Joseph Chaplin   & Sworn
Mr Thomas Brown
Mr Benj Stearns
Mr Jonathan Hartwell
Mr Samvel Poole

Mr David Wood \
Mr John Griffin ∫ were chofen fences viewers
             & fworn

Mr Thomas Carter Chofen Sealer of Leather

Mr David Wood \
Mr Samvel Commings } were Chofen Tyding men
Mr Ephraim Whitney ∫

Mr James Poole \
Mr Ephraim Whitney ∫ were Chofen Dear Reives

Mr Samvel Johnfon jun \
Mr Richard Fowler
Mr Reuben Dodge   were Chofen Hogge Reives
Mr Jonathan Wood   and Sworn
Mr Benoni Wallis

[119]   Mr Thomas Leitch \ were chofen Surveyors of
       Mr Samvel Davis ∫ Staves and Shingles &c and
                          Sworn

Mr Ifaac Gibfon \
Mr Amos Kimbal
Mr John Darlin   were chofen to take Care of fire
Mr James Poole
Mr John Fitch

Voted that Mr John Bufs Mr Abraham Ireland and Mr George Kimbal be acommitte to agree with Mr John Wyman for a peice of Land for a Buriing place and to take a Deed for the Town

Voted & Granted the Sum of thirty pound for the ufe of the School

Voted and Granted the Sum of Six pound for the ufe of the poor

Voted and Granted the Sum of Sixty pound to mend the High ways withall to be workt out as it was the Laſt year

Voted that the Town Except of atown way two Rods wide Begining at the weſterly Side of John Fitchs Land and Runing in and Near the path as it is now Trood to Iſaac Gibſons and is Described by markt trees on the Northerly Side of ſaid way and was Laid out by

John Buſs
Iſaac Gibſon
John Fitch

A Committee appointed By the Selectmen

Voted and Excepted of a Town way two Rods wide Begining at the way neer the Bottom of the Hill Weſt of James Pooles and Runs from thence to the Bridge over Wenoosnoock Brook and from the Brook by trees markt on the South weſterly ſide of S^d way Through Land of James Pooles to the Line Between S^d Pooles and Thomas Stearns Lands then on Said Stearns Land to the Town Line then Runs Southerly one Rod on S^d Stearns Land and one Rod on william Perkins Land about Seventy five Rod alſo a two Rod way from ſ^d Stearns Houſe to the way where it firſt came to his Land ſaid way was Laid out

By the Selectmen. turn over—

[120] Voted that part of the town way be Discontinued Between the Bridge by Paul Wetherbees and the Land of Edward Hartwell Eſq^r (viz) Begining at a pine tree neer ſ^d Wetherbes fence till it comes to ſaid Hartwells Land and that they Except of away in the Room thereof viz Begining at the aboveſaid pine tree and Runs acroſs ſaid Wetherbes Land till it comes into the way again By Samvel Commings Land and is Deſcribed by markt trees on the northerly ſide of ſaid way and was Laid out two rods wide by the Selectmen and ſaid wetherbe is to Clear ſaid way and make it fit to Travil in

Then voted that this meeting be Ajourned to the ſecond tuesday of May next at two of the Clock in the afternoon

LUNENBURG May the 13th 1755 the Freeholders and other Inhabitants of ſaid Town Being Met again by ajornment

Voted and Excepted of a Town way Laid out by acommite appointed by the Selectmen Between the Lands of Capt Joſhua Hutchins and Benjamin Bellows Eſqr Begining at ye corner of ſaid Hutchins Houſe Lot and ſaid Bellowſes near the new meeting Houſe two Rods wide upon ſaid Bellowſes Land and Runs North eaſterly upon ſaid Bellowſes Land 144 Rods upon a Strait Line to Where ſaid Hutchins Corners upon ſaid Bellows from thence ſet off two Rods wide upon ſaid Hutchins Land & Runs a ſtrait Line 144 Rods to the firſt mentioned Bounds near the new meeting Houſe and from the ſaid Hutchins North Eaſterly Corner two Rods wide upon Mr Daniel Auſtins Land 28 Rods in Length NorthEaſterly then upon ſaid Bellowes' Land two Rods wide by the widow Randalls Eleven Rods in Length till it Comes into the way that Leads to Shirley and Groton the Aboveſaid way was Laid out by

    Capt Joſhua Hutchins ⎫ *A Comttc*
    Mr Daniel Auſtin   ⎬ *appointed*
    Mr Jacob Gould   ⎩ *by the*
              Selectmen

Voted and Excepted of a Town way Begining at Thomas Potters Land one Rod wide on Mr Secretary willards Land and one Rod wide on Caleb Taylors Land and on Land of ſd Taylors Brothers then one Rod wide on David Taylors Land and one Rod wide on Arrinton Gibsons Land then one Rod [121] Wide on Joſiah Bayleys Land and one Rod on Land that Mr Jones Reserved out of Benoni Walliſes Deed then twenty feet wide on ſaid Bayleys Land and Twelve feet wide on Benoni Wallis-es Land till it comes to the Brook then Tapering a Little till at the End of ten Rods it Comes to one Rod on ſaid Bayleys And one Rod on ſaid Wallis es Lands ſo continuing till it comes to ſaid Bayleys Corner then continuing one Rod on ſaid Wallis es Land and one Rod on Land of Nathanael Harris Eſqr till it comes into the way that Gos

The Early Records of the Town of Lunenburg.

by Mr Jones Houſe ſaid way was Laid out and Deſcribed by

Mr Solomon Steward
Mr John Buſs   *Selectmen*

Recorded ⅌ Benj.. Goodridge *town Cler*

At A Legal Meeting of the Freeholders & other Inhabitants of the Town of Lunenburg Aſsembled May the 20th A D 1755

Voted and Choſe Mr John Heywood Modderator

Voted and Choſe Mr George Kimball Mr William Stearns and Mr Joſiah Bayley a committe to provide a Houſe to Set Idle perſons to work in

Voted and Granted the Sum of thirty pound to mend the ways from David Goodridge es to narraganſetts Line and from Samvel Hunts to Narraganſetts Line and from Reuben Gibſons to John Fitches the wages to be Same as Laſt year

Recorded ⅌ Benj. Goodridge *town Cler*

[122] At A Legal meeting of the freeholders and other Inhabitants of the Town of Lunenburg Aſsembled September the ninth 1755

voted and Choſe Capt Joſhua Hutchins Moddr

Voted and Granted the Sum of Sixty pound to the Rev Mr David Stearns for his Sallary for the preſent year

	£ s d
Voted and Granted to Capt John Gibſon ye Sum of	0- 4-4
Voted and Granted to Aſael Hartwell	0- 1-0
Voted & Granted to Edward Hartwell jun	0- 1-0
Voted & Granted to Abijah Stearns the Sum of	0-12-0
Voted & Granted to Abraham Carlton	0- 1-0
Voted & Granted to ye Aſseſsor for the year 1754	1- 6-8

Voted and Choſe

Mr Abraham Sanderſon
Mr Edward Hartwell jun
Mr Reuben Gibſon
Mr Obediah Walker
Mr Jacob Gould

a Committe to provide the Town with School Marſters and mistreſses &c for ye year Inſuing

Voted and Granted the Sum of ten pound for the uſe of the School

Voted that the Selectmen be a committe to Reckon with with the Town Treafurer and to Give him a Difcharge for Such Sums as he has paid

Voted that the abatments of the Rates mentioned in the Sixth article be Refered to the Selectmen

Recorded ℔ BENJ GOODRIDGE Town Cler

[123] At A Legal Meeting of the Freeholders and other Inhabitants of the Town of Lunenburg Afsembled March the firft A D 1756

Voted and Chofe Capt Jofhua Hutchins Modderator

Voted and Chofe

Benj. Goodridge
Capt Jofhua Hutchins   Chofen Selectmen
Mr Jonathan Wood   and
Mr Amos Kimball   Sworn as Afsefsors as the
Mr Afhael Hartwell   Law Directs

Benj. Goodridge Chofen Town Clerk & Sworn as the Directs

Capt Jofhua Hutchins Chofen Town Treafurer & Sworn as the Law Directs.

Mr George Kimball   Chofen Conftables & Sworn
Mr Abijah Stearns   as the Law Directs

Mr Philip Goodridge
Mr David Wood
Mr John White
Mr Joseph Fuller   Chofen Surveyors of
Mr Nathanael Page
Mr Jonathan Parce   Highways
Mr Isaac Gibson   and
Mr Caleb Taylor   Sworn as the Law
Mr James Poole   Directs
Mr Timothy Parker

Mr Thomas Dutton   Chosen fence veiwers
Mr John Hereman   and Sworn as the Law Directs

Mr Ezekiel Goodridge   Chofen Tydingmen
Mr Ephraim Whitney   and Sworn as the
Mr Benj Gary Jun   Law Directs

Mr Jofeph Page
Mr Samvel Hammond   Chofen Hogg reives
Mr David Wood   and Sworn as the
Mr Thomas Brown   Law Directs

Turn over

[124] Mr Isaac Gibson ⎱ chosen to take Care of Deer
Mr James Poole ⎰ and Sworn as the Law Directs

Mr Josiah Dodge Jun ⎱
Mr Reuben Gibson   ⎰ Chosen to take care of fire and Burn the woods and Sworn
Mr David Goodridge   ⎰ as the Law Directs

Mr Moses Ritter   Chosen Sealer of Leather and Sworn as the Law Directs

Mr Jacob Gould   ⎱ chosen Surveyors of Staves and
Mr Philip Goodridge ⎰ shingles and to Measure Boards &c and Sworn as the Law Direct

Voted and Granted the Sum of Seventy pound to mend the High ways in the Town and that the Same be workt out at two Shillings p^r Day for aman and one shilling and four pence for a pair of oxen and eight pence for a cart Between the first of April and the Last of September

Voted and Granted the Sum of forty pound to Mend the ways from Capt Hunts to Narragansett Line and from David Goodridges to Narragansett Line and from Reuben Gibsons to Dorchester Cannady to be workt at two Shillings and Eight pence pr Day for aman and one Shilling and four pence for a pair of oxen and Eight pence for a Cart the whole to be workt out Between the first of April and the Last of September

Voted and Excepted of a Town Way Laid out by order of the Selectmen Begining on the East of the Road that Leads from Lunenburg Meeting House to Lancaster Below Esqr Hartwells Barn through part of Esqr Hartwells Land and through Asael Hartwells and Jonathan Hartwells Land to said Jonathan Hartwells East Line one Rod and half Wide as it is Now fenced out said way was Laid out and Described by

Said way was excepted provided the Land be Given | Mr Asael Hartwell and Mr Jonathan Hartwell who were appointed by the Selectmen

[125] Voted and Excepted of a town way Laid out by order of the Selectmen Begining at the way by Ephraim Kimballs and So Ran through Phineas Stewards and Solomon Stewards jun Land to the Land of M^r Ed-

ward Robins and through S^d Robins Land to Naraganset road Discribed by marked trees on the North Side then Running from Naraganset road on f^d Robins and David Goodridges Land to the Land of James Richardfon juner and on S^d Richardfon Land to Lemenfter Line Discribed by markt trees on the North Side

    Said way was Laid out and Defcribed by
                            Mr David Goodridge
Said way was Excepted   Mr Ephraim Kimbal
provided the Land   Mr Solomon Steward Jun
   be Given

    Voted and Excepted of a Town way Laid out by order of the Selectmen Begining at a Stake by Amos Kimbals Land between him & Land of Timothy Parker running one Rod upon S^d Kimbals Land to a heap of Stones till it comes to Mr Olivers Land then running Two Rod wide upon M^r olivers Land till it Comes to Land of Hezekiah Hodgkins & Ephraim Osbourn by mark'd Trees and runs between Ephraim Osbourns Land and Hezekiah Hodgkins Land two Rods wide till it comes to Land of Samuel Hodgkins & Silas Snow by mark-d Trees and then runs through S^d Samuel Hodgkins & sd Silas Snows Land two Rod wide by markd Trees till ^it goes throû the westermost part of their Land which way was Laid out and Defcribed by

and was Excepted pro-   Mr William Snow   ⎫
vided the Land be Given Mr Abraham Ireland ⎬ *Committe*
                             Mr Amos Kimbal   ⎭ *Appointed*

[126] At A Legal Meeting of the freeholders and other Inhabitants of the Town of Lunenburg Afsembled May the 17th 1756
    Voted and Chofe Mr Jonathan Wood Modderator
        Voted that the firft Article in the Warrant be Dismift
        Voted that Hoggs Run at Large the prefent year

At A Legal Meeting of the freeholders and other Inhabitants of the Town of Lunenburg Afsembled July the firft A D 1756

Voted and Chofe Mr Jonathan Wood Moddrator

Voted that they will chufe a committe to fhew Caufe why the prayer of the petetion fhould not be Granted

Voted that Edward Hartwell Esqr
Benj Goodridge
Capt John Gibfon
Mr Nathan Heywood
William Downe Efq^r
Mr Amos Kimbal
Mr Jonathan Wood
Mr Jacob Gould and
Mr Jofiah Dodge
} Bea Com^{tte}

Fully Impowered to Shew Caufe why the prayer of the petetion of william Little and others Should not be Granted and to Anfwer and Reply thereto in behalf of the Town in all Respects as they think Beft and that any two. of them go to Bofton and wait upon the General Court With their Anfwer

Recorded ℔ BENJ GOODRIDGE
Town Clerk

[127] At A Legal Meeting of the freeholders and other Inhabitants of the Town of Lunenburg Afsembled September the Sixth A D 1756

Voted and Chofe Mr Samvel Johnson Moddrator

Voted and Granted to the Rev Mr David Stearns for His Sallary for the prefent year the Sum of Sixty pound to be paid out of the Town Treafury

Voted and Chofe Benj. Goodridge Mr Jonathan Wood Capt John Gibfon Mr Samvel Johnfon and Mr Mofes Ritter a Committe to provide the Town with a School Mafter &c for the year Enfuing

Voted that ye Committe be Inftructed to place the Gramer School as near the places appointed for the four Quarters as they can and that they confider other parts of the town as Equally as may be

Voted that the Committe may Expend the Sum of fifty five pound for the Support of the Schools the year Enfuing

Voted and Granted the Sum of forty pound to be Afsefsed and paid into the Town Treafury

Voted that the Aſseſsors for the year 1755 be paid 1-6-8 for their Service

Voted and Granted to Benj Goodridge —   0- 6-0
Voted and Granted to Aſahel Hartwell   0- 4-0
Voted and Granted to Abijah Stearns   0-12-0
Voted and Granded Abraham Carlton   0-12-0

              Recorded ℞ BENJ GOODRIDGE
                           Town Clerk

[128] At a Legal Meeting of the freeholders and other Inhabitants of the Town of Lunenburg Aſsembled March yᵉ 7ᵗʰ A: D: 1757

    Voted and Chose Mʳ Asael Hartwell Modderator

Benj Goodridge
Capt Joshua Hutchens   Choſen Selectmen and
Mʳ Asael Hartwell   Sworn Aſseſsors
Mʳ Jonathan Wood   as the Law Directs
Mʳ George Kimball

Benj Goodridge Choſe Town Cleark and Sworn
             as the Law Directs

Mʳ Abijah Stearns Choſe Town Treaſurer and
            Sworn as the Law Directs

Mʳ Stephen Boynton   Choſen Conſtables and
Mʳ Partrick White   Sworn as the Law Directs

Mʳ Samuel Commings
Mʳ Josiah Dodge junʳ
Mʳ Stephen Stickney
Capt Samuel Hunt   Choſen Surveyers
Mʳ Isaac Bayley   of Highways
Mʳ Samuel Larrabee   and
Mʳ Reuben Gibson   Sworn
Mʳ Jacob Gould   as the Law Directs
Mʳ Richard Taylor
Mʳ Nathanel Page
Mʳ Ephraim Parce

Mʳ Nathanael Page
Mʳ Benj Reddington   Choſen fence viewers
Mʳ Abraham Ierland   and Sworn
Mʳ Samuel Johnſon jun   As the Law Directs

Mʳ Philip Goodridge   Surveyers of Boards and Shingles
Mʳ Timothy Parker   and Claboards
             and Sworn as the Law Directs

Mr Thomas Leitch } Chosen Surveyers of Staves and
Mr Paul Crocker } Sworn as the Law Directs
Mr Thomas Carter Chose Sealer of Leather and
                       Sworn as the Law Directs

Mr Abijah Stearns
Mr Richard Taylor } Chosen Tydingmen and
Mr Stephen Stickney } Sworn as the Law
Mr Benj Stearns   Directs

[129] Capt Samuel Hunt } Chosen to take Care of
     Mr Isaac Gibson } Dear and Sworn as
                    the Law Directs

Mr William Chadwick
Mr Charles White
Mr Jonathan Parce } Chosen Hoge reives and
Mr William Alexander } Sworn as the Law Directs
Mr David Goodridge

Mr Samuel Pool
Mr Noah Dodge } Chosen to take Care of fire
Mr Amos Kimball } and Sworn as the Law Directs
Mr Isaac Gibson

    The fourth article was Read and the Request of Samuel Hunt and others and after a debate Voted That Edward Hartwell Esqr Mr Nathan Heywood Mr Amos Kimball Mr Thomas Stearns and Benj Goodridge be A committe to consider the Petetion of Samuel Hunt and others and Papers accompaning the same and Report what they Judge proper for the Town to Do thereon on the third Tusday of May Next at one of the clock in the afternoon to which time This meeting is ajornd

    Voted and Excepted of a Town way Laid out by order of the Selectmen Begining at the End of the way by Mr Josiah Dodges Saw mill at a pitch pine Tree on the hill South of the Saw mill and Runs by markt trees markt on the Northerly side of said way to to David Parces and from thence by Trees Markt on the Easterly Side of said way To George Mcferlands said way was Laid out and Described by

    and Excepted provided the   Jonathan Parce
    Land be Given   George Mc ferlin
    A Commite appointed   David Parce

178   *The Early Records of the Town of Lunenburg.*

[**130**] Voted and Excepted of a town Way provided the Land be Given (viz) Begining at Iſaiah Witts and Runing Eaſterly about 30 rod upon Joſhua Meads Land then upon Timothy Bancrofts Land about 40 Rod and then Runing upon Land of Mr Hobby and John Demary about 80 Rods then Runing about twenty Rods on ſ^d Hobbys Land into the County Road upon the Souther Side of markt trees the whole Length of way ſaid way Being two Rod wide and was Laid out and Deſcribed by

John Demary
Iſaiah Witt

Voted that this meeting Be Ajorn d to the third Tuesday of May Next at one of the Clock in the afternoon

Recorded ℞ BENJ GOODRIDGE
Cler

May ye the 17th A: D: 1757

The free holders and other Inhabitants of the Town of Lunenburg being met on ajournment and after hearing the Report of the Committe on the Requeſt of Samuel Hunt and others and a Debate thereon

Voted that the Report be Recommitted for amendment and that the Committe Report a gain att the Town Meeting in September next

At Legal Meeting of the freeholders and other Inhabitants of the Town of Lunenburg Aſsembled May the 17 A: D: 1757

Voted and Choſe Capt John Gibſon Modderator

Voted that Swine Run at Large the preſent year

Voted and Granted the Sum of fifty pound to mend the Highways in Town withall

Voted & Granted the Sum of forty pounds to Mend High ways withall above the Town the wages the Same as Last year   Recorded ℞ BENJ GOODRIDGE
Cler

[**131**] At a Legal Meeting of the Freeholders and other Inhabitants of the Town of Lunenburg Aſsembled Sept ye 27th 1757

Voted and Chofe Mr John Heywood Modderator

Voted and Granted the Sum of Sixty pounds for the Rev Mr David Stearns es Sallery for the prefent year

Voted and Granted the Sum of forty pound for the ufe of the Schools the year Infueing

Voted that the Selectmen Support the poor out of the Town Treafury as prudently as they can the year Infueing and what is paft

Voted that the two Nurfses that attendded the families of the Simondses when Sick with the Small pox be Alow'd for every twenty four Hours the Sum of two Shillings and Eight pence each

Voted and Granted to Capt Joshua Hutchens   –0–12–0
Voted and Granted to Mr Daniel Austin   0– 2–0
Voted and Granted to Nathaniel Page   0– 2–0
Voted and Granted to the Heirs of Capt Willard   0– 2–0
Voted and Granted to Mr John Heywood   0– 2–0
Voted and Granted to Mr Asael Hartwell   0– 2–0
Voted and Granted to Mr Thomas Heywood   0– 2–0
Voted and Granted to Benj. Goodridge   0– 2–0
Voted and Granted to Benj Goodridge and Capt John Gibfon the sum seven pound   7– 0–0
    six Shilings and Eight pence for their time and Expences in Going to Bofton on the Towns Bufinefs

Voted and chofe Mr Jacob Gould Mr Josiah Bayley Mr Nathaniel Page Mr David Goodridge and Mr Edward Hartwell jun A Committe to provide the Town with Schools the year Infueing

Voted that the Committe be Inftructed to place the Grammer School as near the places appointed for the four Quarters as they can and that they Confider the other parts of the Town as Equally as may be

Voted that the Committe may Expend the Sum of fifty pounds for the ufe of the Schools

Voted and Granted to Abraham Carlton –   0–6–8
Voted and Granted to the Afsefsors for the year 1756   1–6–8

    Recorded p^r BENJ GOODRIDGE *town Cler*

[132] At A Legal Meeting of the Freeholders and other Inhabitants of the Town of Lunenburg Assembled March ye 6th 1758

Voted and Chofe Mr John Heywood Modderator for the Government of f^d Meeting

Mr Jonathan Wood
Mr Afael Hartwell
Mr William Stearns } Chofen Selectmen and Sworn Affefsors as the Law Directs
Mr Amos Kimball
Mr Thomas Carter

Benj Goodridge Chofen Town Clerk and Sworn as the Law Directs

Mr Abijah Stearns Chofen Town Treafurer and Sworn as the Law Directs

Mr John Wyman } Chofen Conftables and Sworn as the Law Directs
Mr Ephraim Whitney

Edward Hartwell Esqr
Mr William Jones
Mr Zecheriah Whitney
Mr Abraham Ireland
Mr William Gillghreaft } Chofen Surveyors of Highways
Mr Paul Wetherbee
Mr Philip Goodridge
Mr Samuel Hunt
Mr John Darling } and Collectors of Highway Rates and Sworn as the Law Directs
Mr Benj^e Reddington
Mr Thomas Leitch
Mr Nathaniel Burnam

Mr Jeremiah Norcrofs
Mr Samuel Davis
Mr Phinehas Whelock } Chofen Fence Veiwers and Sworn as the Law Directs
Mr Nathaniel Burnam jun

Mr Samuel Bradftreet
Mr Mofes Ritter
Mr Patrick White } Chofen Tyding men and Sworn as the Law Directs
Mr Jonathan Parce

[133] Mr Ephraim Kimball
Mr Phinehas Whelock
Mr William Chadwick } Chofen Hog reives and Sworn as the Law Directs
Mr Samuel Parker
Mr Benjamin Reddington

Mr Thomas Carter Chofen Sealer of Leather and Sworn as the Law Directs

Mr Thomas Leitch } Chofen Cullers of Staves and Sworn as the Law Directs
Mr Paul Crocker

Mr Philip Goodridge ⎱ Chofen Surveyors of clabbords
Mr Samuel Davis   ⎰ and Shingles and Sworn as
                    the Law Directs
Mr Isaac Gibfon ⎱ Chofen to take care of Dear
Mr James Poole ⎰ and Sworn as the Law Directs
Capt Samuel Hunt ⎱ Chofen to take care of Fire
Mr Perfon Eaton   ⎰ and burn the Woods and Sworn
             as the Law Directs

Voted and Granted the Sum of forty pounds to Repair and mend the High ways in Town Withal

Voted and Granted the Sum of forty pounds to Repair and mend the High ways in the Woods above the Town withal

At A Legal Meeting of the Freeholders and other Inhabitants of the Town of Lunenburg Affembled May ye 25th A: D 1758

Voted and Chofe Mr Jonathan Wood Modderator

Voted that the affair of Repairing the old Meeting Houfe be left with the Selectmen

Voted that the Wages that Shall be Work'd out on the High ways the prefent year be the Same they were Laft year

Voted that they will Seat the Meeting Houfe

Voted that Swine Run at Large the prefent year

                  Recorded ℈ BENJ GOODRIDGE
                               Town Clerk

[135] At A Legal Meeting, of the Freeholders and other Inhabitants of the Town of Lunenburg Affembled September ye 18th A. D. 1758

Voted and Chofe Mr William Snow Modderrator

Voted and Granted the Sum of Sixty pounds for the Rev Mr David Stearnfes Sallerry the prefent year

Voted and Granted the Sum of Thirty pounds for the Support of Schools in the Town of Lunenburg

Voted and Chofe Mr Mofes Ritter Mr Jonathan Parce Mr Paul Wetherbee Mr Richard Taylor and Mr George Kimball A Committe to provide Schooling for the Town of Lunenburg the year Enfuing

Voted that the Committe be Inftructed to place the Grammer Schools as Near the places Appointed for the four Quarters as they can and that they Confider the other parts of the Town as Equally as may be

Voted that the Committe may Expend the Sum of fifty pounds for the ufe of the Schools

Voted and Granted to the Afsefsors for the
 year 1757 the Sum of   1 = 6 = 8 = 0
Voted and Granted to Mr Abijah Stearns
 Town Treafurer   0 = 12 - 0 - 0
Voted and Granted to Mr Afael Hartwell   0 - 2 - 8 - 0
Voted and Granted to Benj Goodridge   0 = 1 = 4 = 0
Voted and Granted to Mr Phinehas Hartwell 0 = 1 = 4 = 0
Voted and Granted to Capt Samuel Hunt   0 - 6 - 0 - 0

      Recorded ℗ BENJ GOODRIDGE
              town Cler

[**136**] At A Legal Meeting of the Freeholders and other Inhabitants of the Town of Lunenburg Affembled March y^e 5th A: D: 1759 At the Old Meeting Houfe

Voted and Chofe Mr Samuel Johnfon Modderrator and then Ajorn'd to the Houfe of Capt Jofhua Hutchens

Mr Jonathan Wood
Mr Afael Hartwell   Chofen Selectmen and
Mr Thomas Carter   Sworn Afsefors as the
Mr Amos Kimball   Law Directs
Mr Daniel Auftins

Benjamin Goodridge Chofen Town Clerk and
        Sworn as the Law Directs

Mr Abijah Stearns Chofen Town Treafurer and
        Sworn as the Law Directs

Samuel Hunt
Mr William Alexander   Chofen Conftables and
David Chaplin   William Alexander Sworn as
         the Law Directs

Mr Benjamin Fofter
Mr Thomas Peobody
Mr Nehemiah Fuller
Mr Eleazer Houghton   Chofen Surveyors
Mr David Chaplin   of High ways
Mr Patrick White   and Collectors of
Mr William Shadwick   High way Rates
Mr David Goodridge   and all Sworn as
Mr Benjamin Steward   the Law Directs
Mr Nehemiah Lane   Except David Chaplin
Mr Daniel Holt

Mr Jereremiah Norcrofs ⎫ Chofen fence viewers
Mr Jofiah Bayley ⎬ and Sworn as the
Mr Ifaac Reddington ⎪ Law Directs
Mr John Fuller ⎭

[137] Mr Benjamin Reddington ⎫ Chofen Tyding men
     Mr David Wood ⎬ and Sworn
     Mr Jeremiah Norcrofs ⎭ as the Law Directs

Mr Thomas Carter Chofen Sealer of Leather
             and Sworn as the Law Directs

Mr Paul Crocker Chofen Culler of Staves

Jacob Gould ⎫ Chofen Surveyors of Shingles
Mr Philip Goodridge ⎭ and Sworn as the Law Directs

Mr Darius Houghton ⎫
Mr Zebulon Dodge ⎪ Chofen Hog reives and
Mr John Fuller ⎬ all Sworn as the Law
Mr Ephraim Kimball ⎪ Directs Except Ephraim
Mr Benjamin Fofter ⎭ Kimball

Mr James Pool ⎫ Chofen to take Care of
Mr Isaac Gibfon ⎭ Deer and James Pool
        Sworn as the Law Directs

Mr Jonathan Wood jun ⎫
Mr Phinehas Steward ⎪ Chofen to take Care
Mr Caleb Taylor ⎬ of fire and Jonathan Wood
Mr Nathaniel Carlton ⎭ jun and Nathaniel Carlton
        Sworn as the Law Directs

Voted and Granted the Sum of forty pounds to Mend the Highways in Town withal the wages to be the Same as Laft year viz two Shillings a Day for a Man one Shilling and four pence for A pair of Oxen and Eight pence for a Cart

Voted and Granted the Sum of forty pounds to mend the ways Above the Town withal the wages the Same as Laft year viz two Shillings and Eight pence per Day for A man one Shilling and four pence for a pair of oxen and Eight pence for A cart

[138] Voted and Excepted of A Town way Laid out by order of the Selectmem.

Begining at the Road on the Eaft Side of Ifaac Bayleys Land two Rods wide on Efq^r Harris Land twenty five Rods then Coming into Isaac Bayleys Land and Running through his to Jofiah Bayleys jun and Through his to Mr Carltons Land and Runs one Rod on Mr Carltons and one Rod on Mr Goodhues Land to Townfhend Line on the Welterly Side of the Mark't Trees which way was Laid out and Defcribed by David Taylor and Ifaac Bayley

At A Legal Meeting of the Freeholders and other Inhabitans of the Town of Lunenburg Afsembled May ye 21st A: D: 1759

Voted and Chofe Mr John Heywood Moderator

Voted and Accepted of Mr John Wyman to Serve as Conftable in the Room of Capt Samuel Hunt he being Hired by Said Hunt and May ye 21st was Sworn as the Law Directs

Voted and Chofe Benj Goodridge Collector to gather the Half penny Acre Rate who has Since been Sworn as the Law Directs

Voted that the Town will make the Fence on the South Side of the way from the way Near the Meeting houfe between the way and Capt Hutchen's Land till it Comes to Mr Daniel Auftins Land

Voted and Granted to Mr Daniel Holt Eight Shillings old tenor pr Rod for building Said fence provided he makes it Good and finifhes it within four Months

Voted that the place for building a School Houfe Near Mr Stickneys be moved Near the Norweft Corner of Mr Isaac Reddington's Land

Voted that the Town will New build the Bridge over Mulpus Brook Near Mr Bellow's Mill

Voted and Granted Six pound to Rebuild Said Bridge withal and that Mr Thomas Peobody Take Care that f^d Bridge be built

Turn over

[139] Voted That Swine Run at Large the Prefent year

At A Legal Meeting of the Freeholders and other Inhabitants of the Town of Lunenburg Afsembled at the Old Meeting houfe in Said Town September ye 10th 1759

Voted and Chofe Mr Jonathan Wood Modderrator

Voted and Granted the Sum of Sixty pounds
   for the Rev Mr David Stearns-s Sallery the
     prefent year   £60 – 0 – 0

Voted and Granted to Mr Daniel Auftin   00 - 6 - 0
Voted and Granted to Mr Jonathan Page the
   Sum of   00 - 6 - 0
Voted and Granted to Mr Abijah Stearns for
   his Serving Town Treafurer for y^e year 1758   00 - 12 - 0
Voted and Granted to y^e Afsefsors for the year
   1758   01 = 6 = 8
Voted and Granted to Mr Ephraim Kimball   00 = 3 = 0

     Voted and Chofe Mr Mofes Ritter Mr Jonathan Parce Mr Paul Wetherbee Mr Richard Taylor and Mr George Kimball A Committe to provide Schooling for the Town of Lunenburg the year Enfuing

     Voted that the Committe be Inftructed to place the Grammar School as Near the places appointed for the four Quarters as they Can. and that they Confider the other parts of the Town as Eaqually as may bee

     Voted that the Committe may Expend the Sum of fifty pounds for the Ufe of the Schools. And that the Committe Give Orders for the money that was Allowed by the laft years Committe to Any of ye Out fkirts of the Town when it Shall be School'd out

     Voted and Granted to Benjamin Goodridge and Mr Jofiah Dodge the Sum of Nine pounds in full Difcharge of their Trouble in building the New Meeting houfe

     [140] At A Legal Meeting of the Freeholders and Other Inhabitants of the Town of Lunenburg Afsembled March ye 3rd 1760

     Voted and Chofe Mr William Snow Modderrator for the Goverment of Said Meeting

   Benj. Goodridge
   Mr John Heywood
   Capt Jofhua Hutchens   }   were Chofen Selectmen and Sworn Afsefsors as the Law Directs
   Mr Benj: Fofter
   Capt Samuel Hunt

   Benj: Goodridge   Chofen Town Clerk and Sworn as the Law Directs

   Mr George Kimball Chofen Town Treafurer and Sworn as the Law Directs

   Mr Jonathan Hartwell
   Mr Mofes Ritter   }   Chofen Chofen Conftables

Voted and Excepted of Mr John Wyman to Serve as Conftable in the Room of Mr Jonathan Hartwell and Mr Mofes Ritter and Mr John Wyman were Took the Oaths of Conftables as the Law Directs

Mr Josiah Dodge jun
Mr Joseph Chaplin
Mr Richard Peobody
Mr Thomas Peobody
Leiut Josiah Dodge
Mr John Fuller
Mr Benj: Biglow
Mr Stephen Stickney
Mr Benj: Garey
Mr Mofes Mitchael
Mr Jonathan Mefsor
Mr Joseph Spaffard
} were Chofen Surveyors of High ways and Collectors of High way Rates

Mr Thomas Carter
Mr Zecheriah Whitney
Mr William Chadwick
Mr Phinehas Whelock
} were Chofen Fence Viewers and Sworn as the Law Directs

Mr Paul Wetherbee
Mr Amos Hazeltine
Mr Jeremiah Norcrofs
Mr Nathaniel Carlton
} were Chofen Tyding men

[141] Mr Thomas Carter—Chofen Sealer of Leather and Sworn as the Law Directs

Mr Josiah Bayley
Capt Jacob Gould
} chofen Surveyors of Shingles

Mr Jonathan Wood jun Chofen Cullor of Staves and Sworn as the Law Directs

Mr Joseph Wood
Mr Timothy Bancroft
Mr Darias Houghton
} Chofen Hog reives

Mr Ephraim Kimball
Mr William Chadwick
} Chofen to take Care of Deer and Sworn as the Law Directs

Mr Caleb Taylor
Mr Nehemiah Fuller
Mr James Poole
} Chofen to take care of fire and burn the Woods

Voted and Granted the Sum of fifty pounds to mend the High ways in Town withal

Voted and Granted the Sum of fifty pounds to mend the Highways on the Weft Side of the River and the way from Capt Hunts to Narraganſett line towards Dorchester Canada and from Mr Reuben Gibſons to Mr John Fitches and So on to the Town line to Dorchester Canada

Voted that the Higway Rate be work'd by the Hour

Voted that the wages at the High ways be four pence an Hour for a man when they they are on the Spot at work and for Oxen and A Cart as it was the Laſt year Viz one Shilling and four pence per day for a pair of Oxen and Eight pence for a cart

The Question was put upon the fourth Article in the Warrant and it paſsed in the Negative

Voted that Swine Run at Large the preſent year

Voted and Accepted of A town way Laid out by order of the Selectmen Beginning Near Mr Thomas Duttons Houſe and is Laid Through Said Duttons Land by Mark'd trees from thence Acroſs a peice of Common Land by mark'd trees from thence Round Mr Isaiah Witts North East corner from thence acroſs Mr Meeds Land by Mark'd Trees from thence upon the Ends of Mr Eaton's and Chadwick Land till it comes to Scotts Road then on that Road to Spaffords land and from thence Acroſs Spaffords land by mark'd Trees to the Road said way is two Rods wide on the Weſt Side of said mark'd Trees said way was laid out and Described by Thomas Dutton and Isaac Gibſon and is Accepted as set forth provided the land be given

[142] Voted and Accepted of a Town way laid out by order of the Selectmen from Mr Samuel Pools to Mr Amos Kimballs beginning at the Road by Said Pools Runs by Trees Marked on the Weſterly Side of Said way Through part of Said Pools Land and Mr Olivers Land to said Kimballs and Through part of said Kimballs Land Said Way was Laid out and Deſcribed by Mr James Poole and Mr Ephraim Kimball

Voted and Accepted of a Town way Beginning at a Stake Near Mr Samuel Larrabee's Corn Houſe and Runs Straight to the Corner of Jonathan Meſsurs Land then on the line of Sd Meſsurs Land which Devides his Land from Mr Noah Dodges Land to the Weſt Side of the way and So to Run to way Leading from Groton Said way is one Rod wide and was Laid out and Defcribed by Mr Daniel Auftin Mr Samuel Larrabee and Mr Noah Dodge and Mr Noah Dodge appeared in the Town Meeting and Declared that he had Received full Satisfaction of Mr Samuel Larrabee for the land of this way and Said Larrabee Likewife Declared that he Gave the Land to the Town for a way and Defir'd it be So Recorded

At A Legal Meeting of the Freeholders and other Inhabitants of the Town of Lunenburg Afsembled May ye 26th 1760

Voted & Chofe Mr John Heywood Moderrator

Then the Town Voted and Accepted of A lift of Jurymen & put them into the Boxes

Voted that Capt Jacob Gould Mr Daniel Auftin and Mr Thomas Peobody be A Committe to take a deed of Capt Jofhua Hutchens and Benjamin Bellows Esqr in Behalf of the Town of the Land that is fenc'd out for A Town Way Between their Lands and to see that the fence be made Good

Voted that they will Repair the Old Meeting Houfe

Voted and Granted the Sum of thirteen pound six shillings & Eight pence to Repair the Old Meeting Houfe withal

Turn over

[143] Voted that Capt Jofhua Hutchens m^r Thomas Carter and m^r Benjamin Foster be a Committe to Repair the old Meeting Houfe

Voted that the Committe Chofen to Repair the Old Meeting Houfe take Care and Repair the Glafs and Doors of the New Meeting Houfe

At A Legal Meeting of the Freeholders & Other Inhabitants of the Town of Lunenburg Afsembled September ye 23rd 1760

Voted & Chofe m^r John Heywood Moderrator for the Government of Said Meeting

Voted and Granted the Sum of Sixty pounds for the Rev Mr David Stearnss Sallery the prefent year

Voted & Granted the Sum of one pound Six Shillings & Eight pence to the Aſseſsors for the year 1759

Voted & Granted to Mr Abijah Stearns the Sum of Twelve Shillings for his Service as Town Treaſurer for the year 1759

Voted & Granted for the Uſe of the Schools in Said Town the Sum of fifty pounds

Voted & Choſe mr William Stearns Mr Philip Goodridge mr William Snow Mr David Wood & mr Joſeph Hartwell A Committe to provide Schooling for the Town of Lunenburg the year Enſuing

Voted that the Committe be Inſtructed to place the Grammar School as Near the places Appointed for the four Quarters as they Can. And that they Conſider the Other parts of the Town as Equally as may be

[144] At A Legal Meeting of the freeholders and other Inhabitants of the Town of Lunenburg Aſsembled March the nd2 — 1761 ——

Voted and Choſe mr John Heywood Modderator

Voted and Choſe

Benj Goodridge
Capt Joſhua Hutchens | Selectmen and were
Mr John Heywood | Sworn Aſseſsors as
Capt Samuel Hunt | the Law Directs
Mr Benj Foster

Mr Abraham Ireland | were chooſen wardens
Mr Jonathan Hartwell | and Sworn as the
 | Law Directs

Benj. Goodridge chooſen Town Clerk and Sworn as the Law Directs

Mr George Kimball Chooſen Town Treaſurer and Sworn as the Law Directs

Mr David Wood and
Mr Samvel Johnſon junr Choſen Constables then voted that Mr Moſes Ritter be Excepted to Serve as conſtable in the Room of David Wood and Johnſon and Ritter were Sworn Conſtables as the Law Directs

Mʳ Benjamin Reddington ⎫
Mʳ Thomas Dutton ⎪
Mʳ Obediah Walker ⎪
Mʳ Zechariah Whitney ⎬ were Chofen
Mʳ Samuel Poole ⎪ Surveyors of
Mʳ Philip Goodridge ⎬ High ways and
Mʳ Thomas Wetherbe ⎪ were Sworn as
Mʳ Jofiah Dodge ⎪ the Law
Mʳ Benjamin Stearns ⎪ Directs
Mʳ David Taylor ⎪
Mʳ Mofes Mitchael ⎭

Mʳ Patrick White ⎫
Mʳ Caleb Taylor ⎭ were Chofen Tydingmen

Mʳ Samuel Davis ⎫ were chofen fence
Mʳ Richard Peabody ⎭ veiwers and Sworn as
                the Law Directs

Mʳ Thomas Carter Chofen Sealer of Leather
              & Sworn as the Law
              Directs

                                  Turn over

[145] Mʳ Abraham Carlton Chofen Surveyor of Shin-
             gles and Sworn as the Law Directs
Mʳ Jonathan Wood Chofen Culler of Staves and
             Sworn as the Law Directs

Mʳ Ifaac Gibfon ⎫ Chofen to take care of fire
Mʳ James Poole ⎭ and Burn the Woods

Mʳ Amos Hazeltine ⎫
Mʳ Oliver Gould ⎪
Mʳ Phinehas Steward ⎬ were Chofen
Mʳ Silas Snow ⎪ Hogg reveis
Mʳ David Parce ⎪
Mʳ Elijah Grout ⎭

Mʳ Abraham Ireland ⎫ were Chofen a Committe
Mʳ Benj Fofter ⎬ to Buy a Buring place
Mʳ Jonathan Wood ⎭ in the wefterly part of
              the Town

Capᵗ Jacob Gould ⎫ were Chofen a Committe to
Capᵗ John Gibfon ⎬ Enquire into the Bounds of the
Mʳ Afahel Hartwell ⎭ Buring yard and Report what
            they Judge Beft to be Done
            to fence it

Voted and Granted the Sum of one Hundred pound to Repair and Mend the High ways withall fifty pound to be workt out in Town and fifty pound on the weft Side of the River and on the way from Capt Hunts to Weftminter Line and on the way from Reuben Gibfons to Dorchefter Line to be workt out as it was the Last year viz at four pence an Hour for aman on the Spot and one Shilling and four pence for a pair of Oxen pr Day and Eight for a Cart

Voted that Benjamin Goodridge buy a Burying Cloth

Voted & Accepted of A Higway Laid out by order of the Selectmen Begining at the Nor weft Corner of Isaiah Witts Houfe Lott & Runing Eafterly one Rod on Said Witts Land & one on Jofhua Meeds Land to the North eaft Corner of Said Witts Land thence Eafterly one Rod on Said Meeds Land & one Rod on Common Land as is Supposed to a Large Hemloct Tree at the Side of a Brook Mark'd on the South Side from thence About South eaft about Twenty Rods on Common Land as is Suppofed from thence the Same Courfe Acrofs Timothy Bancrofts Land Abot forty Rods from thence Eafterly [146] Acrofs Part of John Demarys Land to Dorchefter farm Line thence Running Southerly one Rod on Said Demary Land and one Rod on Mr Hobbys Land About Fourfcore Rods then Runing Eafterly Acrofs Mr Hobbys Land About Fifteen Rods to the County Rode Leading from Capt Hunts to the Meeting Houfe the Above way is Mark'd on the North & Eafterly Side with Spotts Cut in Trees & was Laid out & Defcribed by

      Benjn Fofter
      Samuel Hunt
      John Demary

At A Meeting of the Freholders & other Inhabitants of The Town of Lunenburg Afsembled March ye 10th — 1761

Voted & Chofe Mr John Heywood Modderator for the Government of Said Meeting

Voted that the Town will pay the Coft of the Late Rev'd Mr David Stearns Dec'd Funeral

Voted that they will Give the Late Revd Mr Stearns Brothers weed & Gloves & his Sifters Vails Handkerchiefs Gloves & Fans & his Sons in Law weeds & Gloves

Voted that the Selectmen Provide for the Funeral According to their Peft Difcrefsion & Lay the Account thereof before the Town at the Next Meeting

Voted & Granted the Sum of Sixty pounds to pay for Preaching for the Town

Voted that the Selectmen Provide preaching for the Town

At A Legal Meeting of the Freeholders & Other Inhabitants of the Town of Lunenburg Afsembled May y^e 26 = 1761

Voted & Chofe Mr John Heywood Modderrator for the Government of Said Meeting

Voted & Granted the Sum of Thirty one pound Eight Shillings & three pence to pay the Coft of the late Revnd Mr David Stearns's Funeral Withal

Voted & Chofe Edward Hartwell Esqr Mr Jonathan Wood and Mr William Stearns a Committe to provide preaching for the Town

Voted & Granted the Sum of Sixty pounds to pay for preaching that has been preached or Shall be preached out

Refolved that the Sixty pound Granted the tenth of March laft be not afsefsed

Turn over

[147] The Fourth Article in the Warrant being Read Containing the Request of Samuel Hunt & Others and the Town taking the Same into Confideration

Voted that their Request be So far Granted that one half of the land Within the Townfhip of Lunenburg & the Wefterly part thereof Running a parrelel Line with the Weft Line of said Townfhip be & hereby is Set off a Separate Parifh by it self Provided they Shall Place their Meeting Houfe as near the Centure of faid Parifh as may be so as to accomodate the whole and that as Soon as they are Able and Do Maintain the Gofpel among themfelves that then they Shall be freed from all Cofts & Charges of Maintaining the Gofpel in the firft Parifh in Said Town Upon A Motion made & seconded by Some of the Requefters Notwithftanding the Above Vote the Queftion was put wheither the Town would not Grant the Requeſt in Full and it paſs'd in the Negative

Voted & Choſe Edward Hartwell Esqr Mr Nathan Heywood & Benjamin Goodridge A Committe to Lay out the School Lands in the Beſt way & manner they can & See that they are put upon Record

Voted that Swine Run at Large the preſent year

At A Legal Meeting of the Freeholders & Other Inhabitants of the Town of Lunenburg Aſsembled Auguſt ye 4.th 1761

Voted & Choſe Mr John Heywood Modderrator for the Government of Said Meeting

Voted that the Committe Appointed to Provide preaching for the Town forthwith wait upon the Rev^d M^r Joſiah Bridge to See if he will preach any more for the Town

Said Committe Return'd & Reported that he muſt be away two Sabbaths after the Next Sabbath & then knew not but that he might preach for the Town again

Then the Town Taking into Conſideration the Requeſt of Amos Kimball & others & after a Debate theron the Queſtion was put wheither the Town will Grant their Requeſt and it paſsed in the Negative

[148] At A Legal Meeting of the Freeholders & Other Inhabitants of the Town of Lunenburg Aſsembled September y^e 21th 1761

Voted & Choſe Mr John Heywood Modderrator for the Government of Said Meeting

Voted & Granted the Sum of Forty pounds to pay for preaching

Voted & Granted to Mr Abraham Ireland –	0 = 18 = 0
Voted & Granted to Mr Patrick White	0 - 18 - 0
Voted & Granted to Mr William Gillchreaſt	0 - 18 - 0
Voted & Granted to Capt Joſhua Hutchens	0 = 7 = 2
Voted & Granted to Mr Jonathan Wood	1 = 19 = 4
Voted & Granted to James Deſcomb	0 - 3 - 0
Voted & Granted to Benj Goodridge	0 - 18 - 0
Voted & Granted to Mr William Stearns	1 - 8 - 0
Voted & Granted to Madam Ruth Stearns for Boarding the Miniſters	6 = 2 = 0

Voted & Granted to Mr George Kimball for
 Serving as Treasurer for the year 1760   0 - 12 - 0
Voted & Granted to the Assessors for taking a
 Valuation   6 - 14 - 0
Voted & Granted to Mr John Heywood   0 - 1 - 6
Voted & Granted to Benj Goodridge   0 - 1 - 6
Voted & Granted for the Use of the Schools the
 Sum of   50 - 0 - 0

 Voted that the Committe that Serv'd the Town the Last year be the Committe to provide the Town with Schooling the year Ensuing and that their Instructions be the Same as Last year

 Voted that the Last Grant made to the Revd Mr David Stearns Dec^d be the whole of it paid to the widdow madam Ruth Stearns

 Voted & Accepted of the Reconing made by the Selectmen with the Town Treasurer Mr George Kimball

 [149] At A Legal Meeting of the Freeholders & other Inhabitants of the Town of Lunenburg Assembled December ye 28th 1761

 Voted & Chose Mr Benjamin Foster Modderrator

 Then the Question was put wheither it was the minds of the Town to Hear m^r Samuel Payson any More than the Time they had Agred with him for and after a Debate

 Voted that the Committe forthwith wait upon Mr Payson & Agree with him for four Sabbaths more if they Can & Report The Committe Returnd & Reported that they had waited upon Mr Payson & Agreed with him to Preach for the Town four Sabbaths more

 Upon Reading the Accompts of Mr Thos Peobody Mr Daniel Austins & Capt Jacob Gould the Question was put wheither they would Grant money to pay the Same & it pass'd in the Negative

 Then Voted that the Meeting be Adjourn'd to the Third Monday of January Next at one o Clock in the Afternoon

 January ye 18th 1762 the Town being Met by Adjournment & then Voted that the Committe wait upon

Mr Samuel Payson & Agree with him to preach for the Town four Sabbaths more if they Can

Voted & Granted to Mr Thos Peobody the Sum of one pound Seven Shillings & the fencing Stuff which was left in Fencing out the Highway Between Capt Hutchens & Bellows s land

Voted & Granted to mr Daniel Auſtin the Sum of Thirteen Shillings & Eight pence for what he Did towards fencing the Above Said way &c.

Voted & Granted to Capt Jacob Gould the Sum of Nine Shillings & Eight pence Two Farthings for what he Did toward fencing Said way &c.

Voted & Granted to Capt Jacob Gould Mr Daniel Auſtin & Mr Thos Peobody the Sum of Sixteen Shillings to pay Mr Nathaniel Haſtings for Setting up the fence of Said way

	£	s.	d
Voted & Granted to the aſseſsors for the year 1760—	1	6	8

[150] At a Legal Meeting of the Freeholders & Other Inhabitants of the Town of Lunenburg Aſsembled February ye 15th — 1762

Voted & Choſe Mr Nathan Heywood Modderrator

Voted that the Town Concur with the Vote of the Church in the Choiſe of Mr Samuel Payſon for their Miniſter

Voted & Granted the Sum of Two Hundred pounds for the Incouragement of Mr Samuel Payſon and for & for his Comfortable Settlement in the work of the Miniſtry in the Town of Lunenburg provided he Shall Accept of the Town's Choiſe One half to be paid within one year after his Settlement and the Other half within Six months after the Time of the firſt payment

Voted that the Sum of Eighty pounds be Granted & Annually paid to Mr Samuel Payſon provided he Shall Accept of the Town's Choiſe & Settle in the work of the Miniſtry in Said Town So long as he Shall Continue their Miniſter Said Sum to be paid as his yearly Sallery

Voted that the Same Committe that waited upon Mr Payſon with the Church Vote wait upon him with the

Votes of the Town & Defire his Anfwer as Soon as may bee

The Fourth Article in the warrant was Read & the Queftion was put wheither they would Grant the Requeft & there was No Vote

1762. At a Legal Meeting of the Freeholders & other Inhabitants of the Town of Lunenburg Afsembled March ye 1st 1762

 Voted and Chofe Capt Jofhua Hutchens Moderator

Mefs^rs William Snow } were chofen Wardens
   Afael Hartwel

Mefs^rs Jonathan Wood }
   William Stearns
   David Wood } were chofen Selectmen &
   Abijah Stearns   Sworn Afsefsors
   Jonathan Low

Thomas Sparhawk was Chofen Town Clerk and Sworn

         Turn over

[151]   Mr George Kimball } was Chofe Town Treafurer and Sworn

Mefs^rs Benjamin Redington } were chofen Constables
   William Gilchrest   Gilchrest Sworn

Mefs^rs Samuel Cummings
   Abraham Sanderfon
   Ephraim Whitney
   Benoni Wallas
   Amos Hazeltine were chofen Surveyors
   Stephen Stickney   of High ways
   James Pool   & Collectors of
   John Litch   High way Rates
   Thomas Peabody
   Mofes Mitchel
   Samuel Sanderfon
   Nehemiah Lane

Mefs^rs Samuell Davis
   Elijah Grout } were chofen Tything Men
   David Taylor

Mefs^rs Samuel Davis } were chofen Fence Viewers
   Ezekiel Wyman and sworn as the Law directs

Mr Thomas Carter was chofen Sealer of Leather & sworn as the Law Directs

Mr Philip Goodridge, was chofen Surveyor of Shingles and sworn as the Law directs

Mr George Martin was chosen Culler of Staves
Messrs Reuben Gibson } were chosen to take
    David Goodridge } care of Fires
Messrs Edward Gary
    William Chadwick
    Solomon Steward } were chosen Hogreeves
    John Fisk
    Ephraim Pearce Junr
Messrs Edward Scot } were chosen to take
    Samuel Sanderson } care of Deer

[152] Voted and granted the same Sum of Money to repair Highways as was granted Last year; and that it be work'd out in the same manner —— ——

Voted, that Swine go at Large this Year —— ——
Voted and Granted Capt Samll Hunt   £1 - 2 - 0
Voted and Granted Dean Benjn Foster   0 - 8 - —
Voted and Granted Mr James Dascomb   0 - 3 - ——
Voted and Granted Leiut George Kimball the }
    Sum of one pound for his service as   }
    Town Treasurer for the Year 1761   }   1-0——

Voted yt Mr David Goodridge's account against the Town for service done at at the Bridge near his House be allowed out of next years High way Rate Viz s4-0

Voted yt Mr Paul Weatherbee's acct for service done at sd Bridge be also allowed out of next Years High- way Rate   Viz £0—3-0

Voted and accepted of a Highway Laid out by order of the Seelectmen: Beginning at the Southerly Line of William Flaggs Land and runs to William Benjamins Land & through sd Benjamins Land, then through the Secratary's Land (so called) then through a part of Browns Farm (so called) to where the Way was before laid out and accepted by the Town, the said Road to be two Rods wide & mark'd on the North westarly side beginning at sd Flaggs South Line, a Red Oak Tree mark'd, and ending with a Hemlock Tree on the Northerly side of the Road already established mark'd with two Spots and Three Notches

The above Road was discribed and laid out by
                    Messrs Benjn Foster
                    and John Fitch
    Recorded Pr Me Thos. SPARHAWK T. Clerk

[153] At a Legal Meeting of the Freeholders and other Inhabitants of the Town of Lunenburg Afsembled April 26th 1762

Voted & Chofe Capt: Jonathan Wood Moderator

Voted to Concur with the Churches Vote Refpecting the Time appointed for the Ordination of Mr Samuel Payson, Viz the Second Wenfday in September next —

Voted to choofe a Com^{tee} to agree with some Perfons to make provifion for the Venerable Council & other Gentlemen of Note and diftinction who shall attend the Ordination of Mr Sam^{ll} Payfon — — —

Voted to Choofe three Perfons as a Com^{tee} for s^d purpofe

Voted that Benjn Goodridge Efq^r } Be a Com^{tee} for
Leiut George Kimball } the purpofe
and Leiut Jonathan Low } aforef^d —

Voted that the Woman's Seats in the body of the Meeting Houfe be referved for the Church to Set in, on the Day Appointed for the Ordination

Voted that the Men's Seats be referved for the Venerable Council and such of the Church as cannot find Room in the Womans Seats

Voted and Choofe

Mefs^{rs} Richard Taylor } A Com^{tee} to keep the
Philip Goodridge } seats in the Meeting
Samuel Johnfon Junr } Houfe referved for the
Obediah Walker } Council and Church on
William Gilchrest } Ordination Day

Voted and choofe Mr Mofes Ritter a Com^{tee} man in the Room of Mr Philip Goodridge who refuf'd serving

Voted & Chofe Mefs^{rs} Jofiah Dodge } a Com^{tee} to
Abraham Carlton } Secure the
Meeting Houfe (upon Ordination Day) by Bracing the Galleries and what ever elfe they shall think proper relating thereto

The Second Article in the Warrant was Read, and the Question put to Vote whether they would Act upon it, & it pafsed in the Negative

Voted to accept of Mr Mofes Ritter to serve as Conftable in lieu of Mr Benjamin Redington who was Chofe at the anual meeting; He being hired by Mr Redington and was Sworn to the faithful discharge of his office as the Law directs

Voted to Erect a Monument over the Grave of the Late Revd Mr David Stearns ——

Voted and Chofe Mefs.^{rs} Josiah Dodge, Benj.ⁿ Foster, Jon.^a Low } a Com.^{tee} for the purpofe afore f.^d

[154] The Queftion was put to Vote whether the Town would Act upon the Fifth Article in the Warrant & it pafs'd in the affirmative

Voted that a Work Houfe be provided

Voted to accept of Mr Auftins offer Viz: of his most northerly old houfe; for a Work Houfe ——

Voted & Chofe Mefs.^{rs} Daniel Auftin, Sam.^{ll} Johnfon Junr } Overfeers of s.^d Houfe

And then the s.^d Meeting was Difmif'd

Recorded P.^r Me Thos SPARHAWK *T. Clerk*

At a Legal meeting of the Freeholders & other Inhabitants of the Town of Lunenburg Afsembled Septr 27.th 1762

Voted and chofe Benj.ⁿ Goodridge Efq: Moderator

Voted that ye Rev.^d Mr Sam.^{ll} Payson's Salery begin at ye time of his ordination

The Second Article in the Warrant being read and ye Question what instructions ye town would give ye Afsefsors refpecting Mr Payson's Salery? & it was thought convenient to conform to ye vote of ye Town in their call to Mr Payson

Voted and Granted Mr Thomas Carter for entertaining the Ordination Council £-6-8

Voted and granted ye Afsefsors for ye Year 1761 - 1-6 8

Granted Joseph Bellows for keep:- Mr Payfons Horfe 16½ weeks 1-2.- —

Voted and Granted; (to defray ye Charges of Erecting a Monument over the Grave of ye Rev.^d Mr Stearns Deceaf.^d) the Sum of £8-

Voted and Granted for ye ufe of ye Schools —— 50. ——

Voted and Chofe Mefs^rs Joshua Goodridge ⎫
Sam^ll Cummings ⎪
Thos Peabody ⎬ School
John Bufs ⎪ Com^tee
Joshua Hutchens ⎭

Voted y^t ye School Com^tees Instructions be ye same as they were Last Year: & y^t ye meeting be difmifsed

Recorded Pr Thos Sparhawk *Town Clerk*

[155] At a Legal meeting of the Freeholders & other Inhabitants of the Town of Lunenburg afsembled January the 21st 1763 ——

Voted & chofe Dea^n William Stearns Moderator

Voted to choofe some Perfon to serve the Town as Conftable for the Year 1762 in Lieu of Mr Mofes Ritter deceaf'd

Voted and Choofe Mr Abijah Hovey to serve as Conftable for the year 1762 in lieu of Mr Mofes Ritter deceaf'd who was accepted as Conftable at a Meeting in April 1762 inftead of Mr Benjn Redington who was chofe at the Annual Meeting 1762

Mr Hovey Being chofe Conftable (not being at the Meeting) the town thought proper to inform him of it immediately; whereupon Mr Wm Gilgrest Conftable was sent immediately, (being inftructed by the Town Clerk & Selectmen) to acquaint Mr Hovey with the Towns proceedings towards him, and to report to the Town whether Mr Hovey would serve the Town as Conftable for the year 1762 or not —— Then Voted that the meeting be adjournd for one Hour to the Houfe of Capt: Joshua Hutchens

The Town being meet on adjournment

Voted y^t ye Settlement of all the Charges & accounts relating to the illnefs of Jonathan Whitney be refer'd to the Selectmen, and to be settled by them: Mr Wm Gilchrest being returned reported to the Town y^t Mr Hovey would not serve the Town as Constable, would be glad if the Town would excufe him if they would not, he would pay His fine; unlefs they would accept of Jonathan Page to serve in his stead ——

Put to Vote whether the Town would accept of Jonathan Page to Serve as Constable instead of Abijah Hovey & it pas'd in the Negative

Voted and Chofe Mr Jonathan Pearce to serve the Town as Conftable for the 1762

Voted to Adjourn the Meeting to Wensday the Twenty Sixth of this Inft: to this place (Viz) at one o'clock Capt: Joshua Hutchens Long Chamber

Recorded Pr Thos. Sparhawk *Town Clerk*

[156] January ye 26th 1763 The Freeholders and other Inhabitants of the Town of Lunenburg being meet on Adjournment

Mr Jonathan Pearce being prefent the Question was propofed to him whether he would serve the Town as a Conftable; he reply'd he did not choofe to serve unlefs he could be Sufficiently authorized to collect the Taxes ——

after a long Disputation and Debate; Mr Pearce was again defired to declare to the Town his acceptance or non-acceptance of the office of a Conftable; He defired Longer time for Confideration; & finally refufed to Serve as Constable then —

Voted and Chofe Mr Jonathan Bradftreet to serve as Constable for the Year 1762

Mr Bradftreet being immediately notified of the Town's Choice by Mr Conftable Gilchreft, prefented himfelf to the Town, & Being ask'd by the Moderator, whether he would accept of the office of a Conftable for the Year 1762 Mr Bradftreet reply'd he scrupled whether the Fine could be recovered of him; the Moderator infisting upon a peremptory anfwer, he reply'd again he Scrupled whether the fine could be recovered & finally refufed utterly to serve the Town as Constable then

Voted and chose Mr Richard Taylor Conftable for the year 1762 —— who being notified thereof by the Conftable above-mentioned — made his appearance & declared he would not serve once & again —— Then by a motion, made and seconded, it was put to Vote whether the Town would excufe Mr Richard Taylor from the service of a Conftable? and it pafs'd in ye affirmative

Voted and Chofe Mr Paul Weatherbee to serve the Town as Con Constable for the Year 1762 & then the meeting was Dismifsed

     Recorded Jany 26th 1763 P^r
       Thos. Sparhawk *Town Clerk*

[157] At a meeting of the Free holders & other Inhabitants of the Town of Lunenburg Afsembled Feby 16th 1763

 Voted and chofe Capt: Jonathan Wood Moderator

 Voted to send for The Revd Mr Ebenezer Sparhawk to come and pray with the Town

 Voted to send to the Revd Mr Timothy Harrington the Revd Mr John Mellen the Rev^d M^r: Samuel Dana the Rev^d Mr Jofeph Emerson the Revd Mr Francis Gardner the Rev^d Mr. Ebenezer Sparhawk the Rev^d Mr Samuel Dix and the Revd Mr Phinehas Whitney to attend the interment of the Rev^d Mr Samuel Payson deceaf'd

 Voted to give the Father & Brethren of the deceaf'd Weeds, and Gloves, to the Mother of the deceaf'd & to the ½ Sister Vails Handkerchiefs and Gloves

 Voted to give Mrs Elizabeth Stearns a Neat handfome Suit of Mourning

 Voted that the Selectmen make provifion for thofe Gentle^n who shall attend the Funeral of the Revd Mr Samuel Payson deceaf'd and their Horfes

    Recorded Pr Thos. Sparhawk *Town Clerk*

At a Legal Meeting of the Freeholders and other Inhabitants of the Town of Lunenburg Afsembled March 7th 1763 ——

 Voteded and chofe Dea^n John HeyWood Moderator

Mefs^rs John Bufs   } were chofen Wardens and
  Darius Houghton }   Sworn

Benjn Goodridge Efq^r   }
Capt: Jofhua Hutchens }
Dea^n John Heywood   } Were chofen Selectmen
Capt. James Reed   } and Sworn
Mr Thomas Carter   }

 Thomas Sparhawk was chofen Town Clerk & Sworn

Mr George Kimball was chosen Town Treasurer & Sworn

Mess.rs Abijah Hovey }
Richard Taylor } were chosen Constables & Sworn

Mr Isaac Gibson was chosen Constable before Mr Taylor, but he desiring a Dismission it was Voted ———

[158] Mess.rs John Darling
Ezekiel Goodridge
George Martin
Sam.le Putnam
John White
Caleb Taylor
Jon.a Low
David Goodridge
Jon.a Holt
Joshua Goodridge
George Henry
Sam.ll Johnson Jun.r
Oliver Gould
Elijah Grout
} Were chosen Surveyors, Darling, E: Goodridge Putnam, Taylor, Low, D: Goodridge, Holt, Henry, Johnson and Gould were Sworn Martin Since Sworn

Mess.rs Jedediah Bailey }
Ezekiel Wyman } were chosen Tythingmen & Sworn

Mess.rs Sam.le Davis }
Jeremiah Norcross } were chosen Fence viewers and Sworn

Mr Thomas Carter was chosen Sealer of Leather & Sworn

Mess.rs Philip Goodridge }
Abraham Carlton } were chosen Surveyors of Shingles &c: and Sworn

Mess.rs Thomas Litch & }
George Martin } were chosen Cullers of Staves Hoops &c: & Sworn

Mess.rs W.m Chadwick }
Jon.a Wood }
Edw.d Gary }
W.m Henry } were chosen Hog reeves & Sworn

Mess.rs Eph.m Kimball }
Isaac Gibson } were chosen Deer reeves & Sworn

Mess.rs Reuben Gibson }
Jon.a Pierce }
Caleb Taylor }
James Pool } were chosen to take care of Fires Gibson & Pierce Sworn

Voted and accepted of an Highway laid out by order of the Selectmen as follows, beginning at the End of the Road that runs from M.r Sam.le Cummingss to Daniel

BOOK B,

LUNENBURG TOWN RECORDS.

[1.] Worcefter fs To William Gilchreft Conftable of the Town of Lunenburg Greeting: —

In His Majestys Name you are required to Notify and Warn the Freeholders and other Inhabitants of s^d Town qualifyed by Law to Vote in Town Meetings to afsemble & Meet at the New Meeting Houfe in said Lunenburg on Monday the Seventh Day of March next at Nine o'clock A. M. then and there being meet & duly form'd to act on the following Articles Viz. — — —

1st To choofe Selectmen & all other Town Officers for the prefents Year as the Law directs

2^{ly} To accept of any Roads or Town Ways that have been laid out by the Selectmen or their Order -

3^{ly} To choofe a Committee to provide Preaching & to Give y^m such Instructions as they shall think proper; or to proceed any other way to supply the Pulpit as they shall think best —

4ly To see if the Town will appropriate any Sum or Sums of Money (that is already afsefsed) towards the defraying the charges, y^t have arifen by the late Sicknefs & Funeral of ye Rev^d Mr Sam^{ll} Payfon late of Lunenburg deceaf'd —

5^{ly} To hear the Request of Benjn Foster & Nine others: Viz: if the Town will Vote off from us the West:^{ly} part of the Town, into a distinct precinct by themfelves (Viz) all the Inhabitants on the Westwardly side of Pearl - Hill — Brook, & on the Weftwardly side of Dorchester Farm so called; with their Lands, or to Vote off any part of them & y^r Lands, & to releafe y^m from paying any further Taxes towards the Support of the

Minister or to release them of any part of Taxes to the Minister with us or to make any proposals, or to choose any Com^tee or Com^tees if they think proper to accomodate and settle that Affair ——

6^ly To See if the Town will Vote to have the Grammer-School kept in the middle of the Town at some convenient place during the Term of One Year

7^ly To Grant a suitable Sum of Money to mend the highways & to repair or Build Bridges & to say in w^t manner ye same shall be paid or Work'd out

8^ly To make a Grant of Money suitable to ye support of ye Poor ——

9^ly To Choose a Committee to reckon with the Town Treasurer ——

Hereof fail not and make return of your doings on this Warrant to some one of us the Subscribers, on or before the time of s^d meet^g

Given under our hands & Seals this Sixteenth Day of Feby A. D. 1763
and in the third year of his Majestys Reign

Jon^o Wood
Wm Stearns
Jon^a Low   Select^n of Lunenburg
David Wood
Abijah Stearns

A true Copy
    Attest: Thos Sparhawk *Town Clerk*

N. B. a Return was made by s^d Wm Gilchrest y^t he had fulfild obey^d ye orders of this Warrant
                              Thos Sparhawk

[2] At a Legal Meeting of the Freeholders and other Inhabitants of the Town of Lunenburg assembled March 7th 1763

Voted and chose Dea^n John Heywood Moderator

Messrs John Buss   } were chosen Wardens &
       Darius Houghton   Sworn

Benjn Goodridge Esqr
Capt: Joshua Hutchins   were chosen Selectmen
Dea^n John Heywood   and Sworn Assessors by
Capt: James Reed   the 1st Day of April
Mr Thos Carter

Thomas Sparhawk was chosen Town Clerk & Sworn

Mr George Kimball was chosen Town Treasurer & Sworn

Messrs Abijah Hovey ⎫ were chosen Constables and
Richard Taylor ⎭ Sworn as ye Law Directs

Messrs John Darling
Ezekiel Goodridge
George Martin
Samll Putnam
John White
Caleb Taylor
Jono Low
David Goodridge
Jona Holt
Joshua Goodridge
George Henry
Samll Johnson Junr
Oliver Gould
Elijah Grout

Were chosen Surveyors, Darling, Ezekiel Goodridge, Putnam, Taylor, Low, David Goodridge, Holt Henry, Johnson, & Gould were Sworn Martin since Sworn; Joshua Goodridge Sworn May 18th

Messrs Jedediah Bailey ⎫ were chose Tything men
Ezekiel Wyman ⎭ & Sworn

Messrs Samll Davis ⎫ were chosen Fence
Jeremiah Norcross ⎭ Viewers & Sworn

Mr Thomas Carter was chose Sealer of Leather & Sworn

Messrs Philip Goodridge ⎫ were chose Surveyors of
Abraham Carlton ⎭ Shingles Clapboards &c: & Sworn

Messrs Thomas Litch ⎫ were chosen Cullers of
George Martin ⎭ Staves Hoops &c & Sworn

Messrs William Chadwick
Jono Wood
Edwd Gary
Wm Henry
⎫ were chosen Hog reeves & Sworn

[3] Messrs Ephraim Kimball ⎫ were chosen Dear
Isaac Gibson ⎭ reeves and Sworn

Messrs Reuben Gibson
Jono Pierce
Caleb Taylor
James Pool
⎫ Were chose to take care of Fires Gibson & Pierce Sworn

Voted and accepted of an Highway laid out by order of the Selectmen as follows Viz: beginning at the End of the Road, yt runs from Samll Cummings's to Daniel Stewards Land running South wardly on the Eaſtwardly side of said Stewards Land to Leominſter line & lies wholly upon said Stewards Land who saith he gives the Land for said purpoſe, s^d Road being mark'd on the weſt side & is one Rod and an half wide Laid out by

David Wood
Paul Weatherbee } Com^{tee}
Daniel Steward

Voted to chooſe by Written Votes a Committee of three Perſons to provide preaching

Voted & Choſe Capt: Joshua Hutchens } a Com^{tee} for
Capt: James Reed } the purpoſe
Dea^n John Heywood } afore ſ^d

The Fourth Article in the Warrant being read; after a long Debate, it was thought proper not to act upon it

The 5th Article being read; the Vote was put whether the Town would Act upon it? and it paſs'd in the Negative

The 6th Article was alſo read; & ye Vote was put whether the Grammer School should be kept in the Middle of the Town during the Term of One Year & it paſs'd in the Negative

Voted that the Conſideration of the 7th 8th & 9th Articles in the Warrant be adjourned to Wedneſday the Twenty Third Day of this Inſtant March to the New Meeting Houſe at two o'clock in the afternoon

Recorded P^r

Thos Sparhawk *T Clerk*

[4] March 23 1763 the Freeholders and other Inhabitants of the Town being meet on Adjournment ——

Voted to give the Com^{tee} chooſe to provide preaching some Inſtructions relative thereto ——

Voted to hear Mr Ebenezer Champney 4 Sabbaths & then Mr. Fisk 4 Sabbaths if they may be procured —

Voted & Granted £100. to mend Highways & Bridges for the Year 1763; & that the said Sum shall be work'd out at the same price for Labour and in the same manner as it was last Year — —

The 8th Article being Read and a Vote propoſed, Whether the Town would Grant a Sum of Money for the Support of the Poor? and it paſs'd in the Negative ——

Voted and Choſe a Comtee to reckon with ye Town Treaſurer
- Benjn Goodridge Eſqr
- Capt: Joſhua Hutchens
- Capt: James Reed

Voted and choſe the Surveyors Collectors of their own particular Highway Rates

Then the following Warrant was Read Viz:

Worceſter ſs: To one of the Conſtables of the Town of Lunenburg Greeting — — —

In His Majestys name you are required forthwith to notify and warn the Freeholders & other Inhabitants of sd Lunenburg to meet at this place (Viz the New Meeting Houſe) at four of the Clock this afternoon to agree and Vote whether the Swine shall go at large this preſent Year & to make return of this Warrant and your Doings therein at or before the Time of said Meeting unto us the Subſcribers Dated at Lunenburg March ye 23d 1763

BENJN GOODRIDGE
JOHN HEYWOOD
JAMES REED
Selectmen of Lunenburg

A true Copy
Atteſt THOMAS SPARHAWK *Town Clerk*

Worceſter ſs: March 23d 1763 In Obedience to this Warrant I have warned all the Perſons within Named to meet at time & place.

RICHARD TAYLOR *Conſtable*

The Freeholders and Other Inhabitants being Meet & Legally formd March 23d 1763 at 4 o'clock P. M.

Voted that Swine go at large this Year —

Recorded Pr

THOMAS SPARHAWK *T Clerk*

[5] A Copy of a Warrant for calling a Town Meeting

Worceſter ſs to the Conſtable or Conſtables of the Town of Lunenburg or either of them Greeting:

You are in His Majeſtys Name required to notify and warn the Freeholders and other Inhabitants of the Town of Lunenburg Qualifyed to vote in Town-Affairs to aſſemble and meet at the New Meeting Houſe in said Town on Wednesday the Twenty Third of this Inſtant March at One O, clock P. M. then and there being duly meet and form'd — — —

1st And agreeable to an Act of the Great and General Court To chooſe a Conſtable in the Room of Moſes Ritter Deceaſ'd to finish the Collection of the Rates and Taxes committed to said Ritter, that remain unfiniſhed

2ly To hear the Accounts of the Charges of the Funeral & Sickneſs of the Revd Mr. Samuel Payſon deceaſ'd, if they can be procured, & to agree on and vote any method shall be thought proper for the peacable and quiet Settlement of the same

thereof fail not, & make return of your doings to some one of us the Subſcribers at or before the time of said Meeting

Sealed with our Seal Dated at Lunenburg this Seventh Day of March in the Third Year of His Majesty Reign Anno Domini 1763

A True Copy	BENJN GOODRIDGE	
Attest: THOS SPARHAWK	JOSHUA HUTCHENS	*Selectmen*
Town Clerk	JAMES REED	*of*
	THOS CARTER	*Lunenburg*

Worceſter ſs:
Inobedience to this Warrant I have warned all the Perſons within named to meet at time & place
       RICHD TAYLOR *Conſtable*
 A true copy
  Attest
    THOS SPARHAWK *T Clerk*

At a Legal Meeting of the Freeholders & other Inhabitants of the Town of Lunenburg Aſſembled March 23d 1763

Voted and choſe Dean John Heywood Moderator

Voted and choſe Mr Jonathan Bradſtreet Conſtable in the Room of Mr Moſes Ritter Deceaſed, and he was Sworn to the faithfull discharge of His Office ——

The Second Article in the warrant being read, Voted to hear the Will of the Revd Mr Samll Payſon

The Will being Read, after a long Debate the Meeting was difmifsed ——

      Recorded Pr Thos Sparhawk
            Town Clerk

[6] Worcefter ff To the Conftable or Conftables of the Town of Lunenburg or to any or either of them Greeting ——

In His Majestys Name you are required forthwith to notify and warn the Freeholders and other Inhabitants of said Town of Lunenburg Qualifyed by Law to vote in Town Meetings, to Afsemble and Meet at the Old Meeting-Houfe in said Town, on Thurfday the Nineteenth Day of this Inst: May, at Three O, clock P. M. then and there being duly meet and form'd to act on ye Following Articles Viz:

1st To give the Com^{tee} appointed to provide preach^g for the Town such further inftructions as they shall think proper

2^{ly} To hear any Accounts that shall be bro't by any Perfons to agree & act thereon as they shall think proper

3^{ly} To see, if the Town will agree with the Church in calling a Fast in said Town

4^{ly} To see, if the Town will Vote y^t ye Lands in s^d Lunenburg wh^{ch} lies West and Westwardly of the Line hereafter discribed, should be set off from s^d Town y^t so, ye same Lands & Inhabitants thereon may be formed by the General Court into a Town or District if they think proper: wh^{ch} Line is difcribed as follows, viz, beginning at such place on Leominfter Line as y^t a strait Line therefrom may run between the Lands of Mr Paul Weatherbee & Mr Jonathan Wood to a Stake and Stones a small distance to the Westward of Mary Holts Houfe, then turning & running North 10 Degrees & a half East to Mr Ephraim Whitneys South-East Corner, then to keep the Eastwardly line of said Whitneys Farm, to the North-East Corner thereof, and from thence to continue to run Northwardly on the Eastwardly Line of John Whites Land, to the Northerly Corner of His Farm, and from y^t Corner to run North 4 Deg^r east to Townfhend Line.

Whereas the said Dividing Line will Divide the Lands of sundry Perſons, leaving part on the Eastwardly and part on the westwardly side thereof; to see if yͤ Town by a Vote will manifest it to be their deſire, yͭ whenſoever the aforeſᵈ Lands West & Westwardly of said Line shall be formed into separate Town or District, that it may be done in such manner that all thoſe Perſons whoſe Lands by the said Line shall be Divided, and all Perſons for the future who shall own Improved Lands which Shall lie acroſs said Line, partly on one side & partly on the other side thereof, shall pay Rates & Taxes for the whole thereof, to that Town or District in which such Perſon or Perſons shall dwell, provided they shall dwell on any part of their Lands which may happen to be divided by said Line, that so the said propoſed Town or District may be formed under theſe Reſtrictions by the General Court if they think proper —— hereof fail not, and make return of this Warrant with your doings thereon, unto some one of us the Subſcribers at or before the Time of meeting Given under our Hands and Seals at Lunenburg afore ſᵈ this Third Day of May in the Third Year of his Majestys Reign A. D. 1763

BENJᴺ GOODRIDGE ⎫ *Selectⁿ*
JOSHUA HUTCHINS ⎬ *of*
JOHN HEYWOOD ⎪ *Lunenburg*
THOˢ CARTER ⎭

Worcester ſs. Lunenburg May 19ᵗʰ 1763

In Obedience to the within written I have notified and Warned all the Perſons within named to meet at time and place for the purpoſes within mentioned

RICHARD TAYLOR ⎬ *Constable of Lunenᵍ*

A true Copy
   Attest, THOˢ SPARHAWK
         Town Clark

[7] At a Legal Meeting of the Freeholders and other Inhabitants of the Town of Lunenburg aſsembled May 19ᵗʰ 1763 —

Voted and Choſe Mʳ Nathan Heywood Moderator

Voted yt ye spplying ye Pulpit be left to the difcretion of the Committee chofen to provide preaching

Voted and Granted Mm Ruth Stearns 6/8 for boarding Minifters Three Sabbaths

Voted to concur with the Vote of the Church in calling a Fast in this Town on Tuefday come Fortnight

The 4th Article in the Warrant was Read & the Question put whether the Town would comply with said Article as set forth in the Warrant? & it pafsed in the Negative ——

Then the Meeting was dismifsed ——

Recorded Pr Thomas Sparhawk
Town Clerk

At a Legal Meeting of the Freeholders & other Inhabitants of the Town of Lunenburg afsemd Augt 22d 1763

Voted and chofe Benjn Goodridge Efqr Moderator

Voted to hear Mr Nathan Davis preach a longer Time

Voted and Chofe Dn Benjn Fofter, Mr Samll Putnam & Edwd Hartwell Efqr a Comtee to wait upon Mr Davis to see whether he would engage to preach a longer Term —— then voted that the said Comtee agree with Mr Davis to preach four Sabbaths more

Voted yt the Meeting be adjournd one hour — being meet on adjournment the aforefd Comtee reported to the Town that Mr Davis would Supply the pulpit four Sabbaths, and yt is was likely he should preach himfelf excepting One Day then the Meeting was dismifsd.

Recorded Pr Thos Sparhawk
Town Clerk

At a Legal Meeting of the Freeholders and other Inhabitants of the Town of Lunenburg Afsembled Septr 26th 1763.

Voted and Choofe Capt: Jofhua Hutchens Moderator

Voted and Granted the Sum of Eighty Pounds to provide preaching the enfuing Year

Voted to accept the report of the Committee chofen to reckon with the Town Treafurer & yt ty see it recorded —

Verte.

[8] Voted and Granted the Sum of Fifty pounds for the ufe and support of the School the enfuing Year ——

Voted and choofe the same Committee to take Care of the School this year as was last and that their Inftructions be the Same alfo Viz: to place the Grammar School as Near the Center of each Quarter of the Town as may be; and that they Confider the other parts of the Town as equally as pofsibly they can

Voted that the Account exhibited to the Town by Mrs. Elizabeth Stearns Administratrix to the Eftate of the Rev^d Mr Samuel Payson late of Lunenburg deceaf'd (being Forty Nine pounds, Nineteen Shillings & Three pence one Farthing, bearing date this Twenty Sixth Day of September 1763) be allow'd, accepted and pay'd out of the One Hundred pounds already Afsefsed for Mr Payfons Settlement, and that she be discharg'd, in full, from the Legacy bequeath'd in s^d deceafed's Will to the Town, she giving the Town a difcharge in full as Adminiftratrix to said deceafeds Will —

Voted that the Selectmen be impowered to give Mrs Elizabeth Stearns Adminiftratrix to Mr Payfons Will a full discharge from the Legacy by him bequeathed to the Town of Lunenburg, and alfo to receive from s^d adminiftratrix a full difcharge as Adminiftratrix to s^d deceafeds Will —— ——

Voted and granted the afsefsors for the year 1762 the Sum of £1. 6. 8. for their Service ——

Voted and Granted Mr George Kimball £1-0-0-0 for serving as Treafurer for the Year 1762

Voted and granted Benjn Goodridge Efq^r and Capt. Jofhua Hutchens ^{s}4/ for their Service and Trouble in reckoning with the Town Treafurer

Voted and Granted Mr George Kimball ^{s}2/Shillings for his Trouble and Service Reckon^g with ye Com^{tee}

Voted and Granted Dea^n John Heywood 6 Shillings for going to Hire Mr. Davis to Come and Preach with us

Voted and Granted Mr Patrick White Three 3/Shilling for carrying Some of the Towns Money to Bofton to paying a Debt

Voted and Granted Thomas Sparhawk the Sum of 7/8^d for providing a Book for the Town Records ——

Voted that the Town concur with the Vote of the Church in the Choice of Mr Nathan Davies for their Minifter

[9] Voted the Sum of Two Hundred pounds Lawful Money for the Settlement of Mr Nathan Davies provided he shall Settle in the Work of the Miniftry in the Town of Lunenburg ——

Voted and Granted the Sum of Seventy Five pounds to be paid annually to Mr Nathan Davies as his Sallery provided he shall accept the Towns propofals and Settle among us in the Work of the Miniftry and alfo the ufe of the Minifterial Lands in said Town

Voted and Choofe D^n Foster
                D^n Heywood
                D^n Kimball
                D^n Putnam
                Benjn Goodridge Efq^r

A Committee to wait upon Mr Nathan Davies with the propofals of the Town refpecting their Choice of him to the work of the Miniftry amongft them

        Recorded P^r Me
            THOMAS SPARHAWK *Town Clerk*

At a Legal Meeting of the Freeholders and other Inhabitants of the Town of Lunenburg Afsembled Novr ye 15th 1763

Voted and Chofe Benjn Goodridge Esqr Moderator

Voted that the Com^{tee} Chofen to provide Preaching Apply to Mr Adams first and engage him to preach four Sabbaths if pofsible; and if he is not at liefure Voted that they apply to Mr Williams and Engage him if at liefure if not that they ufe their Judgment in providing a Minifter for the Town ——

Voted to Choofe Agents to Meet and Confer with the Agents of the several Towns about to petition to the Court to be form'd into the County, and to make report of the several propofals that shall be made by said Towns respecting said affair

Voted and Chofe Benj︠n︡ Goodridge Efq︠r︡ } agents
& Deacon John Heywood } to transact the aforefaid affair

Voted the the Article in the Warrant refpecting the old Meeting Houfe be defer'd to some future Meeting — and the the Meeting was dismifs'd

      Recorded P︠r︡ THOMAS SPARHAWK
         T Clerk

[10] At a Legal Meeting of the Freeholders and other Inhabitants of the Town of Lunenburg afsembled Jan︠y︡: 25th 1764

Voted and Choofe Dea︠n︡ John Heywood Moderator

Voted to adjourn the Meeting forthwith to the New-Meeting Houfe where being meet upon Adjournment

Voted that the first article in the Warrant be dismifsed

Voted to hear Mr Adams preach a Longer Term if he may be obtain'd

Voted to choofe a Com︠tee︡ to wait upon Mr Adams forthwith to acquaint him with the Mind of the Town and to enquire something whether it would be worth while to proceed upon anything further refpecting him

Voted and Choofe Benj︠n︡ Goodridge Efq︠r︡ Leiut: Nathan Heywood & Dea︠n︡ Benjamin Foster a Com︠tee︡ to wait upon Mr Adams for the purpofes aforesaid

Voted that the Request of Deacon Benj︠n︡ Foster, Dea︠n︡ Samuel Putnam and others (Viz: To see whether the Town will Vote that the Lands in said Lunenburg which ly West and westwardly of the Line hereafter difcribed should be set off from said Town that so the same Lands and Inhabitants thereon may be formed by the General Court into a Town or Diftrict if they shall think proper, which Line is discribed as followeth Viz: beginning at such place on Leominfter Line as that a strait Line therefrom may run between the Lands of Mefs︠rs︡ Paul Weatherbee & Jonathan Wood to a Stake and Stones a Small Diftance to the Westward of Mary Holts Houfe then turning and running North 10½ degrees east to the South

East Corner of Mr Ephraim Whitney's Land then to keep the Eastwardly Line of said Whitneys Land to the North east Corner thereof, and from that Corner to run Northwardly on the Eastwardly Line of Mr John White's Land to the Northeastwardly Corner thereof and from that Corner to run North four Degrees East to Townfhend Line) be granted as set forth in the Warrant provided the Inhabitants on said Lands shall pay their Minifters Tax as heretofore they have done untill they shall be formed Into a Town or District

Voted that the Meeting be adjourned till 5 o'clock to the Houfe of Capt: Joshua Hutchens

Being meet on Adjournment voted that the Meeting be adjourned to Monday 30th Inst: 11 o'clock A. M. to the New Meeting Houfe

Recorded Pr THOMAS SPARHAWK
Town Clerk

[11] The Freeholders and other Inhabitants of the Town of Lunenburg being met on Adjournment Jany 30th 1764 ——

Voted that the Confideration of the Article for supplying or providing for the pulpit be adjourned to ½ after Three in the afternoon — — —

At a Legal Meeting of the Freeholders and other Inhabitants of the Town of Lunenburg Afsembled Jany: 30th 1764

Voted and Choofe Dean John Heywood Moderator

Voted to Concur with the Church in the Choice of Mr Zabdiel Adams to the Work of the Gofpel Miniftry in this Town — —

Voted the Sum of Two Hundred pounds for the Encouragement of Mr Zabdiel Adams, and for his Comfortable Settlement in the Work of the Miniftry in the Town of Lunenburg, provided he shall accept of the Towns Choice one half to be paid in Twelve Months after his Ordination, the other in Eighteen Months after the time of his Ordination ——

The Early Records of the Town of Lunenburg. 219

Voted Mr Zabdiel Adams the Sum of Eighty pounds for his Yearly Sallery & Support, provided he shall settle in this Town in the Work of the Gofpel Miniftry, solong as he shall continue our Minifter —

Voted to choofe a Com^tee to prefer the propofals of the Church and Town to Mr Adams ——

Voted & Choofe

Benjn Goodridge Efq^r
Dea^n Benjn Foster
Dea^n Sam^ll Putnam
Leiut Nathan Heywood
Capt: Joshua Hutchens
Dea^n John Heywood
Capt James Reed

} A Com^tee for the purpofes aforefd.

Voted that the Supplying of the Pulpit untill such time as Mr Adams gives his Anfwer be referred to the standing Com^tee (to provide preaching) and Mr Adams

Recorded P^r

THO^s SPARHAWKE
T. Clerk

Isaac Farnsworth Town Clerk
1728 - 1736

Benj: Goodridge Town Cler
1737 - 1739   1741 - 1752
1755 - 1762

Benj᷂ Bellows Jr Town Clark
1740 - 1741.

William Doune Town Clerk
1753 - 1754.

Thoˢ Sparhawk T. Clerk
1762 - 1764.

David Hearns-

Minister of the Town of Lunenburg.
1733 to 1760.

INTENTIONS OF MARRIAGE

INTENTIONS OF MARRIAGE

COPIED FROM THE

RECORDS OF THE TOWN OF LUNENBURG,

FROM 1732 TO 1764.

A.

B. S. L. T.

Purpose of marriage between William Alexander, and Elizabath Bradley enterd August ye 26th 1743.

Purpose of marriage enterd between William Adam of Dunstable and Mary Speer of Lunenburg, April ye 13th 1744.

Intentions of marriage between Daniel Austin Jun and Phebe Lovejoy both of Lunenburg was entered October 9th 1756.

Intentions of marriage betwen Amos Ardeway of Fitchburge and Lidya Thurla of Lunenburg, was entered December 27 1774.

B.

W. R. G. L. H. F.

Porpose of marriage between Jonathan Broadstreet of Lunenburg, and Olive Wheelock of Leominster entered May 16. 1741.

Purpose of marriage between Eliphelet Brown of Coventree and Elizabath Retter of Lunenburg entered August ye 18th 1744.

Pupose of marriage between Franice Buttric and Hannah Gilson entred November ye 10th 1744.

Pupose of marriage entered between Nehemiah Bowers and Sarah Larrabee both of Lunenburg.*

Purpose of marriage entered between Jerahmeel Bowers of Lancaster, and Meriam Houghton of Lunenburg Sept. ye 27th 1745.

Purpose of marriage betwixt Capt Jonathan Bradstreet of Lunenburg and Mrs. Abigail Flecher of Concord was entered September the 17th 1751.

---

*John R. Rollins, transcriber of Lunenburg records, states that the rest is lost, but that the date, no doubt, is 1744. [W. A. D.

B. (cont.)

G. L. L. F. L. B. C. W. G. D. H. G. B. J. A. R. W.

Purpose of marriage betwixt Benoni Boynton Jun, and Elizabeth Going both of Lunenburg was entered September the 28th 1751.

Purpose of marriage betwixt Isaac Bayley of Lunenburg and Mary Lovejoy of Andover was entered October ye 26th 1751.

Purpose of marriage betwixt William Baron of the Ashulot and Isabella Larrabee of Lunenburg was entered June the 4th 1752.

Purpose of marriage betwixt Joseph Brown of Cambridge and Abigail Foster of Lunenburg was entered December 11th 1752.

Purpose of marriage betwixt Stephen Boynton and Elizabeth Lovejoy both of Lunenburg was entered February 7th 1753.

Purpose of marriage between Nathaniel Burnam Junr of Lunenburg and Elizabeth Brown of Lunenburg was entered this (thirteenth) 13th day of July A. D. 1754.

Purpose of marriage between Benjamin Bigelow and Elisabeth Colman both of Lunenburg was entered this 30th day of September A. D. 1754.

Purpose of marriage between William Bemus of Narragansett No. 2 and Rezoma Wilder living on the courntry land was entered May ye 14th 1755.

Purpose of marriage between Jonathan Bennet of Groton, and Mary Going of Lunenburg was entered June ye 12th 1755.

Purpose of marriage betwixt William Brabrook of Lancaster, and Thankful Dutton of Lunenburg, was entered Febuary ye 16th 1757.

Intentions of marriage betwixt Timothy Bancroft & Mary Harriman both of Lunenburg were entered August ye 16th A. D. 1757.

Intentions of marriage betwixt Elisha Bigelo of Narragansett nu··ber two, so called, and Sarah Goodridge of Lunenburg was entered August ye 30th 1757.

Intentions of marriage betwixt Benoni Boynton Jun. of Lunenburg and Mary Buttrick of Leominster was entered December ye 24th A. D. 1757.

Intentions of marriage betwixt Benjamin Bellows Esq. of Wallpole and Mrs. Mary Jenison of Lunenburg was entred February ye 24th A. D. 1758.

Intentions of marriage between Unite Brown of a place called Dorchester Canada and Rebeckah Arno —— of Shrewsbury was entered June ye 30th 1759.

Intentions of marriage betwixt Josiah Bayley and Mary Reed both of Lunenburg was entered March ye 29th 1760.

Intentions of marriage betwixt Kendall Boutwell of Lunenburg & Mary Wilder of Leominster, was entered November ye 26th Annoq Domini 1761.

Intentions of Marriage.

B. (cont.)

F. C. W. H. W. W. M.

Intentions of marriage between James Bennet & Elizabeth Fuller both of Lunenburg was entred May 6th 1762.*

Intentions of marriage between Josiah Bailey Junr and Sarah Carter both of Lunenburg were entred Septr 11th 1762.

Intentions of marriage between Ebenezer Bridge & Mehitable Wood both of Lunenburg was entred April 16th 1763.

Intentions of marriage between Thomas Burns of Monson in the Prov^{ce} of New Hampshire, and Elizabeth Harkness of Lunenburg were entred July 25th 1763.

Intentions of marriage between Joseph Bellows, and Lois Whitney both of Lunenburg was entred April 28th 1764.

Intentions of marriage between John Buss Junr of Fitchburgh and Mary Wood of Lunenburgh was entered May 28th 1766.

Intentions of marriage between Jonathan Boynton Jr of Fitchburg & Sally Martin of Lunenburg entred May 2^d 1796.

C.

F. B. A. H. G. F. H. S. F.

Porpose of marriage between Jacob Cory Junr of Tewksbury and Keziah Foster of Lunenburg entered Sept 5th 1741.

Purpose of marriage between James Colbourn Ju^r and Sarah Braodstreet, both of Lunenburg June ye 1st——.†

Purpose of marriage between Paul Crocker and Lydia Austin both of Lunenburg was entered April the 12th 1750.

Purpose of marriage between Benjamin Corey Junr of Lunenburg and Beulah Holden of Shirley was entered this nineteenth of October Anno Domini 1753.

Intentions of marriage betwixt William Chadwick of Lunenburg and Eunice Goss of Stow was entered September the 16th 1756.

Intentions of marriage between Nathanael Carlton and Olive Farwell both of —— was entered October ye 9th 1756.

Intentions of marriage betwixt William Cowdin of Worcester and Mary Henery of Lunenburg was entered Febuary ye 17th 1757.

Intentions of marriage betwixt Moses Childers and Sarah Stiles both of Lunenburg was entered Janavary ye 18th 1758.

Intentions of marriage betwixt Jesse Carlton of Lunenburg and Sarah Foster of Andover was entered October ye 27th 1759.

---

*J. R. Rollins, transcriber of the Lunenburg records, thinks this was a mistake for 1763. [W. A. D.

†John R. Rollins, transcriber, says this date is, no doubt, 1742. [W. A. D.

C. (cont.)

G. B. L. F. H. F. R. G. F.

Intentions of marriage betwixt James Carter and Sarah Gillson both of Lunenburg were entered October ye 30th 1761.

Intentions of marriage betwixt Asa Carlton & Ruth Bailey both of Lunenburg were entred July 29th 1762.

Intentions of marriage between Robert Crawford of Worcester and Elizabeth Litch of Lunenburg was entred Decr 11th 1762.

Intentions of marriage between William Cambell of Malborough & Catharine Fitch of Lunenburg was entred Decr 14th 1762.

Intentions of marriage between Joseph Chaplain and Lois Hastings both of Lunenburg was entred Decr 10th 1763.

Intentions of marriage between Jona Conant of Dorchester Canada and Eunice Farewell of Shirley District was entred Decr 24th 1763.

Intentions of marriage between Thos. Carter Junr & Priscilla Reed of Lunenburg was entred Decr 29th 1764.

Intentions of marriage between Elijah Carter of Fitchburg & Jane Goodridge of Lunenburg ware enterd September ye 7th 1769.

Intentions of marriage between Thomas Cowdin Junr of Fitchburgh and Mary Farrington of Lunenburg was entered August ye 10th 1774.

D.

B. W. L. F. S. H. P. B. B.

Purpose of marriage between John Darlin Jun and Ruth Boynton both of Lunenburg entered September ye 29th 1744.

Purpose of marriage between Arthur Darrah of Nottingham and Margaret Wallis of Lunenburg entered September the twenty first 1745.

Purpose of marriage entered between Samvel Davis of Lunenburg and Rebekah Lakin of Groton Janvary ye 13th 1746/7

Purpose of marriage entered between Dr John Dunsmore of Lunenburg and Ruth Fisher of Hatfield, Janvary ye 17th 1746/7.

Purpose of marriage entered between John Divol and Susannah Smith both of Lunenburg, February ye 28th 1746/7.

Purpose of marriage between Nicholas Dike and Mary Hastings both of Lunenburg entered June ye 10th 1748.

Purpose of marriage between Richard Day and Ruth Pouchee bouth of Lunenburg was entered November ye 18th 1748.

Purpose of marriage between Timothy Darlin of Lunenburg and Johanna Blood of Groton was entered June the 17th 1752.

Purpose of marriage between Timothy Dorman of Boxford and Eunice Burnam of Lunenburg was entered April the 6th A. D. 1754.

D. (cont.)

S. F. F. S. F. C. W. W. S. S. W. K. W. B. W.

Purpose of marriage between William Dodge of Lunenburg and Elizabeth Salmon of Harvard was entered the 9th day of January A. D. 1755.

Intentions of marriage betwixt Thomas Dutton and Sarah Fitch both of Lunenburg was entered August ye 12th A. D. 1756.

Intentions of marriage betwixt Joseph Davis and Elizabeth Foster both of Lunenburg was entred October ye 22d 1757.

Intentions of marriage betwixt Seth Dodge of Lunenburg and Sarah Smith of Ipswich was entered March ye 18th A. D. 1758.

Intentions of marriage between James Dascomb of Lunenburg and Elizabeth Farrington of Andover was entered May ye 4th 1758.

Intentions of marriage betwixt Josiah Dodge jun now resident in Lunenburg & Hannah Conant of Leominster were entered October ye 24th 1761.

Intentions of marriage between Thomas Dodge & Keziah Willard both of Lunenburg were entred April 24th 1762.

Intentions of marriage between Silas Dutton and Sarah Whitney both of Lunenburg were entred Octor 22d 1762.

Intentions of marriage between Thomas Dodge of Lunenburg & Abigail Smith of Ipswich were entred Novr 19th 1762.

Intentions of marriage between Phinehas Divol and Abigail Stockwell both of Lunenburg was entred May 13th 1763.

Intentions of marriage between Noah Dodge junior and Sarah Wetherbee were entred May 21st 1763.

Intentions of marriage between John Dunsmoor Junr of Lunengh and Mary Kimball of Fitchburgh was entred Augt 6th 1766.

Intentions of marriage between Joseph Downe of Fitchburgh and Martha Wood of Lunenburgh was entered Augt 18th 1768.

Intentions of marriage betwen Oliver Davis of Fitchburg, and Anne Boynton of Lunenburg was entered June 25th 1776.

Intentions of marriage between Solomon Day of Fitchburg & Lucy Whitney of Lunenburg entred December 24th 1796.

E.

P.

Intentions of marriage between John Endecott of Danvers, and Martha Putnam of Lunenburg was enterd Febr 24th 1763.

F.

B. H. K. S. W. R. H. S. P. D. R. G. W. C. C. J. J. W.

Intentions of marriage betwixt Joseph French of Ipswich Canada & Sarah Burns of Concord, was entred March 31st 1732.

Porpose of marriage between Stephen Farnworth of number four, a new Town so called, and Eunice Hastings of Lunenburg entered December the 5th 1741.

Purpose of marriage between Richard Fowler and Ruth Kendel both of Lunenburg entered January 15th.*

Purpose of marriage between Michael Fuller of Upton, and Lois Sattle of Lunenburg, entered October ye 31th 1744.

Purpose of marriage between William Farmer of Lunenburg and Ruth Willard of Harvard, entered November ye 3rd 1744.

Purpose of marriage entered between Isaac Forster and Mary Rice both of Lunenburg, September ye 28th 1745.

Purpose of marriage entered between Robert Fletcher of Lancaster and Elizabeth Houghton of Lunenburg, Janvary ye first 1747/8.

Purpose of marriage between Benjamin Foster jun, and Lucy Stiles both of Lunenburg, was entered, March ye 4th 1748/9.

Purpose of marriage betwixt John Fitch and Elizabeth Parce was entered December ye 18th 1750.

Purpose of marriage between Thomas Farnsworth of Lunenburg and Elizabeth Davis of Littleton was entered this twenty third day of Octor 1753.

Purpose of marriage between Stephen Foster of Lunenburg and Mary Rice of Stratford in the Colony of Connecticut was entered May 7th 1754.

Purpose of marriage between John Fuller and Prudence Gilson was entered September the 4th 1755.

Intentions of marriage betwixt John Farwell of Lunenburg and Susanah White of Townshend was entered November the 22d 1755.

Intentions of marriage between Nehemiah Fuller, and Mary Connant both of Lunenburg was entered, March ye 20th 1756.

Intentions of marriage between Jonas Fletcher of Groton and Johannah Crocker of Lunenburg was entered March ye 9th Annoq. Domini 1759.

Intentions of marriage betwixt Joseph Foster and Sarah Jones both of Lunenburg was entered July ye 20. 1759.

Intentions of marriage betwixt John Fosket jun of Bolton and Abigail Jones of Lunenburg was entered March ye 5th 1761.

Intentions of marriage betwixt Benjamin Foster of Lunenburg and Sarah Whitney of Littleton were entered, October ye 30th 1761.

---

*John R. Rollins says that the year is lost, but that it is, no doubt, 1742. [W. A. D.

F. (cont.)

C. B. H. B. D. S.

Intentions of marriage between Tim⁰ Farley of Fitchburgh and Sarah Colburn of Lunenburgh was entred Septr 14th 1765.

Intentions of marriage between Ezekiel Fowler of Fitchburgh & Dorcas Bradstreet of Lunenburgh was entered Jany 30th 1768.

Intentions of marriage between John Farewell of Fitchburgh and Sarah Hovey were entered Feby 25th 1769.

Intention of marriage betwen Edmond Frost of Lunenburg and Lydia Boynton of Fitchburg was entered December ye 26, 1772

Intentions of marriage between Joseph Farnsworth Juner of Lunenburg & Hannah Danforth of Fitchburg was entred February 16th 1782.

Intentions of marriage between Eben Fullam of Fitchburg & Nabby Stiles of Lunenburg, entered September 3^d 1791.

G.

J. W. B. J. F. S. S. D. W. F. B.

Purpose of marriage between Thomas Gearfie —— of Weston and Rebekah Johnson of Lunenburg entered April the 7th 1742.

Purpose of marriage between William Gilchrest and Elizabath White both of Lunenburg, entered May ye 6. 174—*

Purpose of marriage enter^d between Philip Goodridge and Jane Boynton both of Lunenburg October ye 3rd 17——†

Purpose of marriage between Isaac Gibson and Keziah Johnson both of Lunenburg enter^d Janvary ye 5th 1744/5.

Purpose of marriage entered between Joseph Goodridge and Sarah Foster both of Lunenburg December ye 14th 1745.

Purpose of marriage entered between Reuben Gibson of this town and Lois Smith of Sudbury September ye 11th 1746.

Purpose of marriage betwixt John Grout Jun and Phebe Spafford both of Lunenburg were entered October ye 6th 1750.

Intentions of marriage betwixt Jonas Gilson and Sarah Divol both of Lunenburg was entered December the 6th 1755.

Intentions of marriage between Elijah Grout and Mary Willard both of Lunenburg were entered June ye 29th 1757.

Intentions of marriage betwixt Thomas Gary of Lunenburg and Elizabeth Farewell of Townshend, was entered July ye 20th 1759.

Intentions of marriage betwixt Jonathan Going of Lunenburg and Anne Bennet of Shirley District was entered February ye 22nd 1760.

---

*John R. Rollins states that this date is, no doubt, 1743. [W. A. D.
†John R. Rollins gives this date as probably 1743. [W. A. D.

G. (cont.)

H. W. G. S. F. G. P. B. B.

Intentions of marriage betwixt Silas Gates of Stow, and Anna Hammond of Lunenburg was entered Novr ye 13th 1760.

Intentions of marriage betwixt Ephraim Gibson & Lucy Wyman, both of Lunenburg was entered April ye 23. 1761.

Intentions of marriage between Mr. Francis Gardner of Stow and Mrs. Sarah Gibson of Lunenburg were entred Septr 18th 1762.

Intentions of marriage between Eliphalet Goodridge and Rebekah Snow both of Lunenburg was entred Oct^o 28th 1763.

Intentions of marriage between Benjamin Gould of Rowley Canada in the Province of New Hampshire and Sarah Foster of Lunenburg was entred Jany 14th 1764.

Intentions of marriage between Mr. Jacob Gates of Harvard and Mrs. Elizabeth Gibson of Lunenburg were entred April 5th 1764.

Intentions of marriage between Joseph Gilson of Lunenburgh & Esther Parce of Fitchburgh was entered Feby 20th 1768.

Intention of marriage betwen Silas Gibson of Lunenburg & Damaris Benit of Fitchburg was entered December ye 7th 1772.

Intentions of marrage between Abraham Gibson of Fitchburg & Mary Brown of Lunenburg was entred May ye 30th 1778.

H.

H. A. M. W. T. K. G. D. J.

Porpose of marriage between Jonathan Hammond of Lower Ashulott, and Abigail Hastings of Lunenburg, entered July 10th 1741.

Purpose of marriage enter^d betwixt Joseph Holt of Lunenburg and Mary Abbott of Andover Septr ye 4th 1742.

Purpose of marriage enter^d between William Holt and Mary Martin both of Lunenburg July 14 1744.

Purpose of marriage entered between Amos Hezeltine, and Susanna Willard both of Lunenburg, Janvary ye 6th 1745/6.

Purpose of marriage entered between Mr. Jonathan Hartwell and Mrs. Elizabeth Tarball both of Lunenburg, August ye 5th 1745.

Purpose of marriage entered between Goerge Henery and Elizabeth Kanady both of Lunenburg December ye 14th 1745.

Purpose of marriage entered between Amos Hazeltine and Eunice Gilson both of Lunenburg Jany ye 10th 1746/7.

Purpose of marriage entered between Joseph Hartwell and Tabatha Dodge both of Lunenburg July ye 30th 1747.

Purpose of marriage between John Hubbard and Hannah Johnson both of Lunenburg was entered February, the twenty first 1748/9.

Intentions of Marriage.

H. (cont.)

H. T. F. S. P. G. D. R. H. P. D. F. H. R. P. D. F. C.

Purpose of marriage entered between Daniel Holt of Lunenburg and Mehetable Holt of Andover June ye 11th 1748.

Purpose of marriage between John Henderson of Lancaster and Jane Turner of Lunenburg was entered May ye 4th 1749.

Purpose of marriage between Joseph Holt of Lunenburg and Dorcas Frost of Dunstable *was entered* May ye 20th 1749.

P. of m b. Darius Houghton and Jerusha Stearns both of Lunenburg was entered December ye 8th 1749.

Purpose of marriage between Thomas Henderson, late of Lunenburg and Bethsheba Preist of Stow was entered February the 16th 1750/1.

Purpose of marriage between Joseph Hammond of Lower Ashulott and Esther Gould of Lunenburg was entered August ye 14th 1752.

Purpose of marriage betwixt Gershom Hubbard of Dunstable and Lipha Dodge of Lunenburg was entered December ye 20th 1752.

Purpose of marriage between Thomas Heywood of Lunenburg and Elizabeth Richardson of Lancaster, was entered this 23d day of March A. D. 1753.

Purpose of marriage between William Henery Junr and Mary Harper both of Lunenburg was entered this second day of October Anno Domini 1753.

Purpose of marriage between Phinehas Hartwell and Mary Peirce both of Lunenburg was entered this eighth day of November A. D. 1754.

Purpose of marriage between Henry Hogskins & Mary Dutton both of Lunenburg was entered April 19th 1755.

Purpose of marriage between Zimri Heywood of Dorchester Cannada (was entered) and Jane Foster of sd Dorchester Cannada was entered Sept ye 6th 1755.

Intentions of marriage betwixt Joseph Hartwell of Lunenburg and Phebe Hart of Readen was entered Janavary ye 14 A. D. 1757.

Intentions of marriage betwixt Samuel Hogskins and Rebeckah Rice both of Lunenburg were entred July ye 16th A. D. 1757.

Intentions of marriage betwixt Ebenezer Hart and Sarah Poole both of Lunenburg was entered Janavary ye 6th A. D. 1758.

Intentions of marriage betwixt Thaddeus Harrington of Shirley and Thankful Dodge of Lunenburg was entered March ye 18th 1758.

Intentions of marriage betwixt Samuel Hart and Mary Fuller both of Lunenburg was entered April ye 1st 1758.

Intentions of marriage between Daniel Harper and Rachael Colman both of Dorchester Canada so called was entered August ye 4th A. D. 1758.

H. (cont.)

H. W. I. B. R. S. H. B. L. H. S. F.

Intentions of marriage betwixt George Huet of Rowley Canada so called and Triphene Hodgskins of Lunenburg was entered April 26th 1760.

Intentions of marriage betwixt John Heywood of Lunenburg and Silence White of Lancaster was entered December ye 12th 1760.

Intentions of marriage betwixt Abijah Hovey of Lunenburg & Lydia Inggols of Andover was entered Octr ye 9th 1761.

Intentions of marriage between Henry Hodgskins of Ipswich Canada and Jemima Ball of Princetown were entred Octr 9th 1762.

Intentions of marriage between Phinehas Hutchens & Abigail Reed both of Lunenburg was entred Octo 22d 1763.

Intentions of marriage between Samuel Hilton and Rebekah Stickney both of Lunenburg was entred Octo 22d 1763.

Intentions of marriage betwixt Eleazar Houghton Jur and Susannah Holman both of Lunenburg was entred Octo 28th 1763.

Intentions of marriage between Aaron Hodgskins and Eunice Bigsbee both of Ipswich Canada was entred Decr 18th 1763.

Intentions of marriage between Saml Hazen junr of Stow & Elizabeth Little of Shirley was entred Augt 26th 1764.

Intentions of marriage between William Holt of Fitchburg & Bettey Hutchinson of Lunenburg was entred April 22d 1782.

Intentions of marriage between Samuel Hutchinson of Fitchburg & Charlotte Stiles of Lunenburg was entred June 30th 1783.

Intentions of marriage between John Hartwell of Lunenburg & Polly Farwell of Fitchburg was entred April 24th 1792.

I.

B.

Intentions of marriage betwixt Abraham Ireland & Marabah Boynton both of Lunenburg was entered Febr ye 13th 1761.

J.

W. B. P.

Purpose of marriage between James Johnson of Lunenburg and Susannah Willard of Harvard entered May ye 30th 1747.

Intentions of marriage betwixt Abner Jackman and Elizabeth Bayley both of Lunenburg was entered October ye 2nd 1756.

Intentions of marriage between Ezekiel Jewet and ——— Plats both of a place called Rowley Canada May ye ——— [Probably 1759.— J. R. Rollins.]

J. (cont.)

G. S.

Intentions of marriage between William Judevine and Patience Grout both of Lunenburg was entered June —— 1759.

Intentions of marriage betwixt William Jones of Luneng and Sarah Stone of Groton were entred July 29th 1762.

K.

W. P. M. P. S. F. H. M.

Purpose of marriage entered between Ephraim Kimball and Mary Wetherbe both of Lunenburg July the 18th 1746.

Purpose of marriage entered between Uzziah Kendel of Leominster and Elizabeth Parce jun. of Lunenburg April ye second 1748.

———— between George Kimball of Lunenburg and Sarah Mullickin of Bradford was entered Oct ye 1th 1748.

———— Samuel Kennedy and Sarah Page both of Lunenburg —— June ye 29th 1749.

Purpose of marriage betwixt Richard Kimball jun of Boxford and Elizabeth Sectown of Lunenburg was entered December ye 28th 1750.

Intentions of marriage betwixt William Kimball and Jane Farewell both of Lunenburg was entered February ye 23d 1760.

Intentions of marriage betwixt Benjamin Kidder of Billrica & Ruth Heywood of Lunenburg was entred January ye 6th 1761.

Intentions of marriage between William Kilburn Junr of Lunenburg & Polly Mace of Fitchburg was entred Novr 14th 1795.

L.

W. W. P. K. W. C.

Puposeof marriage entered between Samvel Larrabee of Lunenburg and Anne Williams of Groton March ye 3rd 1745/6.

Purpose of marriage between William Little of Lunenburg and Elizabeth Wallis of Worcester was entered November ye 4th 1748.

———— John Lovejoy and Sarah Parce both of Lunenburg ———— December ye 8th 1749.

Purpose of marriage between Thomas Leitch & Jane Kannady both of Lunenburg were entered August ye 20, 1750.

Purpose of marriage betwixt Benjamin Larrabee of Lunenburg and Margarett Williams of Groton was entered August ye 15th 1752.

Intentions of marriage betwixt Samuel Larrabee and Johannah Crocker both of Lunenburg was entered September ye 18th 1758.

L. (cont.)

S. S. F. E. P.

Intentions of marriage between Samuel Larribee of Lunenburg and Mary Simonds of Shirley was entered November annoq Domini 1758.

Intentions of marriage between Nehemiah Lane of Lunenburg and Sarah Shaddock of Pepperell was entered February ye 6th Anno Domini 1759.

Intentions of marriage betwixt Nehemiah Lane of Lunenburg and Sarah Fletcher of Groton was entered March ye 3^d 1760.

Intentions of marriage betwixt John Larrabee of Lunenburg & Abiah Erven of Shurley was entered May ye 12th 1760.

Intentions of marriage betwixt William Larkin of Lunenburg and Hannah Parce of Groton was entered March ye 21th 1761.

M.

H. S. H. F. T. P. K. W. P. H.

Purpose of marriage entered between Robert Mitcheal of Lunenburg and Alice Harice of Lancaster March ye 10th 1743/4.

Pupose of marriage entered between Hugh Moors, and*

Purpose of marriage entered between John Marsh of Notthingham and Martha Seaverans of Lunenburg April ye 20th 1748.

Purpose of marriage between Thomas Matthews and Elizabeth Heborn both of Lunenburg was entered December ye 21th 1748.

Purpose of marriage betwixt William Moors of Lunenburg and Elizabeth Foster of Dorchester Cannada so called was entered December ye 10th 1751.

Purpose of marriage betwixt George Mc ferlin of Lunenburg and Margarett Terrance of Lancaster was entered March ye 7th 1752.

Purpose of marriage between Joseph Moffett of Ipswich Canady so called, and Dorithy Priest of Stow was entered this 23^d day of June A. D. 1753.

Purpose of marriage between William Machan jun^r of Worcester and Mary Kennedy of Lunenburg was entered this seventeenth day of September A. D. 1753.

Intention of marriage betwixt John Moors jun of Bolton and Unity Willard of Lunenburg were entered July ye 13th A. D. 1757.

Intentions of marriage betwixt Jonathan Messer of Lunenburg and Abigail Parker of Groton was entered October ye 13th 1759.

Intentions of marriage betwixt John Moffat of a place called Ipswich Canada, and Hannah Hodgskins of Lunenburg was entered January ye 5th 1760.

---

*John R. Rollins says the remainder is lost. [W. A. D.

M. (cont.)

C. C.

Intentions of marriage betwixt John Martin and Betty Chaplin both of Lunenburg was entered Febry ye 14th 1761.

Intention of marriage between Saml McCraken of Worcester & Lettice Carlifle of Lunenburg was entred Octor 29th 1762.

N.

B. W.

Intentions of marriage between Page Norcross and Elizabeth Bailey both of Lunenburg ware entred Septr 11th 1762.

Intentions of marriage between Hananiah Newton of Lunenburg & Chloe Wood of Fitchburg was entred July 8th 1785

O.

F. T. F.

Intentions of marriage between Ephraim Osbourn and Sarah Fisk both of Lunenburg was entered July ye 20th 1759

Intentions of marriage betwen Amos Ardeway of Fitchburge and Lydya Thurla of Lunenburg was entered December 27 1774.*

Intentions of marriage between Jacob Osburn of Lunenburg & Sibel Farwel of Fitchburg, entred September 14th 1786.

P.

H. D. D. N. R. P.

Purpose of marriage between Daniel Page of Lunenburg, and Ruth Haskell of Harvard entered October the 13th 1744.

Purpose of marriage entered between Jonathan Parce, and Sarah Dodge both of Lunenburg Janvary ye 19th 1745/6.

Purpose of marriage entered, between Amos Phillips of Dunstable and Abigail Dodge of Lunenburg February ye 8th 1745/6.

Purpose of marriage entered between William Porter and Mary Nickalls both of Lunenburg March ye 7th 1745/6.

Purpose of marriage entered between David Parce jun and Anne Retter both of Lunenburg April ye 5th 1746.

Purpose of marriage between Mr. Samvel Page of Lunenburg and Mrs. Sarah Peirce of Leominster June ye 20th 1747

---

*John R. Rollins says this was probably intended for Ordway. See letter A. [W. A. D.

P. (cont.)

G. J. P. W. B. H. P. P. W. N. B. S. S. M. R. F. H. H.

Purpose of marriage entered between Timothy Parker and Johannah Grout both of Lunenburg May ye 21st 1748.

Purpose of marriage betwixt Thomas Prentice Esq of Lunenburg and Madam Borredell Jackson of Newton was entered May the 25th 1751.

Purpose of marriage betwixt Joseph Platts of Rowley Canada and Deborah Page of Lunenburg was entered, September ye 30th 1752.

Purpose of marriage between Thomas Putnam of Charlestown in the Province of New Hampshire & Rachel Wetherbee of Lunenburg was entered January 5th A. D. 1754.

Purpose of marriage Jonathan Parker of Boston and Martha Brown of Lunenburg was entered this 8th day of Aug^st A. D. 1754.

Purpose of marriage between Thomas Page of Lunenburg and Dorothy Houghton of Leominister, was entered September ye 18th 1755.

Intentions of marriage betwixt Samuel Poole and Sarah Potter both of Lunenburg was entered November ye 19th 1756.

Porpose of marriage betwixt Nathan Pouchee of Ipswich Canada so called and Elizabeth Preist of Stow, was entered December ye 18th 1756.

Intentions of marriage between Abel Plats jun of a place called Rowley Canada, and Phebe Wetherbee of Lunenburg was entered March ye 7th A. D. 1759.

Intentions of marriage betwixt Ephraim Parce and Sarah Norcross both of Lunenburg was entered August ye 11th 1759.

Intentions of marriage betwixt Joseph Platts of Rowley Canada, and Sarah Bowers of Lunenburg, was entered September ye 12th 1760.

Intentions of marriage betwixt Samuel Parce and Mary Steward both of Lunenburg was entered November the 27th 1760.

Intentions of marriage betwixt Ebenezer Prat of Lunenburg and Lydia Stone of Groton were entered Sept ye 1th 1761.

Intentions of marriage betwixt David Poor of Ipswich Canada and Jane Martin of Lunenburg wer entered October ye 30th 1761.

Intentions of marriage between Bertholomew Pearson of Ipswich Canada and Lydia Randal of Lunenburg was enterd Septr 24th 1763.

Intentions of marriage between Joshua Pearce of Lunenburg and Molley Foss of Fitchburg ware enter^d October ye 14th 1769.

Intentions of marriage between James Paterson of Fitchburg & Miriam Hovey of Lunenburg was entered May ye 1. 1778.

Intentions of marriage between Amos Putnam of Fitchburg & Lydia Hovey of Lunenburg was entred May 2^d 1781.

Intentions of Marriage.

R.

S. W. H. M. H. S. M. M. B. M.

Porpose of marriage between Benjamin Randal and Lydia Stevens both of Lunenburg, entered Octo' 31th 1741.

Purpose of marriage entered between Amos Robbinson of Lunenburg and Lydia Wintworth of Topsfield, October ye 29 1743.

Purpose of marriage entered between John Russel of Lunenburg, and Thankfull Harris of Lancaster, March ye 4th 1744/5.

Purpose of marriage entered between George Russell, and Jane Mitchel both of Lunenburg March ye 29th 1746.

Intentions of marriage between Daniel Rugg of Lancaster, and Sarah Hastings of Lunenburg was entered April the 6th 1756.

Intentions of marriage betwixt Benjamin Reddington, and Ruth Stearns both of Lunenburg was entered November ye 17th 1756.

Intentions of marriage betwixt John Richards and Elizabeth Mitchael both of Lunenburg was entred Janvary 1th (A. D.) 1757.

Intentions of marriage betwixt Samuel Rufsel and Susannah Mitchael both of Lunenburg was entred April ye 30th A. D. 1757

Intentions of marriage betwixt Isaac Redington of Lunenburg, and Ruth Bodwell of Methuen, was entered November ye 30th Anno Domini 1759.

Intentions of marriage betwixt Mitchael Richards of Shirley and Esther Mitchael of Lunenburg was entered February ye 24th 1761.

S.

L. J. D. W. T. H. P.

Purpose of marriage entered betwixt John Sharer of Kingstown so called and Jane Little of Lunenburg December ye 15 174——*

Purpose of marriage entered between William Stearns and Elizabeth Johnson both of Lunenburg December ye 21th 1745.

Purpose of marriage entered between Hezekiah Sattle of Groton and Margaret Dodge of Lunenburg, Janvary ye 30th 1746/7

Purpose of marriage entered between Gustavus Swan of Lunenburg and Isabella Will of Townfhend October ye 2nd 1747.

Purpose of marriage betwixt Benjamin Steward and Rebeckah Taylor both of Lunenburg was entered September ye (13th) thirteenth 1751.

Purpose of marriage betwixt Abijah Stearns, and Sarah Heywood both of Lunenburg was entered Sept the 28th 1751.

Purpose of marriage betwixt Bradstreet Spafford of No. 4 and Mary Page of Lunenburg was entered September ye 30 1752.

---

*John R. Rollins says this date is, no doubt, 1742. [W. A. D.

S. (cont.)

L. H. T. H. F. T. P. I. S. F. B. I. M. D. I. S. P. H.

Purpose of marriage betwixt David Steel of Londondery and Jenet Little of Lunenburg was entered December ye 22d 1752.

Purpose of marriage between John Smith of Petersborough and Mary Harkneſs of Lunenburg was entered this 11th day of August A. D. 1753.

Purpose of marriage between Benjamin Stearns and Anna Taylor both of Lunenburg was entered this twentieth day of October, Anno Domini 1753.

Purpose of marriage between Moses Stearns of Narragansett No. 2. and Ruth Houghton of Lunenburg was entered February 4th A. D. 1754.

Purpose of marriage between Jonas Spafford and Dorcas Frost both of Lunenburg was entered this 19th day of October A. D. 1754.

Purpose of marriage between Solomon Steward Junr and Elizabeth Taylor both of Lunenburg was entered this third day of Febry Anno Domini 1755.

Purpose of marriage between John Simonds & Mercy Page both of Lunenburg was entered Febry 19th 1755.

Purpose of marriage between Phinehas Steward and Anne Ireland, both of Lunenburg, was entered July the 25th 1755.

Intentions of marriage betwixt Levi Stiles and Patience Smith both of Lunenburg was entered October the 25 1755.

Intentions of marriage betwixt Alexander Swan, and Lucy Foster both of Lunenburg was entered Feburary ye 11th 1756.

Intentions of marriage betwixt Benjamin Shed of Lunenburg and Elizabeth Blower of Lancaster was entered June ye 15th 1756.

Intentions of marriage betwixt Daniel Steward and Mary Ireland was entered October ye 16th 1756.

Intentions of marriage betwixt Joseph Spafford of Lunenburg and Mary Marble of Stow was entered Febuary ye 11th 1757.

Intentions of marriage betwixt Jonas Stearns and Submit Davis both of Lunenburg was entered April ye 15th 1758.

Intentions of marriage betwixt William Steward and Abigail Ireland both of Lunenburg was entered May ye 16th 1758.

Intentions of marriage between Thomas Sparhawk and Rebeckah Stearns both of Lunenburg, was entered June ye 24th Annoque Domini 1758.

Intentions of marriage betwixt Jonathan Stevens of Lunenburg and Elizabeth Parker of Pepperel was entered March ye 2nd 1761.

Intentions of marriage betwixt Jonathan Stedman of Westminster District, and Tabatha Hart of Lunenburg, was entered July ye 25th 1761.

S. (cont.)

P. P. B. A. L. S. P. M. W. B. A.

Intentions of marriage between Reuben Smith and Prudence Parce both of Lunenburg were entred Augt 20th 1762.

Intentions of marriage between Thomas Sweetland & Abigail Pushee both of Ipswich Canada were entred Novr 1st 1762.

Intentions of marriage between Solomon Shed of Lunenburg and Elizabeth Boynton of s^d Town ware entred March 11th 1763.

Intentions of marriage between Abraham Smith of Lunenburg & Lucy Allen of Weston was entred June 29th 1763.

Intentions of marriage between David Stearns and Mary Low both of Lunenburg was entred July 10th 1763.

Intentions of marriage between the Rev^d Mr. Ebenezer Sparhawk of Templetown & Mrs. Abigail Stearns of Lunenburg was entred July 19th 1763.

Intentions of marriage between Jacob Steward of Fitchburgh and Elizath Parce of Lunenburg was entred May 29th 1766

Intentions of marriage between Joseph Symonds of Fitchburgh & Mary Martin of Lunenburgh was entered Octo^r 17th 1767.

Intentions of marriage between Edmond Stone of Fitchburg and Susanna Whitney of Lunenburgh was enter^d April 8th 1768.

Intentions of marriage by William Small of Fitchburg & Mary Bigelow of Lunenburg was entered Janu^y ye 23^d 1777.

Intentions of marriage between Doct. Peter Snow of Fitchburg and Mrs. Betsey Adams of Lunenburg was entred October 2^d 1789.

T.

H. S. G. G.

Purpose of marriage between David Taylor of Lunenburg and Bette Houghton of Lancaster were entred September ye 8th 1750.

Purpose of marriage between Caleb Taylor of Lunenburg and Susannah Shadock of Littleton was entered October ye 6th 1750.

Purpose of marriage betwixt Aaron Taylor and Mercy Gould both of Lunenburg was entered May the 30th 1752.

Purpose of marriage betwixt Zechariah Tarball and Mary Gould both of Lunenburg was entered February ye 22^d 1753.

U.

S.

Intentions of marriage between Oliver Upton of Fitchburg & Susanna Stiles of Lunenburg was entred November ye 8th 1777.

W.

W. W. B. H. G. B. P. B. P. R. M. P. S. W. H. H. W. B. M.

Porpose of marriage between Joseph Wood and Ruth Wetherbee, entered July 4th 1741. both of Lunenburg.

Purpose of marriage between Patrick White of Lunenburg and Jane White of Chesher entered December the 24th 1741.

Purpose of marriage enterd between Jonathan Willard jun of Lunenburg and Phebe Ballard of Concord, September ye 17th 1743.

Purpose of marriage entered between David Wood of Lunenburg, and Mary Hovey of Boxford Janvary ye 3rd 1745/6.

Purpose of marriage entred between Obediah Walker of Lunenburg and Abbigaill Gary of Lynn August the 16th 1745.

Purpose of marriage entered, between Daniel Willard of Lancaster, and Lucy Butler of Lunenburg, September the 10th 1745.

Purpose of marriage entered between Michael Wood and Mary Platts both of this town November ye first A. D. 1745.

Purpose of marriage entered between Ephraim Whitney, and Jane Bancroft both of Lunenburg December ye 27th 1745.

Purpose of marriage entered between Paul Wetherbee and Hannah Parce both of Lunenburg May ye 10th 1746.

Purpose of marriage entered between Jacob Waren of Lunenburg and Melther Russell of Littleton June ye 21th 1746.

Purpose of marriage betwixt Archebald White of the place called New-Ipswich, and Margaret Mc'Clary of Lunenburg was entered November the third 1750.

Purpose of marriage betwixt Joseph Wheelock jun of Lancaster and Allice Page of Lunenburg was entered September ye 14th 1751.

Purpose of marriage betwixt Joseph Wood of Lunenburg and Ruth Simons of Littleton was entered September ye 16th 1752.

Purpose of marriage betwixt John White and Mary Whitney both of Lunenburg was entered November ye 10th 1752.

Purpose of marriage betwixt Abner Whitney of Shirley, and Sarah Hilton of Lunenburg was entered this 23d day of March A. D. 1753.

Purpose of marriage between Josh Wilder Tertius of Lancaster and Elizabeth Heywood of Lunenburg was entered this 18th day of May A. D. 1754.

Purpose of marriage between Jonathan Wood junr of Lunenburg, and Rachel Wood of Uxbridge was entered this 10th of September A. D. 1754.

Purpose of marriage between Benoni Wallis of Lunenburg and Rebecah Brown of Lyn was entered Febry 19th 1755.

Purpose of marriage between Benjamin Wetherbee of Lunenburg and Keziah Munroe of Carlile was entered September the 24th 1755.

Intentions of Marriage.

W. (cont.)

F. M. G. R. F. B. B. W. T. S. H. H. W. L.

Intentions of marriage between Thomas Wheeler, and Abigail Foster, both of Dorchester Canada was entered January 29th 1756.

Intentions of marriage betwixt Thomas Wetherbe of Lunenburg and Hannah Munroe of Carlile was entered April ye 22d 1756.

Intentions of marriage betwixt Jonathan Wood and Sarah Gary both of Lunenburg were entered March ye 30th 1757.

Intentions of marriage betwixt Berzillai Willard and Hepsibeth Reddington both of Lunenburg, was entered September ye 10th 1757.

Intentions of marriage betwixt Winkcal Right of Dunstable, and Sibel Farewell of Lunenburg was entered February ye 25th A. D. 1758.*

Intentions of marriage betwixt Abner Whelock of Leominster and Mary Brown of Lunenburg, was entered March ye 11th 1758.

Intentions of marriage betwixt Reuben Wyman & Elizabeth Bancroft both of Lunenburg was entered January ye 15th 1761.

Intentions of marriage between Michal Wood of Lunenburgh & Lois Wilson of Leominster was entred July 28th 1764.

Intentions of marriage between John Wood of Lunenburgh & Sarah Thurston of Fitchburg was entered July 27th 1767.

Intentions of marriage between Israel Wyman of Lunenburg & Mary Stratton of Fitchburg ware enterd Ocber ye 7th 1769.

Intentions of marriage between Paul Wetherbee of Fitchburg, and Dorcas Hovey of Lunenburg was entered October ye 14th 17——.†

Intentions of marriage between Joseph Wyman of Lunenburg and Hannah Hilton of Fitchburg was entered December ye 28th 1776.

Intentions of marriage between James Wood of Fitchburg & Sarah Walker of Lunenburg was entred May 13th 1780.

Intentions of marriage between Seth Wyman of Lunenburg & Sarah Littlefield of Fitchburg was entred February 16th 1782.

NOTE.

"Dorchester Canada" is what is now known as Ashburnham.
"Narragansett No. 2" is what is now known as Westminster.
"Upper Ashuelott" is what is now known as Keene, N. H.

---

*J. R. Rollins says this name was probably intended for Wright. [W. A. D.
†John R. Rollins gives this date as, no doubt, 1774. [W. A. D.

MARRIAGES

MARRIAGES

COPIED FROM THE

RECORDS OF THE TOWN OF LUNENBURG,

FROM 1727 TO 1764.

A.
S.

William Adams of Dunstable and Mary Speer of Lunenburg were married May 31th 1744 by the Revd Mr. David Stearns minister of Lunenburg.

B.
S. J. W. G. L. R. H.

Benjamin Bellows junr and Abigail Stearns both of Lunenburg were married by ye Rev. Mr. David Stearns, minister of Lunenburg October ye 7th 1735.

Stephen Boynton and Sarah Johnson both of Lunenburg ware married November ye 14th 1737 by the Revnd Mr. David Stearns.

Jonathan Broadstreet of Lunenburg and Olive Wheellock of Leominster were married July the second 1741 by Mr. David Stearns minister of Lunenburg.

Francis Buttrick of Lancaster, and Hannah Gilson of Lunenburg were married by ye Rev Mr. David Stearns minister of Lunenburg December ye 4th 1744.

Nehemiah Bowers and Sarah Larrabee both of Lunenburg were married March ye 18th 1744/5 by ye Rev. Mr David Stearns minister of Lunenburg.

Eliphelet Brown of Coventree and Elizabeth Retter of Lunenburg were married June ye 13th 1745 by ye Rev Mr David Stearns, minister of Lunenburg.

Jerahmeel Bowers of Lancaster, and Miriam Houghton of Lunenburg were married March ye 19th 1745/6 by the Rev Mr David Stearns, minister of Lunenburg.

B. (cont.)

G. L. F. L. B. C. K. G. D. H. G. J. J. R. C. F.

Benoni Boynton Jun and Elizabeth Going both of Lunenburg were married March ye 24th 1752 by ye Rev Mr David Stearns, minister of Lunenburg.

William Barron of Upper Ashuelot ("so called,,) and Isabella Larrabee of Lunenburg were married September 28th 1752 by the Rev Mr. David Stearns minister of Lunenburg.

Joseph Brown of Cambridge and Abigail Foster of Lunenburg were married January 18th 1753 by the Rev Mr David Stearns minister of Lunenburg.

Stephen Boynton and Elizabeth Lovejoy both of Lunenburg were married March 6th 1753, by the Revd Mr David Stearns minister of Lunenburg.

Nathaniel Burnam Junr & Elizabeth Brown, both of Lunenburg were married July 29th 1754 by the Rev Mr David Stearns minister of Lunenburg

Benjamin Bigelow and Elizabeth Colman both of Lunenburg were married Octor 31st 1754 by Rev. Mr Stearns.

Joseph Beman and Hannah Knight both of Lancaster were married July the 23rd 1755 by Edward Hartwell Justice of the Peace.

Jonathan Bennett of Groton and Mary Going of Lunenburg were married October ye 15th 1755 by the Rev Mr David Stearns minister of Lunenburg.

William Barbrook of Lancaster and Thankful Dutton of Lunenburg were married together March ye 24 1757 by William Downe Justice of the peace.

Timothy Bancroft & Mary Harriman both of Lunenburg were married Novm ye 1st A. D. 1757 by William Downe Justice of pacis.

Elisha Bigelow of Narragansett No 2. and Sarah Goodridge of Lunenburg were married Decm ye 1st 1757 by the Rev Mr. David Stearns minister of Lunenburg.

Benjamin Bellows Esqr of Wallpole in the Province of New Hampshire and Mrs Mary Jenisson of Lunenburg were married April ye 21st 1758 by the Rev Mr David Stearns minister of Lunenburg.

Caleb Ball and Elizabeth Joyner both of a place called Narragansett No 2 were married December ye 4th 1758, by Edward Hartwell Justice of the peace.

Josiah Bailey & Mary Reed both of Lunenburg were married April 15th 1760 by ye Rev Mr. David Stearns minister of Lunenburg.

Josiah Bailey Junr & Sarah Carter both of Lunenburg were married by Edward Hartwell Justice of the peace Octor 7th 1762.

James Bennet and Elizabeth Fuller both of Lunenburg were married by Edward Hartwell Esqr Septr 6th 1763.

Marriages.

B. (cont.)
W. W.

Ebenezer Bridge and Mehetable Wood both of Lunenburg were married by Edward Hartwell Esqr Novr 3^d 1763.

Joseph Bellows & Lowis Whitney both of Lunenburg were married by the Rev^d Mr Adams Octo^r 3^d 1764.

C.
R. B. A. H. F. H. F. S. W. G. B. H.

Mr. Robart Clark and Mrs. Mary Reed both of Lunenburg ware married by ye Rev^d Mr. David Stearns minister of Lunenburg July the 31th 1738.

James Colburn and Sarah Bradstreet were married August ye 12th 1742 by the Rev Mr David Stearns minister of Lunenburg.

Paul Crocker and Lydia Austin both of Lunenburg, were married June the 4th 1750 by Thomas Prentice Justice of the peace.

Benj^a Corey Junr of Lunenburg & Beulah Holden of Shirley were married Decr 26th 1753 by the Rev^d Mr David Stearns, minister of Lunenburg.

Nathaniel Carlton jun and Olive Farewell both of Lunenburg were married November ye 1 1756 by the Rev^d Mr David Stearns minister of Lunenburg.

William Cowdin of Worcester and Mary Henry of Lunenburg were married September ye 7th 1757 by Edward Hartwell Justice of the peace.

James Clark and Anne Freeman both of Lancaster were married January ye 5th 1758 by Edward Hartwell Justice of pea——

Moses Child and Sarah Stiles both of Lunenburg were married March ye 28th 1758 by the Rev Mr David Stearns minister of Lunenburg.

Elias Carter & Deborah White both of Leominster were married March ye 12th 1761 by Edward Hartwell Justice of ye peace.

James Carter and Sarah Gilson both of Lunenburg were married by Edward Hartwell Justice of ye peace, December 3^d 1761.

Asa Carlton & Ruth Bailey both of Lunenburg were, married Feby 8th 1763 by the Rev^d Mr Samuel Payson.

Joseph Chaplain & Lois Hastings both of Lunenburg, were married by Edward Hartwell Esqr April 5th 1764.

D.

B. B. W. S. H. P. B. B. S. F. F. C. W. S.

Jacob Davis of Concord and Anne Boynton of Lunenburg were married by ye Revd Mr. David Stearns minister of Lunenburg on ye 19 day of April 1733.

John Darlin & Ruth Boynton both of Lunenburg were married October the 13th 1744 by the Rev Mr. David Stearns minister of Lunenburg.

Authur Darrah of Nothingham and Margaret Wallis of Lunenburg were married December ye 11th 1745 by ye Rev Mr David Stearns minister of Lunenburg.

John Divol and Susannah Smith both of Lunenburg were married March the 31th 1747 by the Rev Mr David Stearns minister of Lunenburg.

Nicholas Dike and Mary Hastings both of Lunenburg were married July ye 20th 1748 by Thomas Prentice, Justice of ye peace.

Richard Day and Ruth Pouchee both of Lunenburg were married by the Rev Mr. David Stearns minister of Lunenburg December ye 8th 1748.

Timothy Darling of Lunenburg and Joanna Blood of Groton were married Febry 8th 1753 by the Revd Mr. David Stearns, minister of Lunenburg.

Timothy Dorman of Boxford, and Eunice Burnam of Lunenburg were married May 27th 1754 by the Revd Mr. David Stearns minister of Lunenburg.

William Dodge of Lunenburg and Elizabeth Salmon of Harvard were married Janvary ye 28th 1755 by the Rev Mr David Stearns minister of Lunenburg.

Thomas Dutton and Sarah Fitch both of Lunenburg were married together September ye 9th 1756 by the Rev Mr David Stearns minister of Lunenburg.

Joseph Davis & Elizabeth Foster both of Lunenburg were married Novm ye 8th A. D. 1757 by William Downe Justice of peace.

Josiah Dodge Junr resident in Lunenburg & Hannah Conant of Leominster were married by Edward Hartwell Justice of the peace November 8th 1761.

Silas Dutton and Sarah Whitney both of Lunenburg were married by Benjn Goodridge Esqr March 3d 1763.

Phinehas Divol & Abigail Stockwell both of Lunenburg were married by Benjn Goodridge Esq June 6th 1763.

F.
H.

David Farnsworth and Hannah Hastings both of Lunenburg were married by ye Revd Mr. David Stearns, minister of Lunenburg August ye 15th 1735.

Marriages.

F. (*cont.*)

E. B. F. H. H. K. S. R. S. P. G. C. J.

Andrew Fleming of Lunenburg and Ann Ellit of Dunstable were married by ye Rev^d Mr David Stearns, minister of Lunenburg November ye 5th 1735.

Thomas Frost of Billerica and Dorcas Boynton of Lunenburg were married by the Rev^d Mr. Stearns June ye 6th 1737.

Jonathan Fisk and Jemima Foster both of Lunenburg ware married July the 28th 1738 by the Rev^d Mr. David Stearns.

Oliver Farewell of Dunstable and Abigail Hubbard of Lunenburg ware married by ye Rev^d Mr. David Stearns minister of Lunenburg December the 25th 1738.

Stephen Farnworth of (number four, so called) and Eunice Hastings of Lunenburg were married by Mr David Stearns, minister of Lunenburg December the 22^d 1741.

Richard Fowler and Ruth Kendell both of Lunenburg were married March the 17th 1741/2 by Mr. David Stearns minister of Lunenburg.

Micah Fuller of Upton and Lois Sattle of Lunenburg were married November ye 21th 1744 by ye Rev Mr. David Stearns minister of Lunenburg.

Isaac Foster & Mary Rice both of Lunenburg were married December ye 2nd 1745 by ye Rev Mr David Stearns minister of Lunenburg.

Benjamin Foster Jun and Lucy Stiles both of Lunenburg were married March ye 24th 1748/9 by the Rev Mr David Stearns minister of Lunenburg.

John Fitch and Elizabeth Parce both of Lunenburg, February the fourteenth 1750/1 by Thomas Prentice Justice of the peace.

John Fuller and Prudence Gilson both of Lunenburg were married December the 18th 1755 by the Rev Mr David Stearns minister of Lunenburg.

Nehemiah Fuller and Mary Connant both of Lunenburg were married May ye 4th 1756 by the Rev Mr. David Stearns minister of Lunenburg.

Joseph Foster & Sarah Jones both of Lunenburg were married January ye 17th 1760 by the Rev. Mr David Stearns minister of Lunenburg.

G.

B. B.

Mr. John Grout and Johannah Boynton married November ye 23th 1727.

Moses Gould and Mary Bellows married Novr 7th 1728.

G. (cont.)

G. H. S. P. W. J. W. B. J. F. S. D. W. S. F.

Mr. Jacob Gould of Lunenburg were married to Mrs. Dorothy Goodridge of Lunenburg by ye Revnd Mr. Andrew Gardner minister of Lunenburg Feb^r 4 1730/1.

John Gibson and Elizabeth Hartwell both of Lunenburg were married by Edward Hartwell Esqr on ye 9th of November 1737.

Joshua Goodridge and Lydia Stearns both of Lunenburg ware married by the Rev^d Mr. David Stearns minister of Lunenburg June the 25th 1739.

Benjamin Gould and Esther Pearce both of Lunenburg was married by the Revnd Mr David Stearns minister of Lunenburg October the 17th 1739.

William Grimes of Winchester and Mary White of Lunenburg were married by the Revnd Mr. David Stearns minister of Lunenburg September the 9th 1740.

Thomas Gearfield of Weston and Rebekah Johnson of Lunenburg were married October ye 21th 1742 by the Rev Mr David Stearns minister of Lunenburg.

William Gillchrest and Elizabeth White both of Lunenburg were married June ye 21th 1743 by the Rev. Mr David Stearns minister of Lunenburg.

Philip Goodridge and Jane Boynton both of Lunenburg were married November ye 3th 1743 by the Rev^d Mr. David Stearns minister of Lunenburg.

Isaac Gibson and Keziah Johnson both of Lunenburg were married Feb^{ry} ye 4th 1744/5 by the Rev Mr. David Stearns minister of Lunenburg.

Joseph Goodridge and Sarah Forster both of Lunenburg were married Janvary ye 30th 1745/6 by ye Rev Mr. David Stearns minister of Lunenburg.

John Grout Jun and Phebe Spafford both of Lunenburg were married October ye 22nd 1750 by ye Rev Mr. David Stearns minister of Lunenburg.

Jonas Gilson and Sarah Divol both of Lunenburg were married Janvary ye 29th 1756 by the Rev. Mr David Stearns minister of Lunenburg.

Elijah Grout and Mary Willard both of Lunenburg were married July 17th A. D. 1757 by William Downe, Justice of the peace.

Elisha Gibs and Abigail Stevens both of the district of Westminster were married by Edward Hartwell Justice of the peace December ye 18th 1759

Thomas Gary of Lunenburg & Elizabeth Farewell of Townshend were married February ye 21st 1760 by the Rev Mr David Stearns minister of Lunenburg.

Marriages.

G. (cont.)

B. H. G. S. G. F.

Jonathan Going of Lunenburg & Anne Bennet of Shirley District were married April ye 15th 1760 by the Rev Mr David Stean minister of Lunenburg.

Silas Gates of Stow & Anna Hammond of Lunenburg were married December ye 1st 1760 by ye Rev. Mr. David Stearns minister of Lunenburg.

Mr. Francis Gardner of Stow & Mrs Sarah Gibson of Lunenburg were married by Edward Hartwell Justice of the peace Octo^r 5th 1762.

Eliphelet Goodridge & Rebekah Snow both of Lunenburg were married by Benjn Goodridge Esqr Decr 29th 1763.

Mr. Jacob Gates of Harvard & Miss Elizabeth Gibson of Lunenburg were married by Ed^d Hartwell Esqr May 9th 1764.

Benjn Gould of Rowley Canada in the Prov^{ce} of New-Hampshire, and Sarah Foster of Lunenburg were married by Benjn Goodridge Esqr May 14th 1764.

H.

K. G. W. H. H. M. K. T.

Edward Hartwell Junr and Elizabeth Kneeland both of Lunenburg ware married by the Rev^d Mr. David Stearns minister of Lunenburg August ye 7th 1739.

Jonathan Hubburd Junr of Lunenburg and Abigail Genison of Watertown was married by the Revnd Mr. David Stearns minister of Lunenburg September ye 24th 1739.

John Hill and Jane Walles both of Lunenburg was married by the Revnd Mr. David Stearns minister of Lunenburg March ye 19th 1739/40.

Nathaniel Hastings and Lois Houghton both of Lunenburg were married May the 21th 1741 by Edward Hartwell Justice of the peace.

Jonathan Hammond of Lower Ashulott so called, and Abigail Hastings of Lunenburg were marryed July the 29th 1741 by Mr. David Stearns minister of Lunenburg.

William Holt and Mary Martin both of Lunenburg were married July 30th 1744 by the Rev^d Mr David Stearns minister of Lunenburg.

George Henry and Elizabeth Kenedy both of Lunenburg were married Feb^{ry} ye 13th 1745/6 by the Rev. Mr. David Stearns minister of Lunenburg.

Jonathan Hartwell and Elizabeth Tarbal both of Lunenburg were married December ye 3rd 1745 by ye Rev. Mr. David Stearns minister of Lunenburg.

H. (cont.)

G. D. J. S. T. P. G. D. H. P. D. F. R. W. D. F.

Amos Hazeltine and Eunice Gilson both of Lunenburg were married March the 5th 1746/7 by ye Rev. Mr. David Stearns minister of Lunenburg.

Joseph Hartwell and Tabitha Dodge both of Lunenburg were married September ye 22nd 1747 by Edward Hartwell Justice of ye peace.

John Hubburd and Hannah Johnson both of Lunenburg were married March ye 20th 1748/9 by the Rev. Mr. David Stearns minister of Lunenburg.

Darius Houghton and Jerusha Stearns both of Lunenburg were married by ye Rev. Mr. David Stearns, minister of Lunenburg, Janvary ye 24th 1749.

John Henderson of Lancaster and Jane Turner of Lunenburg were married August ye 4th 1749 by Thomas Prentice Justice of peace.

Thomas Henderson late of Lunenburg and Bethsheba Prist of Stow were married April the third 1751 by Thomas Prentice Justice of the peace.

Joseph Hammond of Lower Ashuelot so called, and Esther Gould of Lunenburg were married Novr 2d 1752 by the Revd Mr. David Stearns minister of Lunenburg.

Gershom Hubbard of Dunstable and Lipha Dodge of Lunenburg were married January 18th 1753 by the Revd Mr. David Stearns minister of Lunenburg.

William Henry Junr and Mary Harper both of Lunenburg were married December the sixth 1753; by Edward Hartwell Esqr Justice of the peace.

Phinehas Hartwell and Mary Peirce both of Lunenburg were married November 28th 1754 by Edward Hartwell Esqr Just~ Pacis.

Henery Hodgskins and Mary Dutton both of Lunenburg were married May the 8th 1755 by the Rev. Mr. David Stearns minister of Lunenburg.

Zimri Heywood and Jane Foster both of Dorchester Canada so called were married June ye 5th 1756 by Edward Hartwell Justice of the peace.

Samuel Hodgskins and Rebeckah Rice both of Lunenburg were married August ye 8th A. D. 1757 by William Downe Justice of peace.

Joseph Houghton and Mary Willson both of Leominster were married January ye 31st 1758 by Edward Hartwell, Justice of the peace.

Thaddeus Harrington of Shirley and Thankful Dodge of Lunenburg were married April 6th 1758 by the Rev. Mr. David Stearns minister of Lunenburg.

Samuel Hart and Mary Fuller both of Lunenburg were married April ye 20th 1758 by the Rev. Mr David Stearns minister of Lunenburg.

H. (cont.)

P. C. H. B. S. R. H.

Ebenezer Hart and Sarah Poole both of Lunenburg were married May ye 4th 1758 by the Rev. Mr. David Stearns, mininster of Lunenburg.

Daniel Harper and Rachel Colman both of Dorchester Canada so called were married November ye 23rd 1758 by ye Rev. Mr. David Stearns minister of Lunenburg.

George Hewett of Rowley Canada & Triphena Hodgskins of Lunenburg were married October ye 2nd 1760 by the Rev^d Mr. David Stearns minister of Lunenburg.

Henry Hodgskin of Ipswich Canada & Jemima Ball of Princetown were married by Benjn Goodridge Jus^{ce} Peace Novr 17th 1762.

Sam^{ll} Hilton and Rebekah Stickney both of Lunenburg were married by Benjn Goodridge Esqr Nov.r 17th 1763.

Phinehas Hutchens and Abigail Reed both of Lunenburg were married by Benjn Goodridge Esqr Novr 24th 1763.

Eleazar Houghton Junr and Susannah Holman both of Lunenburg were married by Edwd Hartwell Esqr March 8th 1764.

J.

H. W. B. G.

John Jenison and Mary Hubburd were married by the Rev^d Mr. David Stearns July 21st 1740

James Johnson of Lunenburg and Susanna Willard of Harvard were married June ye 15th 1747 by Thomas Prentice Justice of the peace.

Abner Jackman and Elizabeth Bayley both of Lunenburg were married February ye 10th 1757. by the Rev Mr. David Stearns minister of Lunenburg.

William Judevine and Patience Grout both of Lunenburg were married June ye 26th 1759 by the Rev. Mr. David Stearns minister of Lunenburg.

K.

M. P. P.

John Kelsey of Groton and Martha Mc farlen of Lunenburg was married by the Revnd Mr. David Stearns minister of Lunenburg Jenevary the 10th 1739/40.

Uzziah Kendel of Leominister and Elizabeth Parce of Lunenburg ware married July the 6th 1747. by the Rev. Mr. David Stearns minister of Lunenburg.

Samuel Kennedy and Sarah Page both of Lunenburg, were married July 24th 1749 by Thomas Prentice Justice of ye peace.

K. (cont.)

S. F. H.

Richard Kimbal of Boxford and Elizabeth Sectown [Seaton?] of Lunenburg were married January ye 23rd 1750/1 by ye Rev. Mr. David Stearns minister of Lunenburg.

William Kimball & Jane Farewell, both of Lunenburg were married March ye 13th 1760 by ye Rev. Mr. David Stearns minister of Lunenburg.

Benjamin Kidder of Billrica & Ruth Heywood of Lunenburg were married February ye 12th 1761 by the Rev^d Mr David Stearns minister of Lunenburg.

L.

W. P. K. W. S. F. A. P.

Samuel Larrabee jun^r of Lunenburg and Anne Williams of Groton were married April ye 23rd 1746 by ye Rev^d Mr. David Stearns minister of Lunenburg.

John Lovejoy and Sarah Parce both of Lunenburg, were married January ye 25th 1749 by the Rev. Mr. David Stearns minister of Lunenburg.

Thomas Lietch and Jane Kennedy both of Lunenburg, were married September the 19th 1750 by Edward Hartwell Justice of the peace.

Benj^a Larrabee of Lunenburg and Margaret Williams of Groton were married December 7th 1752 by the Rev^d Mr David Stearns minister of Lunenburg.

Mr. Samuel Larrabee of Luneburg and wid^w Mary Simonds of Shirley District were married December ye 19th 1758 by the Rev. Mr. David Stearns minister of Lunenburg.

Nehemiah Lane of Lunenburg, & Sarah Fletcher of Groton were married April 17th 1760 by the Rev^d Mr. David Stearns minister of Lunenburg.

John Larrabee of Lunenburg & Abiel Arven of Groton, were married June ye 19th 1760 by the Mr. David Stearns, minister of Lunenburg.

William Larken of Lunenburg & Hannah Parce of Groton were married May ye 7th 1761 by Edward Hartwell Justice of ye peace.

M.

S. M.

Thomas Morrison of Londonderry and Mary Smith of Lunenburg was married by the Rev^nd Mr. David Stearns, minister of Lunenburg, October ye 2th 1739.

Hugh Moors and Ruth Mitchael both of Lunenburg, were married December ye 28th 1743 by the Rev^d Mr. David Stearns of Lunenburg.

M. (cont.)

H. K. W. C. C.

Thomas Matthews and Elizabeth Heborn both of Lunenburg were married Janvary ye 4th 1748/9 by Edward Hartwell Justice of ye peace.

Willm Machane Junr of Worcester & Mary Kennedy of Lunenburg, were married Decr 4th 1753 by the Rev^d Mr. David Stearns minister of Lunenburg.

John Moors jun of Bolton & Unity Willard of Lunenburg were married August ye 30th A. D. 1757 by William Downe Just pac.

John Martin and Betty Chaplin both of Lunenburg were married March ye 3rd A. D. 1761 by Edward Hartwell Justice of the peace.

Sam^{ll} Mc'Craken of Worcester & Lettice Carlisle of Lunenburg were married by Edwd Hartwell Justice of the peace Decr 8th 1762.

N.

B.

Page Norcross & Elizabeth Bailey both of Lunenburg, were married by Edwd Hartwell Esqr Feby 15th 1763.

O.

F.

Ephraim Osbourn and Sarah Fisk both of Lunenburg were married November ye 26th 1759 by the Rev^d Mr. David Stearns minister of Lunenburg.

P.

L. G. B. W. P.

Mr. John Prescott of Concord married to Mrs. Anne Lynde of Lunenburg by ye Revnd Mr. Andrew Gardner, minister of Lunenburg, November ye 25 1730.

Nathaniel Page and Marcy Gould both of Lunenburg were married by ye Revnd Mr. David Stearns minister of Lunenburg on ye 25 day of December A. D. 1733.

David Page and Priscilla Boynton both of Lunenburg were married by ye Reverand Mr. David Stearns minister of Lunenburg on ye 22 day of January A. D. 1734/5.

Thomas Prentice of Lancaster and Abigail Willard of Lunenburg were married by ye Rev^d Mr Stearns, August ye 2^d 1737.

Josiah Parker and Elizabeth Page, both of Lunenburg, were married October 31th 1737 by the Revnd Mr. David Stearns.

P. (cont.)

W. D. R. N. P. G. P. W. B. F. P. P. W. N. B.

Asael Phelps and Elizabeth Wilder both of Lancaster, were married February ye 15th 1743/4 by Edward Hartwell Justice of ye peace.

Jonathan Parce and Sarah Dodge both of Lunenburg, were married Febry ye 4th 1745/6 by ye Rev Mr. David Stearns minister of Lunenburg.

David Parce Jun and Anne Retter both of Lunenburg were married April ye 20th 1746 by ye Rev. Mr. David Stearns minister of Lunenburg.

William Porter and Mary Nichols both of Lunenburg, were married May the first 1746 by the Rev. Mr. David Stearns minister of Lunenburg.

Mr. Samvel Page of Lunenburg and Sarah Parce of Leominster were married July ye 9th 1747 by the Rev^d Mr. David Stearns minister of Lunenburg.

Timothy Parker and Johannah Grout both of Lunenburg were married September the 6th 1748 by the Rev. Mr. David Stearns minister of Lunenburg.

Joseph Platts of Rowley Canady (so called, and Deborah Page of Lunenburg were married Novr 16th 1752 by the Rev^d Mr. David Stearns minister of Lunenburg.

Thomas Putnam of Charlestown in the Province of New-Hampshire & Rachel Wetherbee of Lunenburg were married Janry 24th 1754 by the Rev^d Mr. David Stearns minister of Lunenburg.

Jonathan Parker of Boston and Martha Brown of Lunenburg were married Novr 8th 1754 by ye Revd Mr David Stearns.

Jacob Peabody and Dorothy Foster both of Leominster, were married March the 4th 1756 by William Downe, Justice of the peace.

Samuel Pool and Sarah Potter both of Lunenburg were married together December ye 14th 1756 by William Downe Justice of the peace.

Nathan Pushee of Ipswich Canada and Elizabeth Priest of Stow were married together Janavary ye 13th 1757 by William Downe Justice of the peace.

Abel Plats of Rowley Canada so called, and Phebe Wetherbee of Lunenburg were married April 26th 1759 by the Rev. Mr. David Stearns minister of Lunenburg.

Ephraim Parce & Sarah Norcross both of Lunenburg, were married January ye 3rd 1760 by the Rev. Mr. David Stearns minister of Lunenburg.

Joseph Platts of Rowley Canada, and Sarah Bowers of Lunenburg were married October ye 2nd 1760 by the Rev^d Mr. David Stearns minister of Lunenburg.

P. (cont.)

S. S. M.

Samuel Parce & Mary Steward both of Lunenburg, were married March ye 19th 1761 by Edward Hartwell, Justice of the peace.

Ebenezer Pratt of Lunenburg & Lydia Stone of Groton were married by Edward Hartwell Justice of ye peace September ye 22^d 1761.

David Poor of Ipswich Canada so called & Jane Martin of Lunenburg were married by Edward Hartwell, Justice of the peace December 2^d 1761.

R.

B. W. S. S. M. M.

Samuel Reed and Mary Ballard both of Lunenburg ware married by the Rev^d Mr. David Stearns, minister of Lunenburg, October ye 26th 1738.

John Russel and Elizabeth Wallis both of Lunenburg were married by ye Rev Mr. David Stearns, minister of Lunenburg Novr the 13th 1740.

Benjamin Randal and Lydia Stevens, both of Lunenburg, were married December the 2nd 1741, by Mr. David Stearns minister of Lunenburg.

Benjamin Reddington and Ruth Stearns, both of Lunenburg were married March ye 24th 1757 by the Rev. Mr David Stearns, minister of Lunenburg.

John Richards and Elizabeth Mitcheal, both of Lunenburg were married October ye 17th 1757 by David Stearns minister of Lunenburg.

Samuel Russel and Susannah Mitchael both of Lunenburg, were married November ye 28th 1757 by the Rev. Mr. David Stearns minister of Lunenburg.

S.

H. S. L. J.

April 7th 1736 The Rev^d Mr. David Stearns and Mrs. Ruth Hubbard were married by the Rev^d Mr. John Prentice of Lancaster.

William Steward and Margaret Sanderson of Lunenburg were married by the Rev^nd Mr. Stearns November 10th 1736.

John Sharer of Kingstown (so called) and Jane Little of Lunenburg were married Janvary ye 4th 1742/3 by the Rev. Mr. David Stearns minister of Lunenburg.

William Stearns and Elizabeth Johnson both of Lunenburg were married Janvary ye 22nd 1745/6 by ye Rev. Mr. David Stearns minister of Lunenburg.

S. (cont.)

W. R. T. H. P. L. H. T. H. F. P. T. S. F. I. I.

Gustavus Swan of Lunenburg and Isabella Willson of Townshend were married Novr ye 4th 1747 by Thomas Prentice Justice of ye peace.

William Swan of Petersbouroh so called and Mary Russell of Lunenburg were married February the twenty sixth 1750/1 by Thomas Prentice Justice of the peace.

Benjamin Steward and Rebecca Taylor, both of Lunenburg were married Janvary ye 9th 1751/2 by the Rev. Mr. David Stearns minister of Lunenburg.

Abijah Stearns and Sarah Heywood both of Lunenburg were married November ye 12th 1751 by the Rev. Mr. David Stearns minister of Lunenburg.

Bradstreet Spafford of N° 4 so called and Mary Page of Lunenburg were married October 16th 1752 by the Rev^d Mr. David Stearns, minister of Lunenburg.

David Steel of Londonderry and Jennet Little of Lunenburg were married Febr^y 8th 1753 by the Rev^d Mr. David Stearns minister of Lunenburg.

John Smith of Petersborough & Mary Harkness of Lunenburg were married October 2^d 1753 by the Rev^d Mr. David Stearns minister of Lunenburg.

Benj^a Stearns & Anna Taylor both of Lunenburg were married Janr^y 15th 1754 by the Rev^d Mr. David Stearns minister of Lunenburg.

Moses Stearns of Narragansett No 2 and Ruth Houghton of Lunenburg were married June 13th 1754 by the Rev^d Mr David Stearns minister of Lunenburg.

Jonathan Spafford and Dorcas Frost both of Lunenburg were married Novr 13th 1754 by the Rev^d Mr. David Stearns.

John Simonds and Mercy Page both of Lunenburg were married March ye 13th 1755 by the Rev. Mr. David Stearns minister of Lunenburg.

Solomon Steward Jun. and Elizabeth Taylor, both of Lunenburg were married May ye 28th 1755 by the Rev. Mr. David Stearns, minister of Lunenburg.

Levi Stiles and Patience Smith both of Lunenburg, were married December ye 16th 1755 by the Rev. Mr. David Stearns minister of Lunenburg.

Alexander Swan and Lucy Foster both of Lunenburg were married March the 7th 1756 by William Downe Justice of the peace.

Phinehas Steward and Anne Ireland both of Lunenburg were married April 22^d 1756 by the Rev. Mr. David Stearns minister of Lunenburg.

Daniel Steward and Mary Ierland both of Lunenburg were married March ye 14th 1757 by ye Rev. Mr. David Stearns minister of Lunenburg.

Marriages.

S. (*cont.*)

G. D. S. I. G. L. F. H. P. S. L.

Ephraim Stockwell & Sarah Grout both of Petersham, were married Nov^m 21st A. D. 1757 by William Downe, Justice of pacis.

Jonas Stearns and Submit Davis, both of Lunenburg were married May ye 4th 1758 by the Rev. Mr. David Stearns minister of Lunenburg.

Mr. Thomas Sparhawk and Mrs. Rebecca Stearns both of Lunenburg were married July ye 10th 1758 by ye Rev. Mr. David Stearns minister of Lunenburg.

William Steward and Abigail Ireland both of Lunenburg were married July ye 25th 1758 by the Rev. Mr. David Stearns minister of Lunenburg.

Samuel Sanderson and Sarah Gould both of Lunenburg were married December ye 27th 1759 by the Rev. Mr. David Stearns minister of Lunenburg.

William Symonds of Shirley District & Abigail Larrabee of Lunenburg were married March ye 11th 1760 by ye Rev. Mr. David Stearns, minister of Lunenburg.

Silas Snow of Lunenburg & Anna Farwell of Groton were married November ye 20th 1760 by the Revnd Mr. David Stearns, minister of Lunenburg.

Jonathan Stedman of Westminster and Tabitha Hart of Lunenburg were married by Edward Hartwell, Justice of the peace, Septr ye 8th 1761.

Reuben Smith & Prudence Pearce both of Lunenburg were married by Edward Hartwell Justice of the peace Septr 6th 1762.

The Reverend Mr. Ebenezer Sparhawk of Templetown, and Mrs. Abigail Stearns of Lunenburg were married by the Rev^d Mr. Timothy Harrington of Lancaster, September the first, seventeen hundred and sixty-three.

Mr. David Stearns and Mrs. Mary Low both of Lunenburg were married by the Rev^d Mr. Timothy Harrington of Lancaster Octo^r ye 20th 1763.

T.

G. G.

Aaron Taylor and Mercy Gould both of Lunenburg were married December 21th 1752 by the Rev^d Mr. David Stearns minister of Lunenburg.

Zechariah Tarboll & Mary Gould both of Lunenburg, were married March 27th 1753. by the Rev^d Mr. David Stearns minister of Lunenburg.

W.

B. B. W. B. B. P. B. P. W. M. P. W. H. B. G.

Mr. Ephraim Wetherbe & Mrs. Johannah Bellows both of Lunenburg were married by ye Revnd Andrew Gardner, minister of Lunenburg (as he saith) Septr ye 18th 1732.

Zachariah Whitney and Sarah Boynton both of Lunenburg ware married by the Revd Mr. David Stearns minister of Lunenburg the 11th of April 1739.

Joseph Wood and Ruth Wetherbe both of Lunenburg were married July 30th 1741 by Mr. David Stearns minister of Lunenburg.

Jonathan Willard Junr & Phebe Ballard both of Lunenburg were married October ye 24th 1743 by the Revd Mr. David Stearns minister of Lunenburg.

Daniel Willard of Lancaster and Lucy Butler of Lunenburg were married November the 19th 1745 by the Rev. Mr. David Stearns minister of Lunenburg.

Michel Wood and Mary Platts both of Lunenburg were married December ye 2nd 1745 by ye Rev. Mr. David Stearns minister of Lunenburg.

Ephraim Whitney and Jane Bancroft both of Lunenburg were married Janvary ye 16th 1745/6 by ye Rev. Mr. David Stearns minister of Lunenburg.

Paul Wetherbe and Hannah Parce both of Lunenburg were married June ye 11th 1746 by ye Rev. Mr. David Stearns minister of Lunenburg.

John White and Mary Wallis both of Lunenburg were married December ye 9th 1747 by Thomas Prentice, Justice of the peace.

Archibald White of Townshend & Margarett McClary of Lunenburg were married December ye 12th 1750 by ye Rev. Mr. David Stearns minister of Lunenburg.

Joseph Wheelock Jun of Lancaster and Alice Page of Lunenburg were married November ye 14th 1751 by ye Rev. Mr. David Stearns minister of Lunenburg.

John White and Mary Whitney both of Lunenburg were married Febry 22d 1753 by the Revd Mr. David Stearns minister of Lunenburg.

Abner Whitney of District Shirley & Sarah Hilton of Lunenburg were married June 21st 1753 by the Revd Mr. David Stearns minister of Lunenburg.

Benoni Wallis of Lunenburg and Rebecca Brown of Lynn were married July the 2nd 1755 by the Rev. Mr. David Stearns minister of Lunenburg.

Jonathan Wood and Sarahrah Gary both of Lunenburg, were married April ye 19th 1757 by the Rev. Mr. David Stearns minister of Lunenburg.

Marriages.

W. (cont.)

R. F. B. M. P. B. F. W.

Barzillai Willard & Hepsabath Reddington both of Lunenburg were married Nov^m ye 18th A. D. 1757 by William Downe Justice pea.

Wincal Wright of Dunstable and Sibil Farewell of Lunenburg were married April ye 7th 1758 by the Rev. Mr. David Stearns minister of Lunenburg.

Abner Wheelock of Leominster and Mary Brown of Lunenburg were married April ye 12th 1758 by Edward Hartwell Justice of the peace.

Jesher Wyman of Lancaster and Dorrothy Moffat of Stow were married November ye 28th 1758 by Edward Hartwell Justice of the peace.

Joseph Wyman of Lunenburg and Keziah Parker of Lexington were married June 21th 1759 by Nathaniel Russel Justice of the peace for the County of Middlesex.

Reuben Wyman & Elizabeth Bancroft both of Lunenburg were married February ye 5th 1761 by the Rev^d Mr. David Stearns minister of Lunenburg.

Jacob Wilson & Margaret Freeman both of Leominster were married by Edwd Hartwell Justice of the peace Decr 6th 1762.

Michal Wood of Lunenburg & Lois Wilson of Leominster were married by Benjn Goodridge Esqr August 21st 1764.

LUNENBURG, 1857.

The following is a Copy of Certificates of Marriages Received and Recorded in compliance with the provisions of Chapter 84, Section 4, of the Acts of 1857.

CITY CLERK'S OFFICE WORCESTER Sept 14, 1857

To the Clerk of the Town of Lunenburg,

In compliance with the provisions of Chapter 84 Section 4 of the Acts of 1857, I herewith transmit to you a certified copy of the record of all Marriages recorded in the books of this City, where either or both of the parties married were resident of your Town at the time of said Marriages, to wit:

Date of Marriage.   Names and Residence of Parties Married.   By whom Married
"Decr 1st 1748.   William Little of Lunenburg and }
                    Elizabeth Wallis of Worcester by }   Thad Maccarty,,

A copy of the Record,
                    Attest.   SAMUEL SMITH, *City Clerk.*
A true copy,   Attest.   JAMES PUTNAM *Town Clerk.*

Samuel Johnson of Lunenburg & Mary Cooledge of Weston ware Married in Weston April the 12th 1732 per William Williams, Minist^r of s^d Town.

A true copy from the Records of Weston.
See Acts of 1857 Chap 84, Sec 4. Attest, NATHAN HAGAR *Town Clerk*
Oct. 6 1857.
A true copy attest. JAMES PUTNAM *Town Clerk*

TOWN CLERK'S OFFICE BOLTON Oct 15, 1857
To the Clerk of the Town of Lunenburg -

In compliance with the provisions of Chapter 84 Section 4 of the Acts of 1857, I herewith transmit to you a certified copy of the record of all Marriages recorded in the books of this town where either or both of the parties married were resident of your town at the time of said Marriage, to wit,

John Fosket of Bolton, Abigail Jones of Lunenburg, by whom Married Rev. Thomas Goss. Date May 28, 1761.

A true copy of record.
Attest RICHARD S. EDES, *Town Clerk*
A true copy.
Attest. JAMES PUTNAM *Town Clerk.*

TOWN CLERK'S OFFICE LANCASTER Oct 2. 1857.
To the Clerk of the Town of Lunenburg.

In compliance with the provisions of Chapter 84 Section 4 of the Acts of 1857, I herewith transmit to you a certified copy of the record of all Marriages recorded in the books of this Town, where either or both of the parties Married were resident of your Town at the time of said Marriage, to wit:

Date of Marriage.	Names & Residence of Parties Married.	By whom Married
May 23. 1733.	Benjamin Corey. Lunenburg.	
	Judith Beaman Lancaster	Rev. John Prentice
Apr. 7 1736.		
	Rev. David Stearns	
	Ruth Hubbart Lunenburg	Rev. John Prentice
Nov. 29. 1750.		
	David Taylor Lunenburg	
	Betty Houghton Lancaster.	Rev. Tim^o Harrington.
Apr. 16, 1752.		
	George McFarling. Lunenburg	
	Margaret Torrence Lancaster	Joseph Wilder Jr. J. P.
July 19. 1756		
	Benjamin Shed Lunenburg	
	Elizabeth Bowers Lancaster	Rev. Tim. Harrington.

Marriages.

Date of Marriage.	Names and Residence of Parties Married.	By whom Married.
July 2. 1761.	Mitchel Richards. Shirley. Ester Mitchel Lunenburg	Joseph Wilder J. P.
Apr. 1. 1762.	Kendall Boutel Lunenburg. Mary Wilder. Leominster.	Joseph Wilder J. P.
Jan 13. 1763.	Robert Crawford Worcester Elisebeth Leitch Lunenburg	Abijah Willard J. P.
May 24. 1763.	Solomon Shead Lunenburg Elisa Bornton Lunenburg.	Joseph Wilder J. P.

A true copy of Record.
    Attest, J. L. S. THOMPSON *Town Clerk.*

A true copy.
    Attest JAMES PUTNAM *Town Clerk.*

To the Clerk of the Town of Luningburg.

 Pursuant to a law of the Commonwealth of Massachusetts passed by the Legislature of 1857, (see Chapter 84, Section 4 of the General Laws.)

 I herewith transmit to you a certified list of all Marriages recorded in the Records of the Town of Woburn where one or both of the parties were at the time of said Marriage resident in the town of Luningburg.

William Jones of Luningburg and Sarah Locke of Woburn were Married December 25 1733.

 (From the present ch. Rec^d.)

William Henderson of Luningburg and Sarah Smith were married Mar. 13 1740.

Woburn Oct. 13. 1857.
  Attest   N. WYMAN *Town Clerk.*

A true copy. Attest.
     JAMES PUTNAM. *Town Clerk.*

Stephen Holden of Groton and Sarah Wheeler of Lunenburg were joined in Marriage in Boxford Before David Wood Esq. March 21. 1739.

A true copy of Record.
    Attest, W^M H. WOOD, *Town Clerk of Boxford.*

BOXFORD October 28. 1857. See Act of /57 Chap. 84. Sec. 4.

Married February ye 19th 1745.

 David Wood of Lunenburg and Mary Hovey of Boxford before Mr. John Cushing as recorded in Boxford W^M H. WOOD. *Town Clerk*

  A true copy, Attest,
     JAMES PUTNAM *Town Clerk.*

264   *The Early Records of the Town of Lunenburg.*

Married by Rev. Caleb Trowbridge Nov. 2d 1732
    Daniel Farmer of Luningburg to Elizebeth Woods of Groton.

Nov. 23d 1732.   Josiah Willard of Luningburg to
                   Hannah Hubburd of Groton.

June 21st 1733.   John Gridridge of Lunenburg to
                   Eunice Scripture of Groton.

May 1st 1759.   Jonas Fletcher of Groton &
                  Wid. Johanna Crocker of Lunenburg.

Feb. 15, 1763.   By Rev. Samuel Dana,
                  William Jones of Lunenburg to
                  Sarah Stone of Groton.

    A true copy from the Records of Groton.
                     Attest.   Geo. D. Brigham, *Town Clerk.*

Chap. 84. Sec. 4 of the Acts of 1857
To the Town Clerk of Lunenburg.
              A true copy. Attest. James Putnam *Town Clerk*

Oliver Gould of Lunenburg and Mary Stockwell of Petersham were Married May ye 3rd 1759. By Aaron Whitney a Minister of the Gospel.
      A copy of the Record.
           Attest, Lewis Whitney, *Town Clerk of Petersham*
      A true copy.
               Attest James Putnam *Town Clerk–*

1755. Dec 25.   Thomas Page of Lunenburg and
                    Dorothy Houghton of Leominster.

1758. Feb. 2d   Benoni Boynton of Lunenburg &
                    Mary Butrick of Leominster.

                                  Leominster, Nov. 2, 1857.

    I certify the foregoing to be true copies from the Church Record of Marriages by Rev. John Rogers first pastor of the Church in Leominster.
                                J. C. Allen. *Town Clerk*
      A true copy.   Attest.
                          James Putnam *Town Clerk*

              Town Clerk's Office, Ipswich, November 16, 1857.
To the Clerk of the town of Lunenburg,

    In compliance with the provisions of Chapter 84 Section 4 of the Acts of 1857, I herewith transmit to you a certified copy of the record of all Marriages which I find recorded in the books of this town prior to the year 1800, where either or both of the parties married were resident in Lunenburg at the time of the marriage. viz,—

    1740. March 19th David Goodridge of Lunenburg & Eliza Martin of
        Ipswich, were joined in Marriage, By Theophilus Pickering. V. D. M.

Marriages.

The foregoing are true copies from the records of the town of Ipswich.

       Attest. ALFRED KIMBALL, *Town Clerk.*
A true copy. Attest.   JAMES PUTNAM, *Town Clerk.*

"Reuben Gibson of Lunenburg, and Lois Smith of Sudbury were Married at Sudbury by Israel Loring Nov. 13, 1746."

A true copy from Records of Sudbury.
Sudbury Nov. 1857.   Attest I. S. HUNT, *Town Clerk –*
   A true copy. Attest JAMES PUTNAM *Town Clerk.*

To the Town Clerk of Lunenburg.

I herewith transmit to you the following Marriages in Conformity with Chapt. 84, Sec. 4 of Laws of 1857. The orthography is given as it appears on the Records.

October ye 10. 1754. Then were Married Jonathan Wood of Luninbourg & Rachel Wood of Uxbridge by Y^r Mr N. Webb

A copy of record. Attest. H. CAPRON *Town Clerk.*
A true copy. Attest. JAMES PUTNAM *Town Clerk.*

"Mr Bartholemew Pearson of Ipswich Cannada and Mrs. Lydia Randal of Lunenburg *bouth* in the County of Worcester were Married November ye 3^d 1763 by the Rev^d Mr. Daniel Stimson."

A Copy from the Town Records of Winchendon.
    Attest
        WEBSTER WHITNEY *Town Clerk.*
In compliance with Chap. 84 Sec. 4 of the Acts of 1857.
To the Town Clerk of Lunenburg.

  A true copy. Attest JAMES PUTNAM *Town Clerk.*

MARRIAGES.

1759 Mar 26. Nehemiah Lane of Lunenburg &
      Sarah Shattuck of Pepperell by Rev.
      Joseph Emerson.
1761. June 25. Jonathan Stevens of Lunenburg &
      Elizabeth Parker of Pepperell by Rev.
      Joseph Emerson.

A true copy from the Record of Marriages.
      Attest, CHAS. CROSBY. *T. Clerk*
See Acts 1857. Ch. 84.
Pepperell Jan 12, 1858.

   A true copy. Attest. JAMES PUTNAM *Town Clerk*

1733. July 11. William Page of Lunenburg &
               Sarah Stevens of Andover were married
               by Rev. John Barnard.

1739. Oct 8. Jonathan Abbott Junr of Lunenburg &
               Martha Lovejoy of Andover ware Married
               by Rev. Samuel Phillips.

1742. Oct. 14. Joseph Holt of Lunenburg and
               Mary Abbott of Andover ware Married
               by Rev. Samuel Phillips-

1748. Oct 13. Daniel Holt of Lunenburg &
               Mehetibel Holt of Andover married
               by Rev. Samuel Phillips.

1758. Nov. 23. James Descomb of Lunenburg &
               Elizth Farrington of Andover Married
               by Rev. William Symmes.

1759. Nov. 29. Jesse Carlton of Lunenburg and
               Sarah Foster of Andover married
               by Rev. Samuel Phillips.

1761 Dec. 3. Abijah Hovey of Lunenburg &
               Lydia Ingalls of Andover Married
               by Rev. William Symmes.

From the Marriage Records of the Town of Andover. Andover Dec. 17, 1857. See General Laws 1857 Chap 84.

    A true copy.   Attest   JAMES PUTNAM *Town Clerk.*

Isaac Redington of Lunenburg and Ruth Bodwell of Methuen Married Dec. 27, 1759, By Rev. Christopher Sargent.

Copy from the Marriage Records of the Town of Methuen Methuen, Jany 4. 1857.

                  Attest, CHAS. SHED *Town Clerk of Methuen*

    A true copy.   Attest,   JAMES PUTNAM, *Town Clerk.*

                                          HARVARD Jany 4. 1858.

Dear Sir:

    Below please find a copy of record which I transmit to you in compliance with the requirements of Chap. 84 Sec. 4 of the Acts of 1857.

Names & Residence.	By Whom.	Date of.
Daniel Page of Lunenburg	Rev Mr	Nov. 22nd
Ruth Haskell	John Seecomb	1744-

                A true Copy   TRUMBULL BULL *Town Clerk.*

           A true Copy. Attest, JAMES PUTNAM *Town Clerk.*

Marriages.

Joseph Wood of Lunenburg and Ruth Symonds of Littleton were married Oct 5th 1752.

Benj<u>n</u> Foster of Lunenburg & Sarah Witney of Littleton were Married Dec. 31. 1761.

Dea Benjⁿ Foster of Lunenburg and Mrs. Sarah Whitney of Littleton were joined in Marriage by Rev. Daniel Rogers of Littleton Dec 3d 1761.

From the Records of Littleton
Littleton Jan. 27/58   B. EDWARDS *Town Clerk.*

A true copy.   Attest   JAMES PUTNAM, *Town Clerk.*

               TOWN CLERK'S OFFICE, NEWTON, Jan 22d 1858.
To the Clerk of the Town of Lunenburgh.

In compliance with the provisions of Chapter 84 Section 4 of the Acts of 1857, I herewith transmit to you a certified copy of the record of all Marriages recorded in the books of this town, where either or both of the parties married were residents of your Town at the time of said Marriage, to wit:

"Thomas Prentice Esqr of Lunenburgh & Mrs Borridel Jackson of Newton were Marryed June 27—1751 by the Rev. Mr. John Cotton."

"Middlesex S. S. Newtown July 26th A. D. 1763

Abraham Smith of Luningburg & Lucie Allen of Weston were Joyned in Marriage by Thos. Greenwood Justice of Peace."

      Attest.   MARSHALL S. RICE – *Town Clerk of Newton*

A true copy.   Attest.   JAMES PUTNAM *Town Clerk.*

Extracts from Marriage records of the town of Topsfield Massachusetts.

"December 3rd 1730 Joseph Page of Lunenburg & Deborah Gould of Topsfield were married."

"Amos Robinson of Lunenburgh & Priscilla Lake of Topsfield were married on ye 3rd day of Sept. 1733."

"Amos Robinson of Lunenburgh and Lydia Wentworth of Topsfield were married on ye 24th of November 1743—"

From Marriage records of the town of Topsfield
Topsfield, Feb. 1858.   Attest   I. P. TOWNE *Town Clerk*

A true copy   Attest.   JAMES PUTNAM *Town Clerk*

BIRTHS

BIRTHS

COPIED FROM THE

RECORDS OF THE TOWN OF LUNENBURG,

FROM 1707 TO 1764.

A.

AUSTEN. AUSTIN.

Priscilla ye daughter of Daniel Austen and Priscilla his wife born at Andover February ye 11 1725/6

Daniel ye son of Daniel Austen and Priscilla his wife born at Lunenburg Apriel ye 13 1727

Lydia ye daughter of Daniel Austen and Priscilla his wife, born at Lunenburg June ye 3, 1729.

Timothy ye son of Daniel Austen and Priscilla his wife, born at Lunenburg March ye 2, 1731

Ruth ye daughter of Daniel Austen, and of Priscilla his wife, born at Lunenburg April ye 1th 1733.

Hannah Austen ye daughter of Daniel Austen and of Priscilla his wife, born at Lunenburg February ye 1th 1734/5.

Phebe Austen ye daughter of Daniel Austen, and of Priscilla his wife, born at Lunenburg October ye 24th 1736.

Phebe Austin the daughter of Daniel Austin and of Phebe his wife, was born at Lunenburg April ye 15th 1758.

Timothy Austin the son of Daniel Austin and of Phebe his wife, was born at Lunenburg June ye 2nd 1759.

Daniel Austin son of Daniel Austin Jr. & Phebe, his wife was born January 6th 1761.

Samuel Austin son of Daniel Austin Jr. & Phebe, his wife was born February 12th 1762

Hannah Austin daughter of Daniel Austin Jr. & Phebe his wife was born January 2d 1765

AUSTIN. ABBOTT. ALEXANDER.

John Austin son of Daniel Austin Jr. & Phebe his wife was born November 7th 1766.

Ruth Austin daughter of Daniel Austin Jr. & Phebe his (wife) was born October 2d 1768.

Jonathan Abbott the son of Jonathan Abbott and of Matha his wife was born at Lunenburg, August the twenty-ninth 1740.

Nathan Abbott the son of Jonathan Abbott, and of Mattha his wife, was born at Lunenburg, Janvary ye 22nd 1743/.4.

William Abbott the son of Jonathan Abbott, and of Mattha his wife, was born at Lunenburg, November the 24th 1745.

John Alexander, the son of William Alexander, and of Elizabeth his wife born at Lunenburg August ye 14th 1744.

Franice Alexander, the son of William Alexander and of Elizabeth his wife, born at Lunenburg March ye 18th 1745/6.

William Allexander, the son of William Allexander and of Elizabeth his wife, was born at Lunenburg November ye first A. D. 1749.

B.

BOYNTON.

Sarah Boynton ye davghter of Benoni Boynton and of Anne his wife born at Rowley March ye 9th 1707.

Sarah Boynton (a surviving) daughter of Benoni Boynton and of Anne his wife born at Rowley June ye 17th 1708

Stephen Boynton ye son of Benoni Boynton and of Anne his wife, born at Rowley April 9th 1710.

Anne Boynton ye davghter of Benoni Boynton and of Anne his wife, born at Rowley November ye 21th 1713.

Dorcas Boynton ye davghter of Benoni Boynton and of Anne his wife, born at Groton December ye 21th 1715.

Jane Boynton ye davghter of Benoni Boynton & of Anne his wife born at Groton August ye 3th 1717.

Mary Boynton ye davghter of Benoni Boynton & of Anne his wife born at Groton November 27th 1718.

Elezebeth Boynton ye davghter of Benoni Boynton & of Anne his wife born at Groton July ye 10th 1720.

Mehittibel Boynton ye davghter of Benoni Boynton & of Anne his wife born at Groton November ye 1th 1721.

Mary Boynton ye davghter of Benoni Boynton & of Anne his wife born at Groton February ye 20th 1722/3.

Births.

BOYNTON.

Benoni Boynton ye son of Benoni Boynton & of Anne his wife born at Lunenburg June ye 1th 1726.

Joseph Boynton ye son of Benoni Boynton & of Anne his wife born at Lunenburg May ye 28th 1727.

The birth of ye Children of Hilkiah Boynton and of Priscilla his wife
- (1.) Sarah born January ye 1th 1718/19
- (2.) Jane born March ye 4th 1722/3
- (3.) Ruth born March ye 31th 1727.
- (4.) Jewet Boynton ye son of Hilkiah Boynton and of Priscilla his wife, born Feb^r ye 14th 1735/6

Sarah Boynton the daughter of Stephen Boynton and of Sarah his wife born at Lunenburg October ye 13th 1738

Joseph Boynton ye son of Stephen Boynton and of Sarah his wife born at Lunenburg January ye 30th 1740/1.

Stephen Boynton the son of Stephen Boynton, and of Sarah his wife, born at Lunenburg February the fifth 1743/4.

Susanna Boynton the daughter of Stephen Boynton and of Sarah his wife born at Lunenburg, September ye 1th 1746.

Elizabeth Boynton the daughter of Stephen Boynton (&) Sarah his wife was born at Lunenburg March the 26th 1749.

Sarah Boynton ye daughter of Stephen Boynton & Sarah his wife was born at Lunenburg February ye 19th 1751/2.

Joseph Boynton the son of Stephen and of Elizabeth his wife was born at Lunenburg April ye 30th 1755.

Samuel Boynton the son of Stephen Boynton and of Elizabeth his wife was born at Lunenburg August ye 28th A. D. 1757.

William Boynton ye son of Stephen Boynton & of Elizabeth his wife was born at Lunenburg March the 29th 1761.

Susannah Boynton daughter of Stephen Boynton & Elizabeth his wife was born at Lunenburg July 13th 1765.

Elizabeth Boynton, the daughter of Benoni Boynton Junr and Elizabeth his wife was born at Lunenburg the 21st day of Novr A: D: 1752.

Mary Boynton the daughter of Benoni Boynton Jun and Elizabeth his wife was born at Lunenburg December ye 20th A. D. 1754.

David Boynton the son of Jonathan Boynton and of Elizabeth his wife was born at Lunenburg February ye 25th 1759.

Mary Boynton the daughter of Jonathan Boynton and of Elizabeth his wife was born at Lunenburg October the 19th 1761.

BOYNTON. BIGELOW. BOWERS. BUTTRICK. BANCROFT.

Jonathan Boynton son of Jonathan Boynton Ju^r and of Elizabeth his wife was born at Lunenburg, October ye 12th 1771.

Solomon Learnard Boynton son of Solomon Boynton & Abigail his wife was born at Lunenburg October 18th 1778 with an uncommon mark on one of his ears.

Hannah Bigelow, daughter of Benjamin Bigelow and Love his wife was born at Lunenburg March the 5th A. D. 1754.

Benjamin Bigelow ye son of Benjamin Bigelow, and of Elisebeth his wife was born at Lunenburg, October ye 4, 1755.

Nehemiah Bowers the son of Nehemiah Bowers, and of Sarah his wife was born at Lunenburg, February the 26th 1752.

Esther Bowers the daughter of Nehemiah Bowers, and of Sarah his wife was born at Lunenburg 28th of May 1754.

Elizabeth Bowers the daughter of Nehemiah Bowers & of Sarah his wife, was born at Lunenburg August ye 29th 1756.

Susannah Bowers the daughter of Jerahmeel Bowers and of Meriam his wife, born at Lunenburg, February ye 4th 1746/7.

Francis Buttrick the son of Francis Buttrick, and of Hannah his wife, was born at Lunenburg April the 7th 1748.

Jonathan Buttrick the son of Francis Buttrick and of Hannah his wife was born at Lunenburg May ye 6th 1750.

Hannah Buttrick the daughter of Francis Buttrick and of Hannah his wife was born Lancaster Janvary 14th 1746.

Lucy Buttrick the daughter of John Buttrick & Mary his wife, was born at Lunenburg, Decr 18th 1752.

Timothy Bancroft ye son of Timothy Bancroft and of Elizabeth his wife, was born at Lunenburg, November ye 18th 1746.

John Bancroft ye son of Timothy Bancroft and of Elizabeth his wife, was born at Lunenburg November ye 14th 1753

Timothy Bancrofft ye son of Timothy Bancrofft and of Elizabeth his wife was born at Lunenburg, August the 14th 1755.

Molley Bancroft the daughter of Timothy Bancroft & of Mary his wife was born at Lunenburg June ye 5th 1761.

Births. 275

BAYLEY. BAILEY.

Isaac Bayle ye son of Josiah Bayle and of Elezabath Bayle his wife born August 8th 1729

Elezabath Bayle ye davghter of Josiah Bayle, and of Elezabath his wife, born March ye 4th 1730/31

Josiah Bayle ye son of Josiah Bayle and of Elezabath Bayle his wife born July ye 14 1734

Ruth Bayley ye daughter of Josiah Bayley and of Elizabeth his wife, was born at Lunenburg Janvary the seventh 1740/1.

Molly Bayley ye daughter of Isaac Bayley & of Mary his wife was born at Lunenburg February ye 14th 1753 new style.

Isaac Bayley the son of Isaac Bayley and of Mary his wife was born at Lunenburg February ye 27 A. D. 1757.

John Bayley the son of Isaac Bayley & of Mary his wife was born at Lunenburg March ye 7th 1760.

Betty Bailey ye daughter of Isaac & Mary Bailey was born at Lunenburg June 2d 1762.

Hannah Bailey daughter of Isaac Bailey and Mary his wife was born at Lunenburg June ye 30th 1764.

Samuel Bailey son of Isaac Bailey and Mary his wife was born at Lunenburg October ye 12th 1771.

Ruth Bailey daughter of Isaac Bailey & Mary his wife was born at Lunenburg August 23, 1775.

Molley Bailey daughter of John Bailey Junr and of Mary his wife was born at Lunenburg August 25th 1762.

John Bailey son of John Bailey Junr and of Mary his wife, was born at Lunenburg Octor 9th 1763.

Joseph Bailey son of Josiah Bailey Junr and of Sarah his wife was born at Lunenburgh June 20th 1763.

Benjn Bailey son of Josiah Bailey Junr and of Sarah his wife was born at Lunenburgh March 6th 1765.

Sarah Bailey daughter of Josiah Bailey Junr and of Sarah his wife was born at Lunenburg Decr 6th 1766

Josiah Bailey Tertius son of Josiah Bailey Junr and of Sarah his wife was born at Lunenburgh Jany 27th 1768.

Sarah Bailey daughter of Josiah Bailey Junr and Sarah his wife, was born at Lunenburg March ye 31st 1770.

Molly Bailey daughter of Josiah Bailey Junr & Sarah his wife, was born at Lunenburg April 1st 1772.

BAILEY. BURNAM. BELLOWS. BUTLER. BRADSTREET.

Joseph Bailey son of Josiah Bailey Junr & Sarah his wife was born at Lunenburg Septr ye 12th 1774.

Ruth Bailey daughter of Josiah Bailey Junr & Sarah his wife was born at Lunenburg May 15th 1777.

Thaddeus Bailey son of Josiah Bailey juner & Sarah his wife born at Lunenburg April 30th 1779.

Ruth Burnam daughter of Nathanael Burnam Jun and of Elizabeth his wife, was born at Lunenburg, December the 17th 1754.

Thomas Burnam the son of Nathanael Burnam Jun and of Elizabeth his wife was born at Littleton September the 9th 1756.

John Burnam the son of Nehemiah Burnam & of Elisabeth born at Lunenburg June the 25th 1745.

Abegail Bellows daughter of Benj^a Bellows Junr and of Abigail his wife born December ye 10th 1736.

Peter Bellows son of Benj^a Bellows Junr and of Abigail his wife born December ye 26th 1738.

Benjamin Bellows the son of Benjamin Bellows Jr and of Abigail was born September ye 25th 1740.

John Bellows the son of Benjamin Bellows and of Abigail his wife born October 22^d 1742.

Joseph Bellows the son of Benjamin Bellows and of Abigail his wife born May ye 26th 1744

Jonathan Bellows ye son of Benjamin Bellows and of Abigail his wife was born at Lunenburg March ye 29th 1746.

Abijah Bellows ye son of Benjamin Bellows & of Abigail his wife was born at Lunenburg March ye 20th 1748/9.

Lucy Butler the daughter of William Butler and of Lucy his wife, born at Lunenburg June the 25th 1738.

Rachel Butler the daughter of William Butler and of Lucy his wife, born at Lunenburg October ye 23th 1739.

Abigail Butler the daughter of the widow Lucy Butler born at Lunenburg November the 25th 1741; one and twenty day after her Father's decease.

John Bradstreet ye son of Samvel Bradstreet and Dorcas his wife was born at Rowley September ye 12th 1737.

Sarah Bradstreet the daughter of Samvel Bradstreet and Dorcas his wife, was born at Lunenburg July ye 24th 1740.

Births.

BRADSTREET. BUSS. BROWN.

Dorcas Bradstreet the daughter of Samvel Bradstreet and of Dorcas his wife, born at Lunenburg April ye 7th A. D. 1743.

Abigail Bradstreet ye daughter of Samvel Bradstreet and Dorcas his wife was born at Lunenburg May ye 19th 1745.

Olive Bradstreet ye daughter of Samvel Bradstreet and Dorcas his wife was born at Lunenburg May ye 19th 1748.

Phebe Bradstreet ye daughter of Samvel Bradstreet and of Dorcas his wife, was born at Lunenburg September ye 10th 1750.

Mary Bradstreet ye daughter of Samuel Bradstreet and Dorcas his wife, was born at Lunenburg Augst ye 1st 1752.

Releif Bradstreet the daughter of Samuel Bradstreet and of Dorcas his wife, was born at Lunenburg, June ye 2nd 1754.

Samuel Bradstreet the son of Samuel Bradstreet and of Dorcas his wife was born at Lunenburg June ye 17th 1757.

Abigail Bradstreet ye daughter of Samuel Bradstreet and of Dorcas his wife, was born at Lunenburg January ye 2nd 1759.

Vashtai Bradstreet the daughter of Samuel Bradstreet & of Dorcas his wife, was born at Lunenburg July ye 2nd 1761 after her Father's death.

Stephen Buss the son of John Buss and of Eunice his wife born at Lunenburg March ye 8th 1743/4.

Silas Buss the son of John Buss and of Eunice his wife was born at Lunenburg May ye 27th 1746.

Eunice Buss ye daughter of John Buss and of Eunice his wife was born at Lunenburg, September ye 7th 1748.

Aaron Buss the son of John Buss and of Eunice his wife was born at Lunenburg March ye 27th 1751.

Mellicent Buss the daughter of John Buss and Eunice his wife, was born at Lunenburg August 22^d 1753.

Jonathan Buss, the son of John Buss, and of Eunice his wife, was born at Lunenburg December ye 30th A. D. 1756.

Aaron Brown the son of Aaron Brown and of Abigail his wife, born at Lunenburg, Janvray the 31st 1744/5.

David Brown the son of Aaron Brown and of Abigail his wife, was born at Lunenburg, February ye 17th 1746/7.

Jonathan Brown ye son of Aaron Brown and of Abigail his wife, was born at Lunenburg, December the 13th 1754.

Hepsibeth Brown, the daughter of Aaron Brown and of Abigail his wife, was born at Lunenburg February ye 2nd 1757.

Jonathan Brown the son of Aaron Brown and of Abigail his wife, was born at Lunenburg October ye 1st 1759.

C.

CHADWICK. CARLTON. CORCKER. CARLILE. CARLTON.

Bette Chadwick the daughter of William Chadwick and of Eunice his wife, was born at Lunenburg, January ye 30th 1758.

Unice Chadwick the daughter of William Chadwick and of Unice his wife, was born at Lunenburg August ye 19th 1759.

The births of ye children of Asa Carlton and of Ruth his wife.
Asa Carlton born at Lunenburg Feby 14th 1764
Betty Carlton born at Lunenburg June 14th 1766.
Ruth Carlton daughter of Asa Carlton and Ruth his wife, was born at Lunenburg July ye 24th 1768.
Calven Carlton son of Asa Carlton and Ruth his wife, was born at Lunenburg June ye 26th 1770.
Luther Carlton son of Asa Carlton and Ruth his wife, was born at Lunenburg August ye 26th 1772.

Timothy Carlton the son of Abraham Calton and Mary his wife was born at Lunenburg May the 1st 1753.

Abigail Carlton daughter of Abraham Carlton and of Mary, his wife, was born at Lunenburg August ye 23^d 1756.

Mary Carlton ye daughter of Abraham Carlton, and of Mary his wife, was born at Lunenburg January ye 7th Annoque Domini 1759.

Nathaniel Carlton son of Abraham and Mary Carlton was born at Lunenburg March 27th 1763.

Abigail Carlton daughter of Abraham & Mary Carton was born at Lunenburg June 5th 1765.

Mary Corcker the daughter of Paul Corcker and of Lydia his wife was born at Lunenburg March ye 19th 1750/1.

Daniel Carlile ye son of David Carlile and of Leatis his wife, was born at Harvard October ye 30th 1738.

David Carlile ye son of David Carlile and of Leatis his wife was born at Lunenburg Feburary ye 20th 1740/1.

Leatis Carlile ye daughter of David Carlile and of Leatis his wife was born at Lunenburg September ye 6th 1742.

John Carlile ye son of David Carlile and of Leatis his wife, was born at Lunenburg January ye 24th 1745/6.

Bette Chaplin the daughter of David Chaplin and of Mary his wife, born at Lunenburg June ye 9th 1740.

Joseph Chaplin, the son of David Chaplin and Mary his wife, born at Lunenburg January ye 23rd A. D. 1741/2.

Births.

CHAPLIN. CORY. COREY. CUMMINGS.

Mary Chaplin y[e] daughter of David Chaplin, and of Mary his wife born April y[e] 8th 1744.

Sarah Chaplin the daughter of David Chaplin and of Mary his wife, born at Lunenburg Janvary y[e] 9th 1746/7.

David Chaplin y[e] son of David Chaplin and of Mary his wife, was born at Lunenburg March y[e] 5th 1748/9.

Mercy Chaplin the daughter of Joseph Chaplin and of Sarah his wife, was born at Lunenburg August the 27th 1748.

Anna Chaplin the daughter of Joseph Chaplin and of Sarah his wife, was born at Lunenburg May 14th 1753.

Sarah Chaplin daughter of Joseph Chaplin & Sarah his wife, was born at Lunenburg September y[e] 10th 1758.

Joseph Chaplin, son of Joseph Chaplin & Sarah his wife was born at Lunenburg October y[e] 17th 1760.

Rebekah Cory y[e] davghter of Benj[a] Cory and of Rebekah his wife, born Janewary 17th 1718/19

Mary Cory y[e] daughter of Benj[a] Cory and of Rebekah his wife, born February 10th 1725/6.

Sarah Cory y[e] daughter of Benj[a] Cory and of Rebekah his wife, born April 1, 1728.

Benj[a] Cory y[e] son of Benj[a] Cory and of Rebekah his wife, born June 15th 1731.

Eunice Corey the daughter of Benjamin Corey jun[r] and Beulah his wife was born at Lunenburg April 26th A. D. 1754.

Children of Sam[ll] Commings and of Sarah his wife.

Miriam born at Lunenburg October 1, 1728.

Thomas born in Lunenburg Sept[r] 23. 1731.

Thaddeus Cummings y[e] son of Sam[ll] Commings and of Sarah his wife born December 30th 1734.

Samvel Cummings y[e] son of Samvel Cummings, and of Sarah his wife born at Lunenburg. febb[r] 13th 1736/7.

Sarah Comings y[e] daufter of Samvel Comings & Sarah his wife, was born June y[e] 30, 1740.

Thomas Commings the son of Samvel Commings and of Sarah his wife, born at Lunenburg February y[e] 23th 1742/3.

Thaddeus Cummings y[e] son of Samvel and of Sarah his wife, was born at Lunenburg June y[e] 16th 1746.

Jonathan Commings born November y[e] 20th 1748.

COFFEN. COLBURN. CLARK. CARTER.

Eliezer Coffeen ye son of Michael Coffen and Lydia his wife, born at Lunenburg September ye 14 1731.

Lydia Coffen ye davghter of Michael Coffen and of Lydia his wife, born in Lunenburg September 8th 1733.

Amme Coffen ye davghter of Michael Coffen, and of his wife, born December ye 1th 1735.

Henery Coffen the son of Michael Coffen and of Lydia his wife, was born at Lunenburg April ye 6th 1738.

Daniel Coffen the son of Mical Coffen and Lydia his wife was born April ye 26th 1740.

Abigail Coffen ye daughter of Michael Coffen and Lydia his wife, born April the 7th 1741.

Priscilla Coffen ye daughter of Michael Coffen, and of Lydai his wife born at Lunenburg, September ye 2nd 1742.

Thomas ye son of James Colburn and of Ruth his wife born in Lunenburg December 1th 1729.

Ruth ye davghter of James Colburn and of Ruth his wife, born in Lunenburg July 16th 1732.

Sarah Colburn ye daughter of James Colburn and of Ruth his wife, was born April ye 24th 1737.

Sarah Colburn the daughter of James Colburn, and of Sarah his wife, born August ye 24th 1743.

James Colburn, the son of James Colburn and of Sarah his wife, born at Lunenburg July the 27th 1745.

Sarah Clark the daughter of Mr. Robert Clark and of Mary his wife born at Lunenburg August ye 9th 1739.

Mary Clark the daughter of Mr. Robert Clark and of Mary his wife born at Lunenburg February the eleventh A. D. 1741/2.

William Clark the son of Mr. Robert Clark and of Mary Clark born at Lunenburg November the 30th 1743.

Thomas Carter Junr the son of Thomas Carter & of Bette Carter was born at Lunenburg May ye 4th 1741.

Elijah Carter the son of Thomas Carter and of Bette Carter was born at Lunenburg February the 26 1742/3.

David Carter the son of Thomas Carter and of Bette his wife, was born at Lunenburg April the twenty-sixth 1745.

Prudence Carter ye daughter of Thomas Carter and of Bette his wife, was born at Lunenburg June ye 15th 1746.

Births.

CARTER.

John Carter ye son of Thomas Carter and of Bette his wife, was born at Lunenburg September ye 13th 1748.

Phinehas Carter son of Thomas Carter and of Betty his wife, was born at Lunenburg April 30th 1751

Beatrix Carter daughter of Thos Carter & of Betty his wife, was born at Lunenburg November ye 18th 1753.

Ruth Carter daughter of Thomas Carter & of Betty his wife, was born at Lunenburg December ye 21st A. D. 1756.

Vashti Carter ye daughter of Thomas Carter and of Betty his wife, was born at Lunenburg May ye 17th 1758.

Jonas Carter son of James and Sarah Carter, was born at Lunenburg August 5th 1762.

Keziah, born Jany 25th 1765 daughter of James & Sarah Carter.

Jerusha born April 2nd 1767 daughter of James & Sarah Carter.

D.

DEMARY. DODGE.

John Demary the son of John Demary and of Rebeckah his wife, was born at Lunenburg, August the 27th 1751.

Rebecah Demerry the daughter of John Demerry and of Rebecah his wife, was born at Lunenburg Febry 24th 1754.

Hannah Demary the daughter of John Demary and of Rebecah his wife, was born at Lunenburg Feburay ye 13th A. D. 1756.

Anne Demary the daughter of John Demary and of Rebeckah his wife, was born at Lunenburg April ye 15th 1758.

Sarah Demary ye daughter of John Demary & of Rebecah his wife, was born at Lunenburg June ye 1th 1760.

Thomas Demary ye son of John Demary & of Rebekah his wife, was born at Lunenburg July 15th 1762.

Margaret Dodge ye daughter of Noah Dodge and of Margaret his wife, born October ye 21th 1729.

Miriam Dodge ye davghter of Noah Dodge and of Margaret his wife, born March ye 23th 1732

Lipha Dodge ye daughter of Noah Dodge and of Margaret his wife, born June ye 2th 1734

Thankfull Dodge ye daughter of Noah Dodge & of Margaret his wife, born July 6th 1736.

Rhoda Dodge the daughter of Josiah Dodge and of Susanah his wife, born at Lunenburg August ye 25 A. D. 1744.

DODGE.

Sarah Dodge ye daughter of Josiah Dodge Jun and of Susanna his wife, was born at Lunenburg May the 24th 1749.

Asahel Dodge the son of Josiah Dodge Jun and of Susanna his wife, was born at Lunenburg August the 26th 1752.

Benjamin Dodge son of Josiah Dodge Junr and of Susanna his wife, was born at Lunenburg May 1st 1754.

Phebe Dodge the daughter of Josiah Dodge Jun and of Susana his wife was born at Lunenburg, September ye 23rd 1759.

Elizabeth Dodge the daughter of Zebulon Dodge and of Martha his wife, was born at Lunenburg Novr 14th 1749.

Jemima Dodge the daughter of Zebulon Dodge and of Martha his wife, was born at Lunenburg March 13th 1750/1.

Sewall Dodge the son of Zebulon Dodge and of Martha his wife, was born at Lunenburg July 21st 1752.

Barzillai Dodge the son of Zebulon Dodge and Martha his wife was born at Lunenburg Febry 8th 1753.

Barzilia Dodge son of Zebulon Dodge and Martha his wife was born February ye 8th 1754. This record was don by order of the Father, as their was a mistake in the above record of one year.

GEORGE KIMBALL *Town Clerk.*

Martha Dodge the daughter of Zebulon Dodge and of Martha his wife, was born at Lunenburg November ye 3th 1755.

Keziah Dodge daughter of Zebulon Dodge and of Martha his wife, was born at Lunenburg December ye 8th 1757.

Kerenhappuch Dodge the daughter of Zebulon Dodge and of Martha his wife, was born at Lunenburg August ye 30th 1759.

Hepsibath Dodge the daughter of Zebulon Dodge & of Martha his wife, was born at Lunenburg October ye 30th 1761.

Jesse Dodge the son of Reuben Dodge and of Ruth his wife, was born at Lunenburg August the 28th A. D. 1744.

Mary Dodge the daughter of Reuben Dodge and of Ruth his wife, born at Lunenburg, May ye 6th A. D. 1746.

Tabatha Dodge the daughter of Reuben Dodge and of Ruth his wife, was born at Lunenburg April ye 8th 1748.

Brewer Dodge the son of Reuben Dodge, and of Ruth his wife, was born at Lunenburg, December ye 4th A. D. 1749.

Levi Dodge, the son of Reuben Dodge, and of Ruth his wife, was born at Lunenburg November ye 21th A. D. 1751.

Births. 283

DODGE. DUTTON.

Tabitha Dodge the daughter of Reuben Dodge and of Ruth his wife, was born at Lunenburg December ye 31 175—*

Zadok Dodge the son of Reuben Dodge and of Ruth his wife was born at Lunenburg April ye 19. A. D. 1756.

Ester Dodge daughter of Reuben and Ruth Dodge was born at Lunenburg April 19th 1758.

John Perkins, son of Reuben and Ruth Dodge, was born at Lunenburg, July 27th 1760.

Ruth Dodge daughter of Reuben & Ruth Dodge was born at Lunenburg June 10th 1762.

Eli Dodge the son of Eli Dodge and of Abigail his wife, was born at Lunenburg, September ye 7th 1743.

Rebakah Dodge the daughter of Eli Dodge, and of Abigail his wife, was born at Lunenburg June ye 2nd 1745.

Isaac Dodge ye son of Eli Dodge & of Abigail his wife, was born at Lunenburg March ye 17th 1747/8.

Abigail Dodge the daughter of Eli Dodge and of Abigail his wife, was born at Lunenburg, December ye 25th 1751.

Prudence Dodge the daughter of Eli Dodge and of Abigail his wife, was born at Lunenburg September ye 25th 1752.

The births of the children of Seth Dodge and of Sarah his wife,

John Smith Dodge born at Lunenburg April 22^d 1761.

Hannah Dodge born at Lunenburg Jany 30th 1763.

Sarah Dodge born at Lunenburg Augt 3^d 1765.

Sarah Dodge, daughter of Seth and Sarah Dodge was born August ye 8th 1765 at Lunenburg.

Eunice Dodge daughter of Seth & Sarah Dodge was born September ye 11th 1767 at Lunenburg.

Hannah Dutton ye daughter of Thomas Dutton and of Mary his wife, born at Lunenburg, January the 28th 1744/5.

Sibel Dutton the daughter of Thomas Dutton and of Mary his wife, was born at Lunenburg December ye 9th 1747.

Thomas Dutton the son of Thomas Dutton and of Mary his wife, was born at Lunenburg, March the 18th 1749/50.

Elizabeth the daughter of Thomas Dutton and of Mary his wife, was born at Lunenburg, on the 24th day of December 1752.

Elizabeth Dutton the daughter of Thomas Dutton and of Mary his wife, was born at Lunenburg December the 18th 1752.

---

*John R. Rollins states that the remainder of the date is nearly obliterated, but he should judge it to be 1753. [W. A. D

DUTTON. DIVOL. DARLING.

Joseph Fitch Dutton the son of Thomas Dutton and Sarah his wife, was born at Lunenburg June ye 3rd 1757.

Susannah Dutton the daughter of Thomas Dutton and of Sarah his wife, was born at Lunenburg March ye 7th 1759.

John Dutton the son of Thomas Dutton & of Sarah his wife, was born at Lunenburg July ye 9th 1761.

Ephraim Dutton the son of Ephraim Dutton and of Thankfull his wife, was born at Lunenburg Aug^st the 30th A. D. 1753.

Jerusha Dutton ye daughter of Ephraim Dutton and of Thankfull his wife, was born at Lunenburg, February the 4th A. D. 1755.

Susanna Divol daughter of Manassah Divol & Sarah his wife, was born at Lunenburg January 25th 17—— [Lost.]

Josiah Divol ye son of John Divol and Sarah his wife, born at Lunenburg March the 7th 1736/7.

Levi Divol ye son of John Divol and of Sarah his wife born at Lunenburg April ye 19th 1742.

The births of the children of John Divol and of Phebe his wife
Keziah Divol born at Lunenburg Feby 28th 1748.
Elizabeth Divol born at Lunenburg Feby 22^d 1750.
Phebe Divol born at Lunenburg Jany 14th 1752.
Manasseh Divol born at Lunenburg Novr 17th 1753
Susannah Divol born at Lunenburg Jany 16th 1758.

John Darling ye son of John Darling Jun and of Ruth his wife was born at Lunenburg December ye 11th 1744.

Ruth Darling ye daughter of John Darling jun and of Ruth his wife was born at Leominster December ye 21th 1746.

Lois Darling ye daughter of John Darlin jun and of Ruth his wife, was born at Lunenburg June ye 26th 1749.

John Darling the son of John Darlin jun and of Ruth his wife, was born at Lunenburg October ye 1th 1751.

Unity Darlin was born at Lunenburg July ye 12th 1755.*

Amity Darling daughter of John & Ruth Darling was born at Lunenburg Octr 28th 1757.

Juet Boynton Darling ye son of John Darling jun. and of Ruth his wife, was born at Lunenburg, February ye 23rd 1760.

---

*John R. Rollins says no doubt the daughter of John Jr. and Ruth. [W. A. D,

Births.

DARLING. DAVIS. DESCOMB. DOWNE. DUNSMOOR.

Timothy Darling son of Timothy Darling and of Joanna his wife, was born at Lunenburg April 6th 1754.

James Darlin the son of Timothy Darlin and of Joanna his wife, was born at Lunenburg March ye 7th 1756.

David & Benjamin Darling sons of Timothy Darling and of Joanna his wife, were born at Lunenburg October ye 6th Annoq: Domini 1758.

John Darling son of Timothy Darlin and of Joanna his wife was born at Lunenburg August ye 13th 1759.

Daniel Darling son of Timothy Darling and Joanna his wife, was born at Winchindon July ye 19: 1761.

The birth of ye children of Samll Davis and of Sarah his wife
Samuell born at Lunenburg March ye 20: 1730
Sarah ye davghter of Samll Davis and of Sarah his wife born in Lunenburg December ye 7th 1732.
Samuell Davis ye son of Samll Davis and of Sarah his wife born June ye 7th 1735.
Joseph Davis ye son of Samvel Davis and of Sarah his wife born May ye 20th 1738.

Jacob Descomb the son of James Descomb & of Elizabeth his wife, was born at Lunenburg September ye 15th 1760.

Sarah Dascombe daughter of James and Elizabeth Dascombe was born at Lunenburg July 14th 1762.

Samvel Downe the son of Mr. William Downe and of Margaret his wife, born at Cambridge Janvary ye 17th A. D. 1744/5.

Sarah Downe the daughter of Mr. William Downe and of Margaret his wife, born at Lunenburg December the 20th 1746.

Margaret Downe ye daughter of Mr. William Downe and of Margaret his wife was born at Lunenburg August the 19th 1749.

Elizabeth Downe ye daughter of William Downe and Margaret his wife, was born at Lunenburg December the 18th 1751.

John Dunsmoor the son of Dr. John Dunsmoor and of Ruth his wife, was born at Lunenburg Janvary ye 25th 1747.

Phinehas Dunsmoor ye son of Dr. John Dunsmoor and of Ruth his wife, was born at Lunenburg April ye 4th 1750.

Ruth Dunsmoor the daughter of Dr. John Dunsmoor and of Ruth his wife, was born at Lunenburg May the 25th 1752.

Rebekah Dunsmoor the daughter of Dr. John Dunsmoor and of Ruth his wife, was born at Lunenburg May ye 4th 1754.

DUNSMOOR.

Hannah Dunsmoor daughter of John Dunsmoor, and Ruth his wife was born at Lunenburg May 4th 1756.

Ebenezer Dunsmoor son of John and Ruth Dunsmoor was born at Lunenburg August 29th 1758.

E.

EATON.

Rebekah Eaton daughter of Peirson Eaton and of Anna his wife was born at Lunenburg April 17th 1753.

Peirson Eaton son of Peirson Eaton and of Anna his wife born at Lunenburg June 10th 1754.

Joseph Eaton son of Pearson Eaton and of Anna his wife was born at Lunenburg March ye 29th 1756.

Anne Eaton daughter of Peirson Eaton and of Anna his wife was born at Lunenburg February ye 24th Anno Domini 1758.

John Eaton son of Person Eaton and of Anna his wife was born at Lunenburg February ye 5th 1760.

Benjn Eaton son of Pearson & Anna Eaton was born at Lunenburg March 4th 1762.

William Eatton son of Person Eatton born at Lunenburg March ye 12 1767.

Sarah Eaton daughter of Pearson & Anna Eaton was born at Lunenburg January ye 3^d 1770.

Ebeneazer Eaton son of Pearson Eaton and Anna, his wife, was born at Lunenburg October ye 17th 1772.

Calven Eaton son of Pearson Eaton and Anna his wife was born at Lunenburg Nov: 6th 1774.

F.

FARNSWORTH. FARMER.

The birth of ye children of Isaac Farnsworth and of Sarah his wife.
Isaac born at Groton November 30: 1723.
William born at Lunenburg Feb^r 26. 1725/6.
Sarah born at Lunenburg Novem^{br} 27: 1727.
Lydia born at Lunenburg July 4: 1729 and dyed July 10: 1729
Lydia ye 3^d daughter born at Lunenburg July 25: 1730.
Mary born at Lunenburg June ye 2th 1735.

Rebekah ye daughter of John Farmer & of Rebekah his wife, born at Lunenburg June ye 1th 1732.

Births.

FARMER. FITCH. FOSTER.

Rachel ye davghter of John Farmer & of Rebekah his wife born in Lunenburg, June ye 27th 1733.

Rebekah Farmer ye daughter of John Farmer & of Rebekah his wife, born April ye 8th 1735.

Catherine Fitch ye davghter of John Fitch and of Susannah his wife, born April ye 28th 1735.

John Fitch Junr son of John Fitch and Susannah his wife was born at Lunenburg May ye 16th 1737.

Paul Fitch the son of John Fitch and of Susanna his wife, was born at Lunenburg Janvary ye 4th 1741/2.

Jacob Fitch the son of John Fitch and of Susannah his wife, was born at Lunenburg June ye 29th 1744.

Susanna Fitch the daughter of John Fitch, and of Susanna his wife, was born at Lunenburg Februray the 18th 1746/7.

Molly Fitch daughter of John and Elizabeth Fitch, was born at Lunenburg Novr 23^d 1752.

Sarah Fitch daughter of John and Elizabeth Fitch was born at Lunenburg June 11th 1755.

Benjamin Forster the son of Benjamin Forster and of Mehetabel his wife, was born on Munday January the tweneth 1729.

Stephen Forster the son of Benjamin Forster and of Mehetable his wife was born January y^e (21st) twenty-first, on Thursday, 1731.

Joseph Forster ye son of Benjamin Forster and of Mehetable his wife was born on Satterday, March the twenty fourth 1732/3.

Abbigal Foster ye daughter of Benjamin Forster and of Mehetable his wife, was born on Sabath day March ye thirtieth 1735.

Elizabath Foster the daughter of Benjamin Forster and of Mehetable his wife was born on Friday, Feb^r the twenty first 1736/7.

Dorothy Forster the daughter of Benjamin Foster and of Mehetable his wife, born May the fifth 1739.

Nathan Foster ye son of Benjamin Foster & of Mehetabel his wife was born June ye 7th 1741.

James Foster ye son of Benjamin Foster and of Mehetabel was born April ye 19th 1743.

Enoch Foster the son of Benjamin Foster and of Mehetabel his wife was born August the 16th 1745.

Mehetabel Foster ye daughter of Benjamin Foster, and of Mehetabel his wife, was born at Lunenburg March ye 15th 1747/8.

Sarah Foster ye daughter of Benjamin Foster and of Mehetabel his wife, was born at Lunenburg March ye 7th 1751/2.

FOSTER. FULLER.

Mary Foster daughter of Isaac Foster and Mary his wife was born at Lunenburg November ye 8 1746.

Benj^a Foster son of Isaac Foster and Mary his wife was born at Lunenburg May ye 26. 1748.

Isaac Foster son of Isaac Foster and Mary his wife was born at Lunenburg August ye 15th 1751.

Keziah Foster daughter of Isaac Foster and Mary his wife was born February ye 10th 1753. was born at Lunenburg.

Richard Foster son of Isaac Foster and Mary his wife was born at Luneburg July ye 31 1756.

Rebeckah Foster ye daughter of Joseph Foster and of Sarah his wife, was born at Lunenburg September ye 16th 1760.

Enoch Foster son of Joseph & Sarah Foster was born at Lunenburg August 21st 1762.

James Foster son of Joseph & Sarah Foster was born at Lunenburg April 24th 1764.

Mary Fuller daughter of Joseph Fuller & Abigail his wife was born August the 15 1736.

Abigail Fuller ye daughter of John Fuller and of Prudence his wife, was born at Lunenburg August ye 30th A. D. 1756.

John Fuller ye son of John Fuller and of Prudence, his wife, was born at Lunenburg April ye 26th 1758.

Prudence Fuller, the daughter of John Fuller, and of Prudence his wife, was born at Lunenburg October the 21th 1759.

Elizabeth Fuller daughter of John and Prudence Fuller was born at Lunenburg Octo^r 21st 1764.

John & James Fuller sons of John & Prudence Fuller were born at Lunenburgh March 28th 1768.

Stephen Fuller ye son of Nehemiah Fuller and of Mary his wife, was born at Lunenburg August ye 19, 1757.

Joseph Fuller ye son of Nehemiah Fuller and of Mary his wife, was born at Lunenburg July ye 22nd 1759.

Nehemiah Fuller ye son of Nehemiah Fuller and Mary his wife was born at Lunenburg Jany 23^d 1762.

Azeriah Fuller son of Nehemiah Fuller & Mary his wife was born at Lunenburg May 28th 1764.

Births.

FISK. FOWLER. FLOOD.

Jemima Fisk the daughter of Jonathan Fisk and of Jemima his wife, born at Lunenburg, February the 8th 1738/9.

Ezekiel Fowler the son of Richard Fowler and of Ruth his wife, born at Lunenburg March ye 18th 1742/3

Susanna Fowler ye daughter of Richard Fowler and of Ruth his wife, was born at Lunenburg May ye 31th 1746.

Ruth Fowler ye daughter of Richard Fowler and of Ruth his wife was born at Lunenburg August ye 18th 1748.

Richard Fowler ye son of Richard Fowler and of Ruth his wife was born at Groton September ye 21th 1750.

Elizabeth Fowler the daughter of Richard Fowler and of Ruth his wife was born at Lunenburg Novembr 15th 1752.

Joshua Chever Fowler & Sarah Chever Fowler the son and daughter of Richard Fowler & of Ruth his wife, were born at Lunenburg January ye 16th 1757.

Alice Flood the daughter of Benjamin Flood, and Elizabath his wife was born at Lunenburg, November the 22d; 1743.

G.

GOODRIDGE.

Sarah Goodridge ye daughter of Benjamin Goodridge and of Sarah his wife, born Janewary ye 1th 1730/31

Eliphalet Goodridge ye son of Benjamin Goodridge and of Sarah his wife born March ye 27th 1733.

Olive Goodridge ye davghter of Benja Goodridge and of Sarah his wife, born July 3d 1736.

Daniel Goodridge ye son of Benjamin Goodridge & of Sarah his wife, born at Lunenburg, August ye eleventh, on Fryday 1738.

Benjamin Goodridge Junr the son of Benjamin Goodridge and Sarah his wife, was born at Lunenburg July ye 7th 1740.

Sewall Goodridge the son of Benja Goodridge and of Sarah his wife, was born at Lunenburg July ye 7th 1743 about midnight.

Lois Goodridge the daughter of Benjamin Goodridge and of Sarah his wife, was born at Lunenburg March the 21th 1744/5.

Lucy Goodridge the daughter of Benjamin Goodridge, and of Sarah his wife, was born at Lunenburg, Janvary the 25th 1746/7.

Oliver Goodridge the son of Benjamin Goodridge, and of Sarah his wife, was born at Lunenburg October the 27th 1749.

GOODRIDGE.

Lydia Goodridge the daughter of Joshua Goodridge and of Lydia his wife, was born at Lunenburg, August the first, 1740.

Mehetabel Goodridge the daughter of Joshua Goodridge and of Lydia his wife was born at Lunenburg May ye 9th 1742.

Relief Goodridge the daughter of Joshua Goodridge and Lydia his wife, was born at Lunenburg March ye 25th 1744.

Joshua Goodridge the son of Joshua Goodridge and of Lydia his wife, born at Lunenburg August ye 10th 1746.

Kathrine Goodridge the daughter of Joshua and of Lydia his wife was born at Lunenburg August the 28th 1749.

Ruth Goodridge the daughter of Joshua Goodridge and of Lydia his wife, was born at Lunenburg September the 13th 1751.

Abijah Goodridge the son of Joshua Goodridge & of Lydia his wife was (born) at Lunenburg February the 21th 1754.

Abigal Goodridge the daughter of Joshua Goodridge and of Lydia his wife, was born at Lunenburg November ye 24th A. D. 1756.

Phinehas Goodridge son of Joshua and Lydia Goodridge was born at Lunenburg Octo^r 17th 1759.

Lois Goodridge daughter of Joshua & Lydia Goodridge was born at Lunenburg March 9th 1763.

David Goodridge the son of David Goodridge and of Elizabath his wife, born at Lunenburg March ye 19th 1741/2.

Elizabeth Goodridge the daughter of David Goodridge & of Elizabeth, born November ye 6th 1743.

Mehetabel Goodridge the daughter of David Goodridge, and of Elizabeth his wife, born at Lunenburg, August the sixth A. D. 1745.

David Goodridge the son of David Goodridge and of Elizabath his wife, was born at Lunenburg April ye 23rd 1747.

Ebenezer Goodridge the son of David Goodridge, and of Elizabeth his wife, was born at Lunenburg May the 1th 1749.

Asaph Goodridge the son of David Goodridge and of Elizabeth his wife, was born at Lunenberg June ye 28th 1751.

Hannah Goodridge the daughter of David Goodridge & Elizabeth his wife, was born at Lunenburg, April 7th 1753.

John Goodridge the son of David Goodridge & of Elizabeth his wife, was born at Lunenburg March ye 17th 1755.

Eunice Goodridge the daughter of David Goodridge and of Elizabeth his wife, was born at Lunenburg August ye 6th 1757.

GOODRIDGE.

Abigail Goodridge the daughter of Philip Goodridge and of Jane his wife, was born at Lunenburg July ye 31th A. D. 1745.

Jane Goodridge ye daughter of Philip Goodridge and of Jane his wife, was born at Lunenburg July the 7th A. D. 1747.

Priscila Goodridge ye daughter of Philip Goodridge and of Jane his wife was born at Lunenburg Janvary ye 15th 1748/9.

Philip Goodridge the son of Philip Goodridge, and of Jane his wife, born at Lunenburg October the 4th 1750.

Sibil Goodridge the daughter of Philip Goodridge & of Jane his wife, was born at Lunenburg June the 10th 1752.

Mary Goodridge the daughter of Philip Goodridge & of Jane his wife, was born at Lunenburg February the 16th 1754.

Joseph Goodridge the son of Philip Goodridge and of Jane his wife, was born at Lunenburg September ye 14th 1755.

William Goodridge the son of Philip Goodridge and of Jane his wife, was born at Lunenburg July ye 17th 1757.

Juet Goodridge the son of Philip Goodridge and of Jane Goodridge was born August ye 8th 1759.

Abel Goodridridge son of Phillip and Jane Goodridge was born at Lunenburgh Septr 19th 1761.

Simon Goodridge son of Philip and Jane Goodridge was born at Lunenburgh August 9th 1763.

Sarah Goodridge daughter of Philip & Jane Goodridge was born at Lunenburgh Feby 12th 1766.

Elizebath Goodridge daughter of Philip Goodridge and Jane his wife, was born at Lunenburg July ye 14th 1768.

Ezekiel Goodridge the son of Ezekiel Goodridge and of Rebacca his wife was born at Lunenburg May ye 5th 1755.

Sarah Goodridge, daughter of Eliphalet (Goodridge) & Rebecca his wife, born at Lunenburg Octo^r 15th 1764.

Rebekah Goodridge, daughter of Eliphalet & Rebekah Goodridge was born at Lunenburg March 17th 1766.

Samuel Payson Goodridge son of Eliphelet & Rebekah Goodridge, was born at Lunenburgh Jany 23^d 1768.

Rebekah Goodridge daughter of Eliphelet Goodridge & Rebekah his wife, was born at Lunenburg December ye 7th 1769.

Elizabeth Goodridge daughter of Eliphalet Goodridge & Rebeckah his wife, was born at Lunenburg February ye 17th 1772.

Eliphalet Goodridge son of Eliphalet Goodridge & Rebeckah his wife, was born at Lunenburg August ye 10th 1773.

GILLSON. GOULD.

The Birth of the children of Jonas Gillson and of Hannah his wife,
(1.) Jonas born at Lunenburg August 31 1728
(2.) Evnice born at Lunenburg March 18 1731
(3.) Prudence Gillson ye daughter of Jonas Gillson and of Hannah his wife born May 8th 1734.
(4.) Joseph Gillson ye son of Jonas Gilson and of Hannah his wife born at Lunenburg September ye 16th 1738.

Sarah Gillson ye daughter of Jonas Gillson and of Sarah his wife, was born at Lunenburg Febuary ye 11th 1757.
Unice Gilson daughter of Jonas and Sarah Gilson was born at Lunenburg May 11th 1759.

Children of David Gould and Abigall his wife.
Abigill born at Topsfield February ye 8th 1726/7.
Rebekah born at Lunenburg March 25 1728
Solomon born at Lunenburg Decem^{br} 15 1730
Joseph born at Lunenburg Janewary ye 18th 1732.

Nemiah Gould ye son of Moses Gould and of Mary his wife, born Febrvary ye 19th 1729/30.
Moses Gould ye son of Moses Gould, and of Mary his wife born July ye 4th 1732.
Benj^a Gould ye son of Moses Gould & of Mary his wife born August ye 15th 1734.

Jonathan Gould ye son of Jonathan Gould, and Lydia, his wife, born July ye 24th 1731.
Lydia Gould ye davghter of Jonathan Gould and of Lydia his wife born December ye 21th 1732.
Mary Gould davghter of Jonath Gould & of Lydia his wife born Janvary 1th 1734/5.
Margarate Gould the daughter of Jonathan Gould & of Lydia his wife, was born April ye 16th 1737.

Marcy ye davghter of Jacob Gould, and of Dorotha his wife born in Lunenburg March ye 4th 1731/2.
Oliver Gould ye son of Jacob Gould and of Dorotha his wife, born in Lunenburg October ye 3th 1733.
Sarah Gould ye daughter of Jacob Gould and of Dorrothy his wife, born at Lunenburg April the 6th 1735
Jacob Gould the son of Jacob Gould and of Dorothy his wife, born at Lunenburg October the 16th 1737.

Births. 293

GOULD. GIBSON.

Dorrothy Gould ye daughter of Jacob Gould and of Dorrothy his wife, was born at Lunenburg August ye 27th 1740.

Elijah Gould ye son of Jacob Gould and Dorrothy his wife, born at Lunenburg August ye 8th 1743.

Thomas Gould ye son of Jacob Gould and of Dorrothy, his wife, born at Lunenburg October ye 20th 1745.

Benjamin Gould Junr ye son of Benjamin Gould and of Esther his wife, was born at Lunenburg Janvary the 31th 1740/41.

Amos Gould the son of Benjamin Gould and of Eshter his wife, born February ye 7th 1743/4.

Oliver Gould ye son of Oliver Gould and of Mary his wife was born at Lunenburg, March ye 31th 1760.

Sarah Gould, daughter of Oliver and Mary Gould, was born at Lunenburg August 16th 1762.

Lucy Gould, daughter of Oliver & Mary Gould, was born at Lunenburg Septr 9th 1764.

Mary Gould daughter of Oliver & Mary Gould, was born at Lunenburg Octor 16th 1766.

Samvel Gibson ye son of Arrington Gibson and of Mary his wife, was born at Lunenburg June ye 4th 1741.

Silas Gibson ye son of Arrington Gibson, and of Mary his wife, was born at Lunenburg September the 1th 1747.

Sarah Gibson the daughter of John Gibson and of Elizabath his wife, was born at Lunenburg June ye 8th 1743.

Isaac Gibson ye son (of) Isaac Gibson & of Keziah his wife, was born at Lunenburg November ye 28th A. D. 1745.

John Gibson the son of Isaac Gibson, and of Keziah his wife, was born at Lunenburg July ye 25th 1747.

Abraham Gibson the son of Isaac Gibson and of Keziah his wife, was born at Lunenburg June ye 13th 1749.

Jacob Gibson the son of Isaac Gibson and Keziah his wife, born March the 6th 1751 at Lunenburg.

Nathaniel Gibson the son of Isaac Gibson & Keziah his wife, was born at Lunenburg Febry 22d A. D. 1753.

David Gibson the son of Isaac Gibson & Keziah his wife, was born at Lunenburg Janvary ye 22nd 1757.

Jonathan Gibson the son of Isaac Gibson & of Keziah his wife was born at Lunenburg December ye 22nd 1757

GIBSON. GARY. GARDNER. GROUT.

Solomon Gibson the son of Isaac Gibson and of Keziah his wife, was born at Lunenburg November ye 19th 1758.

Abraham Gibson son of Isaac Gibson & of Keziah his wife was born at Lunenburg June 13th 1760.

Keziah Gibson, daughter of Isaac Gibson & Keziah his wife was born at Lunenburg Febu^y 10th 1762.

Edward Garey the son of Edward Garey & Phebe his wife was born at Wobourn Septr the 2^d 1752.

Phebe Gary the daughter of Edward Gary and of Phebe his wife, was born at Lunenburg September ye 30th 1755.

Mary Garey the daughter of Edward Garey and of Phebe his wife, was born at Lunenburg, February ye 7th 1759.

John Gary son of Edward & Phebe Gary was born at Lunenburg August 25th 1761.

Elizabeth Gary daughter of Edward and Phebe Gary was born at Lunenburg Feby 26th 1764.

Benjamin Gary the son of Thomas Gary & of Elizabeth his wife was born at Lunenburg September ye 19th 1760.

Andrew Gardner ye son of Mr. Andrew Gardner and of Mrs. Susanna Gardner his wife, born at Lunenburg, Nouember ye 2th 1729.

Susanna Gardner ye daughter of Mr. Andrew Gardner and of Mrs. Susanna Gardner his wife, born at Lunenburg September ye 2th 1732.

The Birth of ye children of John Grout and of Johannah his wife.
Hilkiah born July ye 23th 1728
Johannah born Janewary ye 8th 1729/30.
John born June ye 13th 1731
Elijah born October ye 29th 1732
Joel born March the 6th 1734/5.
Jonathan born July the 23, 1737.
Sarah born November the 28 1738
Patience born August 23th 1740.
Peter born October 9 1744.
Abigail born March the 23 1745
Josiah born November 18 1748
Solomon born June 27th 1751
Jehosaphat born August 2^d 1753

Phebe Grout the daughter of John Grout jun and of Phebe his wife, was born at Lunenburg March the 21th 1751.

Births.

GROUT. GOWEN.

Elijah Grout ye son of John Grout jun and of Phebe his wife, was born at Charlestown in the Province of New-Hampshire Janvary ye 26th 1753.

Susannah Grout the daughter of John Grout jun and of Phebe his wife, was born at Lunenburg December ye 12th 1754.

Endymia Grout the daughter of John Grout and of Phebe his wife, was born at Lunenburg Decem ye 23d A. D. 1756.

Theodore Grout son of John & Phebe Grout, was born at Lunenburg August 23d 1759.

Endymia Grout daughter of John & Phebe Grout, was born at Lunenburg August 5th 1761.

John Butler Grout son of John & Phebe Grout was born at Lunenburg April 28th 1763.

Jonathan Gowin son of Jon^a and Anne Gowen was born at Lunenburg Septr 25th 1762

Thos Gowen son of Jon^a and Anne Gowen, was born at Lunenburg April 19th 1764.

Anna Gowen daughter of Jon^a & Anna Gowen, was born at Lunenburgh June 14th 1766

Eliab Gowen son of Jonathan & Anna Gowen, was born at Lunenburg Sept^m ye 6th 1770

Asahel Gowen son of Jonathan & Anna Gowen was born at Lunenburg June ye 30th 1772

Benjamin Gowen son of Jonathan & Anna Gowen, was born at Lunenburg June ye 14th 1774.

John Kendel Gowen son of Jonathan & Hannah Gowen was born at Lunenburg February ye 25th 1777

Hannah Going daughter of Jonathan & Hannah Going was born at Lunenburg January 11th 1779.

James Going son of Jonathan & Hannah Going was born at Lunenburg December 24th 1780.

H.

HAMMOND.

Susannah Hammond ye daughter of Jonathan Hammond and of Abigail his wife, was born at Lunenburg Janvary ye first 1746/7.

Mary Hammond ye daughter of Jonathan Hammond, and of Abigail his wife, was born at Lunenburg September ye 26th 1749.

Avis Hammon the daughter of Samuel Hammon and of Anna his wife, was born at Lunenburg April ye 3rd 1753.

HAMMON. HOUGHTON.

Anna Hammon the daughter of Samuel Hammon and of Anna his wife, was born at Lunenburg September ye 28th 1754.

Samuel Hammon the son of Samuel Hammon and of Anna his wife was born at Lunenburg July ye 25th 1756.

Phinehas Hammon ye son of Samuel Hammon and of Anna his wife, was born at Lunenburg September ye 11th 1758.

Elizabath Houghton ye daughter of Eleazar Houghton & of Elizabath his wife, born at Lunenburg December ye 5th 1728.

Ruth, ye daughter of Eleazar Houghton, and of Elizabath his wife, born at Lunenburg June ye 30th 1732.

Esther Houghton ye daughter of Eleazer Houghton and of Elizabeth his wife, born January ye 17th 1734/5.

Eleazer Houghton ye son of Eleazer Houghton and of Elizabath his wife, born at Lunenburg August ye 26: 1737.

Susanna Houghton the daughter of Eleazer Houghton and of Elizabath his wife, born at Lunenburg May ye 10th 1743.

Darius Houghton, the son of Darius Houghton, and of Jerusha his wife, was born at Lunenburg October the 4th 1751.

Darius Houghton son of Darius Houghton, and of Jerusha his wife, was born at Lunenburg April 12. 1754.

David Houghton the son of Darius Houghton and of Jerusha his wife, was born at Lunenburg April the 8th 1756.

Adonijah Houghton the son of Darius Houghton and of Jerusha his wife, was born at Lunenburg May ye 28th 1758.

Asael Houghton, the son of Darius Houghton and of Jerusha his wife, was born at Lunenburg January ye 11th 1760.

Elizabeth Houghton, daughter of Darius Houghton and Jerusha his wife, was born at Lunenburg November 9th 1761.

John Houghton son of Darius & Jerusha Houghton, was born at Lunenburg, Novr 21st 1763.

Anna Houghton daughter of Darius & Jerusha Hough^n was born at Lunenburg Septr 22^d 1765.

Susannah Houghton daughter of Eleazar Houghton Junr and of Susannah his wife, was born at Lunenburg August 8th 1764.

Manasseh Houghton son of Eleazar Houghton Junr and of Susannah his wife, was born at Lunenburgh Septr 28th 1765.

Judith Houghton daughter of Eleazar Houghton Junr and of Susannah his wife, was born at Lunenburgh Decr 1st 1766.

Births.

HOUGHTON. HARTWELL.

Sarah Houghton, daughter of Eleazar Houghton jun^r and of Susannah his wife, was born at Lunenburgh, March 10th 1768.

Stephen Houghton, son of Eleazer Houghton Junr & of Susanna his wife, was born at Lunenburg October ye 27th 1769.

Eleazer Houghton ye 3^d, son of Eleazer Houghton Junr & of Susannah his wife, was born at Lunenburg, March ye 26 1771.

Esther Houghton, daughter of Eleazer Houghton jun^r & of Susannah his wife, was born at Lunenburg November ye 6th 1772.

Ruth Houghton, daughter of Eleazer Houghton & Susannah his wife, was born at Lunenburg December 13th 1776.

Lois Houghton, daughter of Eleazer Houghton & Susannah his wife, born at Lunenburg December 15th 1778.

Joseph Hartwell the son of Edward Hartwell, and of Sarah, his wife, born May 14th 1727.

Benj^a Hartwell ye son of Edward Hartwell and of Sarah his wife, born October 17th 1729.

Phenihas Hartwell ye son of Edward Hartwell and of Sarah his wife, born Janewary 2th 1731/2.

Thomas Hartwell the son of Edward Hartwell jun^r and Elesibath his wife, was born at Lunenburg, June ye 5th 1740.

Solomon Hartwell son of Edward Hartwell jun^r and Elizabeth his wife, born at Lunenburg December ye 2nd 1741.

Elizabath Hartwell the daughter of Edward Hartwell Junr and of Elizabath his wife, was born at Lunenburg December ye 5th 1742.

Mary Hartwell the daughter of Edward Hartwell and of Elizabeth his wife, was born at Lunenburg October the 22nd 1744.

Edward Hartwell the son of Edward Hartwell jun and of Elizabeth his wife was born at Lunenburg August ye 22nd 1747.

Asahel Hartwell the son of Edward Hartwell jun and of Elizabeth his wife was born at Lunenburg August the 24th 1749.

Solomon Hartwell the son of Edward Hartwell jun, and of Elizabeth his wife, was born at Lunenburg July ye 18 1751.

Mary Hartwell the daughter of Edward Hartwell jun, and Elizabeth his wife, was born at Lunenburg Septr ye 1st 1753.

Martha Hartwell the daughter of Edward Hartwell and of Elizabeth his wife, was born at Lunenburg August the 14th 1755.

John Hartwell the son of Edward Hartwell jun. and of Elizabeth his wife, was born at Lunenburg April ye 2nd 1758.

Samuel Hartwell son of Edward Hartwell jun. and of Elizabeth his wife, was born at Lunenburg April ye 20th 1760.

HARTWELL.

Lydia Hartwell, daughter of Edward and Elizabeth Hartwell, was born at Lunenburg April 11th 1765.

Sarah Hartwell ye daughter of Jonathan Hartwell, and of Elizabeth his wife was born at Lunenburg November ye 23d 1746.

Jonathan Hartwell ye son of Jonathan and of Elizabeth his wife, was born at Lunenburg October ye 25th 1748.

Elisabeth Hartwell, daughter of Jonathan Hartwell and Elisabeth his wife, was born at Lunenburg April the 14th 1751.

Tamar Hartwell daughter of Jona and Elizabeth Hartwell was born at Lunenburg August 5th 1753.

Lucy Hartwell daughter of Jona & Elizabeth Hartwell, was born at Lunenburg August 24th 1758.

Eunice Hartwell daughter of Jona & Elizabeth Hartwell was born at Lunenburg May 20th 1761.

Susanna Hartwell daughter of Jona & Elizabeth Hartwell was born at Lunenburg Septr 22d 1763.

Josiah Hartwell the son of Joseph Hartwell and of Tabatha his wife, was born at Lunenburg August ye 7th 1748.

Prudence Hartwell the daughter of Joseph Hartwell and of Tabatha his wife, was born at Lunenburg February ye 19th 1750/1.

William Hartwell ye son of Joseph Hartwell and of Tabatha his wife, was born at Lunenburg, February ye 15th 1752.

Ruth Hartwell the daughter of Joseph Hartwell and of Tabatha his wife, was born at Lunenburg, April ye 11th 1754.

Ephraim Hartwell son of Phinehas Hartwell & of Mary his wife, was born at Lunenburg Octor ye 7th 1755.

Molly Hartwell, daughter of Phinehas Hartwell & Mary his wife, was born at Lunenburg February ye 7th 1757.

Esther Hartwell daughter of Phinehas Hartwell & of Mary his wife, was born at Lunenburg, January ye 15th 1759.

Abijah Hartwell son of Phinehas Hartwell & of Mary his wife, was born at Lunenburg July ye 28th 1761.

Joseph Hartwell son of Joseph and Phebe Hartwell, was born at Lunenburg, Decr 28th 1757.

Benjamin Hartwell, son of Joseph and Phebe Hartwel was born at Lunenburg July 18th 1759.

Reuben Hartwel, son of Joseph & Phebe Hartwel was born at Lunenburg July 4th 1762.

Births.

HARTWELL. HART. HUNT. HAZELTINE.

Jacob Hartwell son of Joseph & Phebe Hartwell, was born at Lunenburg June 1st 1765.

Tabitha Hartwell daughter of Joseph and Phebe Hartwell was born at Lunenburgh July 14th 1768,

John Heartwell, son of Joseph Hartwell and Phebe his wife, was born at Lunenburg September ye 4th 1770.

Katharine Hartwell daughter of Joseph Hartwell & of Phebe his wife, was born at Lunenburg August ye 27: 1772.

Samuel Hart jun the son of Samuel Hart and of Mary his wife, was born at Lunenburg January ye 26th 1759.

Abigail Hart the daughter of Samuel Hart & of Mary his wife, was born at Lunenburg August ye 27th 1760.

Ebenezer Hart son of Sam^{ll} & Mary Hart, was born at Lunenburg Decr 6th 1762.

Mary Hart daughter of Samuel Hart and Mary his wife, was born at Lunenburg, February ye 25th 1765.

Elizabath Hart daughter of Samuel Hart and Mary his wife, was born at Lunenburg December ye 17th 1766.

Nathaniel Hart, son of Samuel Hart and Mary his wife, was born at Lunenburg September ye 27th 1768.

Jonathan Hunt ye son of Samuel Hunt and of Hannah his wife, was born at Lunenburg July the 2nd 1750.

Hannah Hunt the daughter of Samuel Hunt and of Hannah his wife, was born at Lunenburg July 22d 1754.

Martha Hunt the daughter of Samuel Hunt, and of Hannah his wife, was born at Lunenburg April ye 2nd A. D. 1757.

Ebenezer Hunt the son of Samuel Hunt, and of Hannah his wife, was born at Lunenburg April ye 18th 1760.

Pearley Hunt son of Samuel & Hannah Hunt was born at Lunenburg Novr 22d 1762.

Amos Hazeltine the son of Amos Hazeltine and of Eunice his wife, was born Lunenburg June the 22nd 1748.

Thomas Hazeltine the son of Amos Hazeltine, and of Eunice his wife, was born at Lunenburg December the first 1750.

Jonas Hazeltine son of Amos Hazeltine, and Eunice his wife, born at Lunenburg Febry 7th 1753.

William Hazeltine, son of Amos Hazeltine, and of Eunice his wife, born at Lunenburg May ye 8th A. D. 1755.

HAZELTINE. HUCHINGS. HUTCHENS. HARRINGTON.

Richard Hazeltine son of Amos Hazeltine and of Eunice his wife, was born at Lunenburg April ye 28th 1757.

Joseph Hazeltine, son of Amos Hazeltine and of Eunice his wife, was born at Lunenburg, July ye 1st 1759.

John Hazeltine son of Amos Hazeltine and of Eunice his wife, was born at Lunenburg, March ye 26th 1762

Ebenezer Hazeltine, son of Amos Hazeltine and of Eunice his wife, was born at Lunenburg September ye 19th 1764.

David Hazeltine, son of Amos Hazeltine and of Eunice his wife, was born at Lunenburg February ye 7th 1767.

Eunice Hazeltine daughter of Amos Hazeltine and of Eunice his wife, was born at Lunenburg July ye 11 1769.

Ephraim Hazeltine son of Amos Hazeltine and of Eunice his wife, was born at Lunenburg March ye 29. 1772.

Abraham Heseltine son of Amos & Eunice Heseltine, was born October 15th 1775.

Loas Huchings the daughter of Joseph Huchings and Sarah his wife, was born at Tuxbury Jenevary ye 22th 1737.

John Huchings the son of Joseph Huchings and Sarah his wife, was born at Tuxbury November ye 27th 1739

Sarah Hutchens daughter of Phinehas Hutchens & Abigail his wife, was born at Lunenburg April ye 6. 1764.

Abigail Hutchens, daughter of Phinehas (Hutchens) and Abigail Hutchens was born at Lunenburgh March 14th 1766.

Joshua Hutchens son of Phinehas and Abigail Hutchens was born at Lunenburgh May 27th 1768.

James Reed Hutchens son of Phinehas and Abigail Hutchens, was born at Lunenburg July the 17th 1770.

Ama Hutchens daughter of Phineas and Abigal Hutchens was born at Lunenburg August ye 22d 1772.

Phinehas Hutchens son of Phinehas (Hutchens) and Abigail Hutchens, was born at Lunenburg July ye 6th 1774.

John Sullivan Hutchins son of Phinehas & Abigail Hutchins was born at Fitzwilliam August 15th 1776.

Prudy Hutchins daughter of Phinehas & Abigail Hutchins was born at Fitzwilliam January 16th 1779.

Ammi Harrington ye daughter of Thaddeus Harrington & of Thankful his wife, was born at Lunenburg October ye 28th Annq Domini 1758.

HENDERSON. HARWOOD. HUBBARD.

The births of the children of William Henderson & of Sarah his wife, viz.

William born Jan^{ry} 8th 1744 at Lunenburg.
Henry born at Lunenburg October 22^d 1746
John born at Lunenburg Jan^{ry} 10th 1748
Sarah born at Lunenburg August 3^d 1750.
James born at Lunenburg July 23^d 1753
David born at Lunenburg August 22^d 1757

Jane Henderson the daughter of John Henderson and of Jane his wife, was born at Lunenburg May the 1th 1753.

Thomas Henderson the son of John Henderson, and of Jane his wife, was born at Lunenburg May the 20th 1755.

Mary Harwood ye daughter of Nathaniel Harwood, and of Hannah his wife, born December ye 19th 1728.

James Harwood ye son of Nathaniel Harwood and of Hannah his wife, born October ye 4th 1730.

Hannah ye daughter of Nathaniel Harwood, and of Hannah his wife, born April ye 1th 1732/3.

Sarah Harwood ye daughter of Nathaniel Harwood and of Hannah his wife, born June ye 26th 1735.

Nathaniel Harwood ye son of Nathanil Harwood, and of Hannah his wife, born May ye 7th 1737.

Eliphelett born December the 12th 1739.*

Elizabeth Harwood the daughter of Nathanel Harwood and of Hannah his wife, born at Lunenburg March the 9th 1742/3.

Lucy Harwood the daughter of Nathanael Harwood and of Hannah his wife, was born at Lunenburg Janvary ye 16th 1745/6.

Grace Hubbard the daughter of Jonathan Hubbard Junr and Abigail his wife, was born August ye 22th 1740.

Abigail Hubbard the daughter of Jonathan Hubbard Jr. and of Abigail his wife, was born at Lunenburg Sept the 17th 1742.

Rebekah Hubburd the daughter of Jonathan Hubburd and of Abigail his wife, born at Lunenburg Sept. ye 27th 1744.

Dorcas Hovey the daughter of Abijah Hovey and Lydia Hovey his wife, was born at Lunenburg June the 24th 1751.

Lydia Hovey ye daughter of Abijah Hovey and Lydia Hovey his wife, was born at Lunenburg August ye 17th 1753.

---

*John R. Rollins thinks this is, no doubt, Harwood. [W. A. D.

HOVEY. HOLT.

Miriam Hovey the daughter of Abijah Hovey & of Lydia his wife was born at Lunenburg October ye 8th 1758.

Abijah Hovey ye son of Abijah Hovey & of Lydia his wife, was born at Lunenburg October ye 16th 1760.

Joseph Holt the son of Joseph Holt and Mary his wife born at Lunenburg April ye 8th 1744.

Mary Holt ye daughter of Joseph Holt and of Mary his wife, born at Lunenburg August ye 17th A. D. 1745.

Abiel Holt the son of Joseph Holt and of Mary his wife, was (born) at Lunenburg July ye 18th 1748.

Joseph Holt, son of Joseph Holt and Dorcas his wife was born at Lunenburg Decr ye 18th 1752.

William Holt ye son of William Holt, and of Mary his wife, born at Lunenburg February the 16th 1744/5.

David Holt the son of William Holt and of Mary his wife, born at Lunenburg September ye 26th 1746.

Jonathan Holt the son of William Holt, and of Mary his wife, born at Lunenburg Janvary ye 22nd 1748.

Humphry Holt, the son of William Holt, and of Mary his wife, born at Lunenburg, Janvary ye 1st 1750.

Mary Holt daughter of W^m & Mary Holt, was born at Ipswich Canada Novr 8th 1754.

Sarah Holt daughter of William Holt & of Mary his wife was born at Lunenburg May ye 30th 1756.

Elizabeth Holt the daughter of Daniel Holt and of Mehetabel his wife, was born at Lunenburg November ye 7th 1749.

Mehetable Holt ye daughter of Daniel Holt and of Mehetabel his wife, was born at Lunenburg September the 20th 1751.

Abigail Holt ye daughter of Daniel Holt and of Mehetabell his wife, was born at Lunenburg March the 9th 1753.

Daniel Holt the son of Daniel Holt and of Mehetabel his wife, was born at Lunenburg March ye 26th 1756.

Sibbil Holt daughter of Daniel Holt, and of Mehetabel his wife, was born at Lunenburg April ye 6th 1758.

Rachel Holt the daughter of Jonathan Holt, and of Rachel his wife, was born at Lunenburg April ye 20: A. D. 1753.

Jonathan Holt the son of Jonathan Holt and of Susana his wife was born at Lunenburg May ye 16th 1756.

Births.

HOLT. HENERY. HILTON. HASTINGS.

Susannah Holt ye daughter of Jonathan Holt, and of Susannah his wife, was born at Lunenburg, May ye 29th A. D. 1758.

Elijah Holt son of Jona Holt and Susannah his wife was born at Lunenburg Octor 23 1759.

William Holt son of Jona & Susannah Holt, was born at Lunenburg April 11th 1761.

Hannah Holt daughter of Daniel & Allice Holt, born at Lunenburg February ye 15th 1763.

Thomas Holt, son of Daniel & Allice Holt, born at Lunenburg November ye 25th 1765.

Lydia Holt daughter of Daniel & Alice Holt, born at Lunenburg August ye 29 1767.

Enoch Holt son of Daniel & Allice Holt born at Lunenburg August ye 15th 1770.

Louis Holt daughter of Daniel & Allice Holt, born at Lunenburg September ye 19 1772.

William Henery ye son of George Henery and of Elizabeth his wife, was born at Lunenburg Janvary the 22nd 1746/7.

Mary Henery ye daughter of George Henery and of Elizabeth his wife, was born at Lunenburg September the 1th 1748.

Thomas Hilton the son of Samuel Hilton and of   his wife, was born at Lunenburg June ye 14th 1752.

David Hilton the son of Samuel Hilton, and of   his wife, was born at Lunenburg April ye 12th 1752.

Mary ye daughter of John Hastings and of Sarah his wife born in Lunenburg July ye 6 : 1731.

John Hastings the son of Nathanael Hastings, and Lois his wife, born at Lunenburg October the 20th 1741.

Lois Hastings the daughter of Nathanael Hastings and of Lois his wife, born at Lunenburg May ye 17th A. D. 1743.

Nathaniel Hastings the son of Nathanael Hastings and of Lois his wife, was born at Lunenburg May ye 28th 1745.

Caleb Hastings the son of Nathanel Hastings and of Lois his wife, was born at Lunenburg, March the 31th 1749.

David Hastings the son of Nathanael Hastings and of Lois his wife, was born at Lunenburg, March ye 31th 1751.

HASTINGS. HEYWOOD.

Elizabeth Hastings ye daughter of Nathaniel Hastings and of Lois his wife, was born at Lunenburg April 14th 1753.

Nicholas Hastings the son of Nathanael Hastings and of Lois his wife, was born at Lunenburg, June ye 30th 1755.

Jonathan Hastings the son of Nathaneal Hastings, and of Lois his wife, was born at Lunenburg August ye 16th 1756.

Susannah Hastings the daughter of Nathaniel Hastings and of Loas his wife, was born at Lunenburg March ye 11th 1759.

Samuel Hastings the son of Nathanael Hastings and of Lois his wife, was born at Lunenburg May ye 19th 1761.

Esther Hastings daughter of Nathll & Lois Hastings was born at Lunenburgh July 21st 1765.

Eunice Hastings daughter of Nathaniel Hastings & Lois his wife, was born at Lunenburg June ye 6th 1769.

Relief Heywood daughter to Nathan and Esther Heywood was born July ye 19th 1724 on a Sabbath day morning about break of day.

Willis Heywood son to Nathan Heywood and to Esther Heywood his wife, was born May ye 21th 1726 on a Satterday morning about break of day.

Thomas Heywood son to Nathan and Esther Heywood was born August ye 20th 1728 on a Tuseday morning about one of ye clock.

Zimri Heywood son to Nathan and Esther Heywood was born September ye 5th 1731 on a Sabbath day. sun about half an hour high at night.

Esther Heywood davghter to Nathan and Esther Heywood was born April ye 20th 1734 on a Satterday morning, sun about two houers high in ye morning.

Elizebeth Heywood daughter of Nathan Heywood and Esther Heywood, was born at Lunenburg October ye 6th 1736.

Mary Heywood daughter of Nathan Heywood and Esther Heywood, was born at Lunenburg July the 28th 1739.

William Heywood the son of Nathan Heywood and of Esther Heywood, was born at Lunenburg on Thursday morning before sunrise January ye 17th 1744/5.

Silent Heywood ye son of John Heywood and of Ruth his wife, born August ye 25th 1728.

Ruth Heywood ye davghter of John Heywood and of Ruth his wife, born February ye 15th 1729/30.

Sarah Heywood ye davghter of John Heywood and of Ruth his wife, born December ye 13th 1732.

Births.

HEYWOOD. HILL. HUTCHINSON.

Abigil Heywood ye davghter of John Heywood and of Ruth his wife, born August ye 13th 1733.

Prudence Heywood daughter of John Heywood and of Ruth his wife, born at Lunenburg August ye 26th 1734/5

Lucy Heywood ye daughter of John Heywood and of Ruth his wife, born at Lunenburg February ye 4th 1739.

Ruth Heywood the daughter of John Heywood and of Ruth his wife, born at Lunenburg February ye 4th 1741/2.

Martha Hill ye daughter of John Hill and of Jane his wife born at Lunenburg December ye 24th 1740.

John Hill ye son of John Hill and of Jane his wife, born at Lunenburg March ye fourth 1742/3

William Hill ye son of John Hill and of Jane his wife, was born at Lunenburg June ye 5th 1747.

Thomas Hill the son of John Hill and of Jane his wife, was born at Lunenburg August the 14th 1751.

Robert Hill the son of John Hill and of Jane his wife, was born at Lunenburg, March the 18th 1755.

David Hill the son of John Hill and of Jane his wife was born at Lunenburg October ye 20th 1760.

Samuel Hutchinson son of Samuel Hutchinson and of Elizebath his wife, was born at Lexinton January ye 11th 1761.

Elizebath Hutchinson, daughter of Samuel Hutchinson and of Elizebath his wife was born at Lunenburg October ye 22d 1763.

Thomas Hutchinson, son of Samuel Hutchinson and of Elizebath his wife, was born at Lunenburg October ye 27th 1765.

I.

IRELAND.

Ann Ireland the daughter of Abram Ireland Junior & Meribah his wife, was born at Lunenburg April 13th 1762.

Mary Ireland daughter of Abraham Ireland Junr & Meribah his wife, was born at Lunenburg April 11th 1763.

Abraham Ireland son of Abraham Ireland Jr. & Meribah his wife, was born at Lunenburg January ye 2. 1765.

Abigail Ireland daughter of Abraham Ireland Jun & Meribah his wife, was born at Lunenburg Sept ye 16. 1766.

IRELAND.

Susannah Ireland daughter of Abraham Ireland Junr and Meribah, was born at Lunenburgh Jany 4th 1768.

Jonathan Ireland son of Abraham Ireland Jun & Meribah his wife, was born at Lunenburg July ye 25. 1769.

Elener Ireland daughter of Abraham Ireland & Meribah his wife, was born at Lunenburg August ye 1 1771.

Meribah Ireland daughter of Abraham Ireland Junr and Meribah his wife was born at Lunenburg Apriel ye 12th 1773.

Betty Ireland daughter of Abraham Ireland Jun and Meribah his wife, was born at Lunenburg June 22th 1775.

David Ireland son of Abraham Ireland Jun. and Meribah his wife, was born at Lunenburg August ye 27th 1777.

J.

JOHNSON.

Rebakah Johnson the davghter of Samuell Johnson and of Rebakah his wife, born Nouember ye 2th 1719.

Elifebeth Johnson ye daughter of Samuell Johnson and of Rebakah his wife, born Janeweary ye 2th 1721.

Samvell Johnson ye son of Samuell Johnson and of Rebakah his wife, born Janeweary ye 2th 1723.

Kezia Johnson ye davghter of Samuell Johnson & of Rebakah his wife, born September ye 7th 1725.

Hannah Johnson ye davghter of Samuell Johnson and of Rebakah his wife, born October 8th 1727.

Nathan Johnson ye son of Samuell Johnson and of Rebakah his wife, born August ye 18th 1731.

Mary Johnson ye daughter of Samvel Johnson Junr, and of Hannah his wife, was born at Lunenburg September the eighth 1747.

Benjamin Johnson the son of Samvel Johnson Junr and of Hannah his wife, born at Lunenburg July ye 8th 1749.

Samuel Johnson son of Samuel Johnson Jr. and of Hannah his wife was born at Lunenburg. the 6th of September Anno Domini 1751.

Lucy Johnson, daughter of Samuel Johnson Jr and of Hannah his wife, was born at Lunenburg August the 5th Anno Domini 1753.

Nathan Johnson the son of Samvel Johnson & of Hannah his wife, was born at Lunenburg November the 6th 1755.

Silvanus Johnson ye son of James Johnson and of Susanna his wife, was born at Lunenburg Februay ye 25th 1747/8.

Births. 307

JEWETT. JONES.

Enoch Jewett the son of Thomas Jewett, and of Hannah his wife, was born at Lunenburg July ye 25th A. D. 1757.

Sarah Jones ye davghter of William Jones and of Sarah his wife, born March ye 25th 1735.

William Jones ye son of William Jones and of Sarah his wife, was born May 11th 1737 at Lunenburg.

Abigail Jones ye davghter of William Jones and of Sarah his wife, was born April ye 18th 1740 at Lunenburg.

Hannah Jones and Enos Jones the daughter and son of William Jones and of Sarah Jones, born at Lunenburg the 14th of July 1742.

Josiah Jones the son of William Jones and of Sarah Jones was born at Lunenburg October ye 23rd 1744.

Isaac Jones the son of William Jones and of Sarah his wife, was born at Lunenburg July ye 15th 1747.

Silence Jones daughter of Wm Jones & Sarah his wife, was born at Lunenburg August the 18th 1753.

John Jones, son of William & Sarhah Jones was born at Lunenburg May 22^d 1764.

William Jones son of William & Sarah Jones was born at Lunenburgh May 15th 1765.

Sarah Jones daughter of Wm Jones & Sarah his wife was born at Lunenburgh April 5th 1766.

David Jones son of William Jones and of Sarah his wife, was born at Lunenburg March ye 30th 1773.

Abigail Jones daughter of William & Sarah Jones, was born at Lunenburg June ye 22^d 1775.

Emme Jones daughter of William & Sarah Jones, was born at Lunenburg January ye 29th 1769.

Amos Jones son of Joseph Jones & Mary his wife, was born at Lunenburg February ye 11th 1761.

Mary Jones daughter of Joseph Jones & Mary his wife, was born at Lunenburg June ye 8th 1763.

Amasa Jones, son of Joseph Jones & Mary his wife, was born at Lunenburg June ye 19th 1765.

Ruth Jones, daughter of Joseph Jones & Mary his wife was born at Lunenburg March ye 3^d 1768.

Elizabeth Jones daughter of Joseph Jones & Mary his wife, was born at Lunenburg March ye 28th 1770.

Samuel Jones, son of Joseph and Mary Jones, was born at Lunenburg May ye 1st 1772.

JONES. JENISON.

Elnathan Jones son of Joseph & Mary Jones was born at Lunenburg August ye 12th 1774.

Mary Jenison the daughter of John Jenison and of Mary his wife, was born at Lunenburg March the 12th 1741/2.

John Jenison the son of John Jenison and of Mary his wife, born at Lunenburg June ye 15th 1744.

K.

KENNEDY. KIMBALL.

William Kennedy the son of Samvel Kennedy and of Sarah his wife, was born at Lunenburg April ye 4th 1750.

Sarah Kennedy the daughter of Samvel Kennedy and of Sarah his wife, was born at Lunenburg February the 14th 1752.

Mary Kennedy the daughter of Samuel Kennedy and of Sarah his wife, was born at Lunenburg March the 27th 1754.

Elisabeth Kimball ye daughter of Amos Kimbal, and of Dorothy his wife, was born at Bradford April ye 20th 1745.

Phinehas Kimball ye son of Amos Kimball, and of Dorothy his wife, was born at Lunenburg Janvary ye 6th 174—.

Dolley Kimball ye daughter of Amos Kimbal and of Dorothy his wife, was born at Lunenburg October ye 25th 1749.

Amos Kimball ye son of Amos Kimball and of Dorothy his wife, was born at Lunenburg September ye 25th 1752.

Thomas Kimball ye son of Amos Kimball and of Dorothy his wife, was born at Lunenburg September ye 5th 1754.

Ebenezer Kimball son of Amos Kimball & of Dorothy his wife, was born at Lunenburg June ye 14 1760.

Mary Kimball ye daughter of Ephraim Kimball and of Mary his wife, was born at Lunenburg, Janvary ye 14th 1747/8.

Anne Kimball ye daughter of Ephraim Kimball and of Mary his wife, was born at Lunenburg December ye 24th 1749.

Ephraim Kimball the son of Ephraim Kimball and Mary his wife, was born at Lunenburg Febry 15th 1752.

Hannah Kimball the daughter of Ephraim Kimball and of Mary his wife, was born at Lunenburg December ye 1st A. D. 1758.

Rachel Kimball the daughter of Ephraim Kimball and of Mary his wife, was born September ye 5th 1754.

KIMBALL. KENDALL. KENDEL.

Levi Kimball the son of Ephraim Kimball and of Mary his wife, was born at Lunenburg October 23rd 1756.

Betty Kimball the daughter of Ephraim Kimball and of Mary his wife, was born at Lunenburg March ye 31th 1761.

Abigail Kimball, daughter of Ephraim & Mary Kimball, was born at Lunenburg April 23d 1763.

Thomas Kimball the son of George Kimball and of Sarah his wife was born at Luenburg March the 7th 1749/50.

Benjamin Kimball the son of George Kimball & Sarah his wife, was born at Lunenburg April 2d 1752.

George Kimball son of George Kimball and of Sarah his wife, was born at Lunenburg August ye 6th 1754.

George Kimball the son of George Kimball and of Sarah his wife, was born at Lunenburg August ye 12th 1756.

Sarah, daughter of George & Sarah Kimball was born at Lunenburg May 3d 1763.

William Kendall the son of William Kendall and of Mary his wife, was born at Lunenburg March ye 8th 1758

Hannah Kendall ye daughter of William Kendall and of Mary his wife, was born at Lunenburg May ye 3rd 1759.

Saml Kendall & Mary Kendall son & daughter of Wm Kendall & Mary his wife, were born at Lunenburg Jany 6th 1762.

Eusebia Kendall, daughter of Wm & Mary Kendal, was born at Lunenburg, October 30th 1763.

Alovisa Kendal, daughter of William & Mary Kendall was born at Lunenburg Septr 28th 1765.

Bezaleel Kendel ye son of Uzziah Kendel, and of Elizabeth his wife, was born at Lunenburg April ye 4th 1749.

Abiathar Kendel ye son of Uzziah Kendel & of Elizabeth his wife, was born at Lunenburg November ye 11th 1750.

L.

LOVEJOY.

John Lovejoy the son of John Lovejoy and of Sarah his wife, was born at Lunenburg December the 22nd 1749.

Sarah Lovejoy, the daughter of John Lovejoy and Sarah his wife, was born at Lunenburg April 3d 1754.

Jonathan Lovjoy the son of John Lovejoy and of Sarah his wife, was born at Lunenburg, January ye 17th 1757.

LOVEJOY. LILLY. LARRABEE. LECH. LANE. LOW. LITTLE.

Susannah Lovejoy the daughter of John Lovejoy and of Sarah his wife, was born at Lunenburg August ye 17th 1759.

Prudence Lovejoy daughter of John Lovejoy & of Sarah his wife was born at Lunenburg April 22d 1762.

Ebenezer Lilly the son of John Lilly and of Elizabeth his wife, was born at Lunenburg June ye 20th 1756.

Mary Larrabee the daughter of Timothy Larrabee and of Mary his wife, was born at Lunenburg October ye 19th 1748.

Abigail Larrabee the daughter of Timothy Larrabee and of Mary his wife, was born at Lunenburg Janvary the 21th 1755.

Manasses Lech ye son of James Lech and of Janat his wife, born July ye 25th 1734.

Eleazer Lane the son of Nehemiah Lane and of Sarah his wife, was born at Lunenburg Janvary ye 8th 1761.

Sarah Lain daughter of Nehemiah Lain & Sarah his wife, was born at Lunenburg October ye 15th 1762.

Nehemiah Lain, son of Nehemiah Lain & Sarah his wife, was born at Lunenburg November ye 28th 1764.

Mary Lain daughter of Nehemiah Lain & Sarah his wife, was born at Lunenburg February ye 1st 1767.

Phebe Lain daughter of Nehemiah Lain & Sarah his wife, was born at Lunenburg October ye 21 1769.

The births of the children of Jonathan Low & Sarh his wife, all which war born at Ipswich in the County of Essex.
Benoni Low was born August the 6th 1732.
Sarah Low was born October the 6th 1734.
Elizabeth Low was born April the 1st 1736
Mary Low was born January the 11th 1740.
Hannah Low was born July the 1st 1744.
Joanna Low was born June the 17th 1746
Jonathan Low was born August ye 13th 1748
William Low was born October ye 31st 1750
Abagail Low was born March ye 29th 1753.
Abraham Low was born February 11th 1755.
Francis Low was born January ye 23d 1757.

————ney Little daughter of John Little and Mar [t] his wife [   ]

Births.

M.

MESSUR. MERRILL. MOWERS. MOFFET. MARTIN.

Jonathan Messur son of Jonathan & Abigail Messur was born at Lunenburg Septr 7th 1760.

Abigail Merrill the daughter of Daniel Merrill and of Abigail his wife, was born at Lunenburg Sept ye 24th 1756.

Hitte Merrill the daughter of Daniel Merrill and of Abigail his wife, was born at Lunenburg Sept. ye 15th 1758.

Elizabeth Mowers, daughter of William Mowers and Elizabeth his wife, was born at Dorchester Canady 27 Decr 1752.

Ruth Moors the daughter of Hugh Moors and of Ruth his wife, born at Lunenburg December the 22nd 1744.

Robert Moffet the son of Joseph Moffet, and of Dorothy his wife, was born at Lunenburg August the 16th 1754.

Jon^a Martin son of Jon^a & Mercy Martin, was born at Lunenburg March 18th 1762.

Samvel Martin the son of John Martin and of Elizabeth Martin was born at Ipswich April ye 8th 1738.

John Martin the son of John Martin and of Elizabeth his wife, was born at Lunenburg October ye 12th 1740.

Jane Martin the daughter of John Martin and of Elizabeth his wife, was born at Lunenburg Sept ye 20th 1742.

Elizabeth Martin the daughter of John Martin, and of Elizabeth was born at Lunenburg June ye 12th 1744.

Hannah Martin ye daughter of John Martin and of Elizabeth his wife, was born at Lunenburg October ye 1th 1746.

Martha and Mary Martin the daughters of John Martin and of Elizabeth his wife, were born at Lunenburg October the 26th 1748,

Susana Martin the daughter of John Martin and of Elizabeth his wife, was born at Lunenburg April the first 1751 Annoq: Domini.

Prudence and Patience Martin the daughters of John Martin and of Elizabeth his wife, were born at Lunenburg May ye 6 A. D. 1753.

The Births of the children of George Martin and of Eunice his wife,
Jonathan Martin born at Ipswich Octo^r 26th 1747.
John Martin born at Ipswich Jany 26th 1749
Lucy Martin born at Ipswich July 11th 1751
Joseph Martin born at Ipswich July 24th 1753

MARTIN. MITCHEL.

Eunice Martin born at Ipswich Decr 15th 1758
Mary Martin born at Lunenburgh July 28th 1762.

Children of Andrew Mitchel and of Martha his wife.
Jane born Feb^r ye 14th 1723/4
Ruth born July ye 19th 1726.
Martha born Janewary ye 19. 1727/8.
Elezabath born December ye 12. 1729.
Susannah born December ye 27 1731.
Hannah born September ye 15 1734
Esther born October ye 15th 1740.
Mary born July the 18th 1745.

N.
NORCROSS.

Jabez Norcross ye son Jeremiah Norcross and of Faith his wife born in Lunenburg March ye 10th 1731/2.

Mary Norcross ye davghter of Jeremiah Norcross and of Faith his wife, born Janewary 24th 1733/4.

Sarah Norcross the daughter of Jeremiah Norcross and of Faith his wife, born at Lunenburg February ye 25th 1735/6.

Page Norcross the son of Jeremiah Norcross and of Faith his wife, born at Lunenburg April ye 9th 1738.

Hanah Norcross ye daughter of Jeremiah Norcross and of Faith his wife, was born at Lunenburg November 10th 1741.

Jeremiah Norcross ye son of Jeremiah Norcross and of Faith his wife, was born at Lunenburg February ye 15th 1743/4.

Elijah Norcross ye son of Jeremiah Norcross, and of Faith his wife, was born at Lunenburg March ye 7th 1749/50.

O.
OSBURN.

John Osburn the son of Ephraim Ozburn and of Sarah his wife, was born at Lunenburg August ye 25th 1760.

P.
PARKER.

Johannah Parker the daughter of Timothy Parker and of Johannah his wife, was born at Lunenburg September the 14th 1749.

Sarah Parker the daughter of Timothy Parker and of Johannah his wife was born at Lunenburg March ye 26th 1752.

Births.

PARKER. PRATT. PEIRCE.

Elijah Parker the son of Timothy Parker and Joanna his wife, was born at Lunenburg Novr 18th 1753.

Elijah Parker ye son of Timothy Parker, and of Joanna his wife, was born at Lunenburg February the 1th 1756.

Abijah Parker ye son of Timothy Parker and of Johannah his wife, was born at Lunenburg September ye 24th 1758.

Joanna Parker ye daughter of Timothy & Joanna Parker was born at Lunenburg May 20th 1762.

Sibil Parker, daughter of Timothy & Joanna Parker, was born at Lunenburg Septr 1st 1764.

Abigail Parker daughter of Tim^o Parker & Joanna his wife was born at Lunenburgh Decr 29th 1767.

The births of ye children of Ebenezer & Charity Pratt,
Oliver Prat born at Lunenburg 29th June 1761.

Anna Pratt, daughter of Ebenezer and Lydia Prat was born at Lunenburg July 19th 1762.

Sally daughter of Eben^r & Lydia Pratt was born at Lunenburg August 23^d 1763.

Anna Prat daughter of Eben^r & Lydia Prat, was born at Lunenburg Septr 10th 1765.

Esther Peirce ye davghter of Ephraim Peirce and of Esther his wife, born May ye 29th 1722.

Jonathan Peirce ye son of Ephraim Peirce and of Esther his wife, born November ye 27th 1724.

Ephraim Peirce ye son of Ephraim Peirce and of Esther his wife, born March ye 13th 1726/7

Amos Peirce ye son of Ephraim Peirce and of Esther his wife born July 8th 1729.

Sarah Peirce ye davghter of Ephraim Peirce and of Esther his wife, born Nouember ye 27th 1731.

Mary Peirce ye davghter of Ephraim Peirce and of Esther his wife, born March ye 5th 1733/4.

Benj^a Pierce ye son of Ephraim Pierce & of Esther his wife, born June ye 3^d 1736.

Prudence Parce the daughter of Ephriam Parce and of Esther his wife, born at Lunenburg February the sixth, Anno Dom. 1738/9.

Oliver Parce the son of Ephriam Parce and Esther his wife, born at Lunenburg July the 17th 1741.

Keziah Parce the daughter of Ephraim Parce and of Esther his wife, born at Lunenburg December ye 4th 1743.

Elizabeth Parce ye daughter of Ephraim Parce and of Esther his wife, was born at Lunenburg March ye 25th 1748.

PEARCE. PEIRCE. PARCE.

Children of David Pearce and Elizabeth his wife,
David born at Groton July 19 1726.
Lydia born at Lunenburg July 21 1728.
Elizabath born at Lunenburg Apriel 7. 1730.
Hannah born at Lunenburg March ye 9 1731/2.
Solomon born at Lunenburg Janewary ye 28th 1733/4
Samvel born at Lunenburg November ye 25th 1737
Joshua born at Lunenburg Janvary the 13th 1745/6

Sibel Peirce the daughter of John Peirce and of Hannah his wife, was born at Lunenburg Jan. ye 28th 1746/7

Ephraim Parce the son of Ephraim Parce Jun. and of Sarah his wife, was born at Lunenburg October the 31th 1760.

Sarah Parce daughter of Ephraim Parce Junr & of Sarah his wife, was born at Lunenburg May 26th 1762.

Relief Parce daughter of Eph^m Parce Junr and of Sarah his wife, was born at Lunenburgh Augt 9th 1767.

Elijah Pearce son of Ephraim Pearce Junr & Sarah his wife, was born at Lunenburg September ye 15th 1769.

Phinehas Parce son of Ephraim Parce Junr and of Sarah his wife, was born at Lunenburg March ye 22^d 1773.

Jonathan Parce the son of Jonathan Parce and of Sarah his wife, was born at Lunenburg October ye 27th 1747.

Sarah Parce the daughter of Jonathan Parce and of Sarah his wife, was born at Lunenburg April ye 13th 1750.

Esther Parce the daughter of Jonathan Parce and of Sarah his wife, was born at Lunenburg February ye 5th 1752.

Prudence Peirce the daughter of Jonathan Peirce and of Sarah his wife, was born at Lunenburg November the 14th 1753.

Mary Pierce the daughter of Jonathan Pierce and of Sarah his wife, was born at Lunenburg May ye 21st 1756.

Tabatha Parce ye daughter of Jonathan Parce and of Sarah his wife, was born at Lunenburg March ye 28th 1758.

Benjamin Parce the son of Jonathan Parce and of Sarah his wife, was born at Lunenburg March ye 8th 1760.

Josiah Parce the son of Jonathan Parce, and of Sarah his wife, was born at Lunenburg October ye 28 : 1761.

Susannah Parce daughter of Jon^a & Sarah Parce, was born at Lunenburg Decr 30th 1763.

Abraham Parce son of Jonathan & Sarah Parce was born at Lunenburg Decr 20th 1765.

Births.

PARCE. PLATTS. PAGE.

Lucy Parce daughter of Jon^a & Sarah Parce was born at Lunenburg August 31st 1767.

Nahum Pearce son of Jonathan Pearce & Sarah his wife, was born at Lunenburg May the 4th 1770

Sarah Parce ye daughter of Samuel Parce & Mary his wife was born at Lunenburg June 7th 1762.

Abel Platts the son of Abel Platts and of Mary Platts was born at Lunenburg March the 28th A. D. 1738.

Hannah Platts the daughter of Abel Platts and of Mary Platts, was born at Lunenburg Janvary the 13th A. D. 1741.

Sarah Platts the daughter of Abel Plats and of Mary his wife, born September ye 4th 1744.

Edward Platts the son of Nathan Platts & of Elizabeth his wife, was born at Lunenburg September ye 3rd 1749.

Thomas Platts the son of Nathan Platts & of Elizabeth his wife, was born at Lunenburg November ye 27th 1754.

Jane Platts the daughter of Nathan Platts & of Elizabeth his wife, was born at Lunenburg August ye 3rd 1756.

Elizabeth Page ye davghter of Sam^{ll} Page and of Martha (Page) his wife, born March 23th 1719.

Zachariah Page ye son of Sam^{ll} Page and of Martha Page his wife, born April 10th 1721.

Daniel Page ye son of Sam^{ll} Page and of Martha Page his wife, born August 10th 1722.

Martha Page, ye davghter of Sam^{ll} Page, and of Martha his wife, born May 31th 1725.

Benj^a Page ye son of Sam^{ll} Page, and of Martha his wife born October 12th 1727

Thomas Page ye son of Sam^{ll} Page, and of Martha his wife, born September 6th 1730.

Children of Jonathan Page and of Mary his wife,
(1.) Sarah born at Lunenburg October ye 15 1728
(2.) Alles born at Lunenburg Decemb^r 28. 1730.
(3.) Mary born at Lunenburg September ye 1 1732
(4.) Jonathan born at Lunenburg March ye 13th 1734/5
(5.) Eunice born at Lunenburg August ye 26th 1737
(6.) Peter Page born at Lunenburg June ye 2nd 1739

PAGE.

(7.) Joshua Page son of Jonathan Page & of Mary his wife, born at Lunenburg July ye 10th 1743.

(8.) Prudence Page ye daughter of Jonathan Page & of Mary his wife was born at Lunenburg August ye 25th 1746.

(9.) Benjamin Page ye son of Jonathan Page and of Mary his wife, was born at Lunenburg September the 15th 1747.

Phinehas Page the son of Jonathan Page and of Mary his wife, was born at Lunenburg April the 28th 1751.

The birth of ye children of Joseph Page & of Deborah his wife.

Joseph born at Lunenburg August 10 1731

Deborah Page ye daughter of Joseph Page & of Deborah his wife, born in Lunenburg, April ye 11th 1733.

Marcy Page ye davghter of Joseph Page & of Deborah his wife, born March 2th 1734/5.

Joseph Page ye son of Joseph Page and of Deborah his wife, born at Lunenburg Feb^r ye 21th 1736/7.

Hannah Page ye daughter of Joseph Page, and of Deborah his wife, born March ye 22nd 1738/9.

Elizabeth Page daughter of Joseph Page and of Deborah his wife, born April 24th 1741.

Amos Page the son of Joseph Page and of Deborah Page born at Lunenburg June the 2nd 1743.

Joseph Page ye son of Joseph Page and of Deborah his wife born at Lunenburg June the 22nd 1745.

Susanna Page ye daughter of Joseph Page and of Deborah his wife, was born at Lunenburg April ye 24 A. D. 1747.

Sarah Page ye davghter of William Page and of Sarah his wife born May 14th 1734

William Page ye son of William Page and of Sarah his wife, born November ye 6th 1735.

Samvel Page the son of William Page & of Sarah his wife, born at Lunenburg Janvary ye 15th 1737/8.

Timothy Page the son of William Page and of Sarah born at Lunenburg April ye 5th 1739.

Hannah Page the daughter of William Page and Sarah his wife, born at Lunenburg December ye 17th 1741.

Ruth Page ye daughter of William Page and of Sarah his wife, born at Lunenburg December 25. 1743.

Phebe Page ye davghter of William Page and of Sarah his wife, born at Lunenburg December ye 4th 1745

Phebe Page ye daughter of William Page and of Sarah his wife, born December the 5th 1745. [Also entered in another place Decr ye 4th 1745.]

PAGE.

Priscilla Page davghter of David Page, and of Priscilla his wife, born October ye 22^d 1735.

Solomon Page ye son of David Page, and of Priscilla his wife, born June ye 6th 1737.

David Page the son of David Page, and of Priscilla his wife, born at Lunenburg August ye 6th 1738.

Caleb Page ye son of David Page and of Priscilla his wife, born at Lunenburg Febuary ye 29 1739/40.

Matha Page ye daughter of David Page and of Priscilla his wife, born at Lunenburg April the 26th 1741.

Sarah Page the daughter of David Page and of Priscilla his wife was born at Lunenburg August ye 8th 1743.

Mehetabel Page the daughter of David Page and of Priscila his wife, born at Lunenburg March ye fifth 1743/4.

David Page the son of David Page and of Priscila his wife, born at Lunenburg June ye 5th 1745.

Ruth Page ye daughter of David Page, and of Priscila his wife, was born at Lunenburg October ye 26th 1747.

Johannah Page ye daughter of David Page and of Priscila his wife, was born at Nichawogg February the 17th 1748/9

Ruth Page the daughter of Daniel Page and of Ruth his wife, born at Groton August the 25th 1746.

Sibil Page daughter of Nathanael Page and of Mercy his wife, was born at Lunenburg April ye 19th 1749.

Rachel Page, the daughter of Nathanael Page and of Marcy, his wife, was born at Lunenburg Janvary the 21th 1750/1.

Prudence Page the davghter of Nathaniel Page and of Mercy his wife, was born at Lunenburg March ye 29th 1752.

Nathaniel Page ye son of Nathaniel Page and of Marcy his wife, born Feb^r 7th 1734/5.

Marcy Page ye daughter of Nathaniel Page & of Marcy his wife, born June 26th 1736.

Nathaniel Page ye son of Nathaneel Page and of Mercy his wife, born Sept. ye 15th 1738.

Abner Page ye son of Nathaniel Page and of Mercy his wife, born March ye 31th 1740.

John Page ye son of Nathaniel Page, and of Mercy his wife, born July ye 16th 1741.

Moses Page the son of Nathanael and of Marcy his wife, born at Lunenburg April y^e (5th) fifth 1743.

PAGE. POOLE. PRIEST.

Aaron (Page) born May Janvary ye 13th 1745.

Samvel (Page) born July ye 26th 1747.

Reuben Page ye son of Nathanael Page and of Mercy his wife, was born at Lunenburg February the 3rd 1753.

Caleb Page the son of Nathanael Page, and of Mercy his wife, was born at Lunenburg May ye 11th 1756.

Sarah Poole the daughter of Samvel Poole and of Prudence his wife, born at Lunenburg April the fifteenth 1740.

Bette Poole the daughter of Samvel Poole and of Prudence his wife, born at Lunenburg March ye twenty-seventh 1742.

Samvel Poole the son of Samvel Poole and of Prudence his wife, born at Lunenburg, February the second 1743/4

Jacob Poole the son of Samvel Poole and of Prudence his wife, born at Lunenburg March ye 11 1745/6.

Bette Pooole ye daughter of Samvel Poole & of Prudence his wife, was born at Lunenburg, March ye 12th 1747/8.

Judith Poole ye daughter of Samvel Poole & of Prudence his wife, was born at Lunenburg March ye 16th 1749/50.

Susanna Poole the daughter of Samvel Poole and Prudence his wife, was born at Lunenburg Janvary the 30th 1752.

James Poole Junr ye son of James Poole and of Elizabath his wife, was born at Lunenburg April the 30th 1741.

Joshua Poole the son of James Poole and of Elizabeth his wife, born at Lunenburg Sept ye 12th 1744.

Elizabeth Poole ye daughter of James Poole and of Elizabeth his wife, was born at Lunenburg Janvary ye 6th 1746/7.

James Poole ye son of James Poole and of Elizabeth his wife, was born at Lunenburg July ye 4th 1749.

Ruth Poole ye daughter of James Poole and of Elizabeth his wife, was born at Lunenburg August the 14th 1751.

Ruth Poole the daughter of James Poole and of Elizabeth his wife, was born at Lunenburg May the 27th 1754.

Prudence Poole the daughter of James Poole and of Elizabeth his wife was born at Lunenburg August the 19th 1756.

Sarah and Susannah Poole, twins, the daughters of James Poole and of Elizabeth his wife, was born at Lunenburg May ye 30th 1759.

Joseph Priest the son of Joshua Priest and of Sarah his wife, was born at Lunenburg Dec^mr ye 4th 1752.

Births.

PRIEST. PUTNAM. POWERS. PATERSON.

Samuel Priest the son of Joshua Priest and of Sarah his wife, was born at Lunenburg Dec^m ye 12th 1754

Molley Priest the daughter of Joshua Priest, and of Sarah his wife, was born at Lunenburg September ye 22^d A. D. 1756.

Hephzibah Putnam the daughter of Thomas Putnam and of Rachel his wife, was born at Lunenburg February the 2^d 1755.

Susannah and Seth Putnam, the daughter and son of Thomas Putnam and of Rachel his wife, was born at Lunenburg September ye 16th A. D. 1756.

Thomas Putnam the son of Thomas Putnam and of Rachel his wife was born at Lunenburg February ye 27 A. D. 1758.

Mary, the daughter of Jonas & Lydia Powers, was born at Framingham Jany 3^d 1763.

Jonas son of Jonas & Lydia Powers, was born at Lunenburg July 30th 1764.

Lovisa Paterson, daughter of James Paterson & Miriam his wife, was born at Fitchburg July 4th 1779.

Lydia Paterson daughter of James Paterson & Miriam his wife, was born at Lunenburg February 6th 1781, and died March 19th 1781.

James Patterson son of James Paterson & Miriam his wife, was born at Lunenburg March 9th 1782.

R.

REED.

Samvel Reed Junr the son of Samvel Reed and Mary his wife, was born at Lunenburg July ye 13th 1740.

Mary Reed the daughter of Samvel Reed & of Mary his wife, was born at Lunenburg July the 30th 1742

Hannah Reed the davghter of Samvel Reed & of Mary his wife, was born at Lunenburg April the 12th 1745.

Sarah Reed the daughter of Samuel Reed & of Mary his wife, was born at Lunenburg 23^d of July 1747.

Priscilla Reed the daughter of Samuel Reed & of Mary his wife, was born at Lunenburg Augst 10th 1749.

Jesse Reed the son of Samuel Reed & of Mary his wife was born at Lunenburg July 23^d 1751.

REED. REDINGTON.

Rebecah Reed the daughter of Samuel Reed & of Mary his wife was born at Lunenburg June 5th 1753.

Joshua Reed the son of Samuel Reed and of Mary his wife was born at Lunenburg February the 18th 1757.

James Reed ye son of James Reed and of Abigail his wife, was born at Lunenburg August ye 25th 1746.

Priscilla Reed the daughter of James Reed, and of Abigail his wife, was born December ye 17th 1748.

Fredrick Reed ye son of James Reed and of Abigail his wife, was born at Lunenburg August ye 16th 1752:

Sylvanus Reed son of James Reed and Abigail his wife, born at Lunenburg January 7th 1755.

Barzillai Reed son of James Reed and of Abigail his wife was born at Lunenburg Janvary ye 23d 1756.

Hinds Reed the son of James Reed and of Abigail his wife was born at Lunenburg November the 29th 1757.

Joseph Reed son of James Reed and of Abigail his wife was born at Lunenburg Feby 17th 1763.

Shefomith Reed daughter of James Reed and of Abigail his wife, was born at Monadnock No. 4 May 23d 1766.

Lucy Redington the daughter of Benjamin Redington and of Ruth his wife, was born at Lunenburg February ye 8th 1758.

Mary Reddington daughter of Benjamin Reddington and of Ruth his wife was born at Lunenburg September ye 15th Annoq: Domini 1759.

David Reddington the son of Benjamin Reddington & of Ruth his wife was born at Lunenburg July ye 1st 1761.

Benjn Redington son of Benjn and Ruth Redington, born at Lunenburg April 7th 1763.

Ruth Redington daughter of Benja Redington and Ruth his wife, was born at Lunenburg April ye 30th 1764.

Thomas Redington son of Benja Redington and Ruth his wife, was born at Lunenburg March ye 29th 1766.

Rebecca Redington daughter of Benja Redington and Ruth his wife was born at Lunenburg November ye 13th 1767.

Hannah Redington, daughter of Benja Redington and Ruth his wife, was born at Lunenburg November ye 6th 1769.

Isaac Redington son of Benja Redington and Ruth his wife, was born at Lunenburg October 10th 1771.

Births.

REDINGTON. ROBINSON. ROBBE. RICHARDS. RITTER.

John Redington son of Benj^a Redington & of Ruth his wife, was born at Lunenburg July ye 3^d 1774.

Elizabeth Redington ye daughter of Isaac Redington and of Ruth his wife, was born at Lunenburg. April 22^d 1762.

Susannah Redington daughter of Isaac and Ruth Reddington was born at Lunenburg 2^d March 1763.

Sophia Redington daughter of Isaac & Ruth Reddington was born at Lunenburg August 22^d 1765.

Amos Robinson ye son of Amos Robinson and of Priscilla his wife, born July ye 26th 1734.

Eliezer Robinson ye son of Amos Robinson and of Priscilla his wife, born March ye 17th 1735/6.

Daniel Robinson ye son of Amos Robinson and Priscilla his wife, born at Lunenburg April the 13th 1738.

John Robbinson the son of Amos Robbinson & Lydia his wife, born August ye 14th 1744.

Margaret Robbe ye daughter of William Robbe and of Elizebath his wife, born August ye 10th 1717 in ye kingdom of Ireland.

Elizibath Robbe ye davghter of William Robbe and of Anne his wife, born October ye 2th 1733.

Mitchael Richards the son of Charles Richards, and of Jane his wife, born at Wenham October the seventh 1737.

Edward Richards the son of Charles Richards and of Jane his wife, was born at Lunenburg August 25th 1740.

Hannah Ritter the daughter of Moses Ritter and Hannah his wife, was born at Lunenburg February ye 11th 1749.

Marcy Ritter the daughter of Moses Ritter and of Hannah his wife, was born at Lunenburg March ye 15th 1751.

Moley Ritter the daughter of Moses Ritter and of Hannah his wife, was born at Lunenburg Janavary ye 29th 1753.

Abner Ritter the son of Moses Ritter and of Hannah his wife, was born at Lunenburg February ye 8th 1755.

S.

SPAFFORD. STEWART. STEWARD.

John Spafford son of Joseph and Mary Spafford, was born at Lunenburg Feby 19th 1758.

Sarah Spafford daughter of Joseph and Mary Spafford was born at Lunenburg June 25th 1761.

Judah Spafford son of Joseph & Mary Spafford, was born at Lunenburg August 25th 1762.

Hannah Spafford the daughter of Jonah Spaffard, and of Dorcas his wife, was born at Lunenburg Janavary ye 11th A. D. 1756.

John Stewart ye son of William Stewart and of Margeret his wife, born at Lunenburg August ye 28th 1737.

William Stewart ye son of William Stewart and of Margeret his wife, was born November y^e (5th) fifth 1740.

Thomas Stewart the son of William Stewart and Margeret his wife, born at Lunenburg May ye 3rd 1743.

Charles Stewart the son of William Stewart and of Margeret his wife, was born at Lunenburg October ye 8th 1745.

Elizabeth Stewart ye davghter of William Stewart, and of Margeret his wife, was born April ye 8th 1748.

Mary Stweert the daughter of Saloman Stwart and of Martha his wife, born September ye 7th 1740.

Jacob Stweart the son of Solomon Stweart and of Matha his wife born at Lunenburg April ye 22nd A. D. 1743.

Martha Steward, the daughter of Benjamin Steward and of Rebeckah his wife, was born at Lunenburg, March the 18th 1754.

Samuel Bird Steward the son of Phinehaz Steward and of Anne his wife, was born at Lunenburg March ye 18th 1757.

Anne Steward the daughter of Phinehaz Steward & of Anne his wife, was born at Lunenburg Nov^m ye 23rd 1758.

Phinehas Steward the son of Phinehas Steward & of Anne his wife, was born at Lunenburg October ye 27th 1760.

Abraham Steward the son of Phinehas Steward and Anne his wife, was born at Lunenburg October ye 15th 1762.

Martha Steward daughter of Phineas Steward and Anne his wife, was born at Lunenburg June ye 28th 1772.

Births.

STEWARD. SHED. SHEED.

Mary Steward ye davghter of Solomon Steward Jun and of Elizabeth his wife, was born at Lunenburg June ye 8th 1757.

Betty Steward the daughter of Solomon Steward and of Elizabeth his wife, was born at Lunenburg May ye 10th 1759.

Rebeckah Steward the daughter of Solomon Steward & of Elizabeth his wife, was born at Lunenburg March ye 4th 1761.

Daniel Steward the son of Daniel Steward and of Mary his wife was born at Lunenburg October ye 3rd 1758.

Benjamin Steward the son of Daniel Steward and of Mary his wife, was born at Lunenburg February ye 12th 1761.

Mary Steward daughter of Daniel & Mary Steward was born at Lunenburg May 10th 1763.

John Steward son of Daniel & Mary born at Lunenburgh Augt 18th 1765.

Amasa Steward son of Daniel and Mary Steward was born at Lunenburgh Decr 18th 1768.

Amherst Steward son of Daniel Steward & Mary his wife was born at Lunenburg February the 17th 1770.

Sarah Steward daughter of Daniel Steward & Mary his wife, was born at Lunenburg August ye 22^d 1772.

Betty Steward daughter of Daniel Steward and Mary his wife, was born at Lunenburg, May ye 14th 1775.

Abigail Steward daughter of William Steward and Abigail his wife, was born at Lunenburg May 19th 1762.

Lemuel Shed son of Benjn Elizabeth Shed, was born at Lancaster Feby 2^d 1762.

John Shed son of Benjn & Elizabeth Shed was born at Lunenburg June 9th 1764.

Person Shed the son of Benjamin Shed and of Elizabeth his wife, was born at Lunenburg June ye 22nd 1757.

Hannah Shed daughter of Benjn Shed, and of Elizabeth his wife, was born at Lunenburgh July 4th 1767.

Solomon Sheed son of Solomon & Elizabeth Sheed, born March ye 6: 1764.

James & Bettey Sheed son & daughter of Sollomon Sheed & Elizabeth his wife, born April ye 6th 1766.

SHEED. STEARNS.

Joseph Sheed son of Solomon & Elizabath Sheed, born February ye 19 1768.

Zackiah Sheed son of Sollomon & Elizabath Sheed, born November ye 28, 1769.

Abigal Sheed daughter of Sollomon & Elizabath Sheed, born December ye 1st 1771.

Patty Shed, daughter of Solomon & Elizebeth Shed, born at Lunenburg November ye 28, 1773.

Ebenezer Shed son of Solomon Shed & Elizabeth his wife was born at Lunenburg September ye 6. 1776.

Ruth Stearns the daughter of the Revnd Mr David, and Mrs Ruth Stearns, born at Lunenburg January ye 3rd 1736/7.

Rebekah Stearns the daughter of the Revnd Mr. David Stearns and Mrs. Ruth Stearns, was born at Lunenburg November ye 4th 1738.

Abigail Stearns the daughter of the Revnd Mr. David Stearns and of Ruth his wife, born at Lunenburg July ye 6th 1740.

Elizabeth Stearns ye daughter of ye Rev Mr. David Stearns and of Ruth his wife, was born April ye 20th 1742.

David Stearns ye son of the Rev Mr. David Stearns and of Ruth his wife, was born at Lunenburg January ye 8th 1743/4.

Lucy Stearns ye daughter of the Rev. Mr. David Stearns and of Ruth his wife, was born at Lunenburg November ye 16th 1745.

Jonathan Stearns ye son of ye Rev. Mr. David Stearns and of Ruth his wife, was born at   November ye 2nd 1747.

Hannah Stearns ye daughter of ye Rev. Mr. David Stearns and of Ruth his wife, was born November 21th 1748.

Mary Stearns the daughter of ye Rev^d Mr. David Stearns, and of Ruth his wife, was born March 9th 1749 at Lunenburg.

Jonathan Stearns the son of the Rev^d Mr. David Stearns and of Ruth his wife, was born at Lunenburg April the 19th 1751.

John Stearns the son of the Rev^d Mr. David Stearns, and of Ruth his wife, was born at Lunenburg April 20th 1753.

Thomas Stearns the son of the Rev^d Mr. David Stearns and of Ruth his wife, was born at Lunenburg March the 8th 1756.

Sarah Stearns daughter of the Rev. Mr. David Stearns and Ruth his wife, was born at Lunenburg April 25th 1758.

Sarah Stearns the daughter of Thomas Stearns and of Lydia his wife, born at Lunenburg July ye 2nd 1745.

Thomas Stearns the son of Thomas Stearns and of Lydia his wife, was born at Lunenburg May ye 9th 1747.

Births.

STEARNS.

Daniel Stearns the son of Thomas Stearns and Lydia his wife, was born at Lunenburg July ye 31th 1749.

Lydia Stearns the daughter of Thomas Stearns and of Lydia his wife, was born at Lunenburg July the 24th 1751.

Charles Stearns son of Thomas Stearns & Lydia his wife was born at Lunenburg July 19th 1753

Sarah Stearns the daughter of Thomas Stearns and of Lydia his wife, was born at Lunenburg March the 12th 1755.

Rebeckah Stearns the daughter of Thomas Stearns and of Lydia his wife, was born att Lunenburg March ye 2 1757

William Stearns the son of William Stearns and of Elizabeth his wife, was born at Lunenburg April the twentieth A. D. 1749.

Mary Stearns ye daughter of William Stearns and of Elizabeth his wife, was born at Lunenburg May ye 7th 1751.

Joseph Stearns the son of William Stearns and of Elizabeth his wife, was born at Lunenburg August the 21th 1754.

James Stearns the son of William Stearns and of Elizabeth his wife, was born at Lunenburg September ye 1st 1758.

Benjamin Stearns the son of Benjamin Stearns and of Anna his wife, was born at Lunenburg December the 3rd 1754.

Joseph Stearns ye son of Benjamin Stearns and of Anna his wife, was born at Lunenburg August ye 22nd 1756.

Anna Stearns ye daughter of Benjamin Stearns and of Anna his wife, was born at Lunenburg Feburaary ye 7th Annoq : Domini 1759.

Saml Stearns, son of Jonas & Submit Stearns, was born at Lunenburg Sept 8th 1759.

Jonas Stearns, son of Jonas & Submit Stearns was born at Shirley Septr 9th 1761.

David Stearns son of David & Mary Stearns was born April ye 14th

David Stearns ye 2d son of David Stearns & Mary his wife was born Septr ——

Mary Stearns ye daughter of David Stearns & Mary his wife, was born May ye 9: ——

Thomas Stearns son of David Stearns & Mary his wife was born June ye 2 ——

STILES. SPEAR.

Lucy Stiles ye davghter of Jacob Stiles and of Sarah his wife, born in Lunenburg May ye 6th 1729.

Levi Stiles ye son of Jacob Stiles and of Sarah his wife, born in Lunenburg February ye 18th 1732/3.

Sarah Stiles ye davghter of Jacob Stiles and of Sarah his wife, born in Lunenburg May ye 24th 1735.

Jacob Stiles ye son of Jacob Stiles and of Sarah born att Lunenburg September ye 26th 1737.

Nahum Stiles ye son of Jacob Stiles and of Sarah his wife, April ye 21th 1740.

Hannah Stiles ye daughter of Jacob Stiles and of Sarah his wife, was born at Lunenburg Janvary ye 19th 1742.

Jeremiah Stiles ye son of Jacob Stiles and of Sarah his wife, was born at Lunenburg Febuary ye 23rd 1744/5.

Prudence Stiles ye daughter of Jacob Stiles and of Sarah his wife, was born at Lunenburg April ye 3rd 1747.

John Stiles the son of Jacob Stiles and of Sarah his wife, was born at Lunenburg July ye 27th 1749.

Jonathan Stiles the son of Levi Stiles and of Patience his wife, was born at Lunenburg October ye 5th A. D. 1756.

Susannah Stiles the daughter of Levi Stiles and of Patience his wife, was born att Lunenburg October ye 4th A. D. 1758.

Nahum Stiles ye son of Levi Stiles, and of Patience his wife, was born at Lunenburg May ye 14th 1761.

Patience Stiles daughter of Levi & Patience Stiles born at Lunenburg September 16th 1763.

Peleg Stearns Stiles son of Levi & Patience Stiles was born at Lunenburg March 25th 1766.

Levi Stiles son of Levi & Patience Stiles, was born at Lunenburg March 14th 1768.

Lusa Stiles daughter of Levi & Patience Stiles, was born at Lunenburg September ye 3 : 1770.

Jacob Stiles son of Levi & Patience Stiles, born at Lunenburg July ye 9 : 1772.

Caleb Stiles son of Levi & Patience Stiles, born at Lunenburg August ye 20th 1774.

Hannah Stiles daughter of Levi Stiles & Patience his wife, born at Lunenburg August 31. 1780.

Robert Spear son of Robert Speer and of Martha his wife, was born at Lunenburgh Octo^r 12th 1747.

SNOW. SCOTT. SANDERSON. SMITH.

Silas Snow ye son of William Snow and of Elizabath his wife, born November ye 29th 1733.

Jemima Snow ye davghter of William Snow and Elizabath his wife, born November ye 27th 1735.

Rebackah Snow the daughter of William Snow and of Elizabath his wife, born May ye 24th 1737.

Esther Snow ye daughter of William Snow and of Elizabath his wife, born March ye 8th 1738/9.

Joseph Snow the son of William Snow and of Elizabath his wife, was born at Lunenburg March ye 26th 1741.

Abigail Snow the daughter of William Snow and of Elizabath his wife, born at Lunenburg November the sixth 1742.

William Snow, the son of William Snow and of Elizabeath his wife born at Lunenburg June ye 20th 1744.

Bette Snow ye daughter of William Snow and of Elizabeth his wife, was born at Lunenburg, November the 9th 1746.

Lucy Snow ye daughter of William Snow and of Elizabeth his wife, was born at Lunenburg Nouember ye 8th 1748.

William Snow the son of William Snow and of Elizabeth his wife, was born at Lunenburg, December ye 28th 1752.

Edward Scott ye son of John Scott and of Lydia his wife born May 21th 1734.

Mary Scot ye daughter of John Scot & of Lydia his wife born March ye 23d 1735/6.

Benjamin Scott ye son of John Scott and of Lydia his wife born April ye 21. 1739.

David Scott the son of John Scott and of Lydia his wife, born at Lunenburg April the 1th 1742.

Jonathan Scott the son of John Scott & of Lydia his wife, born at Lunenburg October the 1th 1744.

Elizabeth Scott the daughter of John Scott, and of Lydia his wife, born at Lunenburg August ye third A. D. 1747.

Samuell Sanderson son of Abraham Sanderson, and of Patience his wife, born April 26th 1734.

Abraham Sanderson ye son of Abraham Sanderson, and of Patience his wife, born February ye 23d 1735/6.

Patience Smith the daughter of Jonathan Smith, and of Susannah his wife, was born at Lunenburg April the 28th 1737.

SMITH. SPARHAWK.

Reuben Smith the son of Jonathan Smith and of Susanna his wife, was born at Lunenburg July ye 15th 1739.

Simon Smith ye son of Jonathan Smith and of Susanna his wife, born at Lunenburg Sept ye 20th 1741.

Mary Smith the daughter of Jonathan Smith and of Susanna his wife, born at Lunenburg October ye 19th 1743.

Susannah Smith the daughter of the widow, Susannah Smith, born at Lunenburg March the 3rd 1745/6.

Prudence Smith daughter of Reuben & Prudence Smith was born at Lunenburgh Decr 28th 1762.

Jonathan Smith son of Reuben & Prudence Smith, was born at Lunenburgh March 5th 1764.

Sarah Smith daughter of Reuben & Prudence Smith was born at Lunenburgh Decr 7th 1765.

Reuben Smith son of Reuben & Prudence Smith, was born at Lunenburgh Octo^r 18th 1767.

Thomas Sparhawk the son of Mr. Thomas Sparhawk and of Rebecca his wife, was born at Lunenburg April ye 12th 1760.

Oliver Stearns Sparhawk son of Thos. & Rebekah Sparhawke was born at Lunenburg July 23^d 1764.

Rebecca Sparhawk daughter of Thos & Rebecca Sparhawk was born at Lunenburg July 17th 1768.

T.

TAYLOR.

Mary Taylor the daughter of Caleb Taylor and of Susanna his wife was born at Lunenburg November ye 26th 1751.

Caleb Taylor the son of Caleb Taylor and of Susanna his wife, was born at Lunenburg December the 1st 1754.

Arthur Taylor the son of Caleb Taylor and of Susanna his wife, was born at Lunenburg May ye 1st 1757.

Martha Taylor the daughter of Caleb Taylor and of Susanna his wife, was born at Lunenburg October the 10th 1760.

Susannah daughter of David Taylor and Betty Taylor his wife, was born at Lunenburg April 6th 1752.

Betty Taylor the   David Taylor and of Betty his wife was born at Lunenburg July ye 1th 1760.

TAYLOR. TARBALL. TRULL.

Jonathan Taylor the son of Aaron Taylor & Mercy his wife was born at Lunenburg July 22d 1753.

Aaron Taylor son of Aaron Taylor & Mercy his wife, was born at Lunenburg Janry 16th 1755.

Sarah Taylor the daughter of Aaron Taylor and of Mercy his wife, was born at Lunenburg July ye 24th 1757.

Matha Taylor ye daughter of Aaron Taylor & of Mercy his wife, was born at Rowley Canada September ye 6th 1760.

Rebekah Taylor daughter of Aron & Mercy Taylor, was born at Rowley Canada June 11th 1763.

David Taylor son of Aaron and Mercy Tayor was born at Rowley Canada April 25th 1765.

Molly Tarbal the daughter of Zachariah Tarball and of Mary his wife, was born at Lunenburg May the first 1753.

Zechariah Tarbal the son of Zechariah Tarball and of Mary his wife, was born at Lunenburg November the 9th 1754.

Elizabeth Tarball the daughter of Zechariah Tarball, and of Mary his wife, was born at Lunenburg December ye 5th 1755.

Moley Tarball the daughter of Zechariah Tarball and of Mary his wife, was born at Lunenburg March the 19th 1757.

Sibel Tarball the daughter of Zechariah Tarball, and of Mary his wife, was born at Lunenburg March the 9th 1758.

Sarah Tarball ye daughter of Zechariah Tarball and of Mary his wife, was born at Lunenburg September ye 20th 1760.

Susannah Trull ye davghter of John Trull and of Sarah his wife, born April ye 25th 1734.

Phebe Trull ye daughter of John Trull and of Sarah his wife, born July 4th 1736.

W.

WALLES.

Jane Walles ye davghter of William Walles and of Elizabath his wife born December ye 16th 1719.

Elizabath Walles ye davghter of William Walles and of Elizabath his wife, born December ye 20th 1721.

Martha Walles ye davghter of William Walles and of Elizabath his wife, born September ye 18th 1722.

Mary Walles ye davghter of William Walles and of Elizabath his wife, born April 3dth 1724.

WALLES. WALLIS. WYMAN.

Margarit Walles ye davghter of William Walles and of Elizabath his wife, born June ye 16th 1727.

Anne Walles ye davghter of William Walles and of Elizabath his wife, born February ye 27th 1728/9.

Susannah Walles ye davghter of William Walles and of Elizabath his wife, born March ye 5th 1730/31.

Samuell Walles ye son of William Walles and of Elizabath, born March ye 27th 1732/3.

Hannah Walles ye davghter of William Walles and of Elizabath his wife, born March 27th 1735.

William Walles and David Walles the sons of William Walles and of Elizabeth his wife, were born at Lunenburg March ye 26th 1737.

Sarah Walles the daughter of William Walles & of Elizabeth (his wife) was born at Lunenburg August ye 1th 1739.

The births of the children of Benoni Wallis and of R——kah his wife.
Benjn Wallis born April 15th 1756.
Curwin Wallis born April 21st 1758.
David Wallis born Octo^r 16th 1760.
Molly Wallis born May 31st 1763.
Ebenezer Wallis born April 11th 1765
Frederick Wallis born Octo^r 15th 1768.

Silas Wyman ye son of John Wyman and of Rebeckah his wife, born at Lunenburg December ye 10th 1736.

Ruben Wymon ye son of John Wymon and Rebeckah his wife, was born at Lunenburg April ye 26th 1738.

John Wyman jun^r the son of John Wyman and Rebeckah his wife, was born at Lunenburg September ye 28th 1739.

David Wyman the son of John Wyman and of Rebeckah his wife, born at Lunenburg April ye 30th 1744.

Abigail Wyman the daughter of Ezekiel Wyman and Abigail his wife, was born June ye 9th 1740

Lucy Wyman the daughter of Ezekiel Wyman and of Abigail Wyman born at Lunenburg December ye 15th 1741.

Israel Wyman the son of Ezekiel Wyman and of Abigail Wyman born at Lunenburg February ye 19th 1743.

Susanna Wyman ye daughter of Ezekiel Wyman & of Abigail his wife, born at Lunenburg February the 25th 1744/5.

Ezekiel Wyman the son of Ezekiel Wyman and of Abigail his wife, born July ye 26th 1746.

WYMAN. WHITE.

Stephen Wyman the son of Ezekiel Wyman, and of Abigail his wife, was born at Lunenburg August ye 4th 1748.

Francis Wyman the son of Ezekiel Wyman and of Abigail his wife, was born at Lunenburg December ye 20th 1750.

William Wyman son of Ezekiel Wyman and Abigail his wife, was born at Lunenburg Novr 30th 1752.

Seth Wyman son of Ezekiel Wyman and Abigail his wife, was born at Lunenburg December 1st 1754.

Ruth Wyman the daughter of Ezekiel Wyman, and of Abigal his wife, was born at Lunenburg Dec. ye 30: 1756.

John Wymon son of Joseph Wymon and Keziah his wife, was born at Lunenburg October ye 14th 1760.

David Wyman son of Joseph Wyman & Keziah his wife, was born at Lunenburg April 29th 1762.

Joseph Wyman son of Joseph and Keziah Wyman was born at Lunenburg April 3^d 1764.

Oliver Wyman son of Joseph & Keziah Wyman, was born at Lunenburg 26th March 1766.

Thomas Wymon son of Joseph Wymon & Keziah his wife, was born at Lunenburg September ye 27th 1768.

Sarah Wymon daughter of Joseph Wymon & Keziah his wife, was born at Lunenburg Febuary ye 27th 1771.

Elizabeth Wyman daughter of Joseph Wyman and Keziah his wife, was born at Lunenburg Novr ye 10th 1773.

Silas Wyman son of Reuben Wyman & Elizabeth his wife, was born at Lunenburg Octo^r 6th 1761.

John White the son of John White and of Mary his wife, was born at Lunenburg December ye 3rd 1748.

Charles White the son of John White and of Mary his wife, was born at Lunenburg February ye 5 1749.

William White the son of John White and of Mary his wife, was born at Lunenburg November ye 2nd 1751.

David White the son of John White and of Mary his wife, was born at Lunenburg. October ye 22. 1753.

Elizabeth White the daughter of John White and of Mary his wife, was born at Lunenburg July ye 1st A. D. 1755.

Lydia White the daughter of John White jun and of Mary his wife, was born at Leominster March the 5th 1755.

WHITE. WOOD.

Betty White the daughter of John White ju^r and of Mary his wife was born at Leominster April ye 19th 1757.

Salmon White the son of John White jun and of Mary his wife, was born at Lunenburg June ye 5th 1759.

Salmon White the son of John White jun and of Mary his wife, was born at Lunenburg April ye 3rd 1761.

Bezelial Wood ye son of Jonathan Wood and of Sarah his wife born April ye 4th 1735.

Jonathan Wood ye son of Jonathan Wood and of Sarah his wife, born October ye 8th 1738.

Mehetabel Wood ye daughter of Jonathan Wood and Sarah his born December ye 23. 1741

John Wood ye son of Jonathan Wood and of Sarah his wife, born at Lunenburg Feburay ye 2nd 1743/4.

Barnabus Wood the son of Jonathan Wood and of Sarah his wife, was born at Lunenburg May the 21th 1746.

Sarah Wood ye daughter of Jonathan Wood and of Sarah his wife, was born at Lunenburg November ye 29th 1748.

Sarah Wood the daughter Jonathan Wood and of Sarah his wife, was born at Lunenburg September ye 26th 1751.

Bezaleel Wood ye son of Jonathan Wood and of Sarah his wife, was born at Lunenburg Septr 10th 1758.

Molly Wood ye daughter of Jon^a Wood & of Sarah his wife was born at Lunenburg August 24th 1761.

Jonathan Wood son of Jonathan & Sarah Wood was born at Lune—— April ye 2. 1767.

Jerusha Wood the daughter of Joseph Wood and of Ruth his wife, born at Lunenburg July ye 24th 1742.

Joseph Wood the son of Joseph Wood and of Ruth his wife, born at Lunenburg June ye 8th 1744.

Elizabeth Wood the daughter of Joseph Wood and of Ruth his wife, was born at Lunenburg April the second 1747.

Bette Wood the daughter of Joseph Wood and Ruth his wife, was born at Lunenburg Novr ye 8th 1749.

Joseph Wood the son of Joseph Wood and of Ruth his wife, was born at Lunenburg October 28th 1753.

David Wood son of Joseph Wood & Ruth his wife, was born at Lunenb——g August ye 31 1760.

WOOD. WHITNEY.

Isaac Wood the son of Michael Wood and of Mary his wife, born at Lunenburg September ye 7th 1746.

Mary Wood the daughter of Michael Wood and of Mary his wife, was born at Lunenburg November ye 1th 1749.

Elizabeth Wood y^e of Michael Wood and of Mary his wife, was born at Lunenburg April ye 20th 1751.

Hannah Wood the daughter of Michael Wood & of Mary his wife was born at Lunenburg Jan^{ry} 18th 1754.

Mary Wood ye daughter of David Wood, and of Mary his wife, was born at Lunenburg July ye 8th 1747.

Martha Wood ye daughter of David Wood, and of Mary his wife, was born at Lunenburg July ye 15th 1749.

Bette Wood ye daughter of David Wood and of Mary his wife, was born October ye 21th 1751.

Sarah Wood the daughter of David Wood & of Mary his wife, was born at Lunenburg June 10th 1754

David Wood the son of David Wood and of Mary his wife was born at Lunenburg December ye 6th 1756.

Zepheniah Wood the son of David Wood & of Mary his wife, was born at Lunenburg July ye 4th 1760.

James Wood ye son of Jonathan Wood and of Rachel his wife, was born at Lunenburg March the 24th 1756.

Esther Wood the daughter of Jonathan Wood jun and of Rachel his wife, was born at Lunenburg March ye 19th A. D. 1758.

Jonathan Wood the son of Jonathan Wood & of Rachel his wife, was born at Lunenburg March ye 25th 1760.

George Wood son of Jon^a & Rachel Wood, was born at Lunenburg June 3^d 1762.

Sarah Whitney ye daughter of Zeckariah Whitney and of Sarah his wife, born at Lunenburg February the 27th 1739/40.

Jane Whitney ye daughter of Zechariah Whitney and of Sarah his wife, born Sept ye 22nd 1742.

Abigail Whitney daughter of Zechariah Whitney and of Sarah his wife, was born at Lunenburg Jan^{ry} 17th 1746.

Zechariah Whitney son of Zechariah Whitney & Sarah his wife, was born at Lunenburg Janry 11th 1747.

Mary Whitney daughter of Zechariah Whitney and Sarah his wife, was born at Lunenburg April 8th 1752.

John Whitney son of Zechariah Whitney and Sarah his wife, was born at Lunenburg April ye 16th 1756.

WHITNEY. WETHERBE.

Moses Whitney ye son of Ephraim Whitney and of Jane his wife, was born at Lunenburg Janvary ye 11th 1747.

Ephraim Whitney ye son of Ephraim Whitney and of Jane his wife, was born August ye 12th 1749.

Molley Whitney the daughter of Ephraim Whitney and of Jane his wife, was born at Lunenburg September ye 25th 1755.

Ezra Whitney son of Ezra Whitney and Agness his wife, was born at Lunenburg November 29th 1760.

Rebekah Whitney daughter of Ezra Whitney and Agness his wife, was born at Lunenburg Jany 2^d 1762.

The birth of ye children of Hezekiah Wetherbe and of Huldah his wife.
Benjamin born at Malborough November 3th 1728.
Thomas born at Lunenburg Nouember 27th 1730.
Phebe born at Lunenburg February ye 12th 1733/4
Phebe born at Lunenburg July 7th 1740.
Sarah Wetherbee ye daughter of Hezekiah Wetherbe and of Huldah his wife born at Lunenburg Novmber seventeeenth 1742.
John born at Lunenburg Septr 14th 1746.
Abraham born at Lunenburg June 5th 1752.

Mary Wetherbe ye davghter of Ephraim Wetherbe and of Elizabath Wetherbe his wife, born at Lunenburg Janeweary ye 6th 1729/30.

Bette Wetherbe ye davghter of Ephraim Wetherbee and of Elizabeth Wetherbe his wife, born at Lunenburg May ye 15th 1732.

Rachel Wetherbe ye davghter of Ephraim Wetherbe, and of Johanah Wetherbe his wife, born at Lunenburg April ye 3th 1733.

Jonathan Wetherbee ye son of Ephraim Wetherbe and of Johannah his wife, born October ye 14th 1734.

Abigail Wetherbe ye davghter of Ephraim Wetherbe and of Joanna his wife, born Feb^r 13th 1735/6.

Susannah Wetherbee ye daughter of Ephraim Wetherbe and of Johannah his wife, born March ye 27th 1738.

Abijah Wetherbe the son of Ephraim Wetherbe and of Johannah his wife, born at Lunenburg April ye 24th 1740.

Johannah Wetherbe the daughter of Ephraim Wetherbe and of Johannah his wife, born at Lunenburg September ye 13th 1742.

Samvel Wetherbee the son of Ephraim Wetherbe and of Johannah his wife born at Lunenburg April ye 3rd 1745.

WETHERBEE. WALKER.

Ephraim Wetherbe the son of Paul Wetherbe and of Hannah his wife, was born at Lunenburg August ye 24th 1747.

Paul Wetherbe the son of Paul Wetherbe and of Hannah his wife, was born at Lunenburg August the 12th 1749.

Hannah Wetherbe ye daughter of Paul Wetherbe and of Hannah his wife, was born at Lunenburg July ye 19th 1751.

Betty Wetherbee the daughter of Paul Wetherbee and of Hannah his wife, was born at Lunenburg December 13th 1753.

David Wetherbee the son of Paul Wetherbee and of Hannah his wife, was born at Lunenburg February ye 16th 1757.

Joab Wetherbee the son of Paul Wetherbee and of Hannah his wife, was born at Lunenburg April ye 26th 1759.

Abijah Wetherbee the son of Paul Wetherbee & of Hannah his wife, was born at Lunenburg August ye 26th 1761.

Esther Weatherbee daughter of Paul & Hannah Weatherbee was born at Lunenburg Decr 3^d 1763.

Daniel Weatherbee son of Paul & Hannah Weatherbe was born at Lunenburg Feby 16th 1766.

The births of the children of Thos & Hannah Weatherbee.
Thomas born August 7th 1757
Daniel born Decr 16th 1758
Hephsibah born Feb^r 28th 1760
Isaac born Sept^m 2^d 1761
Sarah born March 30th 1763.
David born May 31st 1764
Hannah born Feby 16th 1766
Lucy born August 4th 1767
Josiah born March 17th 1769
Patty born October 16th 1771
Molley born Novr 14th 1773.

Rebeccah Walker the daughter of Obediah Walker and of Abigail his wife was born at Lunenburg August the 16th 1746.

Benjamin Walker the daughter of Obediah Walker and of Abigail his wife, was born at Lunenburg, February ye 20th 1749.

Abigail Walker the daughter of Obediah Walker and of Abigail his wife, was born at Lunenburg Janvary ye 21th 1753.

Betty Walker the daughter of Obediah Walker and of Abigal his wife, was born at Lunenburg July the 6th A. D. 1754.

Sarah Walker daughter of Obediah Walker and of Abigail his wife, was born at Lunenburg Novr 12th 1758.

WALKER. WILLARD.

Obediah & Nathaniel Waker sons of Obediah & Abigal Walker were born at Lunenburg March 3^d 1761.

Mary Walker daughter of Obediah Walker and of Abigail his wife, was born at Lunenburg November ye 9th 1770.

Josiah Willard Junr son of Josiah Willard and of Hannah his wife born on Wensday in ———— Janewary ye 21th 1715/16.

Abigall Willard davghter of Josiah Willard and of Hannah his wife, born on Fryday July ye 4th 1718.

Susannah Willard ye davghter of Josiah Willard and of Hannah his wife, born on Satterday July ye 9th 1720.

Lois Willard ye davghter of Josiah Willard and of Hannah his wife, born on Sabbath day December ye 16th 1722.

Nathan Willard ye son of Josiah Willard and of Hannah his wife, born on Tuesday May ye 28th 1726.

Prudance Willard ye davghter of Josiah Willard and of Hannah his wife, born on Satterday September ye 30th 1727.

Oliver Willard ye son of Josiah Willard and of Hannah his wife, born on Fryday March ye 6th 1730.

Sampson Willard ye son of Josiah Willard and of Hannah his wife, born on Tuesday June ye 27th 1732.

Josiah Willard Tersus son of Josiah Willard Junr and of Hannah his wife, born September ye 22th 1734.

Wilder Willard ye son of Josiah Willard and of Hannah his wife, born on Monday June ye 30th 1735.

Jemima Willard ye daughter of Moses Willard and of Susana his wife, born June ye 29th 1728.

Susana Willard ye daughter of Moses Willard and of Susana his wife, born February ye 20th 1729/30

Hulday Willard ye daughter of Moses Willard and of Susanna his wife, born May ye 27th 1732.

James Nutting Willard ye son of Moses Willard and of Susanna his wife, born ye 28th of May 1734.

Moses Willard ye son of Moses Willard and of Susanna his wife, born August ye 15th 1738.

Miriam Willard the daughter of Moses Willard, and Susanna his wife, was born September ye 25th 1740.

Mary Willard, daughter of Jonathan Willard and of Kezia his wife, born Feb^r 13th 1734/5.

Births.

WILLARD. WARRIN.

Unity Willard and Amity Willard the daughters of Jonathan Willard, and of Kezia his wife, born at Lunenburg October ye 31th 1737.

Keziah Willard the daughter of Jonathan Willard Ju^r and of Phebe his wife, was born at Lunenburg March ye 12th 1743/4.

Jonathan Willard ye son of Jonathan Willard Ju^r and of Phebe his wife, was born at Lunenburg September ye 21th 1745.

Jeremiah Willard the son of Jonathan Willard Junr and of Phebe his wife, was born at Lunenburg Aug^st the 3rd 1747.

Phebe Willard the daughter of Jonathan Willard Junr and of Phebe his wife, was born at Lunenburg Aug^st the 4th 1749.

Mary Willard the daughter of Jonathan Willard Jun and of Phebe his wife, was born at Lunenburg Janry 27th 1751/2.

Amity Willard the daughter of Jonathan Willard Junr and of Phebe his wife, was born at Lunenburg Decr 26th 1752.

Mary Willard the daughter of Jonathan Willard Junr and of Phebe his wife was born at Lunenburg Febuary ye 15th 1755.

Thulah Willard the daughter of Jonathan Willard and of Phebe his wife, was born at Lunenburg January ye 14th 1758.

Katharine Willard the daughter of Barzillai Willard and of Hepsibath his wife, was born at Lunenburg July ye 23rd 1759.

Lucy Willard the daughter of Barzillai Willard and of Hepsibah his wife, was born at Lunenburg March 20th 1762.

Sarah Willard daughter of Barzillai Willard & of Hephsibah his wife, was born at Lunenburg March 31st 1765.

Pascal Paoli Willard son of Berzillah Willard & Hapsabath his wife, was born at Lunenburg May ye 10. 1769.

Unity Willard daughter of Barzillia Willard and Hepzibah his wife, was born at Lunenburg May ye 27 1775.

Mary Willard daughter of Berzillia Willard & Hepzibah his wife, was born at Lunenburg April 27th 1778.

Arathusa Willard daughter of Jonathan Willard and Sarah Colburn was born at Lunenburg Decr the 1st 1762.

Jacob Warrin ye son of Jacob Warrin and of Mary his wife was born at Lunenburg December ye 16th 1745.

Isaac Warrin the son of Jacob Warrin and of Matha his second wife, was born at Lunenburg March ye 11th 1746/7.

Elizabeth Warrin the daughter of Jacob Warren and of Matha his wife, was born at Lunenburg December ye 2nd 1748.

WOOLSON.

The births of the children of Asa Woolson & Elizabeth his wife,
Elizabeth born at Weston February ye 22 : 1763.
Lois was born at Weston March ye 13 1765
Asa was born at Townshend February ye 4 1767.
Elijah was born at Lunenburg December ye 1 1769
Ebenezer was born at Lunenburg April ye 18 1773
Amos was born at Lunenburg October ye 11 : 1778
Joseph was born at Lunenburg October ye 23 1783.

DEATHS

DEATHS

COPIED FROM THE

RECORDS OF THE TOWN OF LUNENBURG,

FROM 1707 TO 1764.

B.

BOYNTON.

Sarah Boynton ye davghter of Benoni Boynton & of Anne his wife dyed April 8th 1707.

Mary Boynton ye davghter of Benoni Boynton & of Anne his wife dyed April 13th 1721

Joseph Boynton ye son of Benoni Boynton and of Anne his wife dyed July 1727.

Elizabeth Boynton the wife of Benoni Boynton jun dec^d September ye 26th 1756.

Sarah Boynton ye daughter of Stephen Boynton and of Sarah his wife dec^d November ye 21st A. D. 1749.

Joseph Boynton ye son of Stephen Boynton and of Sarah his wife, dec^d November ye 12th 1749.

Sarah Boynton ye wife of Stephen Boynton dec^d March ye 15th A. D. 1752.

Susannah Boynton daughter of Stephen Boynton and Sarah his wife deceas^d June 3^d 1764 in ye 18th year of her age.

Elizabeth Boynton daughter of Stephen Boynton and Sarah his wife deceas^d June 3^d 1766 in the 18th year of her age.

Susannah Boynton, daughter of Stephen Boynton and Elizabeth his wife, deceas^d June 5th 1766 in her eleventh month.

Elizebath Boynton wife of Stephen Boynton deceas^d April ye 18 1772 in the 52^d year of her age.

Benoni Boynton deceas^d Decr 30th 1758 in the 77th year of his age.

Anne Boynton wife of Benoni Boynton deceas^d May 31st 1764 78 years old.

BUTLER. BELLOWS. BOWERS. BIGELOW. BANCROFT. BRADSTREET. BROWN. BUSS.

William Butler deceast November the 4th 1741.

Abigail Butler the daughter of the widow Lucy Butler deceast September the 20th 1744 in the third year of her age.

Jonathan Bellows ye son of Benjamin Bellows & of Abigail his wife, deceast April ye 26th 1746.

Abijah Bellows the son of Benjamin Bellows and of Abigail his wife, deceast November ye 17th 1749.

Mrs. Dorcas Bellows ye wife of Mr. Benjamin Bellows deceasd September ye 8th 1747.

Susana Bowers ye daughter of Jerahmeel Bowers and of Miriam his wife, deceasd August ye 7th 1749.

Miriam Bowers wife of Jerahmeel Bowers and daughter of Eleazer Houghton decd July 25th 1752.

Love Bigelow, wife of Benja Bigelow deceased, June 18th A. D. 1754.

Elizabeth Bancroft the wife of Timothy Bancrofft deceast Janvary ye 28th 1756.

Abigal Bradstreet the daughter of Samuel Bradstreet and of Dorcas his wife, deceasd Dec ye 9th A. D. 1754.

John Bradstreet the son of Samuel Bradstreet and of Dorcas his wife, deceas'd August ye 30th 1756.

Capt. Jonathan Bradstreet deceas'd May ye 22nd 1757.

Jonathan Brown the son of Aaron Brown and of Abigail his wife, decd July ye 17th 1759 in the fifth year of his age.

Jonathan Buss, son of John Buss and Eunice his wife, deceas'd Decr 5th 1757.

Zephaniah Buss, son of John Buss and Eunice his wife deceas'd Decr 5th 1759.

C.

COLBURN.

Thomas Colburn dyed February 15th 1728/9.

Deaths.

COREY. COMINGS. COFFEN. CARLILE. CARLTON. CARTER.

Rebekah Cory yᵉ wife of Benjᵃ Cory dyed July 24ᵗʰ 1731.

Rebackah Corey yᵉ daughter of Benjᵃ Corey dyed November the eleventh A. D. 1736.

Marriam Comings the davghter of Samvel & Sarah Comings dyed July yᵉ 9ᵗʰ 1740.

Thaddeus Comings the son of Samvel & Sarah Comings dyed July yᵉ 16ᵗʰ 1740.

Thomas Comings the son of Samvel & Sarah Coming dyed July yᵉ 20ᵗʰ 17—0 [1740 probably].

Thomas Cummings the son of Samvel Cummings & of Sarah Cummings, deceast September the 23ʳᵈ 1746.

Samuel Commings Jun dec'd May yᵉ 10ᵗʰ 1760, in the twenty forth year of his age.

Daniel Coffen the son of Michael Coffen and of Lydia his wife deceast October yᵉ 3ʳᵈ 1740.

Abigail Coffen yᵉ daughter of Michael Coffen and of Lydia his wife, deceast October yᵉ 29ᵗʰ 1741.

Elizabeth Carlile yᵉ daughter of David and Leatis Carlile, deceast April yᵉ 21ᵗʰ 1740.

John Carlile yᵉ son of David and Leatis Carlile, deceast May yᵉ 7ᵗʰ 1740.

David Carlile yᵉ son of David and Leatis Carlile, deceast May yᵉ 12ᵗʰ 1740.

Margaret Carlile yᵉ daughter of David and Leatis Carlile, deceast May yᵉ 26ᵗʰ 1740.

Abigail Carlton yᵉ daughter of Abraham Carlton and Mary his wife, deceas'd October yᵉ 6ᵗʰ 1755.

Abigail Carlton daughter of Abraham Carlton and of Mary his wife deceas'd July 7ᵗʰ 1766.

Abram Carlton deceas'd in the Continental Army September 16 1775.

Mr. Abraham Carlton deceased October yᵉ 1ˢᵗ 1779.

Vashtai Carter the daughter of Thomas Carter & of Betty his wife dece'd October yᵉ 20ᵗʰ 1760.

D.

DAVIS. DODGE. DIVOL. DARLING. DOWNE.

Samuell Davis Jr. ye son of Samll Davis died October 19th 1734.

Sarah Davis the daughter of Samvel Davis and of Sarah his wife, dyed February ye 10th 1737.

Meriam Dodge ye daughter of Noah Dodge & of Margarit his wife dyed June 28th 1736.

Reuben Dodge deceas'd June 15th 1762.

Esther Dodge daughter of Reuben and Ruth Dodge deceased June 15th 1763.

Sarah Divol the wife of John Divol, deceast at Lunenburg April ye 14th 1746.

John Darling ye son of John Darling jun and of Ruth his wife, deceast August ye 27th 1746 at Leominster.

Sarah Downe the daughter of William Downe Esqr and Margaret his wife, deceast March ye 24th 1755 aged, eight years and three months.

F.

FARMER. FITCH. FLOOD. FROST. FOSTER.

Rebekah, daughter of John Farmer died July ye 31th 1732.

Hannah Farmer ye wife of John Farmer died February 22th 1730 : 31.

John Farmer of Lunenburg dyed August ye 15th 1735.

Rebekah Farmer, widdow dyed September ye 5th 1736.

Susanna Fitch ye wife of Mr. John Fitch, deceast December ye 24th 1748 at Providence in ye Collony of Rhod Island.

Elizabeth Flood the wife of Benjamin Flood, deceased, April the 1th 1752 in the 30th year of her age.

Hannah Frost deceased May 23d 1753.

Enoch Foster the son of Benjamin Foster and of Mehetabel Foster, deceas't July the 15th 1749 in ye 7th year of his age.

Benjamin Foster Junr deceast Sept ye 8th 1755 in the 27th year of his age.

FOSTER. FULLER.

Nathan Foster ye son of Benjamin Foster and Mehetabel Foster, deceast November ye 10th 1755 in the 15 year of his age.

James Foster the son of Benjamin Foster and Mehetabel Foster deceas^t February ye 3rd 1757 in ye 14th year of his age.

Mehetabel Foster ye wife of Benjamin Foster dec^d February ye 1st 1761.

John Fuller the son of John Fuller and of Prudence his wife deceast June ye 12th 1758.

G.

GOODRIDGE. GOULD. GROUT.

Lt. Phillip Goodridge dyed Janewary ye 16th 1728/9.

David Goodridge the son and child of David Goodridge, and of Elizabeth his wife, deceast October the 4th 1744.

Relieff Goodridge, the daughter of Joshua Goodridge and of Lydia his wife, deceas^t October ye 8th 1746.

The widow, Mrs. Mehetabel Goodridge, deceased February the 24th 1755 in the seventy eight year of her age.

Sibil Goodridge the daughter of Philip Goodridge & of Jane Goodridge, deceased September ye 3rd 1754 in the third year of her age.

Amos Gould a son of the widow Esther Gould, deceast September the 10th 1746.

Edymia Grout, daughter of John and Phebe Grout died April 24th 1759.

H.

HARTWELL. HEYWOOD.

Joseph Hartwell son of Edward Hartwell died November 19th 1726.

Solomon Hartwell the son of Edward Hartwell Junr and of Elizebeth Hartwell, deceas^t January ye 1th 1741/2.

Mary Hartwell the daughter of Edward Hartwell Jun and of Elizabeth his wife, deceast September ye 22nd 1746.

Sarah Hartwell the wife of Edward Hartwell Esqr, deceas^d August 7th 1764.

Tabatha Hartwell the wife of Joseph Hartwell deceased April ye 25. 1756.

Esther Heywood daughter of Nathan Heywood and Esther Heywood, deceast December ye 28th 1739.

HEYWOOD. HOUGHTON. HOLT. HUNT. HENDERSON. HILTON.

Relieff Heywood daughter of Nathan Heywood and Esther Heywood, deceast February the 24th 1739/40.

Willis Heywood son of Nathan and Esther Heywood, deceast March the 6th 1739/40.

Mary Heywood daughter of Nathan Heywood and Esther Heywood deceast June ye 13th 1741.

Ruth Heywood the daughter of John Heywood and of Ruth his wife deceast May the 28th 1740.

Abigail Heywood the daughter of John Heywood and of Ruth his wife, deceast May the 28th 1740.

Prudence Heywood the daughter of John Heywood, and of Ruth his wife, deceast May ye 30th 1740.

Lucy Heywood ye daughter of John Heywood and of Ruth his wife, deceast May the 31th 1740.

Ester Heywood wife of Nathan Heywood deceasd June 18th 1765.

Robert Houghton the son of Eleazer Houghton and of Elizabath his wife, deceast August the 7th 1740.

Susanah Houghton ye daughter of Eleazer Houghton and of Elizabeth, deceasted September ye 7th 1746.

Esther Houghton the daughter of Eleazer Houghton and of Elizabeth his wife, deceasd May ye 5th 1759 in the twenty-fifth year of her age.

Darius Houghton son of Darius Houghton and Jerusha his wife, deceased Octor 3d A. D. 1753.

Joseph Holt the son and child of Joseph Holt and Mary Holt, deceast July ye 26th 1744.

Mrs. Dorcas Holt, relict of Mr. Joseph Holt, deceased June ye 11th 1775 in ye sixtyeth year of her age.

Rachel Holt the wife of Jonathan Holt, deceased April 21, 1753.

William Holt deceased Novr 14th 1759.

Hannah Hunt the daughter of Samvel Hunt and of Hannah Hunt, deceast December ye 9th 1749.

John Henderson son of Willm Henderson and Sarah his wife, deceased April ye 9th 1747.

Samuel Hilton deceased March ye 21 1756.

Deaths.

HOVEY.

Lydia Hovey, the wife of Abijah Hovey dec^d November ye 28th 1760.
Abijah Hovey ye son of Abijah Hovey & of Lydia his wife dec^d December ye 1st 1760.

J.

JOHNSON. JEWET. JONES.

Rebakah Johnson ye wife of Sam^ll Johnson dyed August 29 : 1731.

David Jewet the son of Thomas and Hannah Jewet deceased December ye 1st 1757.
Thomas Jewet deceased February ye 20th 1758

William Jones dec'd January ye 26 1761.
Isaac Jones the son of William Jones and of Sarah his wife dec^d ———

K.

KIMBALL.

Thomas Kimball Esqr deceast September the eleventh 1748 at Lunenburg.
George Kimball the son of George Kimball and of Sarah his wife, deceased October ye 16th 1755.
Mrs. Elizabeth Kimball relict of Thos Kimball Esqr deceas'd Octo^r 1st 1765.

M.

MARTIN.

John Martin deceas'd April the 17th A. D 1753.

P.

PAGE.

Zachriah Page ye son of Sam^ll Page and of Martha Page his wife dyed September 2th 1721.
Matha Page dyed April 1, 1728.
John Page the son of Mr. Samvel Page of Lunenburg dyed at Jamaica, being there on ye Spainish expedition, December the twenty-ninth A. D 1740 as they hear.
Mrs Martha Page ye wife of Mr. Samvel Page, deceas^t September ye 22nd 1746.
Mr. Samvel Page deceast September ye 7th A. D. 1747.

PAGE. PARCE.

Marcy Page ye daughter of Joseph Page & of Deborah his wife, dyed June ye 21th 1736.

Joseph Page Junr son of Joseph Page & of Deborah his wife, dyed July ye 1th 1736.

Nathaniel Page Junr ye son of Nathaniel Page and of Marcy his wife, dyed August ye 12th 1736.

Abner Page ye son of Nathanel Page and of Mercy his wife, deceast August the 4th 1740.

Nathaniel Page Jun the son of Nathaniel Page and of Mercy his wife dec'd November ye 24th 1759.

Aaron Page ye son of Nathanael Page deceast May ye 28th 1746.

Caleb Page the son of David Page and of Priscilla Page, deceast November the 4th 1741.

David Page the son of David Page and of Priscilla Page, deceast November the 12th 1741.

Solomon Page the son of David Page and of Priscilla Page, deceast November the 15th 1741.

Samuel Page ye son of William Page and of Sarah Page deceast April ye 5th 1746.

Submit Page the daughter of William Page and of Sarah his wife, deceast November the 21th 1748.

Benjamin Page deceast Sept ye 16, A. D 1746.

Prudence Page ye daughter of Jonathan Page, and of Mary his wife, deceast September ye 10th 1746.

Mary Page the wife of Jonathan Page, deceast July the ninteenth A. D. 1756 in the forty-ninth year of her age.

Unice Page the daughter of Jonathan Page and of Mary Page, deceas'd August the sixth A. D. 1756 and in the ninteenth year of her age.

Jonathan Page deceased February the 6th 1770.

Solomon Parce ye son of David Parce and Elizabath Parce, deceast June ye 20th 1740.

Lydai Parce the daughter of David Parce and of Elizabeth Parce, deceast September ye 3rd 1746.

David Parce of Lunenburg deceast September ye 19th 1746.

Amos Parce the son of Ephraim Parce and Esher Parce, deceast January (y^e) the 11th A. D. 1741/2.

Keziah Parce, the daughter of Ephraim Parce & of Esther his wife, deceast September the 18th 1746.

Benjamin Parce son of Ephraim Parce and of Esther his wife, deceased Decr 23^d 1757.

Ester Parce, wife of Deacon Ephraim Parce, deceased June 28th 1768.

Deaths.

POOLE. PEABODY. PAYSON.

Judith Pool the daughter of Samuel Pool & Prudence his wife, deceased August the 5th 1752.

Samvel Poole Jun the son of Samvel Poole, deceast May the 8th A. D. 1756, in the 13th year of his age.

Prudence Poole the wife of Mr. Samvel Poole, deceas^d April the sixth A. D. 1756 in 30 year of her age.

The widow. Dorrathy Peabody deceas'd at Lunenburg March ye 29th 1758.

Samuel Peabody son of Thomas Peabody & Ruth his wife, deceas'd Octor 1760.

Ruth Peabody the wife of Thomas Peabody, deceased June 15th 1766.

The Rev^d Mr. Samuel Payson deceased Feby 14th 1763.

R.
REED. RITTER. REDINGTON.

Rebecca Reed daughter of Samuel Reed and Mary his wife, deceased June ye 10th A. D. 1753.

Mary Ritter the daughter of Moses Ritter and of Hannah his wife, deceased May ye 3rd 1753.

Mr. Thomas Redington of Lunenburg, deceas'd August ye 10th A. D. 1755.

S.
STEARNS.

Sarah Stearns ye daughter of Thomas and Lydia Stearns, deceast August ye 31th 1746 in ye second year of her age.

Jonathan Stearns ye son and child of ye Rev. Mr. David Stearns, deceast November ye 12th 1747.

Mary Stearns the daughter of the Rev^d Mr. David Stearns and of Ruth his wife, deceased March 19th 1749.

Lucy Stearns the daughter of the Rev^d Mr. David Stearns and of Ruth his wife, deceas^d Febry 21th 1750.

The Rev^d Mr. David Stearns deceas'd March 9th 1761.

Mr. Benjamin Stearns deceas'd November 22^d 1761.

Joseph Stearns the son of William Stearns and of Elizabeth his wife, deceased September the 25th 1754 aged one month and four days.

STEARNS. STILES. SPAFFORD. SMITH.

Mr. William Stearns son of Deacon William Stearns deceased October 28th 1783 at Worcester in the thirty-fifth year of his age.

Mrs. Elizabeth Stearns the wife of Deacon William Stearns, deceased February ye 25th 1784 in the sixty-third year of her age.

Mr. Jacob Stiles of Lunenburg, deceast April the twenty-first 1750.

Jonah Spaffard deceased November ye 17: A. D. 1755.

Sarah Smith deceased Novr 15th 1746.

W.
WETHERBEE. WYMAN. WARRIN. WOOD.

Elizabath Wetherbe wife of Ephraim Wetherbe dyed in Lunenburg June 17th 1732.

Capt. Ephraim Wetherbee died at Boston November ye 7th A. D. 1745.

Abigail Wyman the daughter of Ezekiel and of Abigail deceast May 30th 1741.

Ezekiel Wyman the son of Ezekiel Wyman & of Abigail his wife, dec'd December ye 6th 1761 & in ye 16th year of his age.

David Wyman ye son of John Wyman and of Rebekah his wife, deceast August ye 1th 1744.

John Wyman Jun dec'd in September 1759 in his Majesty's service up Mohawk River being about twenty years of age.

John Wyman deceas'd Septr 9th 1762.

Mary Warrin ye wife of Jacob Warrin of Lunenburg deceast, December ye 23rd 1745.

Sarah Wood the daughter of Jonathan Wood and of Sarah his wife, deceast July ye 23rd 1749.

Sarah Wood daughter of Jonathan Wood and Sarah his wife, deceas'd Septr 21st 1756.

Sarah Wood the wife of Jonathan Wood, deceas'd September 22d 1756.

Bezaleel Wood ye son of Jonathan Wood & of Sarah his wife, deceas'd July 9th 1758.

Jonathan Wood ye son of Jonathan & Sarah Wood, deceas'd October ye 9th 1758.

Joseph Wood Jun ye son of Joseph Wood and of Ruth his wife, deceas'd March ye 26th A. D. 1758.

ANCIENT NAMES OF TOWNS.

Petapawag,	Groton.
Nashobah,	Littleton.
Musketaquid,	Concord.
Quaboag,	Brookfield.
Nichewoag,	Petersham.
Upper Ashuelot,	Keene, N. H.
Lower Ashuelot,	Swanzey, N. H.
Number Four,	Charlestown, N. H.
Nottingham,	Hudson, N. H.

NARRAGANSETT TOWNS.
GRANTED TO THE HEIRS OF THE SOLDIERS IN THE KING PHILIP WAR.

Narragansett No. 1,	Buxton, Me.
Narragansett No. 2,	Westminster, Mass.
Narragansett No. 3,	Amherst, N. H.
Narragansett No. 4,	Hatfield, Mass., or Goffstown, N. H.
Narragansett No. 5,	Bedford, N. H.
Narragansett No. 6,	Templeton, Mass.
Narragansett No. 7,	Gorham, Me.

CANADA TOWNS.
GRANTED TO MEN ENGAGED IN THE CANADA EXPEDITION.

Ipswich Canada,	Winchendon, Mass.
Rowley Canada,	Rindge, N. H., also called Monadnock No. 1.
Dorchester Canada,	Ashburnham, Mass.
Salem Canada,	Peterborough, N. H., or Lyndeborough, N. H.
Beverly Canada,	Weare, N. H.

MONADNOCK TOWNS.
GRANTED BY THE MASONIAN PROPRIETORS, N. H.

Monadnock No. 1,	Rindge.
Monadnock No. 2,	Jaffrey.
Monadnock No. 3,	Dublin.
Monadnock No. 4,	Fitzwilliam.
Monadnock No. 5,	Marlborough.
Monadnock No. 6,	Nelson.
Monadnock No. 7,	Stoddard.
Monadnock No. 8,	Washington.

This list of towns is appended for the ready reference of those who may be examining the records of Marriages, Births and Deaths. [*W. A. D.*]

INDEX

INDEX OF NAMES.

ABBIT, see Abbott.
Abbott, 115.
——, Jonathan, Jr., 94, 100, 106, 122, 128, 266, 272.
——, Jonathan, 272.
——, Martha (J.), 266, 272.
——, Mary (Holt), 230, 266, 302, 346.
——, Nathan, 272.
——, William, 272.
Adam, see Adams.
Adams, Betsey, 239.
——, William, 223, 245.
——, Rev. Zabdiel, 216–219, 247.
Alexander, Elizabeth (W.), 272.
——, Franice, 272.
——, John, 272.
——, William, 177, 182, 223, 272; 272.
Allen, J. C., 264.
——, Jeremiah, 16, 20, 23, 56, 114.
——, Joseph, 15, 23, 56.
——, Lucie or Lucy (Smith), 239, 267.
Allien, see Allen.
Ames, John, 8, 9.
Amey, John, 15, 22.
——, Philip, 15.
Anger, 10.
——, Mrs., 33.
Ardeway, Amos, 223, 235.
Arno, Rebeckah (Brown), 224.
Arven, Abiah or Abiel (Larrabee), 234, 254.
Asten and Austen, see Austin.
Austin, Daniel, 36, 56, 66, 69, 72, 74, 79, 96, 106, 114, 126, 146, 149, 152, 153, 165, 168, 170, 179, 182, 184, 185, 188, 194, 195, 199, 271.
——, Daniel, Jr., 223, 271, 272.
——, Daniel, 271.
——, Hannah, 271.
——, John, 272.
——, Lydia (Crocker), 225, 271, 278.
——, Phebe (D. Jr.), 223, 271, 272.
——, Phebe [2], 271.
——, Priscilla (D.), and dau. do., 271.
——, Ruth, 271; 272.
——, Samuel, 56; 271.

Austin, Timothy [2], 271.
Austing, see Austin.

BAILEY, Benjamin, 275.
——, Betty, 275.
——, Elezabath (Josiah), 275.
——, Elizabeth (Jackman), 232, 253, 275.
——, Elizabeth (Norcross), 235, 255.
——, Hannah, 275.
——, Isaac, 176, 183, 184, 224, 275; 275.
——, Jedediah, 203, 208.
——, John, 275.
——, John, Jr. [2], 275.
——, Joseph, 275, 276.
——, Josiah, 36, 56, 72, 80, 87, 88, 90, 91, 99, 103, 104, 107–109, 128, 137, 141, 147, 151–155, 163, 170, 171, 179, 183, 186, 224, 246, 275.
——, Josiah, Jr., 183, 225, 246, 275, 276.
——, Josiah, Tertius, 275.
——, Mary (I.), 275.
——, Mary (John, Jr.), 275.
——, Molly [3], 275.
——, Ruth (Carlton), 226, 247, 275, 278.
——, Ruth, 275; 276.
——, Samuel, 275.
——, Sarah (Josiah, Jr.), 225, 246, 275, 276.
——, Sarah, 275.
——, Thaddeus, 276.
Ball, 31.
——, Caleb, 246.
——, Jemima (Hodgskins), 232, 253.
——, Jonathan, 57.
——, Joseph, 15, 23, 56.
Ballard, Jeremiah, 92, 96, 99, 101, 102, 104.
——, Mary (Reed), 257, 319, 320, 349.
——, Phebe (Willard), 240, 260, 337.
Ballord, see Ballard.
Bancroft, Elizabeth (T.), 274, 342.
——, Elizabeth (Wyman), 241, 261, 331.

Bancroft, Jane (Whitney), 240, 260, 334.
——, John, 274.
——, Mary (Dea. T.), 224, 246, 274.
——, Molly, 274.
——, Dea. Timothy, 129, 131, 133, 148, 163, 178, 186, 191, 224, 246, 342.
——, Timothy [2], 274.
Barbrook, Thankful (W.) 224, 246.
——, William, 224, 246.
Barnard, Gov. Francis, 205.
——, Rev. John, 266.
Baron, see Barron.
Barron, Elias or Elles, 14, 22, 55, 57.
——, William, 224, 246.
Baylay, Bayle, Baylee, Bayley, see Bailey.
Beaman, Judith (Corey), 262.
——, see Beman.
Becth, 67.
Bees, Walter, 15, 23, 29, 50, 56.
Bellows, 184.
——, Abegail, 276.
——, Abigail (Benj., Jr.), 245, 276, 342.
——, Abijah, 276, 342.
——, Benjamin, 87, 95, 342; 276.
——, Benjamin, Jr., 99, 103, 106–113, 116–118, 121–123, 125, 126, 128, 130, 131, 136, 138, 141–145, 147, 149, 153, 159, 170, 188, 195, 224, 245, 246, 276, 342.
——, Dorcas (B.), 342.
——, Johannah (Wetherbee), 260, 334.
——, John, 276.
——, Jonathan, 276, 342.
——, Joseph, 199, 225, 247, 276.
——, Lois, (Jos.), 225, 247.
——, Mary, (B., Esq.), 246.
——, Mary, (Gould), 249, 292.
——, Peter, 276.
Beman, Hannah (Jos.), 246.
——, Joseph, 246.
——, see Beaman.
Bemus, William, 224.
Benit, Damaris (Gibson), 230.
—— and Benith, see Bennett.
Benjamin, William, 197.
Bennett, Anne (Going), 229, 251.
——, Elizabeth (Jas.), 225, 246.
——, James, 225, 246.
——, Jonathan, 224, 246.
——, Mary (Jona.), 224, 246.
——, Samuel, 27, 29, 43, 44, 56.
Berry, Col. Thomas, 119, 120.
Bigelow, Benjamin, 186, 224, 246, 274, 342; 274.

Bigelow, Elisha, 224, 246.
——, Elizabeth (B.), 224, 246, 274.
——, Hannah, 274.
——, Love (B.), 274, 342.
——, Mary, 239.
——, Sarah (E.), 224, 246.
Biglow, see Bigelow.
Bignal, Mark, 29.
Bigsbee, Eunice, 232.
Blair, Mr., 151.
Blood, Johanna (Darlin), 226, 248, 285.
Blount, David, 15.
——, William, 15, 22, 55.
Blower, see Bowers.
Blunt, see Blount.
Bodwell, Ruth (Reddington), 237, 266.
Borman, 44, 46, 55.
Boutell, see Boutwell.
Boutwell, Kendall, 224, 263.
——, Mary (Kendall), 224, 263.
Bowers, Elizabeth (Shed), 238, 262, 323.
——, Elizabeth, 274.
——, Esther, 274.
——, Jerahmeel, 223, 245, 274, 342.
——, Miriam (J.), 223, 245, 274, 342.
——, Nehemiah, 223, 245, 274; 274.
——, Sarah (Platts), 236, 256.
——, Sarah (N.), 223, 245, 274.
——, Susannah, 274, 342.
Boyden, Lieut. Jonathan, 8, 9, 11, 15, 19, 23, 26, 56.
——, Josiah, 15.
Boynton, Abigail (Solomon), 274.
——, Anne (B.), 272, 273, 341.
——, Anne (Davis), 227, 248, 272.
——, Benoni, 37, 39, 40, 57, 341, 272, 273.
——, Benoni, Jr., 224, 246, 273, 264.
——, David, 273.
——, Dorcas (Frost, Holt), 231, 249, 272, 302, 346.
——, Eleazer, 67.
——, Elezebeth, 272.
——, Elizabeth (B., Jr.), 224, 246, 273, 341.
——, Elizabeth (Jona., Jr.), 273, 274.
——, Elizabeth (Shed), 239, 263, 323, 324.
——, Elizabeth (Stephen), 224, 246, 273, 341.
——, Elizabeth [2], 273, 341.
——, Hilkiah, 56, 64, 65, 72–75, 79, 81, 82, 84, 91, 106, 120–122, 124–126, 273.
——, Jane, 272; 273; (Goodridge), 229, 250, 291, 345.

Index. 357

Boynton, Jewet, 273.
—, Johannah (Grout), 249, 294.
—, Jonathan, 273, 274.
—, Jonathan, Jr., 225.
—, Joseph, 273, 341.
—, Lydia (Frost), 229.
—, Mary, 273; 272, 273, 341.
—, Mary (B.), 224, 264.
—, Mehittibel, 272.
—, Meribah, 232, 305, 306.
—, Priscilla (Page), 255, 317, 348.
—, Priscilla (Hilkiah), 273.
—, Ruth (Darlin), 226, 248, 273, 284, 344.
—, Samuel, 273.
—, Sarah (Stephen), 245, 273, 341.
—, Sarah (Whitney), 260, 273, 333.
—, Sarah, 272, 341.
—, Solomon, 274.
—, Solomon Learnard, 274.
—, Stephen, 94, 107, 124, 137, 176, 224, 245, 246, 272, 273, 341; 273.
—, Susannah, 273, 341.
—, William, 273.
Brabrook, see Barbrook.
Bradley, Elizabeth (Alexander), 223, 272.
Bradstreet, Abigail, 277; 277, 342.
—, Dorcas (Fowler), 229, 277.
—, Dorcas (S.), 276, 277, 342.
—, John, 276, 342.
—, Capt. Jonathan, 106, 110, 111, 113, 115, 117, 118, 120-122, 133, 136, 137, 140, 142, 146, 223, 342.
—, Jonathan, 223, 245.
—, Jonathan, Jr., 130, 150, 201, 211.
—, Mary, 277.
—, Olive, 277.
—, Phebe, 277.
—, Releif, 277.
—, Samuel, 180, 276, 277, 342; 277.
—, Sarah (Colburn), 225, 247, 280.
—, Sarah, 276.
—, Vashtai, 277.
Braudstreet, see Bradstreet.
Brewer, John, 56.
Bridge, Ebenezer, 225, 247.
—, John, 167.
—, Rev. Josiah, 193.
—, Mehitable (E.), 225, 247.
Brigham, George D., 264.
Broadstreet, see Bradstreet.
Brown, 197.
—, Aaron, 277, 342.
—, Abigail (Aaron), 277, 342.
—, Amos, 16, 23, 56.
—, David, 277.
—, Eliphelet, 223, 245.

Brown, Elizabeth (Burnam) 224, 246, 276.
—, Hepsibeth, 277.
—, Jonathan, 277, 342; 277.
—, Joseph, 224, 246.
—, Martha (Parker), 236, 256.
—, Mary (Gibson), 230.
—, Mary (Wheelock), 241, 261.
—, Rebeckah (Arno), 224.
—, Rebecca (Wallis), 240, 260.
—, Thomas, 113, 117, 118, 124, 127, 128, 130, 133, 137, 141, 149, 152, 168, 172.
—, Unite, 224.
Bull, Trumbull, 266.
Burbeen, James, 16, 24, 56, 67.
Burnam, Elisabeth (Nehemiah), 276.
—, Elizabeth (Nathaniel, Jr.), 224, 246, 276.
—, Eunice (Dorman), 226, 248.
—, John, 276.
—, Nathaniel, 180.
—, Nathaniel, Jr., 180, 224, 246, 276.
—, Nehemiah, 276.
—, Ruth, 276.
—, Thomas, 276.
Burnap, Joseph, 40.
Burnet, Gov. William, 63.
Burnham—see Burnam.
Burns, Sarah (French), 228.
—, Thomas, 225.
Burrill, John, 16, 23, 56.
Buss, Aaron, 277.
—, Eunice (John), 277, 342.
—, Eunice, 277.
—, John, 121, 137, 148, 156, 162, 165, 168, 169, 171, 200, 202, 207, 277, 342.
—, John, Jr., 225.
—, Jonathan, 277, 342.
—, Mellicent, 277.
—, Silas, 277.
—, Stephen, 277.
—, Zephaniah, 342.
Butler, Abigail, 276, 342.
—, Lucy (Willard), 240, 260.
—, Lucy (W.), 276, 342.
—, Lucy, 276.
—, Rachel, 276.
—, William, 276, 342.
Buttric, see Buttrick.
Buttrick, Francis or Franice, 130, 133, 150, 152, 223, 245, 274.
—, Francis, 274.
—, Hannah, 274.
—, John, 274.
—, Jonathan, 274.
—, Lucy, 274.
—, Mary (Boynton), 224, 264.

Buttrick, Mary (John), 274.

CALF or CALFE, John, 15, 22, 55, 57.
Calton—see Carleton.
Cambell, William, 226.
Cannada, William, 118; see Kennedy.
Capron, H., 265.
Carlile, Daniel, 278.
——, David, 104, 141, 278, 343; 278, 343.
——, Elizabeth, 343.
——, John, 278; 343.
——, Leatis (David), 278, 343.
——, Lettice (McCraken), 235, 255, 278.
Carlisle, see Carlile.
Carlton, 125, 183.
——, Abigail, 278, 243.
——, Abraham, 171, 176, 179, 190, 198, 203, 208, 278, 343.
——, Abram, 343.
——, Asa, 226, 247, 278; 278.
——, Betty, 278.
——, Calven, 278.
——, Jesse, 225, 266.
——, Luther, 278.
——, Mary (Abraham), 278, 343.
——, Mary, 278.
——, Nathaniel, Jr., 148, 154, 183, 186, 225, 247.
——, Nathaniel, 278.
——, Olive (Nathaniel, Jr.), 225, 247.
——, Ruth (Asa), 226, 247, 278.
——, Ruth, 278.
——, Sarah (J.), 225, 266.
——, Timothy, 278.
Carter, Beatrix, 281.
——, Betty (T.), 280, 281, 343.
——, David, 280.
——, Elias, 247.
——, Elijah, 226, 280.
——, James, 226, 247, 281.
——, Jerusha, 281.
——, John, 281.
——, Jonas, 281.
——, Keziah, 281.
——, Phinehas, 281.
——, Prudence, 280.
——, Ruth, 281.
——, Sarah (Bayley), 225, 246, 275, 276.
——, Sarah (Jas.), 226, 247, 281.
——, Thomas, 101, 114, 123, 126, 128, 137, 141, 152, 157, 162, 163, 168, 177, 180, 182, 183, 186, 188, 190, 196, 199, 202, 203, 207, 208, 211, 213, 280, 281, 343.
——, Thomas, Jr., 226, 280.
——, Vashti, 281, 343.
Cartter, see Carter.

Chadwick, 187.
——, Bette, 278.
——, Ebenezer, 15, 23, 56.
——, Eunice (W.), 225, 278.
——, Unice, 278.
——, William, 177, 180, 182, 186, 197, 203, 208, 225, 278.
Champney, Rev. Ebenezer, 209.
Chandler, Henry, Jr., 15, 22, 55, 56.
——, John, Jr., 71.
Chaplain, see Chaplin.
Chaplin, Anna, 279.
——, Betty (Martin), 235, 255, 278.
——, David, 130, 162, 163, 182, 278, 279; 279.
——, Joseph, 168, 186, 279; 226, 247, 278; 279.
——, Lois (J.), 226, 247, 303.
——, Mary (D.), 278, 279.
——, Mary, 279.
——, Mercy, 279.
——, Sarah (J.), 279.
——, Sarah, [2], 279.
Child, John, 22, 55, 57.
——, Jonathan, 14.
——, or Childers, Moses, 225, 247.
——, Sarah (M.), 225, 247.
Clark, 80.
——, Anne (J.), 247.
——, James, 247.
——, Mary (R.), 247, 280.
——, Mary, 280.
——, Robert, 247, 280.
——, Sarah, 280.
——, William, 16, 20, 23, 56, 114, 134; 280.
Coffen, Abigail, 280, 343.
——, Amme, 280.
——, Daniel, 280, 343.
——, Eliezer, 280.
——, Henery, 280.
——, Lydia (M.), 280, 343.
——, Lydia, 280.
——, Michael, 280, 343.
——, Priscilla, 280.
Colbern, Colbourn, see Colburn.
Colburn, Lt. James, 56, 64, 65, 68, 69, 72, 79, 80, 81, 83, 85, 87, 91, 93, 94, 96, 97, 99, 104, 107, 112, 280.
——, James, Jr., 225, 247, 280; 280.
——, Ruth (J.), 280.
——, Ruth, 280.
——, Sarah (Farley), 229, 280.
——, Sarah (J., Jr.), 225, 247, 280.
——, Sarah (Willard), 337.
——, Sarah, 280.
——, Thomas, 280, 342.
Colman, Elizabeth (Bigelow), 224, 246, 274.

Colman, James, 133.
—, Rachael (Harper), 231.
Commings, Jonathan, 279.
Coming, Comings, Commins, Commings, see Cummings.
Conant, Hannah (Dodge), 227, 248.
—, Jonathan, 226.
—, Mary (Fuller), 228, 249, 288.
Connant, see Conant.
Converse, Robert, 38.
Cooledge, Mary (Johnson), 262.
Coory, see Cory.
Corcker, see Crocker.
Corey or Cory, Benjamin, 56, 66, 67, 69, 73, 91, 262, 279, 343.
—, Benjamin, Jr., 225, 247, 279.
—, Beulah (B., Jr.), 225, 247, 279.
—, Eunice, 279.
—, Jacob, Jr., 225.
—, Judith (B.), 262.
—, Mary, 279.
—, Rebekah, 279, 343.
—, Rebekah (B.), 279, 243.
—, Sarah, 279.
Cotton, Rev. John, 267.
—, Tm. Jno., 205.
Cowdin, Mary (T., Jr.), 226.
—, Mary (W.), 225, 247.
—, Thomas, Jr., 226.
—, William, 225, 247.
Crawford, Elizabeth (R.), 226, 263.
—, Robert, 226, 263.
Crocker, 135.
—, Johannah (Fletcher), 228, 233, 264.
—, Lydia (P.), 225, 271, 278.
—, Mary, 278.
—, Paul, 163, 177, 180, 183, 225, 247.
Crosby, Charles, 265.
Cummings, Miriam, 279, 343.
—, Samuel, 84, 99, 101, 106, 117, 123, 124, 148, 156, 168, 176, 196, 200, 203, 208, 279, 343.
—, Samuel, Jr., 279, 343.
—, Sarah (S.), 279, 343.
—, Sarah, 279.
—, Thaddeus, 279, 343; 279.
—, Thomas, 279, 343.
Cushing, John, 263.

DANA, Rev. Samuel, 202, 264.
Danforth, Hannah (Farnsworth), 229.
Darlin, see Darling.
Darling, Amity, 284.
—, Benjamin, 285.
—, Daniel, 285.
—, David, 285.
—, Johanna (T.), 226, 248, 285.

Darling, John, Jr., 130, 137, 168, 189, 203, 208, 226, 248, 284, 344.
—, John, 285; 284, 344.
—, Juet Boynton, 284.
—, Lois, 284.
—, Ruth (John, Jr.), 226, 248, 273, 284, 344.
—, Ruth, 284.
—, Timothy, 226, 248, 285; 285.
—, Unity, 284.
Darrah, Arthur, 226, 248.
Dascomb or Dascombe, Elizabeth (Jas.), 227, 266, 285.
—, Jacob, 285.
—, James, 193, 197, 227, 266, 285.
—, Sarah, 285.
Davies, see Davis.
Davis, Anne (Jacob), 248, 272.
—, Anne (O.), 227.
—, Daniel, 14, 22, 55, 57.
—, Elizabeth (Farnsworth), 228.
—, Elizabeth (Joseph), 227, 248, 287.
—, Jacob, 248.
—, Joseph, 227, 248, 285.
—, Mathew, 163.
—, Rev. Nathan, 214–216.
—, Oliver, 227.
—, Rebekah (S.), 226.
—, Samuel, 72, 73, 84, 88, 92, 117, 124, 128, 131, 133, 141, 152, 167, 168, 180, 181, 190, 196, 203, 208, 226, 285, 344.
—, Samuel, Jr., 285, 344.
—, Sarah (S.), 285, 344.
—, Sarah, 285, 344.
—, Submit (Stearns), 238, 259, 325.
Day, Richard, 226, 248.
—, Ruth (R.), 226, 248.
—, Solomon, 227.
Demary, Anne, 281.
—, Hannah, 281.
—, John, 178, 191, 281; 281.
—, Rebecah, 281.
—, Rebekah (J.), 281.
—, Sarah, 281.
—, Thomas, 281.
Descomb, see Dascomb.
Dike, Mary (N.), 226, 248, 303.
—, Nicholas, 141, 148, 226, 248.
Divel, see Divol.
Divol, Abigail (P.), 227, 248.
—, Elizabeth, 284.
—, John, 90, 96, 99, 106, 109, 126, 226, 248, 284, 344.
—, Josiah, 284.
—, Keziah, 284.
—, Levi, 284.
—, Manassah, 284.
—, Manasseh, 284.

Divol, Phebe (John), 284.
——, Phebe, 284.
——, Phinehas, 227, 248.
——, Sarah (Gillson), 229, 250, 292.
——, Sarah (J.), 284, 344.
——, Sarah (M.), 284.
——, Susannah (John), 226, 248, 328.
——, Susanna, 284.
——, Susannah, 284.
Dix, Rev. Samuel, 202.
Dodge, Abigail (E.), 283.
——, Abigail (T.), 227.
——, Abigail, 235; 283.
——, Asahel, 282.
——, Barzillai, 282.
——, Brewer, 282.
——, Benjamin, 282.
——, Eli [2], 283.
——, Elizabeth (W.), 227, 248.
——, Elizabeth, 282.
——, Esther, 283, 344.
——, Eunice, 283.
——, Hannah (Josiah, Jr.), 227, 248.
——, Hannah, 283.
——, Hepsibath, 282.
——, Isaac, 283.
——, Jemima, 282.
——, Jesse, 282.
——, John Perkins, 283.
——, John Smith, 283.
——, Joseph, 84, 104.
——, Lt. Josiah, 121, 124, 127, 128, 130, 132, 133, 138–141, 143–145, 148, 150, 152, 154, 156, 159–161, 165, 175–177, 185, 186, 190, 198, 199, 281.
——, Josiah, Jr., 141, 162, 163, 173, 176, 186, 227, 248, 282.
——, Kerenhappuch, 282.
——, Keziah, 282.
——, Levi, 282.
——, Lipha (Hubbard), 231, 252, 281.
——, Margaret (N.), 281, 344.
——, Margaret, 237, 281.
——, Martha (Z.), and dau. do., 282.
——, Mary, 282.
——, Miriam, 281, 344.
——, Noah, 64–66, 96, 126, 148, 177, 187, 188, 281, 344.
——, Noah, Jr., 227.
——, Phebe, 282.
——, Prudence, 283.
——, Rebakah, 283.
——, Reuben, 157, 158, 168, 282, 283, 344.
——, Rhoda, 281.
——, Ruth (R.), 282, 283, 344.
——, Ruth, 283.
——, Sarah (Parce), 235, 314, 315, 256.

Dodge, Sarah (Seth), 227, 283.
——, Sarah, 282; [2] 283.
——, Seth, 227, 283.
——, Sewall, 282.
——, Susanah (Josiah), 281.
——, Susanna (Josiah, Jr.), 282.
——, Tabatha, 282.
——, Tabitha (Hartwell), 230, 252, 298, 345.
——, Tabitha, 283.
——, Thankful, 231, 252, 281.
——, Thomas, 227.
——, William, 227, 248.
——, Zadok, 283.
——, Zebulon, 163, 183, 282.
Dorman, Timothy, 226, 248.
Downe, Col., 128.
——, Elizabeth, 285.
——, Joseph, 227.
——, Margaret (W.), 285, 344.
——, Margaret, 285.
——, Martha (Joseph), 227, 333.
——, Samuel, 285.
——, Sarah, 285, 344.
——, William, 152, 156, 159–167, 175, 246, 248, 250, 252, 255, 256, 258, 259, 261, 285, 344.
Dows, Judge Jonathan, 16, 23, 56, 105.
Dudley, William, 63.
Dunsmore, 126; see Dunsmoor.
Dunsmoor, Ebenezer, 286.
——, Hannah, 286.
——, Dr. John, 146, 226, 285, 286.
——, John, Jr., 227, 285.
——, Mary (J., Jr.), 227.
——, Phinehas, 285.
——, Rebekah, 285.
——, Ruth (Dr. J.), 226, 285, 286.
——, Ruth, 285.
Dupee, 125.
Dutton, Elizabeth, 283.
——, Ephraim [2], 284.
——, Hannah, 283.
——, Jerusha, 284.
——, John, 284.
——, Joseph Fitch, 284.
——, Mary (Hodgkins), 231, 252.
——, Sarah (S.), 227, 248, 333.
——, Sarah (T.), 227, 248, 284.
——, Sibel, 283.
——, Silas, 227, 248.
——, Susannah, 284.
——, Thankful (Barbrook), 224, 246.
——, Thankfull (E.), 284.
——, Thomas, 152, 153, 172, 187, 190, 227, 248, 283, 284; 283.

EATON, 187.
——, Anna (P.), 286.

Index. 361

Eaton, Anne, 286.
—, Benjamin, 286.
—, Calven, 286.
—, Ebeneazer, 286.
—, John, 286.
—, Joseph, 167; 286.
—, Pearson, Peirson or Person, 181, 286; 286.
—, Rebekah, 286.
—, Sarah, 286.
—, William, 286.
Edes, Richard S., 262.
Edmunds, Mr., 41.
Edwards, B., 267.
Ellit, Ann (Fleming), 249.
Emerson, Edward, 14, 22, 55, 57.
—, Rev. Joseph, 202, 265.
Endecott, John, 227.
—, Martha (J.), 227.
Erven, see Arven.
Estey, Richard, 56.

FAIRBANK, Jabez, 23.
Farewell, see Farwell.
Farley, Sarah (T.), 229, 280.
—, Timothy, 229.
Farmer, Daniel, 264.
—, Elizabeth (D.), 264.
—, Hannah (J.), 344.
—, John, 84, 286, 287, 344.
—, Rachel, 287.
—, Rebekah (John), 286, 287, 344.
—, Rebekah, 286, 344; 287.
—, Ruth (W.), 228.
—, William, 228.
Farnworth, see Farnsworth.
Farnsworth, Elizabeth (T.), 228.
—, Hannah (Jos., Jr.), 229.
—, Eunice (Stephen), 228, 249.
—, Isaac, 37, 40, 57, 61–78, 80–91, 93–97, 286; 286.
—, Ensign John, 8–11.
—, Joseph, Jr., 229.
—, Lydia, 286.
—, Mary, 286.
—, Samuel, 27, 56, 57, 80.
—, Sarah (I.), 286.
—, Sarah, 286.
—, Stephen, 228, 249.
—, Thomas, 228.
—, William, 286.
Farrington, Elizabeth (Dascomb), 227, 266, 285.
—, Mary (Cowdin), 226.
Farwell, Abigail (O.), 249.
—, Anna (Snow), 259.
—, Elizabeth (Gary), 229, 250, 294.
—, Eunice (Conant), 226.
—, Jane (Kimball), 233, 254.
—, John, 228; 229.

Farwell, Olive (Carlton), 225, 247.
—, Oliver, 249.
—, Polly, 232.
—, Sarah (J.), 229.
—, Sibel, 235.
—, Sibil (Wright), 241, 261.
—, Susanah (J.), 228.
Fisher, Ruth (Dunsmoor), 226, 285, 286.
Fisk, Jemima (Jonathan), 249, 289.
—, Jemima, 289.
—, John, 52, 57, 64, 88, 118, 122, 123, 126, 197.
—, Jonathan, 249, 289.
—, Rev. Mr., 209.
—, Sarah (Osbourn), 235, 255, 312.
Fitch, Catherine (Cambell), 226, 287.
—, Elizabeth (John), 228, 249, 287, 314.
—, Jacob, 287.
—, John, 94, 99, 122, 152, 157, 158, 168, 169, 171, 187, 197, 228, 249, 287, 344.
—, John, Jr., 287.
—, Molly, 287.
—, Paul, 287.
—, Sarah (Dutton), 227, 248, 284.
—, Sarah, 287.
—, Susannah (John), 287, 344.
—, Susanna, 287.
Flagg, Maj. Eleazer, 16, 23, 56.
—, William, 197.
Flecher, Mrs. Abigail, 223.
Fleming, Andrew, 92, 95, 125, 249.
—, Ann (A.), 249.
Fletcher, Johannah (Jones), 228.
—, John, 14, 21, 55, 57.
—, Jonas, 228, 264.
—, Robert, 228.
—, Sarah (Lane), 234, 254.
—, see Flecher.
Flood, Alice, 289.
—, Benjamin, 289, 344.
—, Elizabeth, (B.), 289, 344.
Forster, Forstor, see Foster.
Fosket, Abigail (J., Jr.), 228, 262, 307.
—, John, Jr., 228, 262.
Foss, Molley, 236.
Foster, Abigail (Brown), 224, 246, 287.
—, Abigail, 241.
—, Dea. Benjamin, 73, 96, 99, 125, 133, 137, 164, 182, 183, 185, 188–191, 194, 197, 199, 206, 214, 216, 217, 219, 228, 267, 287, 344, 345.
—, Benj., Jr., 228, 249, 287, 344.
—, Benjamin, 288.
—, Dorothy (Peabody), 256, 287.
—, Elizabeth (Davis), 227, 248, 287.

362   *Index.*

Foster, Elizabeth (Moors), 234, 311.
——, Enoch, 288; 287, 344.
——, Isaac, 153, 228, 249, 288; 288.
——, James, 287, 345; 288.
——, Jane (Heywood), 231, 252.
——, Jemima (Fisk), 249, 289.
——, Joseph, 228, 249, 288, 287.
——, Keziah, 225; 288.
——, Lucy (B., Jr.), 228, 249, 326.
——, Lucy (Swan), 238, 258.
——, Mary (I.), 228, 249, 288.
——, Mary, 288.
——, Mehetabel (B.), 287, 344, 345.
——, Mehetabel, 287.
——, Nathan, 287, 345.
——, Rebeckah, 288.
——, Richard, 288.
——, Sarah (Dea. B.), 228, 267.
——, Sarah (Carlton), 225, 266.
——, Sarah (Goodridge), 229, 250.
——, Sarah (Gould), 230 251.
——, Sarah (Joseph), 228, 249, 288, 307.
——, Sarah, 287.
——, Stephen, 228, 287.
Fowler, 123.
——, Dorcas (E.), 229, 277.
——, Elizabeth, 289.
——, Ezekiel, 229, 289.
——, Joshua Chever, 289.
——, Richard, 168, 228, 249, 289; 289.
——, Ruth (R.), 228, 249, 289.
——, Ruth, 289.
——, Sarah Chever, 289.
——, Susanna, 289.
Freeman, Anne (Clark), 247.
——, Margaret (Wilson), 261.
French, Joseph, 228.
——, Sarah (J.), 228.
Frost, Dorcas (Spafford), 238, 258, 322.
——, Dorcas (Thos.), 231, 249, 272, 302, 346; see Holt, Dorcas.
——, Edmond, 229.
——, Hannah, 344.
——, Lydia (E.), 229.
——, Thomas, 249.
Fullam, Eben, 229.
——, Francis, 7, 9–12, 16–21, 24–39, 41–43, 57.
——, Jacob, 14, 22, 29, 55, 57.
——, Nabby (E.), 229.
Fuller, 125.
——, Abigail (Joseph), 288.
——, Abigail, 288.
——, Azeriah, 288.
——, Elizabeth (Bennett), 225, 246.
——, Elizabeth, 288.
——, James, 288.

Fuller, John, 183, 186, 228, 249, 288, 345; 288, 345; 288.
——, Joseph, 99, 101, 106, 110, 113–115, 118, 121, 123, 124, 126–128, 130, 133, 137, 148, 152, 153, 168, 172, 288; 288.
——, Lois (M.), 228, 249.
——, Mary (N.), 228, 249, 288.
——, Mary (Hart), 288, 231, 252, 299.
——, Micah or Michael, 228, 249.
——, Nehemiah, 182, 186, 228, 249, 288; 288.
——, Prudence (John), 228, 249, 288, 292, 345,
——, Prudence, 288.
——, Stephen, 288.

Gardner, Rev. Andrew, 57, 61, 62, 68–71, 75, 76, 78, 83, 250, 255, 260, 294.
——, Andrew, 294.
——, Rev. Francis, 202.
——, Francis, 230, 251.
——, Sarah (F.), 230, 251.
——, Susanna (Rev. A.), 294.
——, Susanna, 294.
Garey, see Gary.
Gary, Abigail (Walker), 240, 335, 336.
——, Benjamin, 125, 128–131, 162, 165, 172, 186; 294.
——, Edward, 197, 203, 208, 294; 294.
——, Elizabeth (T.), 229, 250, 294.
——, Elizabeth, 294.
——, John, 294.
——, Mary, 294.
——, Phebe (E.), 294.
——, Phebe, 294.
——, Sarah (Wood), 241, 260, 332, 350.
——, Thomas, 229, 250, 294.
Gates, Anna (S.), 230, 251.
——, Elizabeth (J.), 230, 251.
——, Jacob, 230, 251.
——, Silas, 230, 251.
Gearfield, Rebekah (T.), 229, 250, 306.
——, Thomas, 229, 250.
Genison, Abigail (Hubburd), 251, 301.
Gibs, Abigail (E.), 250.
——, Elisha, 250.
Gibson, Abraham, 230, 293; 294.
——, Arrington, 127, 141, 157, 162, 170, 293.
——, Damaris (Silas), 230.
——, David, 293.
——, Elizabeth (John), 250, 293.
——, Elizabeth (Gates), 230, 251.

Gibson, Ephraim, 230.
—, Isaac, 133, 135, 137, 141, 153, 156, 163, 167–169, 172, 173, 177, 181, 183, 187, 190, 203, 208, 229, 250, 293, 294; 293,
—, Jacob, 293.
—, Capt. John, 91, 104, 106, 109, 110, 113, 122, 130, 133–136, 140, 145, 147, 152, 153, 156, 159, 161, 162, 165, 171, 175, 178, 179, 190, 250, 293.
—, John, 293.
—, Jonathan, 293.
—, Keziah (Isaac), 229, 250, 293, 294, 306.
—, Keziah, 294.
—, Lois (R.), 229, 265.
—, Mary (Abraham), 230.
—, Mary (Arrington), 293.
—, Nathaniel, 293.
—, Reuben, 135, 153, 157, 163, 171, 173, 176, 187, 191, 197, 203, 208, 229, 265.
—, Samuel, 293.
—, Sarah (Gardner), 230, 251, 293.
—, Silas, 230, 293.
—, Solomon, 294.
—, Timothy, 27, 56, 57.
Gilchrest, Elizabeth (W.), 229, 250.
—, William, 152, 180, 193, 196, 198, 200, 201, 206, 229, 250.
Gillson, see Gilson.
Gilson, Esther (Joseph), 230.
—, Eunice (Hazeltine), 230, 252, 292, 299, 300.
—, Hannah (Buttrick), 223, 245, 274.
—, Hannah (Jonas), 292.
—, Jonas, 15, 29, 57, 66, 69, 84, 96, 103, 292; 229, 250, 292.
—, Ensign Joseph, 15, 23, 56, 79.
—, Joseph, 230, 292.
—, Prudence (Fuller), 228, 249, 288, 292, 345.
—, Sarah (Carter), 226, 247, 281.
—, Sarah (Jonas), 229, 250, 292.
—, Sarah, 292.
—, Unice, 292.
Gipson, 67; see Gibson.
Going, 159.
—, Anna, 295.
—, Anna or Anne (Jona.), 229, 251, 295.
—, Asahel, 295.
—, Benjamin, 295.
—, Ebenezer, 152.
—, Eliab, 295.
—, Elizabeth (Boynton), 224, 246, 273, 341.
—, Hannah (Jona.), 295.

Going, Hannah, 295.
—, James, 295.
—, John Kendel, 295.
—, Jonathan, 229, 251, 295; 295.
—, Mary (Bennet), 224, 246.
—, Thomas, 295.
Gold, see Gould.
Goodhue, 184.
Goodridge, 67.
—, Abel, 291.
—, Abigail, 291.
—, Abigal, 290.
—, Abijah, 290.
—, Asaph, 290.
—, Benjamin, 56, 68, 72, 77–79, 82–86, 88, 90, 91, 93, 95–124, 126–133, 135–140, 142–147, 149–152, 154–156, 160–162, 167, 171, 172, 175–182, 184, 185, 189, 191, 193, 194, 198, 199, 202, 207, 210, 211, 213–217, 219, 248, 251, 253, 261, 289.
—, Benjamin, Jr., 289.
—, Daniel, 289.
—, David, 113, 127, 128, 130, 133, 137, 140, 141, 142, 148, 149, 157, 166, 171, 173, 174, 177, 179, 182, 197, 203, 208, 264, 290, 345; 290; 290, 345.
—, Dorothy (Gould), 250, 292, 293.
—, Ebenezer, 290.
—, Eliphalet, 230, 251, 289, 291; 291.
—, Elizabeth (D.), 264, 290, 345.
—, Elizabeth, 290; 291.
—, Elizebath, 291.
—, Eunice, 290.
—, Ezekiel, 172, 203, 208, 291; 291.
—, Hannah, 290.
—, Jane (Carter), 226.
—, Jane (Philip), 229, 250, 272, 273, 291, 345.
—, Jane, 291.
—, John, 57; 290.
—, Joseph, 150, 229, 250; 291.
—, Joshua, 66, 80, 91, 99, 111, 113, 116, 118, 121, 125, 126, 150, 161, 163, 200, 203, 208, 250, 290, 345; 290.
—, Juet, 291.
—, Kathrine, 290.
—, Lois, 289; 290.
—, Lucy, 289.
—, Lydia (Joshua), 250, 290, 345.
—, Lydia, 290.
—, Mary, 291.
—, Widow Mehetabel, 345.
—, Mehetabel, [2], 290.
—, Olive, 289.

Goodridge, Oliver, 289.
——, Philip, 15, 22, 55, 128, 130, 133, 136, 137, 141, 144, 148, 150–152, 156, 157, 163, 172, 173, 176, 180, 181, 183, 189, 190, 196, 198, 203, 208, 229, 250, 291, 345; 291.
——, Lt. Phillip, 345.
——, Phinehas, 290.
——, Priscila, 291.
——, Rebacca (Ezekiel), 291.
——, Rebekah (Eliphalet), 230, 251, 291, 327.
——, Rebekah, 291.
——, Relief, 290, 345.
——, Ruth, 290.
——, Samuel Payson, 291.
——, Sarah (B.), 289.
——, Sarah (Bigelow), 224, 246, 289.
——, Sarah (Joseph), 229, 250.
——, Sarah [2], 291.
——, Sewall, 289.
——, Sibil, 291, 345.
——, Simon, 291.
——, William, 291.
Goold, see Gould.
Gordon, James, 150.
Goss, Eunice (Chadwick), 225, 278.
——, Rev. Thomas, 262.
Gould, Abigail (D.), 292.
——, Abigill, 292.
——, Amos, 293, 345.
——, Benjamin, 106, 118, 250, 293; 292.
——, Benjamin, Jr., 230, 251, 293.
——, David, 56, 66, 292.
——, Deborah (Page), 267, 316, 348.
——, Dorothy (Jacob), 250, 292, 293.
——, Dorrothy, 293.
——, Elijah, 293.
——, Esther (Benj.), 250, 293, 313, 345; (Hammond), 231, 252.
——, Lt., Capt. Jacob, 66, 82, 84, 96, 97, 102, 106, 110, 118, 121, 122, 124, 125, 127, 128, 131, 133, 137, 147–149, 153, 155, 157, 159, 163, 165, 170, 171, 173, 175, 176, 179, 183, 186, 188, 190, 194, 195, 250, 292, 293.
——, Jacob, 292.
——, James, 15, 23, 56.
——, Jonathan, 80, 292; 292.
——, Joseph, 292.
——, Lucy, 293.
——, Lydia (Jona.), 292.
——, Lydia, 292.
——, Margarate, 292.
——, Mary (M.), 249, 292.
——, Mary (O.), 264, 293.
——, Mary (Tarball), 239, 259, 292, 329.

Gould, Mary, 293.
——, Mercy (Page), 255, 317, 318, 348.
——, Mercy (Taylor), 239, 259, 292, 329.
——, Moses, 57, 159, 249, 292; 292.
——, Nemiah, 292.
——, Oliver, 190, 203, 208, 264, 292, 293; 293.
——, Rebekah, 292.
——, Sarah (Benj., Jr.), 230, 251.
——, Sarah (Sanderson), 259, 292.
——, Sarah, 293.
——, Solomon, 292.
——, Thomas, 293.
Gowen, Gowin, see Going.
Green, Eleazer, 12, 14, 22, 55, 57.
Greenwood, Thomas, 267.
Gridridge, Eunice (J.), 264.
——, John, 264.
Griffin, John, 124, 141, 152, 168.
Grimes, Mary (W.), 250.
——, William, 250.
Grout, Abigail, 294.
——, Elijah, 190, 196, 203, 208, 229, 250, 294; 295.
——, Endymia, 295, 345.
——, Hilkiah, 294.
——, Jehosaphat, 294.
——, Joel, 294.
——, Johannah (John), 249, 294.
——, Johannah (Parker), 236, 256, 294, 312, 313.
——, John, 57, 65, 66, 69, 79, 80, 83–85, 88, 95–97, 99, 102, 106, 111, 113, 116–122, 124, 125, 127–129, 133, 134, 136, 137, 139, 140, 144, 147, 150, 156, 160, 163, 249, 294.
——, John, Jr., 229, 250, 294, 295, 345.
——, John Butler, 295.
——, Jonathan, 294.
——, Josiah, 294.
——, Mary (Elijah), 229, 250, 336.
——, Patience (Judevine), 233, 253, 294.
——, Peter, 294.
——, Phebe (John, Jr.), 229, 250, 294, 295, 345.
——, Phebe, 294.
——, Sarah (Stockwell), 259, 294.
——, Solomon, 294.
——, Susannah, 295.
——, Theodore, 295.
Gutrog, Mr., 46.

HAGAR, Nathan, 262.
Hale, Joshua, 15.
——, Samuel, 20.
——, Thomas, 15, 22, 57.

Index. 365

Hall, Thomas, 55; see Hale.
Hammon, Anna (S.), 295, 296.
——, Anna, 296.
——, Avis, 295.
——, Phinehas, 296.
——, Samuel, 295, 296; 296.
Hammond, Abigail (Jona.), 230, 251, 295.
——, Anna (Gates), 230, 251.
——, Esther (Jos.), 231, 250, 252, 293, 313, 345.
——, Jonathan, 230, 251, 295.
——, Joseph, 231, 252.
——, Mary, 295.
——, Samuel, 162, 172.
——, Susannah, 295.
Harice, Alice, 234; see Harris.
Harkness, Elizabeth, 225.
——, Mary (Smith), 238, 258.
——, Thomas, 104.
Harper, Daniel, 231.
——, Mary (Henery), 231, 252.
——, Rachael (Daniel), 231.
Harres, see Harris.
Harriman, Mary (Bancroft), 224, 246, 274.
Harrington, Ammi, 300.
——, Thaddeus, 231, 252, 300.
——, Thankful (T.), 231, 252, 281, 300.
——, Rev. Timothy, 202, 259, 262.
Harris, 67.
——, Justice, 126, 132, 158, 183.
——, Nathaniel, 14, 21, 55, 57, 154, 170.
——, Roberd, 14, 22, 55, 57.
——, Thankfull, 237.
——, Timothy, 14, 20, 22, 55, 57.
——, see Harice.
Harriss, see Harris.
Hart, Abigail, 299.
——, Ebenezer, 231, 253; 299.
——, Elizabeth, 299.
——, Mary (Saml.), 231, 252, 288, 299.
——, Mary, 299.
——, Nathaniel, 299.
——, Phebe (Hartwell), 231, 298, 299.
——, Samuel, 231, 252, 299.
——, Samuel, Jr., 299.
——, Sarah (Ebenezer), 231, 253, 318.
——, Tabitha (Stedman), 238, 259.
Hartwell, 127.
——, Abijah, 298.
——, Asahel, 128, 133, 136, 155, 156, 163, 167, 171–173, 176, 179, 180, 182, 190, 196.
——, Asahel, 297.
——, Benjamin, 297; 298.

Hartwell, Edward, Lt., Capt., Maj., Justice, 16, 23, 34, 37–39, 56, 57, 62–70, 72, 73, 76, 77, 83–90, 94–99, 103, 104, 106, 108, 110, 111, 115, 117, 119, 122–124, 127, 128, 131, 137, 138, 143–146, 151, 160, 161, 169, 173, 175, 177, 180, 192, 193, 214, 246–248, 250–257, 259, 261, 297, 345.
——, Edward, Jr., 133, 171, 179, 251, 297, 298, 345.
——, Edward, 297.
——, Elisabeth, 298.
——, Elizabath, 297.
——, Elizabeth (E., Jr.), 251, 297, 298, 345.
——, Elizabeth (Gibson), 250, 293.
——, Elizabeth (Jona.), 230, 251, 298.
——, Ephraim, 298.
——, Esther, 298.
——, Eunice, 298.
——, Isaac, 15, 56.
——, Jacob, 299.
——, John, 232, 299.
——, John, 297.
——, Jonathan, 14, 22, 55, 57, 130, 157, 168, 173, 185, 186, 189, 230, 251, 298; 298.
——, Joseph, 189, 230, 231, 252, 297–299, 345; 345.
——, Josiah, 298.
——, Katharine, 299.
——, Lucy, 298.
——, Lydia, 298.
——, Martha, 297.
——, Mary (P.), 231, 252, 298, 313.
——, Mary, 297; 297, 345.
——, Molly, 298.
——, Phebe (Joseph), 231, 298, 299.
——, Phinehas, 182, 231, 252, 297, 298.
——, Prudence, 298.
——, Reuben, 298.
——, Ruth, 298.
——, Samuel, 15, 23, 56; 297.
——, Sarah (Edward), 297, 345.
——, Sarah, 298.
——, Solomon, 297, 345; 297.
——, Susanna, 298.
——, Tabitha (Joseph), 230, 252, 298, 345.
——, Tabitha, 299.
——, Tamar, 298.
——, Thomas, 297.
——, William, 298.
Harwood, Constable, 107.
——, Eliphelett, 301.
——, Elizabeth, 301.
——, Hannah (N.), 301.
——, Hannah, 301.

47

Harwood, James, 301.
—, Lucy, 301.
—, Mary, 301.
—, Nathaniel, 15, 23, 66, 73, 84, 91, 97, 110, 114, 115, 117, 124, 125, 131, 132, 142, 301; 301.
—, Peter, 15, 23, 56.
—, Sarah, 301.
Haskell, Ruth (Page), 235, 266, 317.
Hastings, Abigail (Hammond), 230, 251.
—, Caleb, 303.
—, David, 303.
—, Elizabeth, 304.
—, Esther, 304.
—, Eunice (Farnworth), 228, 249.
—, Eunice, 304.
—, John, 15, 23, 56, 303; 303.
—, John, Jr., 101.
—, Jonathan, 304.
—, Lois (Chaplain), 226, 247, 303.
—, Lois (N.), 251, 303, 304.
—, Mary (Dike), 226, 248, 303.
—, Nathaniel, 195, 251, 303, 304; 303.
—, Nicholas, 304.
—, Samuel, 304.
—, Sarah (John), 303.
—, Sarah, 237.
—, Susannah, 304.
Haward and Haywood, see Heywood.
Hazeltine, 125.
—, Abraham, 300.
—, Amos, 152, 186, 190, 196, 230, 252, 299, 300; 299.
—, David, 300.
—, Ebenezer, 300.
—, Ephraim, 300.
—, Eunice (Amos), 230, 252, 292, 299, 300.
—, Eunice, 300.
—, John, 300.
—, Jonas, 299.
—, Joseph, 300.
—, Richard, 300.
—, Thomas, 299.
—, William, 299.
Hazen, Samuel, 232.
Heartwell, see Hartwell.
Heborn, Elizabeth (Matthews), 234, 255.
Henderson, Bethsheba (Thos.), 231, 252.
—, David, 301.
—, Henry, 301.
—, James, 301.
—, Jane (John), 231, 252, 301.
—, Jane, 301.
—, John, 231, 252, 301; 301, 346.

Henderson, Sarah (Wm.), 263, 301, 346.
—, Sarah, 301.
—, Thomas, 231, 252; 301.
—, William, 158, 159, 263, 301, 346; 301.
Henery, see Henry.
Henry, Elizabeth (G.), 230, 251, 303.
—, George, 203, 208, 230, 251, 303.
—, Mary (Cowdin), 225, 247.
—, Mary (Wm., Jr.), 231, 252.
—, Mary, 303.
—, William, 149, 203, 208; 303.
—, William, Jr., 231, 252.
Hereman, John, 172.
Heseltine, see Hazeltine.
Hewett, George, 232, 253.
—, Triphena (G.), 232, 253.
Heywood, Abigail, 305, 346.
—, Elizabeth, 240, 304.
—, Esther (N.), 304, 345, 346.
—, Esther, 304, 345.
—, Jane (Z.), 231, 252.
—, Dea. John, 56, 62, 66, 67, 72, 76, 79, 87, 90, 91, 96, 97, 99, 102, 103, 105, 108, 113, 115, 116, 118, 128, 129, 133, 136, 143-146, 151, 152, 156, 162-164, 166, 167, 171, 179, 180, 184, 185, 188, 189, 191-194, 202, 204, 207, 209-211, 213, 215-219, 232, 304, 305, 346.
—, Lucy, 305, 346.
—, Mary, 304, 346.
—, Nathan, 14, 22, 55, 57, 64, 65, 67, 69, 74, 77, 79, 87, 89, 94, 96, 97, 105, 120-122, 125, 129, 141, 144, 147, 150, 151, 153, 155, 160, 175, 177, 193, 195, 219, 304, 345, 346.
—, Petter, see Harwood, Peter.
—, Prudence, 305, 346.
—, Relief, 304, 346.
—, Ruth (John), 304, 305, 346.
—, Ruth, 304, 346,
—, Ruth (Kidder), 233, 254, 305.
—, Sarah (Stearns), 237, 258, 304.
—, Silence (John), 232.
—, Silent, 304.
—, Thomas, 179, 231, 304.
—, William, 304.
—, Willis, 304, 346.
—, Zimri, 231, 252, 304.—
Hill, David, 305.
—, Jane (J.), 251, 305, 329.
—, John, 57, 73, 126, 162, 251, 305; 305.
—, Martha, 305.
—, Robert, 305.
—, "Old Mr." Thomas, 48, 56.
—, Thomas, 305.

Hill, William, 305.
Hilton, David, 303.
——, Hannah, 241.
——, Rebekah (S.), 232, 253.
——, Samuel, 303, 346; 232, 253.
——, Sarah (Whitney), 240, 260.
——, Thomas, 303.
Hobbard, see Hubbard.
Hobby, Mr., 178, 191.
Hoberd, see Hubbard.
Hodgkins, see Hodgskins.
Hodgskins, Aaron, 232.
——, Henry, 231, 232, 252, 253.
——, Hezekiah, 174.
——, Hannah, 234.
——, Jemima (H.), 232, 253.
——, Mary (H.), 231, 252.
——, Rebeckah (S.), 231, 252.
——, Samuel, 174; 231, 252.
——, Triphena (Hewett), 232, 253.
Hogskins, see Hodgskins.
Holden, 26, 28.
——, Beulah (Cory), 225, 247, 279.
——, Nathaniel, 14, 22, 55, 57.
——, Sarah (S.), 263.
——, Stephen, 263.
Holdin, see Holden.
Holman, Susannah (Houghton), 232, 253.
Holt, 107.
——, Abiel, 302.
——, Abigail, 302.
——, Allice (Daniel), 303.
——, Daniel, 182, 184, 203, 266, 302, 303; 302.
——, David, 302.
——, Dorcas (Jos.), 231, 302, 346.
——, Elijah, 303.
——, Elizabeth, 302.
——, Enoch, 303.
——, Hannah, 303.
——, Humphry, 302.
——, Jonathan, 208, 302, 303; [2], 302.
——, Joseph, 230, 231, 266, 302, 346; 302, 346; 302.
——, Louis, 303.
——, Lydia, 303.
——, Mary (Joseph), 230, 266, 302, 346.
——, Mary (W.), 230, 251, 302.
——, Mary, 212, 217; [2], 302.
——, Mehetable, 302.
——, Mehetibel (Daniel), 266, 302.
——, Rachel (Jonathan), and dau. do., 302, 346.
——, Sarah, 302.
——, Sibbil, 302.
——, Susannah (Jona.), 302, 303.
——, Susannah, 303.

Holt, Thomas, 303.
——, William, 126, 230, 232, 251, 302, 346; 302; 303.
Houghton, Adonijah, 296.
——, Anna, 296.
——, Asael, 296.
——, Betty (Taylor), 239, 262, 328.
——, Darius, 149, 183, 186, 202, 207, 231, 252, 296, 346; 296, 346.
——, David, 296.
——, Dorothy (Page), 236, 264.
——, Eleazer, 64, 73, 80, 81, 91, 99, 103, 104, 106, 107, 111, 113, 122, 126, 131, 133, 141, 147–149, 159, 162, 182, 296, 346.
——, Eleazer, Jr., 232, 253, 296, 297.
——, Eleazer, 3d, 297.
——, Elizabeth (E.), 296, 346.
——, Elizabeth, 228, 296; 296.
——, Esther, 296, 346; 297.
——, Jerusha (Darius), 231, 252, 296, 346.
——, John, 296.
——, Jonathan, 71, 73.
——, Joseph, 252.
——, Judith, 296.
——, Lois (Hastings), 251, 303, 304.
——, Lois, 297.
——, Manasseh, 296.
——, Mary (Jos.), 252.
——, Miriam (Bowers), 223, 245, 274, 342.
——, Robert, 346.
——, Ruth (Stearns), 238, 258, 296.
——, Ruth, 297.
——, Sarah, 297.
——, Stephen, 297.
——, Susannah (E., Jr.), 232, 253, 296, 297.
——, Susannah, 296, 346; 296.
——, Thomas, 83.
Hovey, Abijah, 162, 200, 201, 203, 208, 232, 266, 301, 302, 347; 302, 347.
——, Dorcas, 241, 301.
——, Lydia (A.), 301, 302, 347.
——, Lydia [2d] (A.), 232, 266.
——, Lydia, 236, 301.
——, Mary (Wood), 240, 263, 333.
——, Miriam (Paterson), 236, 302, 319.
——, Sarah (Farewell), 229.
Hubard, see Hubbard.
Hubbard, Abigail (Farewell), 249.
——, Abigail (Jona., Jr.), 251, 301.
——, Abigail, 301.
——, Gershom, 231, 252.
——, Grace, 301.
——, Hannah (John), 230, 252, 306.
——, Hannah (Willard), 264, 336.

Hubbard, John, 230, 252.
—, Jonathan, Lt., Capt., Maj., 12, 14, 16, 22, 24, 26, 31, 32, 55, 57, 83, 85-88, 90, 92, 93, 95-97, 99, 102, 103, 105, 107-110, 112, 116, 119-122, 124-127, 129-136.
—, Jonathan, Jr., 115, 117, 125, 251, 301.
—, Joseph, 14, 22, 55, 57.
—, Lipha (Gershom), 231, 252, 281.
—, Mary (Jenison), 253, 308.
—, Rebekah, 301.
—, Ruth (Stearns), 193, 194, 214, 257, 262, 324, 349.
Hubbart, and Hubbird, and Hubburd, see Hubbard.
Huchings, John, 300.
—, Joseph, 300.
—, Loas, 300.
—, Sarah (Joseph), 300.
—, see Hutchins.
Huet, see Hewett.
Hunt, Ebenezer, 299.
—, Hannah (J.), 299, 346.
—, Hannah, 299; 346.
—, I. S., 265.
—, Jonathan, 299.
—, Martha, 299.
—, Pearley, 299.
—, Capt. Samuel, 141, 148, 153, 156-159, 162-164, 166, 171, 173, 176-178, 180-182, 184, 185, 187, 189, 191, 192, 197, 299, 346.
Hutchens, see Hutchins.
Hutchins, 128.
—, Abigail (P.), 232, 253, 300.
—, Abigail, 300.
—, Ama, 300.
—, James Reed, 300.
—, John Sullivan, 300.
—, Capt. Joshua, 36, 40, 56, 64, 65, 167, 170-172, 175, 179, 182, 184, 185, 188, 189, 193, 195, 196, 200-202, 204, 207, 209-211, 213-215, 218, 219.
—, Joshua, 300.
—, Phinehas, 232, 253, 300; 300.
—, Prudy, 300.
—, Sarah, 300.
—, see Huchings.
Hutchinson, Bettey, 232.
—, Elizebath (S.), and dau. do., 305.
—, Samuel, 232, 305; 305.
—, Thomas, 305.

INGALLS, Lydia (Hovey), 232, 266.
Ireland, Abigail (Steward), 238, 259.
—, Abigail, 305.
—, Abraham, 152, 165, 168, 174, 176, 180, 189, 190, 193, 232, 305, 306; 305.

Ireland, Ann, 305.
—, Anne (Steward), 238, 258, 322.
—, Betty, 306.
—, David, 306.
—, Elener, 306.
—, Jonathan, 306.
—, Mary (Steward), 238, 258, 323.
—, Mary, 305.
—, Meribah (Abraham), 232, 305, 306.
—, Meribah, 306.
—, Susannah, 306.

JACKMAN, Abner, 232, 253.
—, Elizabeth (A.), 232, 253, 275.
Jackson, Madam Borredell (Prentice), 236, 267.
Jenison, John, 105, 111, 116, 117, 122, 125, 128, 253, 308; 308.
—, Mary (J.), 253, 308.
—, Mary, 308.
Jenisson, Mrs. Mary (Bellows), 246.
—, see Genison.
Jewell, James, 64.
Jewett, David, 347.
—, Enoch, 307.
—, Ezekiel, 232.
—, Hannah (T.), 307, 347.
—, Thomas, 307, 347.
Johnson, Benjamin, 306.
—, Elizabeth (Stearns), 237, 257, 306, 325, 350.
—, Hannah (Hubbard), 230, 252, 306.
—, Hannah (Saml., Jr.), 306.
—, James, 232, 253, 306.
—, Keziah (Gibson), 229, 250, 293, 306.
—, Lucy, 306.
—, Mary (S.), 262.
—, Mary, 306.
—, Nathan [2], 306.
—, Rebakah (S.), 306, 347.
—, Rebekah (Gearfield), 229, 250, 306.
—, Dea. Samuel, 56, 64-66, 69, 72, 74, 76-78, 80, 83, 84, 87, 90, 96, 99, 100, 102-106, 110, 111, 113, 115-118, 125, 127, 134-136, 138-140, 142, 145, 151, 160, 161, 175, 182, 262, 306, 347.
—, Samuel, Jr., 168, 176, 189, 198, 199, 203, 208, 306; 306.
—, Sarah (Boynton), 245, 273, 341.
—, Silvanus, 306.
—, Susannah (J.), 232, 253, 306.
Jones, Abigail (Fosket), 228, 262, 307.
—, Abigail, 307.
—, Alnathan, 56.

Index. 369

Jones, Amasa, 307.
——, Amos, 307.
——, David, 307.
——, Elizabeth, 307.
——, Elnathan, 308.
——, Emme, 307.
——, Enos, 307.
——, Hannah, 307.
——, Isaac, 307, 347.
——, John, 307.
——, Joseph, 307, 308.
——, Lt. Josiah, 14, 22, 55, 57.
——, Josiah, 14; 307.
——, Mary (Joseph), 307, 308.
——, Mary, 307.
——, Ruth, 307.
——, Samuel, 9, 11, 17, 19, 21, 24–26, 28, 29, 33, 34, 36, 37; 307.
——, Sarah (Foster), 228, 249, 288, 307.
——, Sarah (W.), 263, 307, 347.
——, Sarah (W., Jr.), 233, 264, 307.
——, Sarah, 307.
——, Silence, 307.
——, William, 66, 73, 80, 83, 88, 93, 94, 96, 97, 105, 109, 110, 113, 118, 122, 125, 132, 137, 141, 156–158, 162, 170, 171, 180, 263, 307, 347.
——, William, Jr., 233, 264, 307; 307.
Jonson, see Johnson.
Joyner, Elizabeth, 246.
Judevine, Patience (W.), 233, 253, 294.
——, William, 233, 253.

KANNADY, William, 131; see Kennedy.
Keen or Keene, William, 14, 22, 28, 55, 57.
Kelsey, John, 253.
——, Martha (John), 253.
Kembal, Kembel, see Kimball.
Kendal or Kendall, Alovisa, 309.
——, Eusebia, 309.
——, Hannah, 309.
——, Mary (William) and dau. do., 309.
——, Ruth (Fowler), 228, 249, 289.
——, Samuel, 20; 309.
——, William [2], 309.
Kendel, Abiathar, 309.
——, Bezaleel, 309.
——, Elizabeth (U.), 233, 253, 309, 314.
——, Uzziah, 233, 253, 309.
Kennedy, Elizabeth (Henry), 230, 251, 303.
——, Jane (Leitch), 233, 254.
——, Mary (Machane), 234, 255.
——, Mary, 308.
——, Samuel, 233, 253, 308.

Kennedy, Sarah (S.), 233, 253, 308, 315.
——, Sarah, 308.
——, William, 308; see Cannada and Kannady.
Kibby, James, 62, 70.
Kidder, Benjamin, 233, 254.
——, Ruth (B.), 233, 254, 305.
Kilburn, William, Jr., 233.
Kimball, Abigail, 309.
——, Alfred, 265.
——, Amos, 131, 133, 134, 137, 147, 152, 153, 155, 157, 158, 162, 163, 165, 168, 172, 174, 175, 177, 180, 182, 187, 193, 308; 308.
——, Anne, 308.
——, Benjamin, 309.
——, Betty, 309.
——, Dea., 216.
——, Dolley, 308.
——, Dorothy (Amos), 308.
——, Ebenezer, 308.
——, Elisabeth, 308.
——, Elizabeth (R., Jr.), 233, 254.
——, Elizabeth (T.), 347.
——, Ephraim, 134, 141, 153, 156, 163, 173, 174, 180, 183, 185–187, 203, 208, 233, 308, 309; 308.
——, Lt. George, 141, 165, 168, 171, 172, 176, 181, 185, 189, 194, 196–198, 203, 208, 215, 233, 282, 309, 347.
——, George, 309, 347; 309.
——, Hannah, 308.
——, Jane (W.), 233, 254.
——, Joseph, 16, 20, 24.
——, Levi, 309.
——, Mary (Dunsmoor), 227.
——, Mary (Ephraim), 233, 308, 309, 334.
——, Mary, 308.
——, Phinehas, 308.
——, Rachel, 308.
——, Capt. Richard, 16, 20, 24, 56.
——, Richard, Jr., 233, 254.
——, Sarah (Geo.), 233, 309, 347.
——, Sarah, 309.
——, Thomas, Jr., 16, 23, 55, 56, 134, 347.
——, Thomas, 308; 309.
——, William, 233, 254.
Kimbel, see Kimball.
Kneeland, Elizabeth (Hartwell), 251, 297, 298, 345.
Knight, Hannah, 246.

LAKE, Priscilla (Robinson), 267, 321.
Lakin, Rebekah (Davis), 226.
Lain, see Lane.
Lane, Eleazer, 310.

370 *Index.*

Lane, Widow Mary, 131.
——, Mary, 310.
——, Nehemiah, 182, 196, 234, 254, 265, 310; 310.
——, Phebe, 310.
——, Sarah (N.), 234, 265.
——, Sarah [2d], (N.), 234, 254, 310.
——, Sarah, 310.
Larkin, Hannah (W.), 234, 254.
——, William, 234, 254.
Larrabee, Abiah or Abiel (J.), 234, 254.
——, Abigail (Symonds), 259.
——, Abigail, 310.
——, Anne (S.), 233, 254.
——, Benjamin, 233, 254.
——, Isabella (Barron), 224, 246.
——, John, 234, 254.
——, Margaret (B.), 233, 254.
——, Mary (S.), 234, 254.
——, Mary (T.), and dau. do., 310.
——, Samuel, 125, 130, 131, 137, 162, 176, 187, 188, 233, 234, 254.
——, Sarah (Bowers), 223, 245, 274.
——, Timothy, 310.
Laurance or Larrance, William, 11, 15, 17, 19, 21, 23, 56.
Lech, James, 310.
——, Janat (Jas.), 310.
——, Manasses, 310.
——, see Leitch and Litch.
Leitch, Elizabeth (Crawford), 226, 263.
——, James, 130, 133, 148, 150, 152, 155, 157, 159.
——, Jane (T.), 233, 254.
——, Thomas, 168, 177, 180, 233, 254.
——, see Lech and Litch.
Lilly, Ebenezer, 310.
——, Elizabeth (John), 310.
——, John, 310.
Litch, James, 103, 104.
——, John, 196.
——, Thomas, 203, 208.
——, see Lech and Leitch.
Little, Elizabeth (W.), 233, 261.
——, Elizabeth, 232.
——, Jane (Sharer), 237, 257.
——, Jennet (Steel), 238, 258.
——, John, 310.
——, Thomas, 114, 128.
——, William, 175, 233, 261.
Littlefield, Sarah, 241.
Locke, Sarah (Jones), 263, 307, 347.
Loring, Israel, 265.
Lovejoy, Elizabeth (Boynton), 224, 246, 341.
——, John, 233, 254, 309, 310; 309.
——, Jonathan, 309.

Lovejoy, Martha (Abbott), 266, 272.
——, Mary (Bayley), 224, 275.
——, Phebe (Austin), 223, 271, 272.
——, Prudence, 310.
——, Sarah (John), 233, 254, 309, 310, 313.
——, Sarah, 309.
——, Susannah, 310.
Low, Abagail, 310.
——, Abraham, 310.
——, Benoni, 310.
——, Elizabeth, 310.
——, Francis, 310.
——, Hannah, 310.
——, Joanna, 310.
——, Jonathan, 146, 196, 198, 199, 203, 207, 208; 310.
——, Mary (Stearns), 239, 259, 310, 325.
——, Sarah (Jona.), and dau. do., 310.
——, William, 310.
Lynde, Mrs. Anne (Prescott), 255.

Maccarty, Thad, 261.
Mace, Polly, 233.
Machane, Mary (W., Jr.), 234, 255.
——, William, Jr., 234, 255.
Mackfeddres, Arch^a, 57.
Mackfatrich, Archibald, 67.
Mansfeild, John, 129, 131.
Marble, Mary (Spafford), 238, 322.
Marsh, John, 234.
Martin, Betty (John), 235, 255, 278.
——, Elizabeth (Goodridge), 264, 290, 345.
——, Elizabeth (John), and dau. do., 311.
——, Eunice (Geo.), and dau. do., 312.
——, George, 197, 203, 208, 311.
——, Hannah, 311.
——, Jane (Poor), 236, 257, 311.
——, John, 117, 123, 124, 133, 137, 141, 142, 148, 150, 152, 157, 311, 347; 235, 255, 311; 311.
——, Jonathan [3], 311.
——, Joseph, 311.
——, Lucy, 311.
——, Martha, 311.
——, Mary (Holt), 230, 251, 302.
——, Mary, 239, 311; 312.
——, Mercy (Jona.), 311.
——, Patience, 311.
——, Prudence, 311.
——, Sally (Boynton), 225.
——, Samuel, 311.
——, Susana, 311.
Matthews, Elizabeth (T.), 234, 255.
——, Thomas, 234, 255.
McClary, Margaret (White), 240, 260.

Index. 371

McCraken, Lettice (S.), 235, 255, 278.
——, Samuel, 235, 255.
McFarlen, Martha (Kelsey), 253.
McFarling, see McFerlin.
Mcferland, George, 177.
McFerlin, George, 177, 234, 262.
——, Margaret (G.), 234, 262.
Mead or Meed, Joshua, 167, 178, 187, 191.
Mellen, Rev. John, 202.
Merrill, Abigail (D.), and dau. do., 311.
——, Daniel, 311.
——, Hitte, 311.
Messer, Messor, see Messur.
Messur, Abigail (Jona.), 234, 311.
——, Jonathan, 186, 187, 234, 311; 311.
Mitchael, Mitcheal, see Mitchel.
Mitchel, 80.
——, Andrew, 111, 150, 312.
——, Elizabeth (Richards), 237, 257, 312.
——, Esther (Richards), 237, 263, 312.
——, Hannah, 312.
——, Jane, 237, 312.
——, Martha (A.), and dau. do., 312.
——, Mary, 312.
——, Moses, 110, 133, 137, 140, 141, 147, 148, 152, 153, 156, 161, 162, 163, 168, 186, 190, 196.
——, Robert, 234.
——, Ruth (Moors), 254, 312.
——, Susannah (Russel), 237, 257, 312.
Moffat, Dorrothy (Wyman), 261.
——, John, 234.
——, Joseph, 234, 311.
——, Robert, 159, 311.
——, William, 114, 153.
Moffett, see Moffat.
Moors, Elizabeth (Wm.), and dau. do., 311.
——, Hugh, 234, 254, 311.
——, John, Jr., 234, 255.
——, Ruth (H.), 254, 311.
——, Ruth, 311.
——, Unity (J., Jr.), 234, 255, 337.
——, William, 234, 311.
Morrison, Mary (T.), 254.
——, Thomas, 254.
Mowers, see Moors.
Mullickin, Sarah (Kimball), 233, 309, 347.
Munroe, Hannah (Wetherbee), 241, 335.
——, Keziah, 240.

NEWTON, Hananiah, 235.

Nichols or Nickalls, Mary, 235, 256.
Norcross, Elijah, 312.
——, Elizabeth (P.), 235, 255.
——, Faith (Jere.), 312.
——, Hanah, 312.
——, Jabez, 312.
——, Jeremiah, 64, 66, 72–74, 78, 87, 88, 92, 103, 106, 109, 111, 113, 122, 137, 148, 152, 160, 180, 183, 186, 203, 208, 312; 312.
——, Mary, 312.
——, Page, 61, 235, 255, 312.
——, Sarah (Parce), 236, 256, 312, 314.

OLIVER, 174, 187.
——, Andrew, 205.
Ordway, see Ardeway.
Osbourn, Ephraim, 174, 235, 255, 312.
——, Jacob, 235.
——, John, 312.
——, Sarah (E.), 235, 255, 312.
Osburn, see Osbourn.
Osgood, Phinehas, 94.

PAGE, Aaron, 318, 348.
——, Abner, 317, 348.
——, Alice (Wheelock), 240, 260, 315.
——, Amos, 316.
——, Benjamin, 315, 348; 316.
——, Caleb, 317, 348; 318.
——, Daniel, 235, 266, 315, 317.
——, David, 94, 103, 120, 127, 133, 255, 317, 348; 317, 348; 317.
——, Deborah (Jos.), 267, 316, 348.
——, Deborah (Platts), 236, 256, 316.
——, Dorothy, 236, 264.
——, Elizabeth (Parker), 255, 315.
——, Elizabeth, 316.
——, Eunice, 315, 348.
——, Hannah [2], 316.
——, Johannah, 317.
——, John, 347; 317.
——, Jonathan, 69, 80, 113, 116–119, 121, 122, 124, 126, 156, 185, 200, 201, 315, 316, 348; 315.
——, Joseph, 15, 26, 29, 52, 56, 66, 114, 118, 123, 131, 133, 172, 267, 316, 348.
——, Joseph, Jr., 316, 348.
——, Joshua, 316.
——, Marcy, 316, 348.
——, Martha (Samuel), and dau. do., 315, 347.
——, Mary (Jonathan), 315, 316, 348.
——, Mary (Spafford), 237, 258, 315.
——, Matha, 317.
——, Mehetabel, 317.

Page, Mercy (N.), 255, 317, 318, 348.
——, Mercy (Simonds), 238, 258.
——, Mercy, 317.
——, Moses, 317.
——, Nathaniel, 73, 74, 80, 111, 11., 116, 117, 121, 133, 137, 141, 147, 152, 153, 157, 165, 172, 176, 179, 255, 317, 318, 348.
——, Nathaniel, Jr., 317, 348.
——, Peter, 315.
——, Phebe, 316.
——, Phinehas, 316.
——, Priscilla (David), 255, 317, 348.
——, Priscilla, 317.
——, Prudence, 316, 348; 317.
——, Rachel, 317.
——, Reuben, 318.
——, Ruth (Daniel), 235, 266, 317.
——, Ruth, 316; [2], 317.
——, Samuel, 12, 15, 19, 23, 28, 29, 37, 56, 64, 68, 69, 71–74, 78–80, 84, 97, 102, 103, 235, 256, 315, 347; 316, 348; 318.
——, Sarah (Kennedy), 233, 253, 308, 315.
——, Sarah (S.), 235, 256.
——, Sarah (W.), 266, 316, 348.
——, Sarah, 316; 317.
——, Sibil, 317.
——, Solomon, 317, 348.
——, Submit, 348.
——, Susanna, 316.
——, Thomas, 236, 264, 315.
——, Timothy, 316.
——, William, 121, 133, 266, 316, 348; 316.
——, Zachariah, 315, 347.
Paine, Timothy, 167.
Parce, see Pearce.
Parker, Abigail (Messur), 234, 311.
——, Abigail, 313.
——, Abijah, 313.
——, Elijah, 313.
——, Elizabeth (Josiah), 255, 315.
——, Elizabeth (Stevens), 238, 265.
——, Joanna, 313.
——, Johanna (T.), 236, 256, 294, 312, 313.
——, Johanah, 312.
——, Jonathan, 236, 256.
——, Josiah, 255.
——, Keziah (Wyman), 261, 331.
——, Martha (Jona.), 236, 256.
——, Phinehas, 9, 11, 15, 17, 19, 21, 23, 56.
——, Samuel, 180.
——, Sarah, 312.
——, Sibil, 313.
——, Timothy, 157, 163, 172, 174, 176, 236, 256, 312, 313.

Paterson, James, 236, 319; 319.
——, Lovisa, 319.
——, Lydia, 319.
——, Miriam (J.), 236, 302, 319.
Paul, Robert, 57.
Payson, Rev. Samuel, 194, 195, 198, 199, 202, 206, 211, 215, 247, 349.
Peabody, Dorothy (Jacob), 256.
——, Widow Dorrathy, 349.
——, Jacob, 256.
——, Richard, 186, 190.
——, Ruth (T.), 349.
——, Samuel, 349.
——, Thomas, 182, 184, 186, 188, 194–196, 200, 349.
Pearce, Abraham, 314.
——, Amos, 313, 348.
——, Anne (D., Jr.), 235, 256.
——, Benjamin, 313, 348; 314.
——, David, 57, 73, 81, 91, 97, 104, 106, 117, 121, 149, 159, 314, 348.
——, David, Jr., 150, 177, 190, 235, 256, 314.
——, Elijah, 314.
——, Elizabeth (D.), 314, 348.
——, Elizabeth (Fitch), 228, 249, 287, 314.
——, Elizabeth, 239, 313.
——, Elizabeth, Jr. (Kendel), 233, 253, 314.
——, Dea. Ephraim, 14, 22, 55, 57, 64, 65, 67, 69, 73, 76, 78, 80, 84, 87, 89, 90, 92, 96, 104, 105, 109, 110, 137, 156, 313, 348.
——, Ephraim, Jr., 149, 176, 197, 236, 256, 313, 314.
——, Ephraim, 14; 314.
——, Esther (Dea. E.), 313, 348.
——, Esther (Gilson), 230.
——, Esther (Gould), 250, 293, 313, 345.
——, Esther, 314.
——, Hannah (John), 314.
——, Hannah (Larkin), 234, 254.
——, Hannah (Wetherbee), 240, 260, 314, 335.
——, John, 129, 314.
——, Jonathan, 172, 177, 180, 181, 185, 201, 203, 208, 235, 256, 313, 314, 315; 314.
——, Joshua, 236, 314.
——, Josiah, 314.
——, Keziah, 313, 348.
——, Lucy, 315.
——, Lydia, 314, 348.
——, Mary (Hartwell) 231, 252, 298, 313.
——, Mary (Samuel), 236, 257, 315, 322.
——, Mary, 314.

Index. 373

Pearce, Nahum, 315.
——, Oliver, 313.
——, Phinehas, 314.
——, Prudence (Smith), 239, 259, 313, 328.
——, Prudence, 314; 328.
——, Relief, 314.
——, Samuel, 236, 257, 314, 315.
——, Sarah (Ephraim, Jr.), 236, 256, 312, 314.
——, Sarah (Jona.), 235, 256, 314, 315.
——, Sarah (Lovejoy), 233, 254, 309, 310, 313.
——, Sarah (Page), 235, 256.
——, Sarah [2], 314; 315.
——, Sibel, 314.
——, Solomon, 314, 348.
——, Susannah, 314.
——, Tabatha, 314.
Pearly, Thomas, 15.
Pearson, Bartholomew, 236, 265.
——, Lydia (B.), 236, 237, 257, 265; as Randal, 153, 170.
Peobody, see Peabody.
Perham, John, 24, 52, 53, 55, 56.
Perkins, William, 169.
Perlin, David, 28.
Perly or Perley, Jeremiah, 15, 22, 55, 56.
——, Lt. Thomas, 16, 22, 24, 48, 56.
——, Capt. Thomas, 55, 56.
Perram, see Perham.
Phelps, Asael, 256.
——, Elizabeth (A.), 256.
Phillips, Amos, 235.
——, Rev. Samuel, 266.
Pickering, Theophilus, 264.
Plats, 232.
Platts, Abel, 119, 315.
——, Abel, Jr., 236, 256, 315.
——, Deborah (J.), 236, 256, 316.
——, Edward, 315.
——, Elizabeth (Nathan), 315.
——, Hannah, 315.
——, Jane, 315.
——, Joseph, 236, 256.
——, Mary (A.), 315.
——, Mary (Wood), 240, 260, 333.
——, Nathan, 150, 315.
——, Phebe (A., Jr.), 236, 256, 334.
——, Sarah (J.), 236, 256.
——, Sarah, 315.
——, Thomas, 315.
Plympton, Joseph, 20.
Ponchee, see Pouchee.
Pool or Poole, 67.
——, Bette [2], 318.
——, Elizabeth (Jas.), and dau. do., 318.

Poole, Jacob, 318.
——, James, 126, 134, 140, 153, 158, 168, 169, 172, 173, 181, 183, 186, 187, 190, 196, 203, 208, 318; 318.
——, James, Jr., 318.
——, Jonathan, 72.
——, Joshua, 318.
——, Judith, 318, 349.
——, Prudence (S.), 318, 349.
——, Prudence, 318.
——, Ruth [2], 318.
——, Samuel, 153, 157, 158, 162, 168, 177, 187, 190, 236, 256, 318, 349.
——, Samuel, Jr., 318, 349.
——, Sarah (Hart), 231, 253, 318.
——, Sarah (S.), 236, 256.
——, Sarah, 318.
——, Susanna, 318.
——, Susannah, 318.
Poor, David, 236, 257.
——, Jane (D.), 236, 257, 311.
——, Jonathan, 15, 22, 55, 56.
Porter, William, 235, 256.
Potter, Sarah (Poole), 236, 256.
——, Thomas, 170.
Pouchee, Abigail, 299.
——, Gabriel, 137, 148.
——, Elizabeth (N.), 236, 256.
——, Nathan, 236, 256.
——, Ruth (Day), 226, 248.
Powers Jonas [2], 319.
——, Lydia (J.), 319.
——, Mary, 319.
Pratt, Anna, 313.
——, Charity (E.), 313.
——, Ebenezer, 236, 257, 313.
——, Lydia (E.), 236, 257, 313.
——, Oliver, 313.
——, Sally, 313.
Prentice, Abigail (T.), 255, 336.
——, Borridel (T.), 236, 267.
——, Rev. John, 257, 262.
——, Thomas, 110, 112, 113, 116–118, 121, 123, 124, 127, 128, 130, 135–137, 139, 141–145, 147, 149, 150, 159, 236, 247–249, 252, 253, 255, 258, 260.
Prescott, 126.
——, Anne (John), 255.
——, Lieut. Benjamin, 8, 9, 11, 15, 23, 56.
——, John, 255.
——, Capt. Jonas, 24.
——, Jonas, Jr., 8.
Prescut, 123.
Priest, Bethsheba (Henderson), 231, 252.
——, Dorothy (Moffett), 234, 311.
——, Elizabeth (Pouchee), 236, 256.
——, Joseph, 318.

Priest, Joshua, 318, 319.
—, Molley, 319.
—, Samuel, 319.
—, Sarah (Joshua), 318, 319.
Pushee, see Pouchee.
Putnam, Amos, 236.
—, Hephzibah, 319.
—, James, 261–267.
—, Martha (Endecott), 227.
—, Rachel (T.), 236, 256, 319, 334.
—, Dea. Samuel, 203, 208, 214, 216, 217, 219.
—, Seth, 319.
—, Susannah, 319.
—, Thomas, 236, 256, 319; 319.

RANDAL, Benjamin, 237, 257.
—, Lydia (Pearson), 153, 170, 236, 237, 257, 265.
Read, 28.
Reddington, Benj., 176, 180, 183, 190, 196, 198, 199, 200, 237, 257, 320, 321; 320.
—, David, 320.
—, Elizabeth, 321.
—, Hannah, 320.
—, Hepsibeth (Willard), 241, 261, 337.
—, Isaac, 183, 184, 237, 266, 321; 320.
—, John, 321.
—, Lucy, 320.
—, Mary, 320.
—, Rebecca, 320.
—, Ruth (B.), 237, 257, 320, 321, 324.
—, Ruth (I.), 237, 266, 321.
—, Ruth, 320.
—, Sophia, 321.
—, Susannah, 321.
—, Dea. Thomas, 162, 164, 349.
—, Thomas, 320.
Redington, see Reddington.
Reed, Abigail (Hutchens), 232, 253.
—, Abigail (Capt. Jas.), 320.
—, Barzillai, 320.
—, Fredrick, 320.
—, Hannah, 319.
—, Hinds, 320.
—, Israel, 126.
—, Capt. James, 202, 204, 207, 208, 210, 211, 219, 320.
—, James, 320.
—, Jesse, 319.
—, Joseph, 320.
—, Joshua, 320.
—, Mary (Bayley), 224, 246.
—, Mary (Clark), 247, 280.
—, Mary (Saml.), 257, 319, 320, 349.

Reed, Mary, 319.
—, Priscilla (Carter), 226.
—, Priscilla, 319; 320.
—, Rebecca, 320, 349.
—, Samuel, 94, 111, 126, 130, 134–137, 147, 152, 156, 257, 319, 320, 349.
—, Samuel, Jr., 319.
—, Sarah, 319.
—, Shefomith, 320.
—, Sylvanus, 320.
Retter, Anne (Parce), 235, 256.
—, Elizabath (Brown), 223, 245.
—, see Ritter.
Rice, Marshall S., 267.
—, Mary (I. Foster), 228, 249, 288.
—, Mary, 228.
—, Rebeckah (Hodgskins), 231, 252.
Richards, Charles, 321.
—, Edward, 321.
—, Elizabeth (J.), 237, 257, 312.
—, Esther (M.), 237, 263, 312.
—, Jane (C.), 321.
—, John, 237, 257.
—, Mitchael, 237, 263, 321.
Richardson, Ebenezer, 67.
—, Elizabeth, 231.
—, James, 27.
—, Capt. James, 15, 23, 56.
—, James, Jr., 174.
—, Phinehas, 16, 24, 27, 56.
—, Samuel, 38, 39, 40.
—, William, 15, 23, 27, 56.
Right, see Wright.
Ritter, Abner, 321.
—, Hannah (M.), 321, 349.
—, Hannah, 321.
—, Marcy, 321.
—, Mary, 349.
—, Moley, 321.
—, Moses, 137, 147, 156, 162, 173, 175, 180, 181, 185, 186, 189, 198, 200, 204, 205, 211, 321, 349.
—, see Retter.
Robbe, Anne (W.), 321.
—, Elizabath (W.), 321.
—, Elizibath, 321.
—, Margaret, 321.
—, William, 321.
Robins, Edward, 174.
Robbinson, Robbingson, see Robinson.
Robinson, Amos, 87–89, 91, 92, 99, 107, 110, 113, 237, 267, 321; 321.
—, Daniel, 321.
—, Eliezer, 321.
—, John, 321.
—, Lydia (A.), 237, 267, 321.
—, Priscilla (A.), 267, 321.
Rogers, Rev. Daniel, 267.

Index. 375

Rogers, Rev. John, 264.
Rugby, Timothy, 205.
Rugg, Daniel, 237.
Russel or Russell, Elizabeth (J.), 257.
—, George, 150, 237.
—, John, 237, 257.
—, Mary (Swan), 258.
—, Widow Mary, 150.
—, Matha or Meltha (Warrin), 240, 337.
—, Nathaniel, 261.
—, Robert, 104.
—, Samuel, 237, 257.
—, Susannah (S.), 237, 257, 312.

SALMON, Elizabeth (Dodge), 227, 248.
Sanderson, Abraham, 94, 111, 119, 121, 133, 148, 153, 156, 168, 171, 196, 327; 327.
—, Margaret (Stewart), 257, 322.
—, Patience (A.), 327.
—, Samuel, 196, 197, 259, 327.
—, Sarah (S.), 259, 292.
Sargent, Rev. Christopher, 266.
Sattle, Hezekiah, 237.
—, Lois (Fuller), 228, 249.
Sautle, David, 14.
—, Ephraim, 14, 22, 27, 36, 37, 55, 57.
—, Zachariah, 14, 22, 55, 57.
Scott, Benjamin, 327.
—, David, 327.
—, Edward, 197, 327.
—, Elizabeth, 327.
—, John, 57, 88, 96, 97, 106, 132, 141, 167, 327.
—, Jonathan, 327.
—, Lydia (John), 327.
—, Mary, 327.
Scripture, Eunice (Gridridge), 264.
Seaton, see Sectown.
Seaverans, Martha, 234.
Sectown, Elizabeth (Kimball), 233, 254.
Seecomb, Rev. John, 266.
Shaddock or Shattuck, Sarah, 234, 265.
Shadock, Susannah (Taylor), 239, 328.
Shadwick, see Chadwick.
Sharer, Jane (J.), 237, 257.
—, John, 237, 257.
Shed, Abigal, 324.
—, Benjamin, 238, 262, 323.
—, Bettey, 323.
—, Charles, 266.
—, Ebenezer, 324.
—, Elizabeth (B.), 238, 262, 323.
—, Elizabeth (S.), 239, 263, 323, 324.

Shed, Hannah, 323.
—, James, 323.
—, John, 323.
—, Joseph, 324.
—, Lemuel, 323.
—, Patty, 324.
—, Person, 323.
—, Solomon, 239, 263, 323, 324; 323.
—, Zackiah, 324.
Sheed, see Shed.
Sheple, Capt. John, 7, 9–12, 16–19, 21, 24–26, 28–42, 57.
Shiple, Shipley, see Sheple.
Shiply, John, Jr., 29.
—, Jonathan, 16, 23, 34.
—, see Sheple.
Shute, Samuel, 8.
Simonds, 179.
—, John, 238, 258.
—, Wid. Mary (Larrabee), 234, 254.
—, Mercy (J.), 238, 258.
—, see Symonds.
Small, William, 239.
Smith, Abigail (Dodge), 227.
—, Abraham, 239, 267.
—, Aron, 14, 22, 55, 57.
—, Elisha, 93.
—, John, 238, 258.
—, Jonathan, 99, 105, 106, 117, 327, 328; 328.
—. Lois (Gibson), 229, 265.
—, Lucie or Lucy, (Abraham), 239, 267.
—, Mary (John), 238, 258.
—, Mary (Morrison), 254.
—, Mary, 328.
—, Moses, 14, 21, 55, 57.
—, Patience (Stiles), 238, 258, 326, 327.
—, Sarah (Henderson), 263, 301, 346.
—, Reuben, 239, 259, 328; 328.
—, Samuel, 261.
—, Sarah (Dodge), 227, 283.
—, Sarah, 328; 350.
—, Simon, 328.
—, Susannah (Divol), 226, 248.
—, Susannah (Jonathan), 327, 328.
—, Susannah, 328.
Snow, Abigail, 327.
—, Anna (S.), 259.
—, Bette, 327.
—, Elizabeth (W.), 327.
—, Esther, 327.
—, Jemima, 327.
—, Joseph, 327.
—, Lucy, 327.
—, Dr. Peter, 239.

Snow, Rebekah (Goodridge), 230, 251, 291, 327.
——, Silas, 174, 190, 259, 327.
——, William, 99, 111, 117, 122, 133, 141, 150, 152, 155–158, 174, 181, 185, 189, 196, 327; [2], 327.
Spafford, 187.
——, Bradstreet, 237, 258.
——, Dorcas (Jonah), 238, 258, 322.
——, Hannah, 322.
——, John, 322.
——, Jonah, Jonas or Jonathan, 238, 258, 322, 350.
——, Joseph, 162, 167, 186, 238, 322.
——, Judah, 322.
——, Mary (B.), 237, 258, 315.
——, Mary (Jos.), 238, 322.
——, Phebe (Grout), 229, 250, 294, 295, 345.
——, Sarah, 322.
Sparhawk, Abigail (Rev. E.), 239, 259, 324.
——, Rev. Ebenezer, 202, 239, 259.
——, Oliver Stearns, 328.
——, Rebecca (T.), 238, 259, 324, 328.
——, Rebecca, 328.
——, Thomas, 196, 197, 199–202, 204, 205, 207–214, 216–219, 238, 259, 328; 328.
Spear, see Speer.
Speer, Martha (R.), 326.
——, Mary (Adam), 223, 245.
——, Robert, 144, 326; 326.
Stearns, Abigail (Bellows), 245, 276, 342.
——, Abigail (Sparhawk). 239, 259, 324.
——, Abijah, 157, 164, 167, 171, 172, 176, 177, 180, 182, 185, 189, 196, 207, 237, 258.
——, Anna (B.), 238, 258, 325.
——, Anna, 325.
——, Benjamin, 168, 177, 190, 238, 258, 325, 349; 325.
——, Charles, 325.
——, Daniel, 325.
——, Rev. David, 62, 63, 76–78, 81, 82, 86, 94, 98, 102, 103, 108, 112, 116, 120, 122, 124, 127, 130, 132, 136, 139, 144, 151, 156, 161, 165, 171, 175, 179, 181, 184, 188, 191, 192, 194, 199, 245–262, 324, 349.
——, David, 239, 259, 324, 325; [2], 325.
——, Elizabeth, 202, 215, 324.
——, Elizabeth (W.), 237, 257, 306, 325, 349, 350.
——, Hannah, 324.
——, James, 325.

Stearns, Jerusha (Houghton), 231, 252, 296, 346.
——, John, 324.
——, Jonas, 238, 259, 325; 325.
——, Jonathan, 324, 349.
——, Joseph, 325, 349; 325.
——, Lucy, 324, 349.
——, Lydia (Goodridge), 250, 290, 345.
——, Lydia (T.), 324, 325, 349.
——, Lydia, 325.
——, Mary (D.), 239, 259, 310, 325.
——, Mary, 324, 349; [2], 325.
——, Moses, 238, 258.
——, Rebecca (Sparhawk), 238, 259, 324, 328.
——, Rebeckah, 325.
——, Madam Ruth (Rev. D.), 193, 194, 214, 257, 324, 349.
——, Ruth (M.), 238, 258, 296.
——, Ruth (Reddington), 237, 257, 320, 321, 324.
——, Samuel, 325.
——, Sarah (A.), 237, 258, 304.
——, Sarah, 324, 349; 324; 325.
——, Submit (Jonas), 238, 259, 325.
——, Thomas, 158, 169, 177, 324, 325, 349; [2], 324; 325.
——, Dea. William, 125, 151, 152, 156, 157, 159, 161–164, 166, 171, 180, 189, 192, 193, 196, 200, 207, 237, 257, 325, 349, 350.
——, William, Jr., 325, 350.
Stedman, Jonathan, 238, 259.
——, Tabitha (J.), 238, 259.
Steel, David, 238, 258.
——, Jennet (D.), 238, 258.
Stevens, Abigail (Gibs), 250.
——, Capt., 116.
——, Elizabeth (J.), 238, 265.
——, Jonathan, 238, 265.
——, Lydia (Randal, Pearson), 153, 170, 236, 237, 257, 265.
——, Sarah (Page), 266, 316, 348.
Steward, Abigail (W.), 238, 259, 323.
——, Abigail, 323.
——, Abraham, 322.
——, Amasa, 323.
——, Amherst, 323.
——, Anne (P.), 238, 258, 322.
——, Anne, 322.
——, Benjamin, 182, 237, 258, 322; 323.
——, Betty [2], 323.
——, Charles, 322.
——, Daniel, 204, 208, 209, 238, 258, 323; 323.
——, Elizabeth (Sol., Jr.), 238, 258, 323.

Index. 377

Steward, Elizabeth, 322.
——, Jacob, 239, 322.
——, John, 322; 323.
——, Margaret (W.), 257, 322.
——, Martha (S.), 322.
——, Martha [2], 322.
——, Mary (D.), 238, 258, 323.
——, Mary (Parce), 236, 257, 322.
——, Mary [2], 323.
——, Phinehas, 173, 183, 190, 238, 258, 322; 322.
——, Rebecca (B.), 237, 258, 322.
——, Rebeckah, 323.
——, Samuel Bird, 322.
——, Sarah, 323.
——, Solomon, 117, 122, 125, 130, 133, 138, 140, 141, 162, 171, 197, 322.
——, Solomon, Jr., 173, 174, 238, 258, 323.
——, Thomas, 322.
——, William, 257, 322; 238, 259, 322, 323.
Stewart, 125; see Steward.
Stickney, Mr., 184.
——, Rebekah (Hilton), 232, 253.
——, Stephen, 176, 177, 186, 196.
Stiles, Caleb, 326.
——, Charlotte, 232.
——, Hannah [2], 326.
——, Jacob, 57, 64, 96, 101, 106, 107, 108, 113, 123, 326, 350; 326.
——, Jeremiah, 326.
——, John, 326.
——, Jonathan, 326.
——, Levi, 238, 258, 326; 326.
——, Lusa, 326.
——, Lucy (Foster), 228, 249, 326.
——, Nabby (Fullam), 229.
——, Nahum [2], 326.
——, Patience (L.), 238, 258, 326, 327.
——, Patience, 326.
——, Peleg Stearns, 326.
——, Prudence, 326.
——, Sarah (Child), 225, 247.
——, Sarah (Jacob), and dau. do., 326.
——, Susanna, 239, 326.
Stimson, Rev. Daniel, 265.
Stockwell, Abigail (Divol), 227, 248.
——, Ephraim, 259.
——, Mary (Gould), 264, 293.
——, Sarah (E.), 259.
Stone, 125.
——, Edmond, 239.
——, Isaac, 14, 22, 55, 57.
——, Lydia (Pratt), 236, 257, 313.
——, Sarah (Jones), 233, 307.

Stow, Nathaniel, 15, 23, 27, 56.
——, Rev. Samuel, 25.
——, Samuel, 160.
——, Thomas, 27.
Stratton, Mary, 241.
Swan, Alexander, 238, 258.
——, Gustavus, 237, 258.
——, Isabella (G.), 237, 258.
——, John, 104.
——, Lucy (A.), 238, 258.
——, Mary (W.), 258.
——, William, 258.
Sweetland, Thomas, 239.
Symmes, Rev. William, 266.
Symonds, Abigail (W.), 259.
——, Joseph, 239.
——, Ruth (Wood), 240, 267, 332.
——, William, 259.
——, see Simonds.

TAILER, Thomas, 15, 23, 55, 56.
——, Col. William, 7, 10–12, 16–19, 21, 24–27, 30–35, 37–42, 57.
——, see Taylor.
Tarball, Eleazer, 117, 124, 127, 129, 132, 137, 141.
——, Elizabeth (Hartwell), 230, 251, 298.
——, Elizabeth, 329.
——, Mary (Z.), 239, 259, 292, 329.
——, Moley, 329.
——, Molly, 329.
——, Sarah, 329.
——, Sibel, 329.
——, Thomas, 9, 11, 15, 19, 21, 23, 56.
——, Zechariah, 239, 259, 329; 329.
Tarbell, Tarbul, see Tarball.
Taylor, Aaron, 239, 259, 329; 329.
——, Anna (Stearns), 238, 258, 325.
——, Arthur, 328.
——, Betty (David), 239, 262, 328.
——, Betty, 328.
——, Caleb, 152, 170, 172, 183, 186, 190, 203, 208, 239, 328; 328.
——, David, 168, 170, 184, 190, 196, 239, 262, 328; 329.
——, Elizabeth (Steward), 238, 258, 323.
——, Jonathan, 148; 329.
——, Martha, 328.
——, Mary, 328.
——, Matha, 329.
——, Mercy (Aaron), 239, 259, 292, 329.
——, Rebecca (Steward), 237, 258.
——, Richard, 176, 177, 181, 185, 198, 201, 203, 208, 210, 211, 213.
——, Sarah, 329.
——, Susanna (Caleb), 239, 328.

Taylor, Susannah, 328.
——, see Tailer.
Tenny, Samuel, 20.
Terrance, see Torrance.
Thaxter, Col. Samuel, 7, 12, 16, 17, 20, 21, 24–28, 31–35, 38–42, 57.
Thirston, 81, 153.
——, Daniel, 15, 22, 50, 55, 57, 67.
——, Jonathan, 15.
Thurla, Lidya (Ardeway), 223, 235.
Thurstin, Thursting, see Thirston.
Thurston, Sarah, 241.
Torrance, Margaret (McFerlin), 234, 262.
Towne, I. P., 267.
Towns, Nathan, 57.
Trowbridge, Rev. Caleb, 264.
Trull, John, 94, 329.
——, Phebe, 329.
——, Sarah (J.), 329.
——, Susannah, 329.
Turner, Jane (Henderson), 231, 252.
——, Joseph, 91.

UPTON, 121.
——, Oliver, 239.

WALKER, 125.
——, Abigail (O.), 240, 335, 336.
——, Abigail, 335.
——, Benjamin, 335.
——, Betty, 335.
——, Mary, 336.
——, Nathaniel, 336.
——, Obediah, 128, 138, 148, 168, 171, 190, 198, 240, 335, 336; 336.
——, Rebeccah, 335.
——, Samuel, 38–40.
——, Sarah, 241, 335.
Wallas, Walles, see Wallis.
Wallis, Anne, 330.
——, Benjamin, 330.
——, Benoni, 158, 168, 170, 196, 240, 260, 330.
——, Curwin, 330.
——, David [2], 330.
——, Ebenezer, 330.
——, Elizabeth (Little), 233, 261.
——, Elizabeth (Russel), 257, 329.
——, Elizabath (W.), 329, 330.
——, Frederick, 330.
——, Hannah, 330.
——, Jane (Hill), 251, 305, 329.
——, Margaret (Darrah), 226, 248, 330.
——, Martha, 329.
——, Mary (White), 260, 329, 331.
——, Molly, 330.
——, Rebecca (Benoni), 240, 260, 330.

Wallis, Samuel, 330.
——, Sarah, 330.
——, Susannah, 330.
——, William, 56, 80, 81, 111, 329, 330; 330.
Ward, Capt., 24.
Warren, Elizabeth, 337.
——, Isaac, 337.
——, Jacob, 240, 337, 350; 337.
——, John, 14, 55, 57.
——, Ensign John, 14, 22.
——, Mary (Jacob), 337, 350.
——, Matha or Meltha (Jacob), 240, 337.
——, Samuel, 57.
Warrin, see Warren.
Weatherbee, see Wetherbee.
Webb, N., 265.
Wentworth, Lydia (Robinson), 237, 267, 321.
Wetherbee, 115, 123, 125.
——, Abigail, 334.
——, Abijah, 334; 335.
——, Abraham, 334.
——, Benjamin, 240, 334.
——, Bette, 334.
——, Betty, 335.
——, Daniel [2], 335.
——, David [2], 335.
——, Elizabeth (E.), 334, 350.
——, Capt. Ephraim, 66, 68–74, 84, 87, 89, 95, 96, 99, 101, 103, 106, 108, 111, 114, 119, 122, 123, 260, 334, 350.
——, Ephraim, 335.
——, Esther, 335.
——, Hannah (P.), 240, 260, 314, 335.
——, Hannah (Thos.), 241, 335.
——, Hannah [2], 335.
——, Hephsibah, 335.
——, Hezekiah, 99, 106, 114, 126, 127, 131, 152, 334.
——, Huldah (H.), 334.
——, Isaac, 335.
——, Joab, 335.
——, Johannah (E.), 260, 334.
——, Johannah, 334.
——, John, 334.
——, Jonathan, 334.
——, Josiah, 335.
——, Lucy, 335.
——, Mary, 233, 308, 309, 334.
——, Molley, 335.
——, Patty, 335.
——, Paul, 165, 169, 180, 181, 185, 186, 197, 202, 204, 209, 212, 217, 240, 260, 335; 241, 335.
——, Phebe (Platts), 236, 256, 334.
——, Phebe, 334.

Index. 379

Wetherbee, Rachel (Putnam), 236, 256, 334.
——, Ruth (Wood), 240, 260, 332, 350.
——, Samuel, 334.
——, Sarah, 227, 334; 335.
——, Susannah, 334.
——, Thomas, 190, 241, 334, 335; 335.
Wheeler, Ebenezer, 57.
——, George, 81.
——, Jethro, 104.
——, Sarah (Holden), 263.
——, Thomas, 241.
——, William, 15, 23, 56.
Wheelock, Abner, 241, 261.
——, Alice (J., Jr.), 240, 260, 315.
——, Joseph, Jr., 240, 260.
——, Mary (A.), 241, 261.
——, Olive (Broadstreet), 223, 245.
——, Phineas, 180, 186.
Whetney, Constable, 107.
White, Archibald, 240, 260.
——, Betty, 332.
——, Charles, 162, 177; 331.
——, David, 331.
——, Deborah (Carter), 247.
——, Elizabeth (Gilchrest), 229, 250.
——, Elizabeth, 331.
——, Jane, 240.
——, John, 172, 203, 208, 212, 218, 240, 260, 331; 331.
——, John, Jr., 260, 331, 332.
——, Jonathan, 167.
——, Lydia, 331.
——, Margaret (A.), 240, 260.
——, Mary (Grimes), 250.
——, Mary (J.), 260, 329, 331.
——, Mary (J., Jr.), 240, 260, 331, 332.
——, Old Mr., 93.
——, Patrick, 113, 137, 157, 162, 163, 176, 180, 182, 190, 193, 215, 240.
——, Salmon [2], 332.
——, Silence (Heywood), 232.
——, Susanah (Farwell), 228.
——, Widow, 127.
——, William, 331.
Whitney, Rev. Aaron, 264.
——, Abigail, 333.
——, Abner, 240, 260.
——, Agness (Ezra), 334.
——, Ephraim, 133, 137, 148, 152, 161, 168, 172, 180, 196, 212, 218, 240, 260, 334; 334.
——, Ezra [2], 334.
——, Isaac, 16, 23, 56.
——, Jane (Ephraim), 240, 260, 334.
——, Jane, 333.
——, John, 14, 22, 55, 57; 333.

Whitney, Jonathan, 16, 23, 40, 56, 64, 67, 80, 81, 90, 91, 200.
——, Jonathan, Jr., 36, 56.
——, Lewis, 264.
——, Lois (Bellows), 225, 247.
——, Lucy, 227.
——, Mary (White), 240, 260, 331, 332.
——, Mary, 333.
——, Molley, 334.
——, Moses, 334.
——, Nathaniel, Jr., 16, 20, 23, 56.
——, Rev. Phineas, 202.
——, Rebekah, 334.
——, Sarah (A.), 240, 260.
——, Sarah (Dutton), 227, 248, 333.
——, Sarah (Foster), 228, 267.
——, Sarah (Z.), 260, 273, 333.
——, Shadrik or Shadrach, 16, 23, 56.
——, Susanna, 239.
——, Webster, 265.
——, William, 9, 14, 22.
——, Zechariah, 131, 147, 153, 157, 180, 186, 190, 260, 333; 333.
Whittemore, Benjamin, 7, 9–12, 14, 16–21, 24–43, 57.
——, Nathaniel, 22, 55, 57.
Wilder, Elizabeth (Phelps), 256.
——, Joseph, Jr., 262, 263.
——, Josh Tertius, 240.
——, Mary (Boutwell), 224, 263.
——, Rezoma, 224.
——, Thomas, 167.
Willard, 115, 127.
——, Abigail (Prentice), 255, 336.
——, Abijah, 263.
——, Amity [2], 337.
——, Arathusa, 337.
——, Barzillai, 241, 261, 337.
——, Daniel, 240, 260.
——, Hannah (Col. Josiah), 336.
——, Hannah (Josiah, Jr.), 264, 336.
——, Hepsibeth (B.), 241, 261, 337.
——, Hulday, 336.
——, J., 63.
——, James Nutting, 336.
——, Jemima, 336.
——, Jeremiah, 337.
——, Ensign, Lieut., Capt. Jonathan, 57, 64, 66, 68, 70, 73, 82, 85, 87, 91, 92, 94, 95, 103, 117, 122, 124, 127, 128, 130, 131, 135, 136, 146, 150, 165, 336, 337; heirs of, 179.
——, Jonathan, 337.
——, Jonathan, Jr., 136, 157, 240, 260, 337.
——, Capt., Col. Josiah, 34–37, 39, 56, 57, 62–66, 68, 69, 71, 74, 76–78, 81–90, 94, 95, 100, 101, 127, 336.

380 *Index.*

Willard, Josiah, Jr., 79, 84, 264, 336.
——, Josiah Tersus, 336.
——, Katharine, 337.
——, Kezia (Capt. Jona.), 336, 337.
——, Keziah, 227, 337.
——, Lois, 336.
——, Lucy (D.), 240, 260.
——, Lucy, 337.
——, Madam, 56.
——, Mary (Grout), 229, 250, 336.
——, Mary [3], 337.
——, Miriam, 336.
——, Moses, 67, 96, 108, 114, 336; 336.
——, Nathan, 336.
——, Oliver, 336.
——, Pascal Paoli, 337.
——, Phebe (Jona., Jr.), 240, 260, 337.
——, Phebe, 337.
——, Prudance, 336.
——, Ruth (Farmer), 228.
——, Sampson, 336.
——, Sarah, 337.
——, Secretary, 100, 101, 135, 170.
——, Susannah (Johnson), 232, 253, 306.
——, Susanna (Moses), and dau. do., 336.
——, Susannah, 230; 336.
——, Thulah, 337.
——, Unity (Moors), 234, 255, 337.
——, Unity, 337.
——, Wilder, 336.
Williams, Rev. Mr., 216.
——, Anne (Larrabee), 233, 254.
——, Margaret (Larrabee), 233, 254.
——, Rev. William, 262.
Wilson, Isabella (Swan), 237, 258.
——, Jacob, 261.
——, Lois (Wood), 241, 261.
——, Margaret (J.), 261.
——, Mary (Houghton), 252.
Witt, Isaiah, 178, 187, 191.
Wood, 125.
——, Barnabus, 332.
——, Bette, 332; 333.
——, Bezaleel, 330.
——, Bezelial or Bezaleel, 332, 350.
——, Chloe, 235.
——, David, 138, 141, 162, 165, 168, 172, 183, 189, 196, 204, 207, 209, 240, 263, 333; 333; 332.
——, Elizabeth, 332; 333.
——, Esther, 333.
——, George, 333.
——, Hannah, 333.
——, Isaac, 333.
——, James, 241, 333.
——, Jerusha, 332.

Wood, John, 29, 56; 241, 332.
——, Capt. Jonathan, 94, 99, 121, 124, 125, 130, 133, 136, 137, 142, 144, 146, 147, 151, 153, 156, 160, 161, 167, 168, 172, 174–176, 180–182, 184, 190, 192, 193, 196, 198, 202, 203, 207, 208, 212, 217, 241, 260, 332, 350.
——, Jonathan, 332, 350; 332; 333.
——, Jonathan, Jr., 163, 183, 186, 240, 265, 333.
——, Joseph, 128, 137, 141, 157, 186, 240, 260, 267, 332, 350.
——, Joseph, Jr., 332, 350.
——, Lois (M.), 241, 261.
——, Martha (Downe), 227, 333.
——, Mary (Buss), 225, 333.
——, Mary (D.), 240, 263, 333.
——, Mary (M.), 246, 260, 333.
——, Mary, 333.
——, Mehitable (Bridge), 225, 247, 332.
——, Michael or Michal, 240, 241, 260, 261, 333.
——, Molly, 332.
——, Nathaniel, 11, 22.
——, Rachel (Jona., Jr.), 240, 265, 333.
——, Ruth (Jos.), 240, 260, 332, 350.
——, Ruth [2d], (Jos.), 240, 267, 332.
——, Sarah (Jona.), and two daus. do., 332, 350.
——, Sarah [2d], (Jona.), 241, 260, 332, 350.
——, Sarah, 333.
——, William, 14, 22, 55, 57.
——, William H., 263.
——, Zepheniah, 333.
——, see Woods.
Woodard, 101.
Woodman, Jonathan, 15, 23, 55, 56.
Woods, Elizabeth (Farmer), 264.
——, Nathaniel, 14, 17, 55, 57.
——, Nathaniel, Jr., 14, 22, 55, 57.
Woodward, Abraham, 14, 22, 55, 57.
——, Stephen, 15.
Woolley, Thomas, 15, 23, 56.
Woolson, Amos, 338.
——, Asa [2], 338.
——, Ebenezer, 338.
——, Elijah, 338.
——, Elizabeth (Asa), and dau. do., 338.
——, Joseph, 338.
——, Lois, 338.
Wright, Joseph, 38.
——, Sibil (W.), 241, 261.
——, Wincal, 241, 261.

Wyman, 119.
—, Abigail (Ezekiel), 330, 331, 350.
—, Abigail, 330, 350.
—, David, 330, 350; 331.
—, Dorrothy (Jesher), 261.
—, Elizabeth (R.), 241, 261, 331.
—, Elizabeth, 331.
—, Ezekiel, 91, 94, 96, 103, 106, 107, 111, 117, 120, 124, 128, 130, 136, 141, 157, 160, 165, 166, 168, 196, 203, 208, 330, 331, 350; 330, 331, 350.
—, Francis, 331.
—, Israel, 241, 330.
—, Jesher, 261.
—, John, 107, 120, 124, 126, 168, 180, 184, 186, 330, 350; 331.
Wyman, John, Jr., 330, 350.
—, Joseph, 241, 261, 331; 331.
—, Keziah (Jos.), 261, 331.
—, Lucy, 230, 330.
—, N., 263.
—, Oliver, 331.
—, Rebeckah (John), 330, 350.
—, Reuben, 241, 261, 330, 331.
—, Ruth, 331.
—, Sarah, 331.
—, Seth, 241, 331.
—, Silas, 330; 331.
—, Stephen, 331.
—, Susanna, 330.
—, Thomas, 331.
—, William, 331.
—, Wymon, see Wyman.

GENERAL INDEX.

ANCIENT Names of Towns, 351.
Andover, 15, 224, 225, 227, 230–232, 266.
Appletree Hill, 134.
Ashburnham, see Dorchester Canada.
Ashulot, The, 224.

BEAVER Dam, 44, 47, 48, 52, 150.
——, Pond, 48.
Benith Brook, 9.
Bennet Brook, 9.
Billerica, 233, 249, 254.
Births, 271-338.
Bolton, 228, 234, 255, 262.
Book B, 206.
Borman's Farm, 44, 46, 55.
Boston, 10, 15, 16, 20, 21, 30, 34, 39, 41, 140, 175, 179, 215, 236, 256, 350.
Boxford, 15, 226, 233, 240, 248, 254, 263.
Bradford, 15, 16, 20, 223.
Bridges, 118, 127, 128, 131, 134, 140, 142, 149, 154, 165, 169, 184, 197, 207, 209.
Brookline, 14.
Burying Place, 63, 74, 92, 150, 165, 166, 168, 190.
By-law in Reference to Pasturage, 93.

CAMBRIDGE, 18, 19, 24, 25, 27, 33, 34, 224, 285.
Carlile, 240, 241.
Cataconamog, 9, 43-47, 55.
Charlestown, N. H., 236, 256, 295.
Cheshire, 240.
Church, 75, 76, 89, 91, 195, 198, 212, 214, 216, 218, 219.
Clay Pit Meadows, 48, 49.
Committee of Town of Groton, 10, 11.
Committee to Allot and Grant Lands, 7-57, 67, 81, 99.
Common Land, 32, 45, 49, 50, 53, 54, 114, 126, 134, 187, 191.
Concord, 10-12, 14-17, 20, 21, 24-31, 42, 223, 228, 240, 248, 255.
Conditions of Settlement, 8, 13, 36.

Continental Army, 343.
Country Land, 224.
Countrey Rode, 81.
County Road, 178, 191.
Coventree, 223, 245.

DANVERS, 227.
Deaths, 341-350.
Deer, 105, 106, 111, 113, 118, 128, 131, 133, 137, 141, 148, 153, 157, 163, 168, 173, 177, 181, 183, 186, 197, 208.
Division of Town, 140, 143, 192, 206, 212, 213, 217, 218.
Dorchester, 18, 30, 38, 191.
—— Canada, 119, 120, 143, 166, 173, 187, 224, 226, 231, 234, 241, 252, 253, 311.
—— Farm, 40, 206.
Dunstable, 9, 223, 231, 235, 241, 245, 249, 252, 261.

EXCISE Bill, 166.

FALLS, The, 51.
Fast, 212, 214.
Fitchburg, 223, 225-227, 229, 230, 232, 233, 235, 236, 239, 241.
Fitzwilliam, 300.
Flat Hill, 104.
Forfeited Lots, 35, 36.
Framingham, 319.

GENERAL Court, 7, 12, 35, 40-42, 62-65, 68, 70, 71, 89, 166, 175, 204, 205, 211-213, 216, 217.
Groton, 7-12, 14-16, 18-20, 22, 25, 27, 31-34, 37, 38, 48, 67, 80, 85, 86, 114, 126, 143, 159, 170, 187, 224, 226, 228, 233, 234, 236, 237, 246, 248, 253, 254, 257, 259, 263, 264, 286, 314, 317.
—— River, 140.
—— Road, 153.

HARTWELL's Company, 127.
Harvard, 227, 228, 230, 232, 235, 248, 251, 253, 266, 278.

Harvard College Lot, 8, 18.
Hatfield, 226.
Highways, 18, 61-63, 67, 68, 72, 74, 80, 81, 85, 88, 90, 92-96, 98-101, 104, 105, 107, 108, 111, 113-115, 118-121, 123, 125-129, 131, 132, 134, 135, 138, 142, 143, 148-150, 153-160, 162, 164, 166, 167, 169, 170-172, 174, 177, 178, 181, 184, 186-188, 190, 191, 195, 197, 203, 204, 206-210.
Holding the South Town Lots, 55-57.
Horsmeat or Horsmeet Meadow, 37, 48, 55.

INTENTIONS of Marriage, 223-241.
Ipswich, 227, 264, 310-312.
—— Canada, 120, 228, 232, 234, 236, 239, 253, 256, 257, 265.
Ireland, Kingdom of, 321.

JAMAICA, W. I., 347.
Jurymen, 62, 70, 71, 152, 188.

KEENE, N. H., see Upper Ashuelot.
Kingston, 237, 257.

LANCASTER, 10, 15, 16, 23, 26, 63, 67, 83, 99, 173, 223, 224, 228, 231, 232, 234, 237-240, 245-247, 250, 255-257, 259-262, 274, 323.
Leominster, 126, 143, 167, 174, 209, 212, 217, 223, 224, 227, 235, 236, 241, 245, 247, 248, 252, 253, 256, 261, 263, 264, 331.
Lexington, 261.
Littleton, 24, 228, 239, 240, 267.
Londonderry, 238, 254, 258.
Lot for First Settled Minister, 8, 18, 57, 75.
Lower Ashulott, 230, 231, 251, 252.
Lynn, 240, 260.

MARLBOROUGH, 14, 24, 226, 334.
Marriage, Intentions of, 223-241.
Marriages, 245-267.
Massapog, 45, 46, 55.
Meadow Lots, 25, 27, 43-54, 77.
Medfield, 20.
Meeting House, 8, 13, 18, 37, 61-63, 65, 67, 68, 72, 75, 76, 82, 84, 86, 87, 89, 90, 91, 94-96, 98-100, 102, 103, 107, 115-118, 122, 130, 134, 136-138, 146, 156, 173, 181, 184, 188, 191, 212, 217.
—— ——, New, 138, 139, 142-148, 150, 151, 154-156, 160, 161, 164, 165, 170, 181, 182, 185, 188, 198, 206, 211, 217.
—— ——, West Parish, 192.

Methuen, 237, 266.
Middlesex County, 65, 85-87.
Mills: Widow White's, 127; Josiah Dodge's, 177; Bellows', 184.
Minister's Salary, 61-64, 68, 75, 76, 78, 94, 98, 103, 108, 112, 116, 124, 127, 130, 132, 136, 139, 144, 151, 156, 161, 165, 171, 175, 179, 181, 184, 188, 192, 194, 195, 199, 214, 216, 218, 219.
Ministerial Lot, 8, 18, 48, 57, 62, 72, 77, 88, 94, 107, 122, 126.
Mohawk River, 350.
Monadnock No. 4, 320.
Monson, N. H., 225.
Monusnut Brook, 158; see Wenoosnock.
Mulpus, Mullepus or Mullipus, 50, 52, 53, 55, 93, 119, 127, 131, 184.

NARRAGANSETT No. 2, 134, 135, 140, 154, 156, 158, 164, 166, 171, 173, 174, 187, 224, 238, 241, 246, 258.
Needham, 14.
Newbery, 14, 15.
New County, 63, 65, 85-87, 216.
New Ipswich, 240.
Newton, 236, 267.
Nichawogg or Nichewoag, 317.
Nistaqualothe or Nissitissit Hill, 8.
Nistiquasit Hill, 10.
North Branch, 123, 127.
—— River, 126.
—— Town, 11, 12, 17, 20, 27, 31, 43.
Northfield Road, 62, 63, 67, 72, 88, 92, 95-97, 118, 135.
Nottingham, 226, 234, 248.
Number Four, 228, 237, 249, 258.

OLIVER'S Land, 174, 187.

PEARL HILL Brook, 67, 128, 206.
—— —— Meadow, 55.
Pearl Hills, 135.
Pepperell, 234, 238, 265.
Peterborough, 238, 258.
Petersham, 259, 264.
Poor, The, 105, 150, 160, 165, 168, 179, 207, 210.
Pound, 61, 68, 112, 116, 117, 137, 151.
Princeton, 232, 253.
Proprietors, 27, 32, 37, 77.
Proprietors' Meetings, 31, 37.
Providence, R. I., 344.
Province Land, 70.

READING, 15, 231.
River, The, 186.
Rock Meadow, 52, 53.
Rowley, 20.

Rowley Canada, 230, 232, 236, 251, 253, 256, 276, 329.

SCHOOLS, 62, 63, 77, 79, 83, 85, 86, 89, 94–96, 98, 102, 105, 108–110, 112, 113, 115, 118, 122, 124, 125, 127, 128, 129, 131–133, 135–137, 139, 141, 142, 144, 150, 155, 161–163, 165, 168, 171, 175, 179, 181, 182, 184, 185, 189, 193, 194, 199, 200, 204, 207, 209, 215.
School Lot, 8, 18, 62, 77.
Scott's Road, 187.
Secretary's Land, 197.
Sergant's Land, 126.
Shirley, 170, 225, 226, 229, 231, 232, 234, 237. 240, 247, 251, 252, 254, 259, 260, 263.
Shrewsbury, 224.
Small-pox, 179.
South Town, 7, 9, 11, 12, 16–21, 24–39, 42, 43, 55.
Spanish Expedition, 347.
Stocks, 73, 132.
Stone Bridge, 118.
Stow, 16, 23, 225, 230–232, 234, 236, 238, 251, 252, 256, 261.
Stratford, Conn., 228.
Sudbury, 229, 265.

TAXES, 63–65, 68, 70, 71, 74, 77, 82, 85, 86, 89, 90, 98, 105, 109, 110, 116, 120, 139, 142, 148, 152, 161, 166, 175, 201, 206, 207, 213, 218.
Templeton, 239, 259.
Tewksbury, 225.
Thunder Bolts, 1749, 61.
Topsfield, 237, 267, 292.
Town Meetings, 61–219.
—— ——, How Warned, 110, 130, 135, 161.

Town Records, 61–350.
—— ——, Book B, 206–219.
Townshend, 94, 127, 184, 212, 218, 228, 229, 237, 250, 258, 260, 338.
Turkey Hill Brook, 150.
—— Meadow, 55.
Turkey Hills, 7, 9, 15, 21, 27–29, 32–40, 55.
Tuxbury, 300.

UNCHAWALAM, Unchechewalunk, or Unkechewalom Pond, 40, 45, 126.
Unimproved Lands, 70, 71, 85, 166.
Upper Ashuelot, 246.
Upton, 228, 249.
Uxbridge, 240, 265.

WAGES, 86, 90, 98, 115, 120, 134, 143, 149, 154, 164, 173, 183, 187.
Walpole, 224, 246.
Watertown, 14, 15, 251.
Weights and Measures, 62, 73, 105, 156.
Wenham, 321.
Wenoosnock Brook, 169; see Monusnut.
Westminster, 238, 241, 250, 259.
Weston, 14–16, 20, 42, 229, 239, 250, 262, 267, 338.
Willard's Company, 127.
Winchendon, 265.
Winchester, 250.
Woburn, 15, 16, 20, 38, 39, 263, 294.
Woburn Farm, 38–40, 100, 101, 107, 126.
Wolves, 153.
Worcester, 70, 71, 79, 119, 166, 225, 226, 233–235, 247, 255, 261, 263, 350.
—— County, 70, 71, 73, 85–87, 166.
Work House, 171, 199.

PLATES.

First Page of Records of General Court's Committee,	frontispiece
Second Page of Same,	to face 9
Isaac Farnsworth's Copy of Rev. Andrew Gardner's Request for Dismission,	to face 75
Signatures of Town Clerks and Rev. David Stearns,	to face 220

www.ingramcontent.com/pod-product-compliance
Lightning Source LLC
Chambersburg PA
CBHW050834230426
43667CB00012B/1992